Hellenic Studies 41

A CALIFORNIAN HYMN TO HOMER

Recent Titles in the

Hellenic Studies Series

Archilochos Heros: The Cult of Poets in the Greek Polis
Master of the Game: Competition and Performance in Greek Poetry
Yearning for the Infinite: Desire and Possession in Three Platonic Dialogues
Black Doves Speak: Herodotus and the Languages of Barbarians
Amphoteroglōssia: A Poetics of the Twelfth-Century Medieval Greek Novel
Victim of the Muses: Poet as Scapegoat, Warrior and Hero
Pointing at the Past: From Formula to Performance in Homeric Poetics
The Life and Miracles of Thekla: A Literary Study
Homeric Conversation
The Culture of Kitharoidia
The Power of Thetis and Selected Essays
Comparative Anthropology of Ancient Greece
Poetic and Performative Memory in Ancient Greece
Weaving Truth: Essays on Language and the Female in Greek Thought
Ritual and Performativity: The Chorus in Old Comedy
The Epic City: Urbanism, Utopia, and the Garden in Ancient Greece and Rome
Plato's Symposium: Issues in Interpretation and Reception
Paradise Earned: The Bacchic-Orphic Gold Lamellae of Crete
Concordia Discors: Eros and Dialogue in Classical Athenian Literature
King of Sacrifice: Ritual and Royal Authority in the Iliad
The Feast of Poetry: Sacrifice and Performance in Aristophanic Comedy
C. P. Cavafy, *The Canon: The Original One Hundred and Fifty-Four Poems*
Sappho in the Making: The Early Reception
The Oral Palimpsest: Exploring Intertextuality in the Homeric Epics
Practitioners of the Divine: Greek Priests and Religious Officials from Homer to Heliodorus
Zeus in the Odyssey
The Politics of Ethnicity and the Crisis of the Peloponnesian League
Genos Dikanikon: Amateur and Professional Speech in the Courtrooms of Classical Athens
Fragments of Sappho: A Commentary
Recapturing a Homeric Legacy:
Images and Insights from the Venetus A Manuscript of the Iliad
Homer the Classic
Hippota Nestor
The New Sappho on Old Age: Textual And Philosophical Issues
Pindar's Verbal Art: An Ethnographic Study of Epinician Style

A CALIFORNIAN HYMN TO HOMER

Edited by
Timothy Pepper

CENTER FOR HELLENIC STUDIES
Trustees for Harvard University
Washington, DC
Distributed by Harvard University Press
Cambridge, Massachusetts, and London, England
2010

A Californian Hymn to Homer
edited by Timothy Pepper

Published by Center for Hellenic Studies, Trustees for Harvard University, Washington, D.C.
Distributed by Harvard University Press, Cambridge, Massachusetts and London, England

Library of Congress Cataloging-in-Publication Data
A Californian hymn to Homer / edited by Timothy Pepper.
p. cm. — (Hellenic studies ; 41)
Includes bibliographical references and index.
ISBN 978-0-674-03605-5
1. Homer—Criticism and interpretation. 2. Epic poetry, Greek—History and criticism. 3. Hymns, Greek (Classical)—History and criticism. 4. Homeric hymns. I. Pepper, Timothy. II. Title. III. Series.

PA4023.Z5C35 2010
883'.01—dc22 2010010204

Contents

Proöimion

Timothy Pepper

NOT UNLIKE ANCIENT GREEK HYMNS, *A Californian Hymn to Homer* begins with the origins of its subject: the contributors to this volume first came together for a seminar given by Gregory Nagy during his Sather Professorship at the University of California at Berkeley in the spring of 2002. The essays here grew from our collaboration in that seminar, our discussions of Nagy's Sather lectures[1] within and without the classroom, and our later exchange of papers and ideas with Nagy's enthusiastic encouragement. Though one may read the title of this volume as a statement of our collective interest in and admiration for the insights Homeric poetry and its scholarship provide, it is significant in another sense as well. All of the contributions engage in some way with Homeric material; most comment on the poems directly, while others find approaches in the study of Homer to apply to other aspects of Mediterranean cultures.

We may press the analogy of the hymn to our scholarly projects a little further when we remember that hymn itself, as prelude to epic or catalogue poetry, offered a place for describing the act of performance of traditional song.[2] The hymnic prologue is in some sense our earliest example of discourse on poetry in Greek, and we see within such presentations of poetry a complex, reciprocal interplay of a notional specific performance and a larger tradition. Just as in archaic Greek poetics as a whole, it is very difficult to untangle recreated traditions in performance from newly created ones.[3] That complex

1 Nagy's Sather lectures themselves are forthcoming in a pair of volumes published by the University of California Press (*Homer the Preclassic*) and the Center for Hellenic Studies (*Homer the Classic*).

2 Most overtly through the self-identification of the poet's persona; see Nagy 1992:54.

3 De Vet 2005:277 suggests the image of a living holiday tree, on which each year old ornaments are shifted or fall off, and new ornaments in the same traditional style are added. As hundreds of years pass, some of those ornaments may even incorporate themselves into the trunk of that tree. Similarly, an epic Kunstsprache can also relate to a process of composition through

interdependence, which both is shaped by the history of the tradition and shapes it, provides either the focus or a major part of the discussion in each of our essays. The *Homeric Hymn to Apollo*, translated at the end of this volume, contains an illustration of such interaction, providing a poetic parallel that is worth sketching out briefly.

At the end of the first, "Delian" part of the hymn, Delian maidens are introduced as an archetypical chorus[4] performing within a timeless festival.[5] When they are asked, "Which singer is it of men wandering hither / who is the sweetest in song, and by whom you most are delighted?" they are exhorted to reply, "It is a blind man dwelling in Chios, rugged and rocky, / whose songs, every one, are the best both now and hereafter" (169–170, 172–173).[6] The poet then says that he will spread the *kleos* of the maidens by means of his performance ("Yours is a fame, in turn, I will carry around as I wander / over the earth to the well-inhabited cities of mankind"); the future tense here is not a promise but rather a signal that the present poem itself is a manifestation and instantiation of that praise, following the conventions of hymnic form.[7] The Delian maidens' role as a foil hinges on the word *aoidos*, which in choral lyric refers to a choral song and dance performer,[8] of which the maidens are

---

writing, with the accretion, falling off, and invention of traditional elements (the ornaments) forming a system. A synchronic "slice" of epic language, much like a cross section of the tree, provides a mixture of different moments in the tradition, with the result that purely linguistic approaches become problematic.

4 See Peponi 2009:65–67. We find further support in Peponi's parallels with the Delian maidens as choral archetype in Euripides *Heracles* 685–690, and with *Iliad* II 485 (Muses) and *Odyssey* xii 39–40, 189–190 (Sirens). Though Nagy 1996:56 also reads the maidens as choral archetypes, he takes those archetypes as being set against dance performance on Delos rather than the poet.

5 As is clear from the series of general and modal clauses in 149–163. The transition from the maidens with a concluding hymnal *khairete* ('farewell') in 166 makes the distinction from the here and now of the present performance of the hymn even clearer: see Bundy 1962:46, 66. The command that the maidens recall "me" in the second half of line 166 (just as the "I" in 177) is a version of the similar hymnic transition to first person noted in Bundy 1962:46n34, contra Dyer 1975:120. Placing from internal evidence the performance context in Delos in 522 BCE, as independently suggested by Burkert and Janko (see Burkert 1987:54 with 61–62n61 and references) or as revised to possibly 523 by West 2007:368–370n17, thus misses the fundamental point of the Delian maidens: they are the foil to the poet rather than part of a report of the festival at which the poet intends to perform.

6 All translations from the *Hymn to Apollo* are by Rodney Merrill and are taken from his translation of the complete hymn elsewhere in this volume.

7 Bundy 1962:21–22, contra Dyer 1975:121; Thucydides understands the convention here: he precedes his quotation of lines 165–172 with ἐτελεύτα τοῦ ἐπαίνου ἐς τάδε τὰ ἔπη ("he makes an end of his praise with the following words"; III 104.5).

8 Not only has the formulation *anēr hēdistos aoidōn* (169) been the primary source for the misconception that *aoidos* is the normative Greek term for a poet-performer (Maslov 2009:5), but it has obscured its historically developed meaning of "[instructed] performer/member of the chorus" in choral poetry, separate from its meaning in hexameter of "professional solo

presented as archetypes. But the term is applied within hexameter to the solo performer, just as the poet here has appropriated their speech to proclaim himself the paradigmatic *aoidos*. Further, the anachronistic description—only within this imagined dialogue and not in the poet's further description of himself—of his singing rather than reciting the performance recasts the traditional role of the rhapsode through "diachronic skewing."[9] The poet thus realigns the tradition in a way integral to shaping the collective identity of performers of Homer, specifically the Homeridai.[10] This realignment finds its historical expression in antiquity in the literary judgment of Thucydides (III 104), who unequivocally reads the poet in this passage as a singing Homer. Just as the poet here shows a sensitivity to the interlocking of performance and tradition that allows him to recast both, the essays in this volume deal with the complex unfolding and changing of traditions within time, sensitive to the insights that the various branches of Homeric scholarship provide, yet still rooted in the particularity of each of their subjects.

Excellent examples of this sensitivity to the changing interaction within traditions can be found in Jack Mitchell's and Thomas Walsh's chapters in this volume. Mitchell's investigation of the role of the prophet Theoclymenus in the *Odyssey* provides a valuable demonstration, on the level of narrative, of the development of the historical relationship between the poet and the prophet, particularly in light of Maslov's recent work on the historical development of the semantics of *aoidos* in Homer.[11] Theoclymenus illustrates the relation of this term for solo performer to magical incantation, for Theoclymenus' prophecies are effective when they affect their audience with "verse-based magical performance," and he more than any figure except Odysseus is shown as exerting control over the course of the narrative. Walsh finds in his study of the Homeric terminology of anger in Athenian drama that Aeschylus' use and

performer" (Maslov 2009:17–19, esp. with table 2).

9 Nagy 1990:21–24. We perhaps should be a little more cautious at reading the internal evidence of this poetry as testimony rather than presentation of poetic practice in light of Maslov 2009.

10 Cf. Durante 1976:197–198, who connects the creation of this poem with the Homeridai, the Chian guild of rhapsodes, whose name he derives from *ὅμᾱρος or *ὅμᾱρις, which he calls a "missing link." From Greek cultic epithet (176), Sanskrit evidence (198–201), and a gloss in Hesychius on the name Thamuris, Durante deduces its meaning as an assembly of the people at which contests are performed, and he connects these to the assembly of the Ionians in 147–148. West 2007 calls Durante's reconstruction the "most coherent that has been offered" (376), but draws on a Pindaric scholium (7.1c Drachmann) for the identification of the poet with Cynaethus (368–369). See, however, Nagy 2000:99n6 for doubts about the historical reliability of that scholion. Note that if we accept the etymology for Homer proposed by Nagy 1996:74–75n45 of *homo-* 'together' + the root of *arariskō* 'fit, join', we find almost an exact analogue in 164: *sunarēren* (< *sun* 'together' + *arariskō*).

11 Maslov 2009:21–33 reconstructs ἀοιδός as a backformation from ἐπαοιδός "performer of incantations."

elaboration of these archaic concepts represents both a realignment of them to the realities of the polis and a link to the archaic past.

By utilizing a comparative approach, David Larsen highlights both the differences between early Islam's and Homeric poetry's incorporation of mantic speech—a demonstration to any Homerist that the hexameter epic's relationship to prophecy is not a cultural inevitability—and the constitutive repurposing of the speech of the seer to the words of the Prophet. Curtis Dozier and Charles Stocking present a different side of the understanding and adaptation of traditional styles of speech in the formula. Both argue that even if we cannot attribute an intellectual understanding of the workings of oral-formulaic theory either to the Roman poet Virgil or to the character Achilles, each shows a practical mastery of the formula not only within the context in which they need it, but for deeper poetic and narrative needs as well. Dan Sofaer and I organize our essays around the repurposing of objects, birds and wine respectively, within culture, and how their reuses and transformations within texts act as tokens of traditions. Many more such correspondences can be drawn across these essays; now, however, it will be worthwhile to run through each of them in turn.

The first three essays examine the opposition and conjunction of prophetic and poetic speech in the performance of authority. David Larsen's "Signs, Omens, and Semiological Regimes in Early Islamic Texts" examines the Qur'ān's preemption of the pre-Islamic oracular tradition—a confrontation that is as formative for early Islam, Larsen argues, as its encounter with Judaism and Christianity. Making a comparison with the emblematic use of oracular vocabulary within Homer, he notes that while both the Qur'ān and Homeric poetry use divinatory language to stage interpretation by their audience, that appropriation within the Qur'ān discredits and is hostile to divination. The interrelation of performance and tradition is constituted through the historical, generative struggle within the appropriation of the semiological concepts and poetics of *saj'*, the performative medium of the *kāhin* or pre-Islamic soothsayer. Within the Qur'ān, the soothsayer's omen is sublated by Prophetic demonstration of evidence of the power of God. Thus, without access to correct belief through the medium of the Prophet, interpretation of the signs is bound to fail: divination has gone from a method for interpreting signs to fully being contained by them. The one type of divination not rejected by Islam, a sign of confirmation (*fa'l*) roughly analogous to the Homeric *phēmē*, is the exception that proves the rule, as it lends itself to the semiological hegemony of the Prophet, available without interpretive mediation and controlled at the level of language by Prophetic fiat. In an appendix, Larsen illustrates the shifting polarities of traditional Arabian oracular signage with two translated entries from the *Lisān al-ʿarab* of Ibn Manẓūr (d. 711/1311 CE).

Jack Mitchell provides a complementary analysis of the intersection of prophetic and performative authority in "Theoclymenus and the Poetics of Disbelief: Prophecy and Its Audience in the *Odyssey*." Mitchell's goal is to understand the portrayal of the seer Theoclymenus, a seemingly minor figure who nevertheless has a prodigiously long narrative introduction, the longest of any figure in Homer. The three prophecies of Theoclymenus provoke different reactions from Telemachus, Penelope, and the suitors, depending on the degree to which the magical power of formal language manipulates the understanding of audiences through their receptivity to the truths of the narrative. Theoclymenus as a hexameter performer of events in the present has strong commonalities with the epic reimagining of its performance through the *aoidos*, and at one significant point he reveals that a narrative description has provided a focalized sign seen only by him, a "perspective zeugma" that provides the basis of his prophecy to the suitors. Theoclymenus colludes with the narrator to perform the story for his own interest, as a well- and ill-treated guest.

Dan Sofaer looks at the significance of Aristophanes' bird-chorus in musical performance in "The Places of Song in Aristophanes' *Birds*." Observing that birds in Greek poetic traditions are the quintessential intermediaries, whether on the metaphorical level of poetic performance or the metonymic level of carriers of the gods' will through signs of mantic significance, yet are not authorities in themselves, Sofaer reads the lyric passages of *Birds* as performances of comedy under scrutiny. The birds' transformation to active agents correspondingly transforms comedy's relation to other traditions of song. He argues that there is something fundamentally novel in the birds' creating a community through song, from the first lyric in which a performing group is forged from a disparate set of voices and styles. They go on to lay claim to a sacred, musical authority from Phrynichus, and reject epinician and dithyramb in the intruder scenes because they are too dependent on the institutions of the human city. The birds, together with their city, thus construct a music divorced from civic or divine dependency, a music connected explicitly with the Muses, a music, Sofaer suggests, that may have implicitly provided the model for the "birdcage of the Muses," the Library of Alexandria.

Both Thomas Walsh's "Some Refractions of Homeric Anger in Athenian Drama" and Charles Stocking's "Language about Achilles: Linguistic Frame Theory and the Formula in Homeric Poetics" address the construction of cultural memory by building on Walsh's earlier work on the ideology of

Homeric anger (Walsh 2002). Walsh looks at the uses of κότος as a term for anger in Aeschylus and argues that the term is central for his portrayal of conflict and emotion, and even more thematically significant in his tragedies than in Homeric epic. For Aeschylus, *kotos* retains its Homeric cultural framework, yet is "refracted" through contemporary public politics to provide an ethical center for archaic values that would otherwise fade. It acts out two interrelated problems: a political one of allegiances and acts of violence that persist even beyond death and a poetic one of the continuity of cultural memory. Walsh notes that, ironically, for all the rhetoric of permanence around archaic *kotos*, it is marginalized and virtually ignored in later Athenian drama. This word not only shows its potential for structuring the institutions of society but also reveals the ultimately fictive nature of such institutions.

Stocking takes the insights of Walsh's work and of frame theory semantics to argue that the narrative associations of the anger term χόλος imply a potential script, or a socially stabilized series of events bound to speech-act(s). He applies his model to a speech by Achilles to his Myrmidons in *Iliad* XVI, and argues that it depicts a practical understanding of the semantics of formulaic language. Achilles projects an imagined, distributed complaint against him through an act of poetic mimesis framing a series of formulaic speech-events that use the conventional language of Homeric poetry. Yet when we look to the context of that imagined complaint, we see Achilles not only creating grammatical and metrical structures not represented elsewhere in the corpus, but also framing the language about his anger with the same formal structures the poet(s) use for his exceptionalism. Stocking illustrates how an exceptional character such as Achilles can be represented as reacting to and recreating generic structures even from within Homeric poetry.

The last two essays treat what might be called the "genre memories"[12] preserved in later traditions: the discourse of hero cult in Homer and archaic lyric, and of Homeric poetry itself within Virgil's *Aeneid*. My own essay, "Skillful Symposia: *Odyssey* ix, Archilochus Fr. 2 West, and the Οἶνος Ἰσμαρικός," examines the legendary Ismaric wine, which surprisingly is directly mentioned only twice in extant archaic and classical Greek literature. To appreciate its appearances within *Odyssey* ix and Archilochus fr. 2 West, I suggest, we must understand the cultural significance of both wine in general and specifically named wines in ancient Greek discourse. Wine, a potential holder of symbolic capital as well as an item of exchange, figures prominently within the construction of social and political identity. Within the *Odyssey*, Ismaric wine operates as a marker of order within divinely sanctioned proto-sympotic rituals of com-

12 Cf. Bakhtin1984:159. The formulation comes from Morson and Emerson 1990:294–299.

mensality, and its characterization as an item of gift-exchange between Odysseus and Maron reflects Maron's suppressed role in cultic worship. This talismanic wine transfers Maron's connection with civilized cultivation and especially colonization, and wine's power to define the city is channeled into an implicit narrative of colony foundation. Turning to Archilochus fr. 2 West, I argue that Archilochus appropriates the heroic and cultic background of Maron and his Ismaric wine within a self-personification as a spokesman of a "middling" ideology, and he adapts language associated with an elite founder of a city to the hoplite tactics of a colonist moving for a better life. His success in this repurposing is perhaps reflected in his *Nachleben* as the object of hero-cult. We thus see two separate strands of archaic Greek poetics transforming material from cult for ideologically very different ends.

Curtis Dozier's "Homeric Poetics and the *Aeneid*" opens with several questions: to what extent can we characterize Virgil's understanding of the oral poetics of Homeric epic and, more particularly, the workings of the formula within Homer? If he does not fully understand the formula, how does he imitate formulaic language? Or if he does, how can he imitate that language within a work that is decidedly not formulaic? Dozier seeks an answer to this query by running an "experiment." By studying the occurrences and variants of the programmatic phrase *arma virum*, he reconstitutes within their contexts their "networks of meaning"—the whirl of intra- and intertexts that the phrase/formula calls forth and doubles back on. In this analysis, then, we see the *Aeneid* operating as a performance within a larger system. Using a linguistic model to characterize the differentiation of the synchronic and the diachronic, Dozier likens the *Aeneid* to a *parole* operating within the larger *langue* of Homer.[13] He sees in Virgil's adaptations of similar formulae within Homer a surprisingly multifarious thematic resonance between their contexts, their often wide-ranging analogues in Homer, and even further themes and formulae elsewhere within the *Aeneid* that the Homeric passages foreground. For instance, the famous occurrence of *arma viri* in Dido's death speech in *Aeneid* IV, already recognized by Ovid to have strong intratextual resonance with the beginning of the poem (*Tristia* II 534), gains its full thematic force only when we consider its formulaic analogues in Homer. Dozier traces them through the *Aeneid* and the *Iliad* to the lyre with which Achilles sings the κλέα ἀνδρῶν, a reference that moves us back again to the first line of the *Aeneid*. Dozier concludes that the use of formula can, at least for certain phrases,

13 For the application of these terms, ultimately from Saussure and Levi-Strauss, to denote the manifestations (= *parole*) of specific epics within the system of the performance of epic (= *langue*), see Nagy 1990:17n2 and 1996:1.

stand up to the same scrutiny as in a traditional, oral-poetic framework. Even if it remains an open question whether Virgil was "the most attentive . . . audience Homer ever had," his imitation is so skilled that the *Aeneid* functions as if he were.

Concluding the volume, Rodney Merrill presents a translation of the *Homeric Hymn to Apollo.* Beyond the thematic resonances of this hymn, Merrill's use of English hexameter and consistent English-language rendering of Homeric formulae provides the closest possible experience in English to the actual audition of Homeric poetry in Greek. And, in a real sense, Merrill provides an artistic analogue to the scholarly project of the essays here, that of making the often subtle and complex effects of Greek verse perceptible to contemporary readers.

I would like to extend my thanks to Gregory Nagy for setting us on this journey and for his help throughout this project; to Curtis Dozier and Wilson Shearin for their input at various stages of the editing process; to Olga Levaniouk, Jill Curry Robbins, and Leonard Muellner at the Center for Hellenic Studies for their invaluable assistance and patient guidance; and to Mary Bellino for her superb, vigilant copyediting.

"And about some other song I will be thinking . . ."

Bibliography

Bakhtin, Mikhail. 1984. *Problems of Dostoevsky's Poetics*. Ed. and trans. Caryl Emerson. Minneapolis.

Bundy, Elroy L. 1962. *Studia Pindarica*. Berkeley.

Burkert, Walter. 1987. "The Making of Homer in the Sixth Century B.C.: Rhapsodes versus Stesichoros." *Papers on the Amasis Painter and His World* (ed. Marion True) 43–62. Malibu, CA.

De Vet, Thérèse. 2005. "Parry in Paris: Structuralism, Historical Linguistics, and the Oral Theory." *Classical Antiquity* 24.2:257–284.

Durante, Marcello. 1976. *Sulla preistoria della tradizione poetica greca*. Vol. 2. Rome.

Dyer, Robert. 1975. "The Blind Bard of Chios (Hymn. Hom. Ap. 171–76)." *Classical Philology* 70.2:119–121.

Morson, Gary Saul, and Emerson, Caryl. 1990. *Mikhail Bakhtin: Creation of a Prosaics*. Stanford.

Maslov, Boris. 2009. "The Semantics of ἀοιδός and Related Compounds: Towards a Historical Poetics of Solo Performance in Archaic Greece." *Classical Antiquity* 28.1:1–38.

Nagy, Gregory. 1990. *Pindar's Homer: The Lyric Possession of an Epic Past*. Baltimore.

———. 1992. *Greek Mythology and Poetics*. Ithaca.

———. 1996. *Poetry as Performance: Homer and Beyond*. Cambridge.

Peponi, Anastasia-Erasmia. 2009. "*Choreia* and Aesthetics in the *Homeric Hymn to Apollo*: The Performance of the Delian Maidens (Lines 156–64)." *Classical Antiquity* 28.1:39–70.

Walsh, Thomas. 2002. *Feuding Words and Fighting Words: Anger and the Homeric Poems*. Lanham, MD.

West, M. L. 1999. "The Invention of Homer." *Classical Quarterly* NS 49.2:64–382.

1

Signs, Omens, and Semiological Regimes in Early Islamic Texts

David Larsen

IN HIS 1983 ARTICLE "Sêma and Nóēsis: The Hero's Tomb and the 'Reading' of Symbols in Homer and Hesiod," Gregory Nagy describes one of the channels through which communication between gods and mortals takes place in the Homeric poems:

> For example, there is the *sêma* sent by Zeus to the Achaeans, as reported in *Iliad* II (308): the event of a snake's devouring eight nestlings and their mother (II.308–19) requires the mantic *interpretation* of Kalkhas the *mántis* 'seer', who recognizes it as a portent of Troy's impending destruction (II.320–32). Or again, there are all the Homeric instances of lightning sent by Zeus as a *sêma* (II.353, IX.236, XIII.244, xxi.413, etc.)—one might say as a *code* bearing distinct *messages* that are to be interpreted in context by both the witnesses and the narrative itself.[1]

While the gods address direct speech to some mortals in dreams and waking visions, to the collectivity their will is made known through *signs and omens* requiring the hermeneutic intervention of a skilled decoder. The faculty demanded of this decoder is above all *noos*, translatable as 'mind' or 'mindfulness' but shown more specifically by Nagy to consist in the allied powers of *recognition* (distinguishing the signifier from a welter of ambient phenomena) and *interpretation* (rendering into speech the information signified by it). And

For their helpful critique of this essay, I thank Margaret Larkin, Leslie Kurke, James Monroe, Jack Mitchell, Rodney Merrill, and Dan Sofaer. Thanks also to Mohammed Sharafuddin and Edgar W. Francis for their responses on its delivery at the 2003 conference of the Middle East Studies Association in Anchorage, Alaska. I also thank the Al-Falah Program of U. C. Berkeley's Center for Middle Eastern Studies for awarding it the 2004 Abduljawad Prize for Best Paper on an Islamic Subject.

1 "Sêma and Nóēsis" first appeared in *Arethusa* 16 (1983): 35–55; text as quoted here is from Nagy 1990a:203–204.

as Hector will hear from his comrade Polydamas, it is a faculty not equally present in all people:

> οὕνεκά τοι περὶ δῶκε θεὸς πολεμήια ἔργα,
> τοὔνεκα καὶ βουλῇ ἐθέλεις περιίδμεναι ἄλλων·
> ἀλλ' οὔ πως ἅμα πάντα δυνήσεαι αὐτὸς ἑλέσθαι.
> ἄλλῳ μὲν γὰρ ἔδωκε θεὸς πολεμήια ἔργα,
> ἄλλῳ δ' ὀρχηστύν, ἑτέρῳ κίθαριν καὶ ἀοιδήν,
> ἄλλῳ δ' ἐν στήθεσσι τιθεῖ νόον εὐρύοπα Ζεύς,
> ἐσθλόν, τοῦ δέ τε πολλοὶ ἐπαυρίσκοντ' ἄνθρωποι,
> καί τε πολέας ἐσάωσε, μάλιστα δὲ κ'αὐτὸς ἀνέγνω.
>
> Just because the god granted that you excel in deeds of war
> you wish also to excel in planning by knowing more than others.
> But there is no way you can get everything all to yourself.
> The god grants that one man excel in deeds of war
> and another in dancing and another in playing the lyre and singing.
> And for yet another man, far-seeing Zeus places *nóos* in his breast,
> a genuine one; and many men benefit from such a man,
> and he saves many of them, and he himself has the greatest powers of recognition.
>
> *Iliad* XIII 727–734 (trans. Nagy 1990a:204)

It is on this idea of the unequal distribution of *noos* that the office of *mantis* or 'seer' apparently rested. The Homeric seer is a noticer and interpreter of signs that elude the community at large. So closely are *anagnōrēsis* ('recognition') and *hypokrisis* ('interpretation') of omens identified with this office that characters who are *not* seers will announce that they are miming a seer's speech when they undertake to interpret a given omen for themselves—whether by way of introduction ("Listen to me, and I will act as *mantis*," Helen commands at *Odyssey* xv 172) or conclusion ("And a seer would perform his interpretation in the same way," Polydamas says to Hector at *Iliad* XII 228).

The truth-value of divinely motivated *sēmata* as interpreted by a qualified *hypokritēs* is generally upheld in the Hesiodic and Homeric poems, so that while a given speaker (such as Hector at *Iliad* XII 237–243) may question the validity of omens in general, the narrative itself tends overwhelmingly to confirm it.[2]

2 Collins 2002:17–41 concludes otherwise, reading the various expressions of distrust in omens that occur in Homer as an outright critique of mantic authority. Like the suitor Eurymachus' spurning of the omen at *Odyssey* ii 146–207, however, Hector's disbelief seems rather a function of his role *within* the narrative than a critique of divination *by* the narrative.

This is not to deny any of the *sēma's* well-known potential for ambiguity and polyvalence, but to declare that the oracular *sēma* is not a site of robust ideological conflict in Homer and Hesiod. "Consider the bird-omens and avoid transgressions" (*ornithas krinōn kai hyperbasias aleeinōn*) is the closing admonition of *Works and Days*.[3] Nor is there any perceptible conflict between poetic and oracular tradition in the Homeric poems. Oracular practice is quite favorably memorialized throughout—a circumstance dryly noted in Augustine's remark that the ancient poets were fonder of commemorating the mantic arts than of actually teaching them.[4]

Far from being in competition with the oracle, then, Homeric poetry appears to draw on oracular tradition as a source of authority and legitimacy. In a later article Nagy goes so far as to argue that "Homeric poetry equates its own performance with that of a seer or *mantis* who performs oracular poetry in responding to questions about omens" (Nagy 2002:142). It does this in the sense that the narratives of the *Iliad* and *Odyssey* both end in fulfillment of key omens whose revelation and translation into speech are staged within the epics themselves. As interpreted by Nestor (and recollected by Odysseus at *Iliad* II 308–332), the devouring of eight nestling sparrows and their mother by a giant snake emblematizes the very plot being narrated by the *Iliad*—just as the rightward flight of the goose-killing eagle at *Odyssey* xv 160–165 combines with the interpretation performed immediately afterward by Helen to encapsulate the denouement of the *Odyssey* itself. If the omen is read as an emblem of the story being narrated in the poem, the seer's interpretive performance is a figure for the poem itself, with which it is coextensive. Or to put it another way, "the prophecy of the seer is not only fulfilled by the epic but also becomes the epic."[5]

The *mise en abîme* that resounds in these scenes of omen-reading depends on the identification of one performance medium (that of the Homeric singer) with another (the medium of oracular speech). For what makes this identification possible a number of ideas might be advanced, but none with more certainty than that performers of Homeric poetry (and, presumably, the institutions that sponsored its performance) did not see themselves as being in conflict with institutionalized divination, and furthermore that the alignment

3 A scholiast notes that *Works and Days* stops at the beginning of a long discourse on bird divination athetized in the third century BCE by Apollonius Rhodius. See Hesiod *Works and Days* 364–365.

4 *[Q]ualia sunt molimina magicarum artium, quae quidem commemorare potius quam docere assolent poetae. De doctrina christiana* II 20.30 (Augustine, *De doctrina christiana* 33).

5 Nagy 2002:145. This is a new way to frame *mise en abîme* in Homer, which is one is more used to thinking about in connection with the *Odyssey*'s scenes of epic singing on Phaeacia and Ithaca. See Foucault 1977:53–67.

of their medium with that of the oracle was felt to be an ennobling one. For a contrasting, antagonistic relationship to the oracle one need only look ahead to fifth-century Athens, and the conflict

> openly expressed in the reflections of those who, in their intellectual activity, entered into the same territory of knowledge in more or less direct competition with oracles and seers. These are, first of all, of course, sophists and philosophers, but they are also historians, doctors, and wise men. In professing to teach the art of rhetoric that could give the power to win the decision on any debated question, what else did the sophists finally claim, if not to substitute a secular technique for an oracular type of procedure, one wholly different but equally efficacious, which in the sectors where it was applied corresponded to a similar final result?[6]

This essay will show how oracular concepts and vocabulary may be co-opted in the service of an oppositional stance toward divination itself. It is likely that such a study could be performed on any number of cultural traditions and historical periods; here it will be carried out on the early Arabic texts of Islam, primarily the Qurʾān. Whereas Homeric poetry affirms an identity between its own performance and that of a seer, the Qurʾān rejects any such identity, and with it the authority of the soothsayer—even as it adapts the Arabian soothsayer's own performance medium (the rhymed speech known as *sajʿ*) to a new Islamic mandate.

The comparison between the Homeric poems and the Qurʾān is far from frivolous. Both could with justice be called the master-texts in which the Greek and Arab nations were first addressed as such. Also, both make use of oracular models and vocabulary in staging their own reception and interpretation by their hearers, with the key difference that the Qurʾān does so in opposition to the divinatory practices it cites. The perceptible forms of this opposition range from negative representations to outright prohibitions, and to the bellicose appropriation of oracular concepts and practices. Prophetic co-option of the hermeneutic and political authority of the pre-Islamic *kāhin* (variously translated as 'soothsayer', 'diviner', and 'seer', and cognate to Hebrew *kōhēn*, 'priest') will in any theory of Islam's Meccan origins be granted as inevitable; what remain to be pointed out are the traces of this co-option in the Qurʾān, and in the Prophet's speech and practice as represented in *ḥadī<u>th</u>* and *sīra* (biography). My examination of these traces will demonstrate the superscription of prophetic authority over oracular semiology as it was enacted in the earliest texts of Islam.

6 Vernant 1991:307.

Prophecy vs. Divination

The formal similarity between oracular and Qurʾānic discourse has been observed by Western Orientalists ever since Julius Wellhausen's still-startling declaration that the best evidence for what pre-Islamic oracular speech was like is located in the earliest *sūras* of the Qurʾān itself.[7] Relative to the expansive verbiage of the later *sūras*, these are distinguished by their cryptic, incantory style and overall brevity, and as such are grouped toward the end of the Qurʾān (whose chapters are arranged in descending order of length).[8] The precise extent to which they actually resemble pre-Islamic oracular speech cannot be judged, as no authentically pre-Islamic sources for this have survived. But the Qurʾān's insistence on its own distinction from oracular speech will alert us that some ritual and/or formal correspondence between them was observable to the Qurʾān's early hearers, as in the Meccan-era *Sūrat al-Ṭūr* ("The Mount"):

52:29. *Fa-<u>dh</u>akkir fa-mā anta bi-niʿmati rabbika bi-<u>kāhinin</u> wa-la majnūn*
52:30. *Am yaqulūna <u>Shāʿirun</u> natarabbaṣu bi-hi rayba ʾl-manūn*

52:29. So make it known that you, by the grace of your Lord, are no <u>soothsayer</u>, nor are you possessed by jinns.
52:30. Or do they say [of you] "<u>Poet</u>! for whose downfall we lie in wait"?[9]

Being more frequent, the denial that the Qurʾān was the work of a *<u>sh</u>āʿir* ('poet') has attracted more attention than the concomitant disavowal of soothsaying. Whereas *kāhin* occurs only twice in the Qurʾān (52:29 and 68:42), *<u>sh</u>āʿir* occurs four times, its plural once more, and the affiliated verbal noun *<u>sh</u>iʿr* once again, each time in an unambiguously negative context.[10] This circumstance has led Michael Zwettler to remark that "the charge that the Prophet was a *kāhin* seems not to have been thought so grave or to have required so vehement a refutation as the one that he was a poet" (Zwettler 1978:157). Though this observatation rings true, it requires some explanation in light of the Qurʾān's lack of similarity in form or content to the extant corpus of

7 Wellhausen 1897:137n4. See also Jones 1994:32–37, Fahd 1966:149–176, Frolov 2000:105–108, Zwettler 1978:157–159, and Zwettler 1990:80–84.

8 Known together as *al-Muʿawwidatayn* or "*Sūras* of Refuge," the last two (*al-Falaq* and *al-Nās*) are renowned as charms against illness and malevolent sorcery.

9 Translations, except where noted, are my own.

10 It will further be noticed that three of *<u>sh</u>āʿir*'s four occurrences (21:5, 37:36, and 52:30 quoted above) fall within in the quoted speech of those who dismiss the Qurʾān as the invention of a "poet."

pre-Islamic Arabic poetry, and its resemblance to Arabian oracular speech. In resolution of this difficulty, Zwettler argues that what made Qur'ānic recitation confundible with poetic performance was not a generic resemblance but a *linguistic* one, in that the Qur'ān was delivered in the "non-vernacular, classical" Arabic language which was up to that point an exclusive vehicle for the performance of poetry, and thus "to the minds of Muḥammad's hearers (and of Muḥammad himself) inextricably bound up with their total experience of poetry, so that they were quite unprepared to hear it enounced competently and coherently in any other genre of comparable length and artistry" (Zwettler 1978:158–160).

Thankfully, it is not my purpose to unravel the long-running debate about the origins of Classical Arabic and its relationship to the tribal dialects in which Zwettler's argument takes its place. I will note that his linguistic turn does not yield the only possible explanation for the Qur'ān's self-distancing from poetry, nor necessarily the most persuasive.[11] But the premise that Qur'ānic revelation must have shared some traits with both poetry and divination for its recurrent disavowals to make sense is quite well founded, and suggestive of other points of likeness than the poetic form and linguistic idiom he adduces. Social and ritual context is another. Another homology between poetry and Qur'ānic recitation is that both are *for performance aloud before an assembly of hearers*, and the Qur'ān's antagonism toward poets may well have been motivated (at least in part) by this homology.

The office of the s͟hā'ir (literally, 'knower') is likely to have comprised an oracular function at some early point, and as a matter of course involves privileged contact with an invisible muse (s͟hayṭān).[12] In the received folklore of the pre-Islamic period, however, the s͟hā'ir is most often encountered as a group spokesman and a dispenser of intertribal praise and blame. Despite the clear formal remove between them, the public performance context of Qur'ānic recitation (which mobilizes a good deal of praise and blame of its own) must have been similar enough to that of poetry to call for the denials that

11 Least convincing is his downplaying of the ritual speech of soothsayers, on the grounds that "their short, enigmatic and highly occasional utterances offered no real precedent for recurrent and sustained use of the poetic idiom outside the realm of poetry, as represented by the Qur'ān." Zwettler 1978:160.

12 Although *al-S͟hayṭān* is regularly identified in Islamic usage with Satan, the name is also given to airborne spirits coeval with the *jinn*. As impish companion spirits, *s͟hayāṭīn* (pl.) may be thought of by analogy to the Socratic *daimōn*—the Prophet is said to have affirmed that everybody has one in Muslim 2007 (*Kitāb Ṣifāt al-munāfiqīn*): 1272—or, in the case of poets, to the muse. "Muse" is clearly its operative sense in the remark by the early poet Jarīr to his rival Farazdaq: "Did you not know we share the same *s͟hayṭān*?" (*a-mā 'alamta anna s͟hayṭānanā wāḥid*). Al-Ḥātimī 1979: II 47.

Muḥammad was in any way a poet. The Qur'ān may be further comparable to pre-Islamic poetry in its function as an *instrument of group formation*, toward the end of superimposing a universalized Islamic community over the tribal kinship structures of traditional Middle Eastern society. By insisting on its remove from poetry, the Qur'ān places itself outside the arena of inter-tribal conflict, and indicates a newly universalized ritual context for its own recitation and reception.[13]

Nor is it the case that divination is treated indifferently in the Qur'ān, or that its treatment is limited to two fleeting occurrences of the word *kāhin*. In fact the Qur'ān's engagement with oracular language is complex and quite tendentious, as one might expect from its assumption of the form most characteristic of the oracular utterance: namely, the stylized rhyming speech called *saj*ʿ.[14] As a genre of perfomed speech, *saj*ʿ is formally distinguished from shiʿr by its variable line length and lack of a fixed metrical structure. It was also in use as a vehicle for *khuṭba*, that is, 'oratory' in the general sense; the Prophet is said to have recollected this piece of *saj*ʿ by the orator Quss b. Sāʿida, whom in his youth he had heard speak at the market-fair of ʿUkāẓ:

Ayyuha 'n-nāsu ijtamiʿū
wa-ismaʿu
wa-ʿū
man ʿāsha māt
wa-man māta fāt
wa-kullu mā huwa ātin āt

13 This is demonstrated in an episode from *al-Sīrat al-nabawiyya* ('Life of the Prophet') by Ibn Isḥāq and Ibn Hishām (discussed by Zwettler 1978:158–159), describing an assembly of Muḥammad's Meccan opponents convened by al-Walīd ibn al-Mughīra in order to determine the exact nature of the Prophet's mission. To their first conjecture that he is a *kāhin*, al-Walīd responds, "No, by God, he is no *kāhin*, for we have seen *kāhins*, and his is not the cryptic muttering [*zamzama*] of the *kāhin*, nor the *kāhin*'s *saj*ʿ." "Then he is *majnūn* [possessed by demons]," they say, to which al-Walīd replies, "He is not *majnūn*, for we have seen demonic possession, and are acquainted with it, and he shows none of the convulsions, choking, or devilish whispering [*waswasa*] of the possessed." "Then he is a poet [*shāʿir*]," to which al-Walīd says, "He is no poet, for we know poetry in all its forms and meters, and [the Qur'ān] is not poetry." "Then he is a sorcerer [*sāḥir*]." "No, he is no sorcerer, for we have seen sorcerers and their magic, and [Muḥammad practices] none of their spitting and tying of knots." And yet al-Walīd concludes, "Your guess that he is a sorcerer comes closest, *in that he has the sorcerer's power to separate a man from his father, his brother, his wife, and his tribe*" (emphasis added). Ibn Isḥāq 1936: I 270–271 ; alluded to in *Sūrat al-Muddaththir* (74:18-25).

14 As Dmitry Frolov has indicated, it was a concern for scholars of the Ashʿarī school to deny the presence of *saj*ʿ in the text of Qur'ān, but even Abū Bakr al-Bāqillānī (d. 403/1013) "had to concede that speech can be patterned as *saj*ʿ 'without turning into it'" (*qad yakūnu 'l-kalāmu ʿalā mithāli 's-sajʿi wa-in lam yakun sajʿan*). Frolov 2000:107–108 (with references).

> O people, gather together
> and listen
> and keep [this] in your memory:
> Who lives, dies
> and who dies is done with
> and all the future holds will come to pass.
>
> al-Jāḥiẓ 1968: I 308–309

The utility of *saj'* was described by the orator 'Abd al-Ṣamad b. al-Faḍl b. 'Īsā b. Abān al-Raqāshī (d. ca. 200/815–816), as related by 'Amr b. Baḥr al-Jāḥiẓ (d. 255/869):

> [When asked] "Why do you esteem *saj'* over prose, when it obliges you to [speak in] rhyme and measure?" he responded, "When my hope is only [to reach] the hearing of those present, my speech differs little from yours. But I am concerned with what is absent and what is past as well as what is present, and [with *saj'*] the recollection of it is faster, and its appeal to the hearing is keener, and it is fixed more truly [in the recollection] and less of it escapes. The Arabs find it easier to express themselves correctly in unconstrained speech than poetry, but no more than one tenth of what is said in unconstrained speech is remembered, and it is diffused only a tenth as widely as measured speech.
>
> al-Jāḥiẓ 1968: I 287

In the pre-Islamic period, *saj'* was principally identified as the performance medium of the *kāhin*. "Heathen incantation" is clearly the word's meaning in *ḥadīth* where the Prophet dismisses a litigant's statement with the remark, "Is this a *saj'* of the Time of Ignorance and its soothsaying?" (*a-saj'u 'l-Jāhiliyyati wa-kahānatuha*). The dismissed statement was a rhymed couplet protesting that no recompense was due in the case of a miscarriage induced by a hurled stone:

> *Innahu kādhibun innahu wa-'llāhi mā istaḥall*
> *Wa-lā sharaba wa-lā akala fa-mithluhu yuṭall*[15]

> He is lying! He is! By God, I swear that it never raised its voice
> Nor did it drink nor eat. Such a death calls for no vengeance.

Several features of the above statement could have invited the comparison to ritual *kāhin* speech—notably, its indulgence in repetition ("*innahu . . . innahu*"),

15 Thus in Abū Dā'ūd 1996 (*Kitāb al-Diyāt*): IV 196, with multiple versions in Muslim 2007 (*Kitab al-Qaṣāma*): 796–797; cited also in al-Jāḥiẓ 1968: I 287, and noted by Frolov 2000:113.

oaths ("*wa-'llāhi*"), and, above all, rhyme. As such they hallmarks not only of the *kāhin*'s performance but, according to Toufic Fahd, of the oracular trance itself: "In origin, *saj*ʿ denoted the *kāhin*'s entry into a trance, the oracular utterance issuing from this state, and then the stylistic form of this utterance." The description given in Fahd's landmark study *La divination arabe* is worth quoting in full:

> In the lexica, *al-saj*ʿ denotes the formal expression of the oracle. Some have sought to see in them an imitation of the repeated, jerky and monotonous cooing of a pigeon or dove, or the drawn-out and monotonous moaning of a camel. But in our traditional sources the term is recognized as a specific designation for the oracular utterance of the *kāhins*, formulated in short, rhymed phrases, with rhythmical cadences and the use of an obscure, archaizing, bizarre and cabalistic vocabulary.
>
> In its most ancient sense, however, *saj*ʿ denoted a state of ecstasy, as we see in Akkadian *šegû* (root *š-g-*ʾ), Hebrew *š-g-*ʿ and Arabic *s-j-*ʿ. The root's meaning in the the Akkadian texts is in fact "fury" or "rage," said most typically of a dog; in Hebrew it serves to designate a state of dementia or unconsciousness, and is in particular used against the prophets by their opponents as an abusive epithet.[16] And some forms of the Arabic root *s-j-*ʿ, which commonly expresses the idea of courage and audacity, still conserve the ancient meaning of "demented, insensate, unbalanced." . . . Nor is a Sumerian origin excluded, given that *šugîtu*, a feminine form of *šegû* borrowed by Akkadian from Sumerian, denotes the hierodule, whose duties included serving as oracle in the temple where she officiated.[17]

Many examples of oracular *saj*ʿ could be culled from the literature at large. Fahd quotes a number of them in *La divination arabe*, including one by the early Khuzāʿite soothsayer ʿAmr b. Luḥayy, which he singles out as an especially archaic specimen.[18] Alan Jones's 1994 article "The Language of the Qurʾān" collects several more (Jones 1994:33–37). Below I offer an example of oracular *saj*ʿ as represented in a tale from the *Kitāb al-Aghānī* ('Book of Songs') of Abu 'l-Faraj al-Iṣbahānī (d. 371/981), in which a man consults the soothsayers Shiqq

16 See 2 Kings 9:11, Jeremiah 29:26, and Hosea 9:7; also Deuteronomy 28:34 and 1 Samuel 21:14–15. If I am not mistaken, Yiddish *meshuggeneh* is formed upon this Hebrew word.

17 Fahd 1966:151–153; see also Fahd art. "Sadjʿ (1)" in *Encyclopaedia of Islam*, 2nd ed. (henceforth EI²) VIII 732–733.

18 Fahd 1966:162–169; for an English translation see Ibn al-Kalbī 1952:46–47.

and Saṭīḥ about his son-in-law's identity. Saṭīḥ and S̲h̲iqq were *kāhins* of pre-Islamic renown to whom Islamic legend attributed fantastically long lives in order to draft them into stories of the Prophetic nativity (traditionally dated to 570 CE). The meaning of Saṭīḥ's name ('He who lies stretched out') is variously understood to suggest prostration, fainting spells, or outright paralysis; early or late, Saṭīḥ came to be described as lacking the ability to move under his own power, or even lacking solid bones altogether (al-Ḥalabī 1989: 131–132). S̲h̲iqq's name, meaning 'Cleft', appears all along to have denoted a being with only one arm, one leg, and one eye.[19] And yet the *bizarrerie* of these personages does not invalidate the following as a representative sample of pre-Islamic oracular speech:

> Ibn al-Kalbī (d. 206/821) said: I was told by my father on the authority of Abū S̲ā̲liḥ, who was told that Ibn ʿAbbās said T̲h̲aqīf and al-Najaʿa were descended from Īyād.[20] T̲h̲aqīf's name was Qasiyy b. Munabbih. . . . [He and] al-Najaʿa had set out together, bringing with them a goat whose milk they were drinking, when they encountered a tax-collector of the king of Yemen who sought to take the goat from them. "But we live on its milk!" they said, and killed him in the act of seizing it. He who fired the arrow said to the other, "You and I must not be found in the same land." Al-Najaʿa journeyed to Bīs̲h̲a, where he remained; Qasiyy arrived at an area near al-Ṭāʾif. There he saw a slave-girl watching over a flock belonging to ʿĀmir b. al-Ẓarib al-ʿAdwānī, which he coveted. "I will kill the slave-girl," he said, "and take possession of the flock." But the slave-girl prevented his plan when she said to him, "I see that you intend to kill me and take the flock. If you do this you will yourself be killed, and the flock will be taken from you. [If you refrain,] I will treat you as a hungry stranger." She led him to her master, and Qasiyy came before him and asked for permission to reside in the area. ʿĀmir gave him his daughter in marriage, and Qasiyy settled at al-Ṭāʾif. It was said: "How easily was he made master!" [*Li-ʾllāhi darruhu mā athqafahu*] when Qasiyy became ʿĀmir's master [*thaqifa ʿĀmiran*] and neighbor. . . . And ʿĀmir was upbraided for having married his daughter to Qasiyy. "You have married [your daughter] to a slave," they said.
>
> So he set off to consult the *kāhins*. The first one he arrived at was S̲h̲iqq ibn Ṣaʿb of the Bajīla, who was closest. On arriving before

---

19 See Levi Della Vida's article "Saṭīḥ b. Rabīʿah" in EI² IX 84–85.
20 The Banū T̲h̲aqīf inhabited the mountainous area of al-Ṭāʾif, south of Mecca.

him, he said, "We have come about a certain matter. What is that matter?" Shiqq said,

> *Ji'tum fī Qasiyy*
> *wa-Qasiyyu ʿabdu Ībād*
> *abaqa laylata 'l-wād*
> *fī Wajjin dhāti 'l-andād*
> *fa-wālā Saʿdan li-yufād*
> *thumma lawā bi-ghayri muʿād*

> "You have come about Qasiyy.
> Qasiyy is a slave of Ībād
> who fled by night to the the river
> in the valley of Wajj of many idols
> and joined with Saʿd in order to be free.
> Then he concealed his unfriendlike behavior."

(Saʿd was a branch of [ʿĀmir's tribe,] Qays b. ʿAylān b. Muḍar.)

ʿĀmir then went to consult Saṭīḥ of Dhi'b. (Dhi'b ['Wolf'] was either a tribe of Ghassān, or a Quḍaʿite tribe living among the Ghassān.)[21] He said to him: "We have come about a certain matter. What is that matter?" Saṭīḥ said,

> *Ji'tum fī Qasiyy*
> *wa-Qasiyyu min waladi Thamūda 'l-qadīm*
> *waladathu ummuhu bi-'ṣ-ṣaḥrā'a Barīm*
> *fa-'ltaqṭahu Īyādun wa-huwa ʿadīm*
> *fa-'staʿabdahu wa-huwa mulīm*

> "You have come about Qasiyy.
> Qasiyy is a descendant of the Thamūd of old
> whose mother bore him in the desert of Barīm.
> Īyād took him in when he was destitute,
> then punished his behavior by enslaving him."

ʿĀmir b. al-Ẓarib returned home, still not knowing what to do about the whole affair. He was held fast in the pact he had made and the marriage agreement, for despite their being deprived of Islam, the men of his day were bound by their word.

al-Iṣbahānī 1969: IV 75 (1517–1519)

21 The Ghassānids were a tribal alliance retained as *foederati* of the Byzantines along the empire's Arabian borders. By virtue of their service, the Banū Ghassān rose to semi-aristocratic status among the northern nomads.

What echoes of the early Qur'ānic style we find in these *saj'* passages (including brevity of line, indulgence in parallelism, and the predominance of the oath) are perhaps unsurprising, given its preservation by generations of transmitters who had the Qur'ān before them as a stylistic model. Of greater interest are the narrative details surrounding the soothsayer's office, beginning with his isolation from society. The *kāhin* is either summoned from elsewhere or made the goal of a long journey, but is in all cases remote from the matters on which he or she (feminine *kāhina*) is consulted.[22] Zwettler observes that "the pre-Islamic *kuhhān*, with few exceptions, were frequently depicted as something of social misfits, sometimes deformed or defective in body, dwelling outside the pale of normal urban and nomadic communities."[23] This isolation seems key to the *kāhin*'s authority, for above all we find the soothsayer resorted to as an arbiter. In addition to his judgments on genealogical matters, Saṭīḥ is elsewhere shown handing down interpretations of dreams and omens, and in one account dividing an inheritance.[24] *Fāṣil al-khuṭṭa*, he is called in one story, that is, 'Divider' or 'Adjudicator of the case'.[25] Poetic flourish though this may be, it is quite in the spirit of the agnomen that the Prophet Muḥammad declared off-limits: Abu 'l-Qāsim, or 'Father of the Apportioner'. In the collection of Muslim b. al-Ḥajjāj al-Qushayrī (d. 261/875) appear several versions of the following *ḥadīth*:

> 'Uthmān b. Abī Shayba and Isḥāq b. Ibrāhīm relate that Jarīr heard from Manṣūr on the authority of Sālim b. Abī Ja'd that Jābir b. 'Abd Allāh said: "A son was born to a man in our community, and he named him Muḥammad. His people told him: 'We urge you not to call [your child] by the name of God's Prophet, God's blessings and peace be upon him.' So he set off with his son on his back and brought him to the Prophet (God's blessings and peace be upon him)

22 The Prophet's grandfather 'Abd al-Muṭṭalib resorts to the arbitration of female soothsayers in two separate incidents related in Ibn Isḥāq 1936: I 144–145 and 153–154; English translation by Guillaume 1955:67–68 and 91–92.

23 Zwettler 1990:78. Vernant 1991:306 makes a similar point about the civic marginalization of oracular activity in classical Greece. *Kuhhān* is the plural of *kāhin*.

24 The story of Saṭīḥ's interpretation of a dream for the king of Yemen is narrated in Ibn Isḥāq 1936: I 15–19, trans. Guillaume 1955:4–6. In another well-known story Saṭīḥ interprets omens for Chosroes, King of Persia, narrated in *Kitāb al-'Iqd al-farīd* by Ibn 'Abd Rabbih 1940: II 28–31, the *Lisān al-'arab* (henceforth *Lisān*) of Ibn Manẓūr 1988: VI 254–256 (article √sṭḥ), and al-Ḥalabī 1969:130–133. In this last source we read that "Some have said Saṭīḥ lived in the days of Nizār b. Ma'add b. 'Adnān, and that it was he who divided Nizār's inheritance among his sons, who were Muḍar and his brothers" (132).

25 Ibn 'Abd Rabbih 1940: II 29, *Lisān* VI 255.

> and said: 'A son is born to me, and I have named him Muḥammad. But my people urge me not to call him by the Prophet's name.' The Prophet (God's blessings and peace be upon him) said: 'You may call [your sons] by my name but not by my agnomen, for Qāsim am I who divide the apportionments among you' [*fa-innamā anā Qāsimun aqsimu baynakum*]."
>
> Muslim 2007 (*K. al-Ādāb*): 1006

To the extent that soothsayers were resorted to as a juridical authority, that authority was by definition in conflict with the institutions of early Islam, beginning with the establishment of Muḥammad's legal mandate at Medina. The Prophet's assumption of any and all juridical authority excerised by the *kāhin* forms a suggestive parallel to the Qur'ānic adaptation of *saj*ʿ, and raises the question of what other ritual and political functions formerly played by soothsayers were taken over by Islam, and which were neutralized outright. The question is hardly scandalous, as the *kāhin*'s spiritual authority is acknowledged by the traditional sources and modern scholarship as a predecessor to the Prophet's own.[26] The Qur'ān's delivery in *saj*ʿ in fact telegraphs the *kāhins*' institutional displacement by the Prophet, as do his reported prohibitions against consulting them and paying them tribute.[27]

Āya vs. *ṭā'ir*

The formal analogies between pre-Islamic *saj*ʿ and Qur'ānic revelation are perhaps of secondary interest, for what really draws attention is the Qur'ān's *transformation* of the oracular medium, and the transvaluation of semiological concepts that accompanied it. Toshihiko Izutsu makes the same point in his 1964 study *God and Man in the Koran*: "Old concepts are there, but they have undergone a drastic semantic transformation by having been put into a new system of values. Something similar happened to *saj*ʿ: the old traditional form of supernatural communication is used, but it is used as a vehicle for conveying a new content" (Izutsu 1964:184). There being no way to check the

26 "The *kuhhān* were widespread among the Arabs before Islam, due to the absence of Prophecy [*al-nubuwwa*] among them" (Fayyūmī 1979:291). For an ancient Hebrew analogue, see 1 Samuel 9:9: "Formerly in Israel, when a man went to inquire of God, he said, 'Come, let us go to the seer [*ro'eh*]'; for he who is now called a prophet was formerly called a seer."

27 Specifically forbidden in more than one *ḥadīth* is the fee paid to the *kāhin* for his or her services; in an echo of Deuteronomy 23:18, the Prophet is said to have ranked such payment with "the price paid for a dog and the wages of a prostitute." Al-Bukhārī 2004 (*K. al-Ṭalāq*): 1121, (*K. al-Ṭibb*): 1194, etc.

Qur'ān against the forms of oracular speech that preceded it, we are left to examine the transformations in Arabian semiological concepts as they are enacted within the text of the Qur'ān itself. Foremost among these concepts is that of the *āya* (pl. *āyāt, āy*), or 'sign'. The Arabic word is cognate with Hebrew *oth*, also 'sign' (and rendered as σημεῖον in the Septuagint), which is used for the mark of Cain, the rainbow of Noah, and the miracles performed by Moses before Pharaoh.[28] *Oth* also occurs in the Lachish ostraka of the sixth century BCE, in reference to the beacon-fires (*massu'oth*) by which coded messages were passed over long distances.[29]

In the pre-Islamic corpus of poetry, *āya* shows a similar flexibility. It can mean 'trace,' as in the traces of an abandoned campsite in the poem by ʿAbīd b. al-Abraṣ (d. ca. 555 CE):

Taghayyarat ad-diyāru bi-Dhī Dafīni
fa-ūdiyati 'l-Liwā fa-rimāli Līn
fa-ḥarjay Dhirwatin fa-qafā Dhayālin
yuʿaffī āyahu salafu 's-sinīn

Altered are the abodes at Dhū Dafīn,
and in the valleys of al-Liwā, and on the sands of Līn,
and in the two narrows of Dhirwa, and on the far side of Dhayāl
the bygone years have effaced their traces.
ʿAbīd b. al-Abraṣ 1994:97

Or the *āya* can be an abstract 'proof,' as in the *Muʿallaqa* of al-Ḥārith b. Ḥilliza:

Man la-nā ʿinda-hu min al-khayri āyā-
tun thalāthun fī kullihinna 'l-qaḍā'
Āyatun shāriqu 'sh-shaqīqati idh jā-
'at Maʿaddun li-kulli ḥayyin liwā'

He has had three proofs of our excellence,
each of them decisive:
One proof was [our valor at] the pass's eastern end, when came
[the tribe of] Maʿadd with a banner for each of their clans.
al-Zawzanī 1972:163–164

28 Genesis 4:15, 9:12, and Exodus 4:8; see Keller 1946:7.

29 Torczyner et al. 1938: I 79 (Letter IV). We find the *massu'oth* described in the *Mishnah Rosh Hashanah* (II 2–3), as translated by Herbert Danby: "They used to take long cedarwood sticks and rushes and oleander wool and flax tow; and a man bound these up with a rope and went up to the top of the hill and set light to them; and he waved them to and fro and up and down until he could see his fellow doing the like on the top of the next hill. And so, too, on the top of the third hill" (quoted in Torczyner et al. 1938: I 83).

It can also mean an intentionally deployed ‘signal’ as in the verse of al-Aʿshā (d. ca. 4/625):

> *Bi-āyati tuqdimūna ʾl-khayla shuʿthan*
> *ka-anna ʿalā sanābikihā mudāman*
>
> At the signal with which you drive on the horses, uncombed
> as if their hooves had never known rest from their burdens . . .
>
> *Lisān* I 283

Some archaic uses of the word *āya* appear to have persisted into the early Islamic period. “The signs of the hypocrite are three,” begins a *ḥadīth* in the first book of *Ṣaḥīḥ Muslim*, a case in which *āya* means ‘identifying mark.’[30] This general meaning is seldom found in post-Qurʾānic Arabic–perhaps in emulation of the specific uses of *al-āya* in the Qurʾān, where (with two exceptions) it is used strictly to indicate a sign of God’s agency.[31] Thus it refers to teratological interventions (such as catastrophes and prophetic miracles), as well as quotidian phenomena such as the sun and moon (10:5), rainwater and the growth of plants (16:10–11), and the safe passage of ships upon the sea (31:31). At the same time, each individual verse of the Qurʾān is called an *āya*, as at 2:106 and in Islamic usage ever since.[32] Unlike omens, which require the intervention of an interpreter for their latent content to be revealed, the *āyāt* of God are named as clear and unmistakable signs, which only those whom God prevents will fail to read as such. The Qurʾān does not interpret these signs so much as it proclaims them, and affirms their source in the Creator whose mastery they in turn signify.

If a mapping of Qurʾānic semiology onto modern Western terms were asked for, one might align the signifying capacity of the *āya* with that of C. S. Peirce’s “index,” that sign “which refers to its object not so much because of any similarity or analogy with it, nor because it is associated with general characters which that object happens to possess, as because it is in dynamical (including spatial) connection both with the individual object, on the one hand, and with the senses or memory of the person for whom it serves

30 The *ḥadīth* continues: “When he speaks, he lies; when he makes a promise, he breaks it; and when trust is placed in him, he betrays it” [*Āyat al-munāfiqi thalāthun: idhā ḥaddatha kadhaba wa-idhā waʿada akhlafa wa-idhā uʾtumina khāna*]. Muslim 2007 (*K. al-Īmān*):87; also in al-Bukhārī 2004 (*K. al-Īmān*): 20.

31 The exceptions are in *Sūrat al-Baqara* (2:248), which speaks of the “sign” of Saul’s kingship, and *Sūrat al-Shuʿarā* (26:128), wherein the prophet Hūd chastises his people: “In vain you build an *āya* on every hill-top.”

32 Not until the mid-twentieth century would *Āyat Allāh* (‘Sign of God’) be adopted as a title by Shīʿite clergy; see Momen 1985:205–206.

as a sign, on the other hand."[33] In other words, the relationship between the index and its object is fundamentally *metonymic*, motivated not by likeness (as is Peirce's "icon") or convention (Peirce's "symbol"), but by virtue of causal association—enforced in the *āya*'s case by the Qurʾān's repeated declarations of God's responsibility for the creation of the heavens, the earth and everything between them. The Qurʾān's application of the word *āya* to all verbal and non-verbal manifestations of God's will effected a permanent transformation in the concept as known in the pre-Islamic poetry. No longer would *āya* be used to mean "sign" in a general sense, but only for those signs indicating God's agency and might. As such it is the basis for the semiological regime ushered in by Prophetic revelation (and by "semiological regime" I mean the set of semiotic norms that govern a community's interaction with the divine). How much Judeo-Christian residue *al-āya* brought with it into Arabic (borrowed, it is thought, from Syriac *āṯā*) is difficult to judge, but any recognizable affiliation to Hebrew *oth* would seem only to have confirmed the *āya* as the preferred vehicle for communication between the God of Moses and His Muslim worshipers.

That the *āya* was not the only semiological model available to the Qurʾān's early hearers is verifiable on internal evidence alone, for alongside it may be observed a set of idioms drawn openly from the lexicon of divination. These are constructed on the verb *ṭayara* ('to fly') by virtue of its being the root of *ṭāʾir*, the word for 'bird' and hence any 'indicator of fate' in the double sense familiar from Greek *ornis* and Latin *avis*. The analogy to Greek and Roman ornithomancy is upheld by Fahd, whose elucidation is again worth quoting in full:

> The technique of *ṭīra* or *ṭayr* (= ὄρνις) consists in observing the spontaneous flights of birds (*auspicia oblativa*) and drawing from them knowledge of future outcomes. It is carried out upon confrontation with the ominous sign, limited not to the activities of birds but drawing on calls, flights and all the other displays made by animate and inanimate beings. Originally the word referred to all portents good and bad, but early Islam—anxious to purify itself of the remnants of paganism and at the same time striving to retain by conversion the good that inheres in *fiṭra*, "*la bonne nature*"—condemned the *ṭīra* as an ornithomantic technique and an omen of fate equally, while adopting the beneficial omens under the rubric of the *faʾl*.[34]

33 Peirce 1955:107; see also Zwettler 1990:214n38.

34 Fahd 1966: 436; see also Fahd's article "Faʾl" in EI² II 758–760.

The Qur'ān's repudiation of *al-ṭīra* is most forcefully expressed in a single narrative template engaged in three separate *sūras*. This is the primal confrontation between God's earlier messengers (two drawn from Hebrew scripture and one from Arabian tradition) and the disbelieving nations they were sent to warn.[35] Repeatedly, the disbelievers of old are heard to reject the prophetic warnings with the remark "We take you to be a bad omen," paying for it in the end with their own destruction. Thus we hear of the Egyptians:

7:130. *Wa-la-qad akhadhnā āla Fir'awna bi-'s-sinīna wa-naqṣin min ath-thamarāt la'allahum yadhdhakkarūn*

7:131. *Fa-idhā jā'athumu 'l-ḥasanatu qālū La-nā hādhihi wa-in tuṣibhum sayyi'atun yaṭṭayyarū bi-Mūsā wa-man ma'ahu a-lā inna-mā ṭā'iruhum 'inda 'llāhi wa lākinna aktharahum lā ya'lamūn*

7:132. *Wa-qālū Mahmā ta'tinā bi-hi min āyatin li-tasḥaranā bi-hā fa-mā naḥnu la-ka bi-mu'minīn*

7:133. *Fa-arsalnā 'alayhimu 'ṭ-ṭūfāna wa-'l-jarāda wa-'l-qummala wa-'ḍ-ḍafādi'a wa-'d-dama āyātin mufaṣṣalātin fa-'stakbarū wa-kānū qawman mujrimīn*

[...]

7:136. *Fa-intaqamnā minhum fa-aghraqnāhum fī-'l-yammi bi-annahum kadhdhabū bi-āyātinā wa-kānū 'anhā ghāfilīn*

7:130. We beset the house of Pharaoh with famine and failure of crops in order that they might take heed.

7.131. For when good things came to them they said, "These are our due," but when bad things befell them they augured ill of Moses and those who were with him. But no, the indicator of their fate lay with God, though most of them were unknowing.

7.132. And they said, "No matter what signs you bring in order to deceive us by, we will not believe in you."

7.133. So We unleashed the flood over then, and the locust and the vermin, and the frogs and the blood: a variety of signs. But they remained proud, for they were a sinning people.

[...]

[35] As such these narratives unite a number of themes listed in the *Motif-Index of Folk-Literature* of Stith Thompson (1989), among them J652, "Inattention to warnings"; J2051, "Wise man short-sightedly scorned for his advice"; and J2285, "Foolish interpretation of omens."

7.136. We took Our vengeance on them, and drowned them in the sea, because they challenged the truth of Our signs, and disregarded them.

Of the Thamūd who dwelt at al-Ḥijr we are told,

27:45. *Wa-la-qad arsalnā ilā Thamūda akhāhum Ṣāliḥan an Iʿbudu ʾllāha fa-idhā hum farīqān yakhtaṣimūn*

27:46. *Qāla Yā qawmi li-ma tastaʿjilūna bi-ʾs-sayyiʾati qabla ʾl-ḥasanati law lā tastaghfirūn Allāha laʿallakum turḥamūn*

27:47. *Qālū Aṭṭayyarnā bi-ka wa-bi-man maʿaka qāla Ṭāʾirukum ʿinda ʾllāhi bal antum qawmun tuftanūn*

[. . .]

27:51. *Fa-unẓur kayfa kāna ʿāqibatu makrihim annā dammarnāhum wa-qawmahum ajmaʿīn*

27.52. *Fa-tilka buyūtuhum khāwiyatan bi-mā ẓalamū inna fī dhālika la-āyatan li-qawmin yaʿlamūn*

27:45. To Thamūd we sent their brother Ṣāliḥ [commanding] that they "Worship God!" But they were a people divided into two warring factions.

27:46. He said, "O people! Why do you hasten what is evil, instead of what is good? Though you do not [now] seek God's pardon, you may [yet] be forgiven.

27:47. They said: "We augur ill of you and those who are with you." He replied: "Your fate's indicator lies with God, but you are a people beguiled away."

[. . .]

27:51. See, then, what sort of end their delusion came to: We destroyed them and their people altogether.

27:52. Yonder lie their dwellings, vacated on account of their sins. Truly, there is a sign in this for a knowing people.

Finally, the story is told of "the Village" (*al-Qarya*) identified with Antioch in Syria:

36:13. *Wa-ʾḍrib la-humu mathalan aṣḥāba ʾl-Qaryati idh jāʾaha ʾl-mursalūn*

36:14. *Idh arsalnā ilayhim ithnayni fa-kadhdhabūhumā fa-ʿazzaznā bi-thālithin fa-qālū Innā ilaykumu mursalūn. . . .*

[. . .]

36:18. *Qālū Innā taṭayyarnā bi-kum la-in lam tantahū la-narjumannakum wa-la-yamassannakum minnā ʿadhābun alīm*

36:19. *Qālū Ṭāʾirukum maʿakum a-in dhukkirtum bal antum qawmun musrifūn*

36:13. As an example, tell them of the people of the Village when messengers came to it.

36:14. When We sent them two, [the villagers] called them liars, and so We strengthened [them] with a third. They said, "Truly have we been sent to you as messengers"...

[...]

36:18. [The villagers] said, "We augur ill of you. If you do not desist we will truly stone you, and grievous punishment will befall you at our hands."

36:19. [The messengers] said, "Your fate's indicator is with you, if you only knew it—but you are a people who go too far."

The pattern is clear: in each case, unbelievers fail to interpret the messengers as bringers of divine *āyāt*, instead taking the messengers' very appearance in their midst as a bad omen, and so reject the message they were sent. Their failure is one of interpretation, in that it is caused by applying the wrong code—the *oracular* code—to the *āyāt* presented to them.

These citations of oracular vocabulary can be construed in two ways. One is to understand the omen as a "dead metaphor," that is, as an archaic concept fossilized in the language as a figure of speech. The other is to conclude that if the Qurʾān persists in dramatizing the superscription of the Islamic *āya* over the ornithomantic *ṭāʾir*, it is because the practice of divination was general enough to pose a challenge to the semiological mandate of Islamic prophecy. From this conclusion there follows a second, which is that a doctrinal and political conflict between the early Muslim community and the oracular institutions indigenous to the Ḥijāz did in fact take place.

The office of the *kāhin* might be better imagined with the help of Toufic Fahd's *Encyclopaedia of Islam* entries for "Faʾl" and "Kāhin." Spurned by Alan Jones for their speculative daring (Jones 1994:32–33), they are here quoted for the same reason:

> *Ṭīrah* is in effect a technique whose origin is pastoral and nomadic; Arabia was therefore a very propitious region for its development, as Cicero had already commented: "Arabes (et Phryges et Cilices),

> quod pastu pecudum maxime utuntur, campos et montes hieme et aestate peragrantes, propterea facilius cantus avium et volatus notaverunt."[36] Its technical character made it the prerogative of a privileged class of men, which in an organized and developed society enjoyed the status of a priesthood.[37]
>
> The Arab *kāhin* had not developed beyond this stage when the advent of Islam brought about his disappearance because of the absence, in the nomadic environment in which he lived, of a permanent stable kingship which, as in neighboring kingdoms and elsewhere, would have organized the priesthood if only to keep it under control.[38]

Conjectural though it is, Fahd's description is hard to dismiss. *Al-kihāna* was, it seems, no monolith, but a constellated and localized field of practice, and perhaps for this reason figures less prominently in the narrative of emergent Islam than do the more organized tribal and mercantile institutions of the Ḥijāz.

And yet this is no grounds for disregarding the terms of conflict between early Islamic institutions and their oracular counterparts, as Fahd himself comes close to doing. After his articulation of the *kāhin*'s numerous functions in Arabian society on the eve of Islam, he gives surprisingly little space to the Islamic ban on divination in its political and juridical aspects.[39] In Fahd's account, it is chiefly for "its pagan character" that divination in most of its forms is banned under Islam, "in the sense that it is conceived as an act of faith in blind forces of nature and the gods which represent them" (Fahd 1966:436–438). I suggest that the Islamic interdiction of divination had not only this cosmological motivation but a political one as well, which was the need to deny all claims to hermeneutic and juridical authority that competed with the Prophet's own, or the claims made in his name by Islamic institutions. I furthermore submit that the Qur'ān's citations of the language of divina-

36 *On Divination* I 42: "Arabs, Phrygians and Cilicians, who are mostly engaged in herding flocks, and wander over the fields and mountains through winter and summer, have therefore found the songs and flights of birds easier to take note of." Collins 2002:19 reminds us that Cicero actually held the augur's office in 53 BCE.

37 EI^2 II 759.

38 EI^2 IV 421.

39 "In Islam, the principle is continually affirmed: *La kihānata ba'da 'n-nubuwwa*, or 'After the Prophet there is no divination.' When the Prophet was sent, it became impossible for soothsayers to dispense knowledge of hidden matters, as these were made obscure to them by the glory of the Prophet's lamp: here one descries the duel between the monotheist prophet and the polytheist diviner." Fahd 1966:64.

tion may be read as artifacts of an historical struggle that took place between the new institutions of Islam and the indigenous oracular institutions that preceded them. As such, the Qur'ānic narratives quoted above are not inert "reflections" of this struggle, but *programmatic and performative representations* mobilized within the selfsame struggle for hermeneutic and political jurisdiction.

Ornithosemantics

The *ṭā'ir* is deployed in a variety of contexts within the Qur'ān, and is not always so polemically marked as in the passages above. In one remarkable example, we find it named as an eschatological indicator:

17:13. *Wa-kulla insānin alzamnāhu <u>ṭā'irahu</u> fī 'unuqihi wa-nukhriju la-hu Yawma 'l-Qiyāmati kitāban yalqāhu manshūran*

17:14. *Iqrā' kitābaka kafā bi-nafsika 'l-yawma 'alayka ḥasīban*

17:13. To every man's neck We have fastened an <u>indicator of his fate</u>, and on the Day of Resurrection we will issue him a text which he will find spread open.

17:14. [And he will be told,] "Read your text! On this day it is all the accounting you need."

Here the *ṭā'ir* is not only placed under God's jurisdiction (as above at 7:131 and 27:47), but accompanies the text each person will be issued on the Day of Resurrection, indicating their earthly deeds and fated afterlife. If this usage does not exactly amount to an Islamic rehabilitation of the omen, it does at least show another rhetorical use for oracular vocabulary within the Qur'ān, which is to say a *co-optional* use. For even as the practice of *al-ṭīra* is forbidden to the Muslim community, the *ṭā'ir* is claimed by the Qur'ān as an indicator over which God's control is complete.[40]

Of the twenty-four Qur'ānic occurrences of *ṭā'ir* and its quasi-plural *ṭayr*, there are few that cannot be construed as having some oracular sense. Even references to "birds" that do not explicitly engage their semiological function do not exclude it, as in *Sūrat al-Naḥl:*

[40] In one *ḥadīth* it is recorded that the Prophet said: "'Divination by omens is idolatry [*Aṭ-ṭīratu shirkun*]. Divination by omens is idolatry.' Saying it a third time, he then said, 'Not one of us is unsusceptible [to belief in them], but God will cause it to pass if we trust in Him.'" Abū Dā'ūd 1996 (*Kitāb al-Ṭibb*): III 16.

16:79. *A-lam yaraw ila 't-ṭayri musakhkharātin fī jawwi 's-samā'i mā yumsikuhunna illa 'llāhu inna fī dhālika la-āyātin li-qawmin yu'minūn*

16:79. Have they not seen that the birds in the upper air are subservient [to Him]? They are held [aloft] by none but God: truly there are signs in this for those who believe.

Where *ṭayr* are mentioned in connection with any of the Biblical prophets, it is always in an oracular or magical context. David and Solomon were favored with armies of *ṭayr* who fought on their behalf (21:79); Solomon was even taught their language (27:16). Abraham is told to perform a rite involving four tame birds when he asks God about raising the dead (2:260), and (as at Genesis 40:16–19) Joseph is called on to interpret his cellmate's ill-omened dream about birds (12:36–41). Most suggestive of all is the *ṭayr* of Jesus, which God will recollect in *Sūrat al-Mā'ida*:

> 5:110. *Idh qāla 'llāhu Yā 'Īsa 'bna Maryama 'dhkur ni'matī 'alayka wa-'alā wālidatika idh ayyadtuka bi-Rūḥi 'l-Qudusi tukallimu 'n-nāsa fi 'l-mahdi wa-kahlan wa-idh 'allamtuka 'l-kitāba wa-'l-ḥikmata wa-'t-Tawrāta wa-'l-Injīla wa-idh takhluqu min aṭ-ṭīni ka-hay'ati 'ṭ-ṭayri bi-idhnī fa-tanfukhu fī-hā fa-takūnu ṭayran bi-idhnī wa-tubri'u 'l-akmaha wa-'l-abraṣa bi-idhnī wa-idh tukhriju 'l-mawtā bi-idhnī wa-in kafaftu Banī Isrā'īla 'anka idh ji'tahum bi-'l-bayyināti fa-qāla 'lladhīna kafarū minhum In hādhā illā siḥrun mubīn*
>
> 5:110. [The Day] when God will say, "O Jesus son of Mary, remember My blessing upon you and your mother: when I fortified you with the Holy Spirit, and from the cradle you spoke to the people, and as a full-grown man; when I taught you the book and and the proverb, and the Torah and the Gospel; when out of clay you molded the likeness of a bird, with My sanction; and you blew into it and with My sanction it became a bird, and you healed the blind and leprous, with My sanction; and when you caused the dead to emerge [from the tomb], with My sanction; and when I held the children of Israel back from you, when you brought the clear proofs to them, and the disbelievers among them said, 'Clear sorcery, this, and nothing more.' "

This verse draws notice for its summary of the so-called "Infancy Gospel of Thomas," a collection of anecdotes about the boyhood deeds of Jesus whose

Greek recension dates to the sixth century.[41] Along with its near double at *Sūrat Āl ʿImrān* 3:49, it may be numbered among several Qurʾānic engagements of post-canonical Christian material, of which *Sūrat Kahf*'s take on the Seven Sleepers of Ephesus (18:9–22) is perhaps the best-known example. As faithfully as the Qurʾān encapsulates these Christian stories, our attention is more attracted to the way they are Islamicized in their new setting, and made consistent with the ongoing semiological project of the Qurʾān. In the first place, God is heard to specify that Jesus's miracles are performed "with My sanction" (*bi-i<u>dh</u>nī*). This phrase (a variation on the formulaic affirmation *bi-i<u>dh</u>ni 'llāhi*: "with God's sanction") is here found in series with the phrase *bi-Rūḥi 'l-Qudusi*, Arabic for τῷ πνεύματι τῷ ἁγίῳ, viz. "[fortified] with the Holy Spirit" (as at Luke 10:21).[42] One might say of this nod to Christian usage that it eases the absorption of monotheist narrative into the fabric of the Qurʾān, and furthermore that it achieves this in a contained way that equates Jesus's teachings to Islam instead of the other way around.

41 The incident of "Jesus and the sparrows" is the very first related in this Infancy Gospel:

Τοῦτο τὸ παιδίον Ἰησοῦς πενταέτης γενόμενος παίζων ἦν ἐν διαβάσει ῥύακος, καὶ τὰ ῥέοντα ὕδατα συήγαγεν εἰς λάκκους, καὶ ἐποίει αὐτὰ εὐθέως καθαρά, καὶ λόγῳ μόνῳ ἐπέταξεν αὐτά. καὶ ποιήσας πηλὸν τρυφερὸν ἔπλασεν ἐξ αὐτοῦ στρουθία δώδεκα · καὶ ἦν σάββατον ὅτε ταῦτα ἐποίησεν. ἦσαν δὲ καὶ ἄλλα παιδία πολλὰ παίζοντα σὺν αὐτῷ.

Ἰδὼν δέ τις Ἰουδαῖος ἃ ἐποίει ὁ Ἰησοῦς ἐν σαββάτῳ παίζων, ἀπῆλθε παραχρῆμα καὶ ἀνήγγειλε τῷ πατρὶ αὐτοῦ Ἰωσήφ· Ἰδοὺ τὸ παιδίον σού ἐστιν ἐπὶ τὸ ῥυάκιον, καὶ λαβὼν πηλὸν ἔπλασεν πουλία δώδεκα, καὶ ἐβεβήλωσεν τὸ σάββατον.

Καὶ ἐλθὼν Ἰωσὴφ ἐπὶ τὸν τόπον καὶ ἰδὼν ἀνέκραξεν αὐτῷ λέγων· Διὰ τί ταῦτα ποιεῖς ἐν σαββάτῳ ἃ οὐκ ἔξεστι ποιεῖν;

Ὁ δὲ Ἰησοῦς συγκροτήσας τὰς χεῖρας αὐτοῦ ἀνέκραξε τοῖς στρουθίοις καὶ εἶπεν αὐτοῖς· Ὑπάγετε, πετάσετε καὶ μιμνήσκεσθέ μου οἱ ζῶντες. καὶ πετασθέντα τὰ στρουθία ὑπῆγον κράζοντα.

"When this boy, Jesus, was five years old, he was playing at the ford of a rushing stream. He was collecting the flowing water into ponds and made the water instantly pure. He did this with a single command. He then made soft clay and shaped it into twelve sparrows. He did this on the Sabbath day, and many other boys were playing with him.

"But when a Jew saw what Jesus was doing while playing on the Sabbath day, he immediately went off and told Joseph, Jesus's father: 'See here, your boy is at the ford and has taken mud and fashioned twelve birds with it, and so has violated the Sabbath.'

"So Joseph went there, and as soon as he spotted him he shouted, 'Why are you doing what's not permitted on the Sabbath?'

"But Jesus simply clapped his hands and shouted to the sparrows: 'Be off, fly away, and remember me, you who are now alive!' And the sparrows took off and flew away noisily." Trans. Hock 1995:104–106.

The Infancy Gospel's ascription to "Thomas the Israelite" would appear to be a medieval development, and indicates no affiliation to the better-known Gospel of Thomas.

42 *Qudus* has been identified as another Arabic borrowing from Christian Aramaic (Jeffrey 1938: 232). In the Qurʾān it appears only within the phrase *bi-Rūḥi 'l-Qudusi*, and in exclusive connection with Jesus (as here and at 2:30, 2:87, and 16:102).

At the same time, the episode of the *ṭayr* is framed so as to keep its ever-present divinatory valences subordinate to the normative semiological mandate of Islam. The necessity of this containment is not hard to comprehend: to the extent one allows the *ṭayr* of 5:110 its continually attested sense of "indicator of fate," it will insinuate the concept of the *omen* alongside the literal bird made out of clay. It was this sense that led Ahmed Ali (in apparent ignorance of the prior Infancy Gospel) to venture a figurative translation: "when you formed the state of your people's destiny out of mire and you breathed [a new spirit] into it, and they rose by My leave."[43] With reason does Khaleel Mohammed single out this passage for critique in his review of Ali's *Al-Qurʾān: A Contemporary Translation*; but this does not invalidate Ali's apprehension of the *ṭayr* as a semiotic entity, and furthermore one that operates as a "proof" (*bayyina*) of Jesus' prophetic mission. English-language translators have variously rendered *al-bayyināt* at 5:110 as "clear proofs" (Pickthall), "clear signs" (Arberry), and "tokens" (Ali). As semiological vehicles, *al-bayyināt* appear in the Qurʾān to be a subspecies of *āyāt*, naming those signs that are adduced in confirmation of a given prophet's authority (*nubuwwa*).[44] In the later Islamic period, this concept would come to form the basis for an entire category of hagiographical narrative devoted to cataloguing the "Signs of Prophecy" (*ʿalāmāt al-nubuwwa*), i.e. the many miracle-tales indicating Muḥammad's divine appointment as the messenger of God. The figure of a *kāhin* was occasionally deployed within these tales in order to dramatize Prophetic supercession of the *kāhin*'s pre-Islamic hermeneutic authority (Fahd 1966:83n8). And at 5:110 we see the *ṭayr* deployed to a similarly subordinated effect.

As evidence for the intricacy and pervasiveness of the concept of the *ṭayr* in classical Arabic culture, two entries from *Lisān* appear in translation as an appendix to this essay. These are the entries for the roots √*snḥ* and √*brḥ*, commonly understood to denote the "auspicious" (*sāniḥ*) and "sinister" (*bāriḥ*) values that a given omen can embody. In other words, they constitute the two main kinds of *ṭayr*. A look at the entry for √*snḥ* will show that these values are by no means fixed, and that Arabian divination is a system of shifting valences where a single sign will indicate different meanings to different beholders. In part this is explained as a function of geography: Ibn Barrī (d. 582/1187) says

43 Ali 1990:112. Ali's gloss, "Apart from 'bird' and other things, *tair* also means 'omen' as in 7:131, 27:47, 36:19, and 'actions' or 'good or evil fate'—'the register of deeds'—as in 17:13. It also means 'destiny' or 'fortune.' As Apostle to the Jews at a time when their state was most deplorable, Jesus instilled new life into them, and raised them up from the mire" (56n1). For a critique, see Mohammed 2002:47.

44 In particular that of Jesus, as is seen at *Sūrat al-Baqara* 2:253.

that the *sāniḥ* was considered a sign of bad omen in the Ḥijāz and a good omen in the Najd, but that Ḥijāzī usage spread to the Najd resulting in the *sāniḥ*'s transvaluation, as is seen in the verse by Najdī poet ʿAmr b. Qamīʾa (d. ca. 540 CE):

> *Fa-bīnī ʿalā ṭayrin sanīḥin nuḥūsuhu*
> *wa-a<u>sh</u>ʾamu ṭayri 'z-zājirīna sanīḥuhā*
>
> Get away from me then, at the winging of the ill-omened *sanīḥ*;
> *al-sanīḥ* is the worst omen known to diviners.
>
> *Lisān* VI 386

Nor is there total agreement on which direction the *sāniḥ* and the *bāriḥ* take in their flight, but the leftward departure is usually indicated for √*brḥ* and a rightward one for √*snḥ*. Ibn Manẓūr explains this in terms of relative difficulty for the bow-hunter:

> The desert Arabs take *al-bāriḥ* as a bad omen because of the difficulty it presents for [the right-handed archer], who must contort his torso in order to get a shot at it. Meanwhile the *sāniḥ* is what passes in front of you from your left to your right; this they interpret as a good omen, because of the ease it presents to hunters and archers.
>
> *Lisān* I 363

The valences *sāniḥ* and *bāriḥ* are not limited to omens but apply to a wide range of phenomena that appear out of nowhere, to the practical advantage or disadvantage of the one experiencing them. An idea may "occur" to one as a *sāniḥ*; so also may a surprise attack. *Al-bawāriḥ* are violent, dust-laden winds that blow in summer, and active participle *al-bāriḥ* means "yesterday"—pointing out that *disappearance into* nowhere is also another key to the occurrence of an omen. Indeed, *rapid alternation of presence and absence*, as described by Martin Heidegger, would appear to be the hallmark by which an omen may be recognized as such:

> The rising of animals into the open remains closed and sealed in itself in a strangely captivating way. Self-revealing and self-concealing in the animal are one in such a way that human speculation practically runs out of alternatives when it rejects mechanistic views of animality—which are always feasible—as firmly as it avoids anthropomorphic interpretations. Because the animal does not speak, self-revealing and self-concealing, together with their unity, possess a wholly different life-essence [*Lebe-Wesen*] with animals.
>
> Heidegger 1984:116

The binary valence given to the non-domestic in its self-revealing and self-concealing is from this perspective not surprising. The startled animal may be said to embody pure contingence, to which assigning negative and positive values is an irresistible reflex of "human speculation" (*menschliches Auslegen*). This same reflex will also explain why disagreement on their signification is so widespread.

There are other variables in *al-ṭīra* besides which direction an animal takes in its flight. Species is another, and here it will suffice to point out the crow's strict valuation as an omen of separation and departure.[45] For a wider-ranging résumé of *ṭayr* and their interpretations, the reader is referred to Fahd's appendix on "Les animaux de présage chez les Arabes" in *La divination arabe* (Fahd 1966:498–518). But to return to *Sūrat al-Māʾida*, if any particular branch of Arab divination is referenced in Jesus's animation of the *ṭayr* at 5:110, it is the well-attested technique of *al-zajr*, as is seen from Fahd's description:

> *Al-zajr* was a method of divination which essentially consisted of throwing a stone at a bird and shouting at it. A bird which flew away to right of the thrower (*zājir*) was taken to be a favorable portent (*tafāʾala bi-hi*), while the leftward-flying bird was taken as an unfavorable one (*taṭayyara*). Testimony for the antiquity of this practice is found in a verse of Labīd, which also indicates that *al-zajr* was practiced by women.[46] This is supported by a *ḥadīth* related by one Umm Karz, who said: "I went before the Prophet and heard him say: 'Let the birds stay in their places' (var. 'in their nests')." Asked about the meaning of this *ḥadīth*, al-Shāfiʿī (d. 204/820) said: "The Arabs were masters at the technique of inducing birds to fly. When one of them wished to make a journey, he would exit his dwelling until he came upon some perching birds, which he would then cause to fly away. If they flew off to the right, he would continue on his journey; but if they flew off to the left, then he would go back home."[47]

The Qurʾān's most obvious reference to this practice is in the eschatological motif of *al-Zajra*, the apocalyptic "Blast" or "Shout" that will ring out on the

45 Ibn Manẓūr gives *Ibn Barīḥ* and *Umm Barīḥ* ('Son' and 'Mother of Barīḥ'] as epithets for the crow; "a flock of crows is called *Banāt* ('daughters of') *Barīḥ*." *Lisān* I 364.

46 The verse runs: *La-ʿamruka mā tadri ʾḍ-ḍawāribu bi-ʾl-ḥaṣā wa-lā zājirātu ʾṭ-ṭayri mā Allāhu ṣāniʿu* ("By your life, the men who toss pebbles and the maids who rouse birds do not know what God designs"), Labīd b. Rabīʿa 1962:172. "The men who toss pebbles" refers to another divinatory technique of the Arabs known as *al-ṭarq*; see Fahd 1966:195–196.

47 Fahd 1966:438. As Fahd points out, the name Umm Karz means 'Falcon-keeper,' or more literally, 'Mother of a Falcon'.

Day of Judgment (as at 37:19 and 79:13). If the Qur'ān does not name *al-zajr* in direct connection with Jesus at 5:110, his animation of the *ṭayr* may still be felt to recollect the traditional practice. The other miracles listed in the verse—revival of the dead, restoration of the blind and leprous—follow either by metonymy (where they are ranked in series with the animation of Jesus's *ṭayr*) or by metaphor (where they are what is heralded by its miraculous flight).

What this brings us to is basically an inversion of the logic of divination. If, as Gregory Nagy writes, "to interpret is really to formalize the speech-act that is radiating from the dream or omen," then what Jesus does is to *produce* the encoded omen, with God's sanction (Nagy 1990b:168n95). It is here that we might locate the difference between divination and prophecy as represented in early Islamic texts: where the *kāhin* is an interpreter of signs, the prophet is the medium through whom signs are themselves performed. The subordination of the mantic *ṭayr* to the prophetic *āya* is more explicitly enacted at 3:49, where the same narrative is referenced within the annunciation to Mary:

> 3:49. *Wa-rasūlan ilā Banī Isrā'īla Innī qad ji'tukum bi-āyatin min rabbikum annī akhluqu lakum min aṭ-ṭīni ka-hay'ati 'ṭ-ṭayri fa-anfukhu fī-hi fa-yakūnu ṭayran bi-idhni 'llāhi wa-ubri'u 'l-akmaha wa-'l-abraṣa wa-uḥi 'l-mawta bi-idhni 'llāhi wa-unabbi'ukum bi-mā ta'kalūna wa-mā taddakhirūna fī buyūtikum inna fī dhālika la-āyatan la-kum in kuntum mu'minīn*
>
> 3:49. "[He will be] a Prophet unto the Children of Israel, [saying] 'I bring you an *āya* from your Lord, which is that out of clay I will mold the likeness of a *ṭayr*, and that with God's sanction it will become a *ṭayr* when I breathe into it. I will heal the blind and the leper, and with God's sanction I will bring the dead to life, and I will inform you of what you are eating and hoarding in your homes. Truly, there is an *āya* for you in this, if you are believers.' "

Here the *ṭayr*'s co-option is complete, its semiological charge fully grounded in the normative sign of the *āya*. As mantic "omen" and Christological "proof" equally, the Qur'ān claims the incident of the *ṭayr* as an *āya*, bracketing the *ṭayr* within that claim, and announces the supercession of the pre-Islamic semiological regimes in which it formerly circulated.

The implications of this transvaluation are sweeping. Disengaged from the occult sign-system of the diviners, the *ṭayr* is established as a clear monument whose decoding hinges not on interpretive technique, but correct *belief*: "Truly there is an *āya* for you in this, if you are believers." The contrast here presented to Homeric semiology, where reception of the *sēma* requires the combined noetic powers of *anagnōrēsis* ('recognition') and *hypokrisis* ('interpretation'), is most instructive. For one thing, a wider range of faculties is involved in recognizing the *āya*, as is seen in the many variations on the formula *inna fī dhālika la-āyatan li-qawmin X* ("Truly, there is an *āya* in this for people who do X"): throughout the Qur'ān, *āyāt* are in this way said to present themselves to those who 'contemplate' (*li-qawmin yatafakkarūna*, 16:11), who 'remember/ reflect' (*li-qawmin yadhdhakkirūna*, 16:13), who 'listen' (*yasma'ūna*, 16:65), 'are cognizant' (*ya'qilūna*, 16:67), 'have knowledge' (*ya'lamūna*, 6:97), 'understand' (*yafhamūna*, 6:98), and 'believe' (*yu'minūna*, 6:99). This last term stands out from the other verbs in the series by virtue of its being a matter of *doctrine*, not cognition; furthermore, in the Qur'ān's every *negative* iteration of the formula, we find that *āmana* is the only verb used: "Truly, there is an *āya* in this, but most of them are not believers" (*inna fī-dhālika la-āyatan wa-mā kāna aktharuhum mu'minīn;* 26:8, 67, 103, etc.). The failure to interpret the *āya* is presented as a failure of belief, not intellect; alternately, it could be said that belief is effectively *merged with* intellect in the conditions the Qur'ān establishes for the *āya*'s reception. It is as if no gap existed between the recognition of the *āya* and its interpretation, or as if no interpretation were needed at all. The only precondition for the correct understanding of the *āya* is acknowledgement of God's supremacy as the transcendent signified of every semiological event.[48]

"A beneficial word"

It would be difficult to prove whether the distinction between the *āya* and the omen long predated its expression in the Qur'ān. The question of divination by earlier prophets does arise as a matter of concern to Muḥammad: when, on entering the Ka'ba, he discovered images of Abraham and Ishmael clutching the featherless arrows used in pre-Islamic divination, he is said to have exclaimed, "By God, never did those two practice divination by arrows!" (*Wa-'llāhi, in istaqsamā bi-'l-azlāmi qaṭṭ*).[49] And yet for the Prophet himself some

48 Thus we are brought back to Peirce's tripartite taxonomy of the sign. If the *āya*'s signifying capacity was said above to be indexical, its predication upon *belief* qualifies it for Peirce's third category of the conventional "symbol": the sign that "refers to the Object that it denotes by virtue of a law, usually an association of general ideas, which operates to cause the Symbol to be interpreted as referring to that Object. It is thus itself a general type of law. . . ." Peirce 1955:102. That the *āya* should span two of Peirce's categories says more about semantics in general than about the *āya* itself, as pointed out by Sebeok 1976:120 (citing Umberto Eco): "It should be clearly understood, finally, that it is not signs that are actually being classified, but, more precisely, aspects of signs: in other words, a given sign may—and more often than not does—exhibit more than one aspect, so that one must recognize differences in gradation."

49 Al-Bukhārī 2004 (*K. Aḥādīth al-anbiyā'*): 680 (*K. al-Maghāzī*): 864 and with slightly different wording in Ibn Isḥāq 1936: IV 413. Mantic sortition of arrows (known as *maysir*) is forbidden in

form of casting lots as a way of determining a course of action was not unthinkable, as is seen in the opening of ʿĀʾisha's account of the slander against her in the year 6/627–628:

> Whenever the Prophet (God's blessings and peace be upon him) was planning a journey, he would choose between his wives, taking with him the one whose arrow emerged [from the bundle]. When the quarrel with Banu 'l-Muṣṭaliq broke out, he chose between his wives as was his custom, and my arrow came out over the others' [*aqraʿu baina nisāʾihi ka-mā kāna yaṣnaʿu fa-kharaja saḥmī ʿalayhinna maʿahu*]. So he took me on his journey, the Prophet on whom be God's blessings and peace.[50]

In the Qurʾān, oracular vocabulary is cited in to order to contain it—that is, to foreclose on the mantic sign-systems and institutions with which Prophetic revelation was in direct competition. In this connection it is worth contemplating the one oracular sign the Prophet is said to have praised, namely *al-faʾl* (pl. *fuʾūl*). The Prophet's predilection for the *faʾl* is reported in a number of *ḥadīths*, such as: "'There is no *ṭīra*. The best thing of its kind is the *faʾl*' [*lā ṭīrata wa-khayruha 'l-faʾl*]. He was asked, 'O messenger of God, what is *faʾl*?' He said: 'A beneficial word [*al-kalimatu 'ṣ-ṣāliḥ*] any one of you may hear' " (Muslim 2007 [*K. al-salām*]: 1041). Toufic Fahd, who calls *faʾl* "a term peculiar to the Arabic," nevertheless explains it by analogy to the Hebrew *neḥashīm* as well as the Greek *phēmē* and *klēdōn*.[51] He writes that it once embraced both good and bad portents:

> [B]ut with early Islam's condemnation of bird divination ("The Messenger of God loved the *faʾl* and never practiced *al-ʿiyāfa*," runs another *ḥadīth*), *al-faʾl* came to signify the favorable omen and *aṭ-ṭīra* was applied strictly to the unfavorable—to the point where it can be said [as in the *Kashf al-ẓunūn* of Ḥājjī Khalīfa (d. 1067/1657)]: "The meaning of the *faʾl* is to continue moving forward. The meaning of the *ṭīra* is to abstain and retreat."[52]

---

the Qurʾān at *Sūrat al-Māʾida* 5:3 and 5:90–91.

50 Ibn Isḥāq 1936: III 297. Other such scenes take place in *al-Sīrat al-nabawiyya*, as when Surāqa b. Mālik is dissuaded from detaining the Prophet in his Flight by the judgment of his divining arrows (II 488–489, noted by Fahd 1966:187).

51 Its best Homeric parallel may be found in the *phēmē* ('prophetic utterance') Odysseus prays for and is vouchsafed in *Odyssey* xx 98–121; see Nagy 1990a:221.

52 Fahd 1966:451 (with references). Thus we read that in the *Murūj al-dhahab* of al-Masʿūdī 1965: IV 110 that al-Jāḥiẓ's nephew Yamūt (whose name in Arabic means "He is dying") avoided paying visits to sick people, lest they take his name as a bad omen. For *al-ʿiyāfa*, see Fahd 1966:432–450.

The *fa'l* "appears in very varied forms, ranging from simple sneezing, certain peculiarities of persons and things that one encounters, to the interpretation of the names of persons and things which present themselves spontaneously to the sight, hearing and mind of man."[53] As such, *fu'ūl* are semiological events that, like *āyāt*, need no mantic interpretation for their meaning to be made manifest. They wear their content on their faces, or rather in their beholder's: any name or word or thing that pleases or displeases can be interpreted as a positive or negative indicator of some endeavor's advisability. Thus we read in *al-Sīrat al-nabawiyya* of one of the Prophet's military campaigns:

> On his approach to al-Ṣafrā', a village located between two mountains, he asked what the names of the mountains were. They told him: "The first one is called Musliḥ ('Crappy'), the other is called Mukhrī' ('Dung-hill')." When he asked who lived there, he was told: "Two clans of the Banū Ghifār named Banu 'l-Nār ('Sons of Fire') and Banū Ḥurāq ('Sons of Kindling')." The Prophet, God's blessings and peace be upon him, found the mountains hateful, even to pass between, detecting an omen in their names and the names of the people living there [*wa-tafā'ala bi-asmā'ihimā wa-asmā'i ahlihimā*]. So he departed, God's blessings and peace be upon him, keeping al-Ṣafrā' on the left-hand side.
>
> Ibn Isḥāq 1936: II 614

Two reasons stand out as to why this method of divination would be accommodated in Islam where others are rejected. The first is that the *fa'l* leaves no gap between sign and sign-reader requiring a soothsayer's hermeneutic intervention. The nature of the *fa'l* is to be instantly apprehended by its "addressee," which is to say anyone who feels warned or encouraged by it. It neither requires interpretive mediation nor allows it, but is to all appearances transparent, and thus poses no threat to Islam's semiological hegemony.

The second reason is that unlike the decisive casting of lots or the minatory activities of wild animals, the *fa'l* could be deliberately managed by fiat of Prophetic authority. So we read in Fahd's EI² entry for "Fa'l":

> Furthermore, he made a considerable number of changes in proper names, with the double design of effacing all traces of Arab paganism from Muslim terminology, and even more of removing from any shocking or unsuitable names of followers which he must hear around him, all baleful influences which might emanate from their

53 EI² II 758.

> meanings. It was for this reason that he changed Qalīl ["paltry"] into Kat͟hīr ["plenty"], ʿĀṣī ["disobedient"] into Muṭīʿ ["compliant"]; and thus also that he gave the future Medina the name of Ṭayyiba ["agreeable"] in place of Yat͟hrib, whose root contained the idea of "calumny" [*tat͟hrīb*].[54]

If the *faʾl* is a semiological event that the Prophet is empowered to produce or control, it finds its antecedent in the *ṭayr* Jesus animates in the Qurʾān. These irruptions of oracular idioms within the Qurʾān and *sunna* (i.e. the precedent of the Prophet's behavior) demonstrate that even as Islamic spiritual authority defined itself in opposition to the oracular institutions of the Ḥijāz, some manipulation of contemporary oracular codes was nevertheless allowable. Insofar as the Prophet's intervention into Arabian toponymy is explained as a safeguard against inauspicious *fuʾūl* radiating from the ignoble or insurrectionist place-name, we see the oracular code being manipulated in defense of Islam's political legitimacy. In other cases, as where the Prophet is said to have disallowed the name G͟hurāb ("Crow") because of its negative ornithomantic associations, the oracular code is shut down altogether.[55]

"The oracle," Joseph Fontenrose wrote, "is a device that one storyteller needs and another does not" (Fontenrose 1978:92). Of legend and folk narrative this is true, but the story of Islam's historical development can scarcely be told without examining the semiological practices and institutions against which it defined itself as a religious and political movement. Though less well explored than the Qurʾān's engagement with the institutionalized traditions of Judaism and Christianity, the Islamic encounter with Arabian oracular tradition was hardly less formative. Indeed, an antagonism toward the prevailing oracular institutions of his day would seem to be a constitutive feature of the Prophet's mission from its very beginning. It is my conclusion that the oracular idioms engaged in the Qurʾān are traces of an historical struggle for hermeneutic and religious authority that took place between indigenous Arabian soothsaying and the new institutions of Islam—a struggle for which, as with so much of early Islamic history, our only surviving evidence is textual.

54 EI^2 II 758–759

55 *Tāj al-ʿArūs* III 466 (article √*g͟hrb*).

Appendix: Good and Bad Omens in *Lisān al-ʿarab*[56]

1. √SNḤ

[Active Ist form participle] *al-sāniḥ* is what comes at you from your right-hand side in the way of gazelles, birds, and things like that. And *al-bāriḥ* is said of any of those things that come upon you from your left. [However,] Abū ʿUbayda (d. 209/824) says that he was present when Yūnus [ibn Ḥabīb (d. 182/798)] asked Ruʾba [ibn al-ʿAjjāj (d. 145/762)] about *al-sāniḥ* and *al-bāriḥ*, and that Ruʾba's answer was "*Al-sāniḥ* is what is what turns toward you its right side, and *al-bāriḥ* is what turns toward you its left side." [Alternately,] it is said that *al-sāniḥ* is what comes from your right side so that its left side is brought next to your left. Abū ʿAmr al-Shaybānī (d. 213/828) says, "*Al-sāniḥ* is what comes from your right-hand side toward your left and turns its left side toward you, also called "the human side" [*al-insiyy*]. *Al-bāriḥ* is what comes from your left-hand side toward your right, turning its right side toward you, also called "the wild side" [*al-waḥshiyy*]." Saying, "*Al-sāniḥ* is preferred to *al-bāriḥ*, insofar as it is [the sign] of good fortune," Abū ʿAmr cites the verse by Abū Dhuʾayb [al-Hudhalī (d. ca. 28/649)]:

Aribtu li-irbatihi fa-inṭalaqtu
urajjī li-ḥubbi ʾl-liqāʾi sanīḥan

My need for him was such that I left off
hoping for an omen, so great was my wish for [the actual] encounter.

The meaning here is "paying no attention to bird-omens, whether *sāniḥ* or *bāriḥ*." But the verse has also been said to mean "I left off wishing for a good omen."[57] Abū ʿAmr also says that for others the *sāniḥ* is a portent of evil, as in the line by ʿAmr b. Qamīʾa (d. ca. 540 CE):

Wa-ashʾamu ṭayri ʾz-zājirīna sanīḥuhā

The worst omen known to diviners is the *sanīḥ*.

And also in the verse of al-Aʿshā (d. ca. 4/625):

56 *Lisān* VI 385–386 and I 361–364, respectively.

57 In his edition of Abū Dhūʾayb's *dīwān*, S. al-Miṣrī makes note of *Lisān*'s version but gives the second hemistich as *uzjī li-ḥubbi ʾl-īyābi ʾs-sanīḥā*: "Scanting the omen, longing instead for [his] return" (Abū Dhuʾayb 1998:63). As noted in al-Iṣbahānī 1969: VI 58–59 (2345–2346), this verse is in praise of the future anti-Caliph ʿAbd Allāh b. Zubayr (d. 73/692).

Ajārahumā Bishrun min al-mawti baʿdamā
jarā la-humā ṭayru ʾs-sanīḥi bi-ashʾami

Bishr protected them both from death, after
the bird of *sanīḥ* sped its ill omen to them.

The Bishr mentioned in this verse is Bishr b. ʿAmr b. Marthad, who was a hunting companion of al-Mundhir Māʾ al-Samāʾ (d. ca. 554 CE). On his [yearly] "Day of Evil," it was al-Mundhir's custom to kill the first person he came across. On that day, when two of Bishr's cousins (sons of his father's brother) appeared, al-Mundhir wanted to kill them, but Bishr pleaded their cause before him, and al-Mundhir gave them over to him.[58] And from Ruʾba come the *rajaz* verses:

Fa-kam jarā min sāniḥin yasnaḥu
wa-bāriḥātin lam taḥri tabraḥu
bi-ṭayrin takhbībun wa-lā tabraḥu

How many of those which present as *sāniḥ*
and those presenting as *bāriḥ*, which are not fulfilled!
In the omen is deception, and no indicator of ill fortune.

Shammar [b. Ḥamdawayh (d. 255/869)] said that Ibn al-Aʿrābī (d. 231/846) recited these lines with the last word as *yasnaḥu*, indicating good fortune and a blessing, as in the verse cited by Abū Zayd [al-Anṣārī (d. 215/830)]:

Aqūlu wa-ʾṭ-ṭayru la-nā sāniḥun
yajrī la-nā aymanuhu bi-ʾs-suʿūd

When the omen presents itself to us as a *sāniḥ*, I say
that its good fortune runs in our favor.

58 Nicholson 1930:43–44 gives the story as follows: "It is related in the *Aghānī* that he had two boon companions, Khālid b. al-Muḍallil and ʿAmr b. Masʿūd, with whom he used to carouse; and once, being irritated by words spoken in wine, he gave orders that they should be buried alive. Next morning he did not recollect what had passed and inquired as usual for his friends. On learning the truth he was filled with remorse. He caused two obelisks to be erected over their graves, and two days in every year he would come and sit beside these obelisks, which were called *al-Ghariyyān*, i.e. the Blood-smeared. One day was the Day of Good [*yawmu naʿīmin*], and whoever first encountered him on that day received a hundred black camels. The other day was the Day of Evil [*yawmu buʾsin*], on which he would present the first-comer with the head of a black polecat, then sacrifice him and smear the obelisks with his blood. The poet ʿAbīd b. al-Abraṣ is said to have fallen a victim to this horrible rite."

Abū Mālik [ʿAmr b. Kirkira] said that the *sāniḥ* is what blesses one, and that the *bāriḥ* is what announces a calamity, but that Zuhayr [ibn Abī Sulmā (d. early 7th c. CE)] interpreted them the other way around, as in the verse:

> *Jarat sunuḥan fa-qultu la-hā Ajīzī*
> *nawan ma<u>sh</u>mūlatan fa-matā al-liqāʾ*

> [The gazelles] presented as omens, and I said to them, "Oblige me
> to cross the distance swept by the north wind—but when will
> the encounter be?"

Here *sunuḥ* are glossed as gazelles of good omen, as well as bad. Among the Arabs, there were differing schools of interpretation brought to such portents; some understood the *sāniḥ* to bode well, and others took it as an evil portent. Al-Lay<u>th</u> [ibn al-Muẓaffar (d. ca. 187/803)] cites the line:

> *Jarat la-ka fī-ha ʾs-sāniḥātu bi-asʿad*

> The omens present you with the happiest of fortunes in the
> matter.

"Who will be my *sāniḥ*, after my *bāriḥ* [has flown]?" is a proverbial expression [discussed ahead in art. √*brḥ*].

As is seen in the verse by al-Aʿ<u>sh</u>ā, [IIIrd-form verb] *sānaḥa* and [Ist-form] *sanaḥa* have the same meaning:

> *Jarat li-himā ṭayru ʾs-sināḥi bi-a<u>sh</u>ʾam*

> There came upon the two of them a bird signifying bad fortune.

There are some who dispute this. The plural of *sāniḥ* is *sawāniḥ*; [adjectival form] *sanīḥ* is its equivalent, as in the verse:

> *Jarā yawma ruḥnā ʿāmidīna li-arḍihim*
> *sanīḥun fa-qāla al-qawmu Marra sanīḥ*

> On the day we departed on course for their land, there flew
> a *sanīḥ*, and the people said, "A *sanīḥ* passes by."

Its plural is *sunuḥ*, as in the verse:

> *A-bi-ʾs-sunuḥi ʾl-ayāmini am bi-naḥsin*
> *tamurru bi-hi ʾl-bawāriḥu ḥīna tajrī*

> Do they come as auspicious *sunuḥ*, or as bad omens
> do the *bawāriḥ* pass by, when they present?

Ibn Barrī said: "The Arabs differ in their reading of omens, that is, in the good or bad fortunes of the *sāniḥ* and *bāriḥ*. The people of Najd [north-central Arabian Peninsula] hold the *sāniḥ* as a good omen, as in the verse by Dhu 'l-Rumma (d. 117/735–736), who was from Najd:

> *Khalīlayya lā lāqaytumā mā ḥayaytumā*
> *min aṭ-ṭayri illa 's-sāniḥāti wa-as'adā*

> My two friends, you did not encounter and did not witness
> any omens, except for the *sāniḥ* and [signs] happier still.

"And al-Nābigha [al-Dhubyānī (d. 602 CE)], who was also from the Najd, held the *bāriḥ* as an ill omen:

> *Za'ama 'l-bawāriḥu anna riḥlatanā ghadan*
> *wa-bi-dhāka tan'ābu al-ghurābi 'l-aswad*[59]

> The *bawāriḥ* claim that our journey is tomorrow,
> and that is the subject of the black crow's croaking.

"And Kuthayyir ['Azza b. 'Abd al-Raḥmān (d. 105/723)], who being from the Ḥijāz read the ill omen in the *sāniḥ*, has the verse:

> *Aqūlu idhā ma 'ṭ-ṭayru marrat mukhīfatan*
> *Sawāniḥuhā tajrī wa-lā astathīruhā*

> When bird-omens pass in a threatening way, I say,
> "Their *sawāniḥ* are presenting," and I do not rouse them.

"These are the original values. Ḥijāzī usage was later to spread to the Najd, from which we get the verse by Najdī poet 'Amr b. Qamī'a:

> *Fa-bīnī 'alā ṭayrin sanīḥin nuḥūsuhu*
> *wa-ash'amu ṭayri 'z-zājirīna sanīḥuhā*[60]

> Get away from me then, at the winging of the ill-omened *sanīḥ*
> —*sanīḥ* is the worst omen known to diviners."

The verbal nouns of *sanaḥa* (imperfect *yasnaḥu*) are *sunūḥ*, *sunḥ*, and *sunuḥ*, and name the passing of a gazelle from your left to your right. Al-Azharī (d.

[59] K. Al-Bustānī's edition of al-Nābigha al-Dhubyānī 1963:38 has *wa-bi-dhāka khabbarana 'l-ghudāfu 'l-aswadu* ("and that was what the black raven informed us").

[60] In C. Lyall's edition of the *Poems of 'Amr Son of Qamī'ah* this verse is given as *Fa-bīnī 'alā najmin shakhīsin nuḥūsuhu / wa-ash'amū ṭayri 'z-zājirīna sanīḥuhā* (1919:14). Lyall's translation: "Go thy way then, with a star that ceases not to carry an evil influence: the most ill-omened bird of the diviners is that which passes form left to right."

370/890) relates that during the Jāhiliyya there was a woman who frequented the market at 'Ukāẓ, and that she was a reciter of sayings and a coiner of new ones, and that she used to ridicule men in the marketplace. One day a man came up to her, and after she had spoken as was her wont, he responded:

Askatāki jāmiḥun wa-rāmiḥu
ka-'ẓ-ẓabyatayni sāniḥun wa-bāriḥu

Shut up, you fractious hurler of barbs,
darting this way and that [in your speech] like two ominous gazelles!

—whereupon the woman went away, herself humiliated. *Sanaḥa* is also used of a thought or a line of poetry, meaning "it presented itself" or "occurred" [to the mind]. In one *ḥadīth*, 'Ā'isha spoke of [her distaste for] passing in front of the Prophet when he was at prayer: *Akrahu an asnaḥahu*, ["I hate to pass before him"]. Where it is reported that [the first Caliph] Abū Bakr said to Usāma: *Aghir 'alayhim ghāratan sanḥā'a* ["Make a surprise attack on them"], it means to "fall upon" someone, or to "occur," as is said of an idea. (Of this instance, Ibn al-Athīr [d. 606/1210] says that *saḥḥā'an* ["Make your attack an inundation"] is better attested.) Ibn al-Sikkīt (d. 244/858) has remarked: "*Sanaḥa* and *sāniḥ* are said of a thing which deters someone from their goal, repelling them and turning them away."

When the particles *bi-* and *'alā* are interposed between *sanaḥa* and its object, it means to dispossess or otherwise afflict someone. It also means to allude or reveal obliquely, as in the verse by Sawwār b. al-Muḍarrib:

Wa-ḥājatin dūna ukhrā qad sanaḥtu la-hā
ja'altuhā li-'llatī akhfaytu 'unwānā

Such a need, like no other! I showed it to her,
concealing its object from her for whom I conceived it (?).

Al-sanīḥ is also the thread on which pearls are strung, before the pearls are strung on it. Afterwards, it is called an *'iqd*. Its plural is *sunuḥ*. According to al-Liḥyānī, in the expression *sunuḥ al-ṭarīq* it means "the middle" of a road. Al-Azharī says that for some speakers *sanīḥ* means "pearls and ornamentation"; and in speaking of women Abū Dū'ād [al-Iyādī, *fl.* 6th c.] spoke the following verse:

Wa-taghālayna bi-'s-sanīḥi wa-lā yas'alna
ghibba 'ṣ-ṣabāḥi ma 'l-akhbār

They are excessive in ornament, and have no care for
what the breaking day's news might be.

The derived [Xth- and Vth-form] verbs *istasnaḥa* and *tasannaḥa* are spoken in rare instances, as are [their anagrams] the similarly formed verbs *istanḥasa* and *tanaḥḥasa*. Their meaning is "to seek an explanation."

The redoubled noun *sanaḥnaḥ* is attributed by Ibn al-Athīr to ʿAlī, who called himself "*sanaḥnaḥ* of the night," meaning "I never sleep at night, but remain watchful." *Samaʿmaʿ* is also related.[61] Of Abū Bakr it is said that his home was in an elevated area of Medina called the Sunuḥ, where the Banu 'l-Ḥārith b. al-Khazraj made their homes. It is also called Sunayḥ and Sinḥān.

2. √BRḤ

Baraḥa (verbal nouns *baraḥ* and *burūḥ*) means "to cease." When its second radical is voweled with *kasra*—i.e. *bariḥa*, meaning "to quit" one's place or station—its verbal noun is *barāḥ*. [There follows a lengthy discussion of the idiom *lā barāḥa*—"There will be no departure/quitting of place"—which can be voweled in the accusative or the nominative.]

[Vth-form] *Tabarraḥa* is similar in meaning to [Ist-form] *baraḥa*, occurring negatively in the verse by Mulayḥ [al-Ḥakam al-Qirdī] al-Hudhalī:

Makathna ʿalā ḥājatihinna wa-qad maḍā
shabābu 'ḍ-ḍuḥā wa-'l-ʿīsu mā tatabarraḥu

[The ladies] are still troubled by their need, when the youths of the morning
have decamped, and the white-haired camels have stayed behind.

[IVth-form] *Abraḥa* is a transitive form. According to al-Azharī, *bariḥa* is said of a man when he leaves his place. The negative expression *mā bariḥa*, followed by an imperfect verb, is equivalent to *mā zāla*, meaning "to persist" in that action or state. (This expression also occurs in the imperfect—i.e. *lā yabraḥu* with following verb also in the imperfect, much like *lā yazālu*.) And when its object is a land or territory, as in *bariḥa 'l-arḍa*, it means to depart from it. In revelation [at *Sūrat Yūsuf* 12:80, Joseph's brother says]: *Fa-lan abraḥa 'l-arḍa*

61 Note by editor ʿAlī Shīrī: "*Sanaḥnaḥu* and *samaʿmaʿu* are formed upon *sanaḥa* and *samaʿa* by redoubling their second and third radicals. As a noun, *sanaḥnaḥ* means a thing frequently in view which presents itself often. Its being appended to *al-layl* ['the night'] means that his nighttime attacks on the enemy were many" (*Lisān* VI 386n3).

ḥattā ya'dhana lī abī: ["I will not depart from this land until my father gives me permission"]. And, God be Exalted [at *Sūrat Ṭā Hā* 20:91, Moses's people say of the golden calf]: *Fa-lan nabraḥa 'alayhi 'ākifayni* ["We will not relinquish it, but remain devoted"].

Ḥabīlu barāḥin ["Who fights to the end"] is an epithet of the lion or the hero who does not retreat, as if bound to the spot by cords [*ḥibāl*].[62] And *barāḥ* can mean a manifestation or appearance. *Bariḥa 'l-khafā'u* ["secrecy departed"] is a synonym for *ẓahara*: "it appeared," and Ibn al-A'rābī says the voweling *baraḥa* also applies in such cases as the line:

> *Baraḥa 'l-khafā'u fa-mā ladayya tajalludun*
>
> Secrecy was dispelled, for I could endure it no longer.

Here the poet's disclosure of the matter is characterized as the departure of secrecy, or in other words its cessation. According to al-Azharī, the meaning of *bariḥa 'l-khafā'u* is that "secrecy came to an end." It is also explained as "what was hidden became revealed, and was uncovered," and that this sense comes from *barāḥ al-arḍi*, which means ground with no cover. The phrase is also glossed as "what I was concealing became revealed." From this comes the expression found in *ḥadīth*: *Jā'a bi-'l-kufri barāḥan* ["He made no concealment of his unbelief"], in which adverbial accusative *barāḥan* means "distinctly" or "openly"; another such expression is *Jā'anā bi-'l-amri barāḥan* ["He made no concealment of the matter from us"]. *Barāḥ* (used adjectivally and substantively) is said of open land that is free of trees, dwellings, tillage or vegetation of any kind. And *Barāḥi* is a name of the sun, formed upon *bariḥa* as the indeclinable name Qaṭāmi is formed from *qaṭama*;[63] it is a name that describes the sun's open visibility. The following lines were transmitted by Quṭrub (d. 206/821):

> *Hādhā maqāmu qadamay Rabāḥi*
> *dhabbaba ḥattā dalakat Barāḥi*
>
> Here stood the two feet of Rabāḥ
> who prolonged his journey until the sun went down.

Al-Farrā' (d. 207/822) gives this verse's ending as *bi-rāḥi*, where *rāḥ* is the plural of *rāḥa*, i.e. the hand. The meaning here is that people's hands were held to

62 This idiom recalls an incident in Herodotus' account of the battle of Plataea wherein an Athenian named Sophanes is said either to have fastened himself to the battleground with an anchor and chain, or to have borne the device of an anchor on his shield (*Histories* IX 74).

63 For this form see Wright 1967: I 243D, 244AB.

their eyes as they watched the setting sun. [There follows more debate on the verse's original sense and vocalization.]

[IInd- and IVth-form verbs] *barraḥa* and *abraḥa* both mean "to bother persistently," where the object is introduced with the particle *bi-*. And in the *Tahdhīb* of al-Azharī it says "to be persist in being bothersome and wearisome." Verbal nouns *barḥ* and *tabrīḥ* are used to describe a wearisome affair, as for example in the verse [by <u>Dh</u>u 'l-Rumma] that ends:

> *bi-nā wa-'l-hawā barḥun ʿalā man yu<u>gh</u>ālibuhu*[64]
>
> . . . passion is a drag for the one overcome by it.

The expression *barḥun bāriḥun* ["a bothersome bother," "grievous grief," etc.], like *barḥun mubriḥun*, is redoubled for emphasis and intensity. When used in an optative sense, the accusative case is preferred, but the nominative is allowable, as in the verse:

> *A-munḥadiran tarmī bi-ka 'l-ʿīsu <u>gh</u>urbatan*
> *wa-muṣʿidatan barḥun li-ʿaynayka bāriḥu*
>
> So the white-haired camels hurry away with you, carrying you off
> and bringing you back? Grievous grief in your eyes!

[This last phrase] functions as a curse and a proposition equally. *Al-barḥ* is malignance and vicissitude of fate. With the particle *bi-* before its object, [IInd form verb] *barraḥa* means to harass. And *al-tabārīḥ* [the plural of *barraḥa*'s verbal noun *al-tabrīḥ*] are "calamities." *Al-tabārīḥ* are also defined as hardships of a toilsome life. The *tabārīḥ* of desire refer to its burning. The redoubled expression "I encountered from him *barḥan bāriḥan*" indicates "a great deal of vexation." In *ḥadīth* we find the phrase "We met with *al-barḥ* from him"—that is, "harshness"—and in an account the people of Nahrawān [site of the <u>Kh</u>ārijites' defeat at ʿAlī's hands in 38/658], "They met with *al-barḥ*." A poet said:

> *A-jaddaka hā<u>dh</u>ā ʿamraka 'llāhu kullumā*
> *daʿāka 'l-hawā barḥun li-ʿaynayka bāriḥu*
>
> Does this inflame you? God grant you long life! All that
> passion calls you to is grievous grief in your eyes.

A blow that is *mubarriḥ* [present active participle of IInd-form verb *barraḥa*] is a forceful one. *Mubarraḥ [passive participle of same] is not used. Also found

---

[64] At <u>Dh</u>u 'l-Rumma 1995:85 the full verse appears as *Matā taẓʿanī yā Mayyu ʿan dāri jīratin / li-nā wa-'l-hawā barḥun ʿalā man yu<u>gh</u>ālibuhu*: "When, O Mayya, you leave the house in our neighborhood, passion is a drag for the one overcome by it."

in *ḥadīth* is the phrase "a blow that was not *mubarriḥ*," i.e. not grievous. *Abraḥ*, the comparative form, means "more grievous" and "harsher," and is found in the verse by Dhu 'l-Rumma:

> *Anīnan wa-shakwā bi-'n-nahāri kathīratan*
> *'alayya wa-mā ya'tī bi-hi 'l-laylu abraḥu*
>
> By day, I am overcome by much wailing and grief,
> and what the night brings is more grievous still.

Although its lexical meaning derives from *barraḥa, abraḥ* is formed upon the root *baraḥa*. Otherwise it must be understood as an anomalous form like *aḥnak*, as in the phrase "the hungrier [*aḥnak*] of the two sheep" [anomalous in that there is no prior adjectival form like **ḥanīk* for *aḥnak* to be the comparative of].

Al-buraḥā' is harshness and difficulty. More specifically, it is held by some to mean the extremity of a fever, and *burāḥāyā* is of this same meaning. In connection with a fever or any other complaint, *buraḥā'* refers to its intensity. Of a person afflicted with fever, one says, "*Al-buraḥā'* has struck him." According to al-Aṣma'ī (d. 213/828), "When a fever is of long duration, it is called *al-muṭawwī* ['the enfolding']. If the fever recurs, it is called *al-ruḥaḍā'* ['the sweats']. If it becomes more intense, it is *al-buraḥā'*." In *ḥadīth* we find the phrase "I was afflicted with an extremity of fever" [*barraḥat bī al-ḥummā*]. And in a *ḥadīth* of the Slander we find *al-buraḥā'* used for the intensity of the distress provoked in the Prophet by the weightiness of the Revelation.[65]

In a *ḥadīth* relating the assassination of Abū Rāfi' al-Yahūdī comes the phrase "His widow assailed us [*barraḥat bi-nā*] with her cries." One says *barraḥa tabrīḥan* of a matter that taxes one's endurance. And we hear the expression "I met with the daughters of harshness [*al-barḥ*] from him," as well as "the sons of harshness."

Al-biraḥīn, al-buraḥīn and *al-baraḥīn* all mean "calamaties and disasters." Their singular form would be **biraḥ*, but this word is never used. [Much discussion of this follows.] Also heard is "I met with *barḥun bāriḥun* from him," and "I

65 "The Slander" (*al-Ifk*) refers to the well-known accusation of infidelity against the Prophet's wife 'Ā'isha, in consequence of which *āyāt* 11–20 of *Sūrat al-Nūr* were revealed. The speaker in this *ḥadīth* is 'Ā'isha herself : *Fa-akhadha mā kāna ya'khudhuhu min al-buraḥā'* ("He was seized by one of the fevers that used to seize him"). al-Bukhārī 2004 (*K. al-Maghāzī*):, etc. Interestingly, the word does not not occur in her account as given by Ibn Hishām (on the authority of a separate chain of transmitters), but the expression *mā bariḥa* does: "God's Prophet (God's blessings and peace be upon him) did not move from where he sat until he was overwhelmed by what used to overwhelm him [when receiving a revelation] from God" (*Mā bariḥa Rasūl Allāh . . . min majlisihi ḥattā taghashshāhu min Allāhi mā kāna yataghashshāhu*). Ibn Isḥāq 1936: III 302.

met with the son of *barīḥ* from him." *Al-barīḥ*, like *al-barḥ*, means "toil" [*taʿab*], as in the line:

> *bi-hi masīḥun wa-barīḥun wa-ṣakhab*
>
> with him are sweat, toil and tumult.

Al-bawāriḥ (singular *al-bāriḥa*) are strong north winds prevailing in summer that bring no rain. It is also said that *al-bawāriḥ* are strong winds that because of the violence of their blowing carry dirt with them, and that their singular is *al-bāriḥ*, which by itself means a hot wind in summer. Abū Ḥanīfa (d. 150/767) named several who defined *al-bawāriḥ* simply as "storms," but himself denied this unspecialized meaning. Abū Zayd relates: "*Al-bawāriḥ* are north winds particular to the summer," on which al-Azharī comments, "I have found that the desert Arabs' usage corresponds with Abū Zayd's." Ibn Kunāsa (d. 209/824) said, "All the winds that blow at the height of summer are called by the Arabs *al-bawāriḥ*. The most plenteous of these are called *al-simāʾim* [sg. *al-simūm*] and blow when the stars of Libra are in ascendance." And Dhu 'l-Rumma said:

> *Lā bal huwa 'sh-shawqu min dārin takhawwanahā*
> *marran saḥābun wa-marran bāriḥun taribu*
>
> Nay, it is only longing provoked by an encampment defaced
> by the passage of rainclouds and dust-laden wind.

The epithet *tarib* ["dusty"] shows that al-*bāriḥ* is a summer wind and not a vernal wind. The winds of summer are always dusty.

Said of [the flight of] a gazelle or bird, *al-bāriḥ* is the contrary of the *sāniḥ*. When used in this sense, the verb's second radical is voweled with *ḍamma* in the imperfect [i.e. *baraḥat tabruḥu*] and given the verbal noun *burūḥ*, as in the *rajaz* verses:

> *Fa-hunna yabruḥna la-hu burūḥan*
> *wa-tāratan yaʾtīnahu sunūḥan*
>
> [At one moment] they present as ill omens, and bad augury
> is his,
> and [at another] they come as good omens.

In *ḥadīth* we find the expression *baraḥa al-ẓaby*: "The gazelle presented as *bāriḥ*," i.e. inversely to the *sāniḥ*. *Al-bāriḥ* is that bird or beast that passes in front of you heading from your right toward your left. The desert Arabs take *al-bāriḥ* as a bad omen because of the difficulty it presents for [the right-handed archer], who must contort his torso in order to get a shot at it. Meanwhile the *sāniḥ* is what passes in front of you from your left to your right; this they interpret as a good omen, because of the ease it presents to hunters and archers. The saying "Who will be my *sāniḥ*, after my *bāriḥ* [has flown]?" [*man lī bi-'s-sāniḥi baʿda 'l-bāriḥi*] became proverbial when it was uttered by one man who was wronged by another. "He will do right by you in the future," he was told by a third, and he responded with the now-proverbial expression. But it originated with a man whose path was crossed by a *bāriḥ* gazelle. When someone said to him, "It will turn *sāniḥ* on you," he responded, "Who will be my *sāniḥ*, after my *bāriḥ* [has flown]?"

In its oracular sense, the verb *baraḥa* is voweled exclusively with *fatḥa*. The *bāriḥ* gazelle is the one that shows its left flank to you as it runs from your right to your left. The saying "Little seen, like the *bāriḥ* of the mountain goat" [*Innamā huwa ka-bāriḥi 'l-urwiyyi qalīlan mā yurā*] was coined to describe the [infrequent] generosity of a man whose hand is slow to open. Its sense comes from the fact that the mountain goat makes its home on the peaks of mountains, and therefore does not present its flank to the viewer, so that people hardly ever see it as either *bāriḥ* or *sāniḥ*.

In the phrase *qatalūhum abraḥa qatlin* ["They made a surprise attack on them"], *abraḥ* means "most astonishing" [*aʿjab*]. In a *ḥadīth* related by ʿIkrima (d. 105/723–724), we are told that the Prophet (God's blessings and peace be upon him) prohibited *al-tabrīḥ* together with *al-tawlīh* ["laying waste"]. *Tabrīḥ* refers to slaughter that does the animal needless harm, as when one throws a living fish into fire; further commentary on it may be found in *ḥadīth*. We are told by Shammar that Ibn al-Mubārak (d. 181/797) mentioned this *ḥadīth* in the course of describing his revulsion at encountering a fish cooked live in fire, saying, "The food was eaten, but I took no pleasure in it." Shammar also tells us that some authorities also refer to the live burning of lice as *tabrīḥ*. And al-Azharī says, "I saw some desert Arabs who filled a vessel with live locusts. They dug a pit in the sand where they kindled a fire, [into which] they dumped the still-vigorous locusts, spilling them into the fire until they were all dead. Then they gathered the locusts from the ashes and set them out under the sun to cure. And when they were throroughly dessicated, they ate them." The root meaning of *al-tabrīḥ* is "grief and violence," after *barraḥa*'s sense of "to cause grief" for someone. In the exclamation *Ma abraḥa hādha 'l-amra* ["What an affecting matter!"], *mā abraḥa* has the sense of *mā aʿjaba* ["How extraordinary!"]. And in the verse by al-Aʿshā,

Aqūlu la-hā ḥīna jadda 'r-raḥīlu
abraḥti rabban wa-abraḥti jāran

I say to [my mount] at the beginning of the journey:
"You have astounded your lord and neighbor."

Abraḥa's meaning here is "to inspire wonder" and "to perform admirably." Others give its meaning here as "You served nobly," where the transitive meaning of *abraḥa* is "to honor" and "to magnify." In his commentary on this same line of al-Aʿshā's, Abū ʿAmr says that a thing or an event is said to have *barḥā* when it delights or astounds the speaker, and that *marḥā* is used the same way. Opinions differ as to whether *abraḥti rabban* here means "You ennobled your master," "You have astounded your master," or "You have served your master well." Al-Aṣmaʿī's judgment was for the meaning "You have gone beyond what was demanded." Another gloss is that it means "to excel in stinginess or generosity"; *abraḥa* is said of one man who gives preference to another, or anything that confers a benefit.

The expression *Barraḥa 'llāhu ʿanka* means "May God dispel your troubles." *Mā ashadda mā baraḥa ʿalayhi* ["How great was what provoked him!"] is said of a man who gets angry with his companion. *Al-bāriḥa* is used by the Arabs to mean "last night," said after the sun has begun descending from its highest point in the sky. Until that time the previous night's events are still discussed as things that happened "on this night" [*al-laylata*]. In the line by Dhu 'l-Rumma:

taballagha bāriḥiyya karāhu fīhi

. . . last night's slumber got the best of him

some have said that *bāriḥiyy* [a relative adjective derived from *al-bāriḥa]* refers to the oppressive drowsiness that muddled his vigil. Others have commented that it simply means "the previous night." The saying *Mā ashbaha 'l-laylata bi-'l-bāriḥati* ["How like this night is to last night!"] means "How like last night, most recent of the nights past and done with, is the night in which we find ourselves tonight." *Al-bāriḥa* is the most recent of all the nights that have passed. "I met with him on *al-bāriḥa*," or "*al-bāriḥa* the first." Its meaning comes from *bariḥa*'s sense of "to pass or come to an end." It has no diminutive form. Thaʿlab [b. Yaḥyā (d. 291/904)] said, "I am told that Abū Zayd said, 'In the period between the rising of the sun and the beginning of its descent, you say [of a dream], "In my sleep tonight I saw . . ." After midday you say, "Last night I saw . . ."' " In his *Tales of the Grammarian of Baṣra*, [al-Ḥasan b. ʿAbd Allāh] al-Sīrāfī (d. 368/979) reports these words of Yūnus: "The Arabs say, 'Such and such a thing happened tonight' until morning is over. At that point they say, 'It happened last night.' "

According to al-Jawharī (d. ca. 400/1009–1010), "The word *barḥā*, construed after the form *faʿlā*, is said for the missed shot of an archer or anyone aiming for a target, and *marḥā* is said for a hit." And Ibn Sīda (d. 458/1066) says, "The Arabs have a pair of words used for shooting and throwing. For the shot that hits its target, they say *marḥā*; and for the shot that misses, they say *barḥā*." And [yet] an utterance that is *barīḥ* is one said [by others] to have hit its mark, as in the line by Abu Dhuʾayb al-Hudhalī:

Arāhu yudāfiʿu qawlan barīḥan[66]

I saw him fending off a harsh talking-to.

Al-burḥa means "the best" of anything, and its plural is *al-buraḥ*. One says, "This one is *al-burḥa* of the *buraḥ*" to mean that it is the best of the best. Said of a she-camel, it means that of all the camels she is the finest. And according to the *Tahdhīb*, it is said of a male camel also.

Ibn ["Son of"] *Barīḥ* and *Umm* ["Mother of"] *Barīḥ* are epithets of the crow, so called because of its call. A flock of crows is called *Banāt* ["daughters of"] *Barīḥ*. Ibn Barrī says that only *Ibn Barīḥ* is heard, and that it may also be used as a general expression for hardship. One says, "I met with the son of *Barīḥ* from him," as in the anonymous verse:

Salā al-qalbu ʿan kubrāhumā baʿda ṣabwatin
wa-lāqayta min ṣughrāhima ʾbna Barīḥi

After a dalliance, your heart turned away from the elder of the
two [sisters]
but you met with Ibn Barīḥ from the younger.

Another form of this expression is: "I met with *Banāt Barḥ*," or "*Banū Barḥ*."

Yabraḥ is a man's name. In a *ḥadīth* related by Abū Ṭalḥa [it is related that the Prophet said], "Of all the territories in my possession, Bayraḥāʾ is the one I love best." Ibn al-Athīr reports differing versions of how this name should be voweled. It is the name of an area of Medina. In *al-Fāʾiq fī gharīb al-ḥadīth*, al-Zamakhsharī (d. 538/1144) states that it is built on *al-barāḥ*, the word for "open land."

66 From the same poem of Abū Dhuʾayb's quoted above in article √*snḥ* (n57); see Abū Dhuʾayb 1998:61.

Bibliography

I. Primary Sources

Augustine, Bishop of Hippo. 1930. *De doctrina christiana, libros quattuor*. Ed. H. J. Vogels. Bonn.

al-Bukhārī, Muḥammad b. Ismāʿīl. 2004. *Ṣaḥīḥ al-Bukhārī*. Ed. A. Zahwa and A. ʿInāya. Beirut.

al-Ḥalabī, Nūr al-Dīn b. Burhān al-Dīn. 1989. *Al-Sīrat al-Ḥalabiyyat al-nabawiyya: Insān al-ʿuyūn fī sīrat al-amīn al-maʾmūn*. Ed. M. al-Tunjī. Damascus.

al-Ḥātimī, Muḥammad ibn al-Ḥasan. 1989. *Ḥilyat al-muḥādara fī ṣinaʿat al-shiʿr*. Ed. J. al-Kitābī. Baghdad.

Hock, R. F., ed. and trans. 1995. *The Infancy Gospels of James and Thomas*. Santa Rosa, CA.

Ibn ʿAbd Rabbih, Aḥmad ibn Muḥammad. 1940. *Kitāb al-ʿIqd al-farīd*. Ed. A. Amīn, A. al-Zayn, and I. al-Abyārī. 7 vols. Cairo.

Ibn Isḥāq b. Yasār, Muḥammad, and Ibn Hishām, Abū Muḥammad ʿAbd al-Malik. 1936. *Al-Sīrat al-nabawiyya*. Ed. M. al-Saqqā, I. al-Abyārī, and ʿA. Ḥ. Shalabī. 4 vols. Cairo.

———. 1955. *The Life of Muhammad: A Translation of Ibn Ishaq's Sīrat Rasūl Allāh*. Ed. and trans. A. Guillaume. London.

Ibn al-Kalbī, Hishām. 1952. *The Book of Idols*. Ed. and trans. N. A. Faris. Princeton.

al-Iṣbahānī, Abu ʾl-Faraj ʿAlī b. al-Ḥusayn al-Qurashī. 1969–1982. *Kitāb al-Aghānī*. Ed. I. al-Abyārī. 31 vols. Cairo.

al-Jāḥiẓ, Abū ʿUthmān ʿAmr b. Baḥr. 1968. *Al-Bayān wa-al-tabyīn*. Ed. ʿA. S. M. Hārūn. 4 vols. Cairo and Beirut.

al-Masʿūdī, Abu ʾl-Ḥasan ʿAlī b. al-Ḥusayn. 1965–1966. *Murūj al-dhahab wa-maʿādin al-jawhar*. Ed. Y. A. Dāghir. 4 vols. in 2. Beirut.

Muslim, al-Ḥusayn b. al-Ḥajjāj. 2007. *Ṣaḥīḥ Muslim*. Ed. Kh. M. Shīḥā. Beirut.

Abū Dāʾūd Sulaymān al-Sijistānī. 1996. *Sunan Abī Dāʾūd*. Ed. M. al-Khālidī. 3 vols. Beirut.

II. Lexica

Lisān al-ʿarab. 1988. Jamāl al-Dīn b. Mukarram b. Manẓūr. Ed. ʿA. Shīrī. 18 vols. Beirut.

Tāj al-ʿarūs min jawāhir al-Qāmūs. 1965–2001. Muḥammad al-Murtaḍā al-Ḥusaynī al-Zabīdī. Ed. ʿA. al-S. A. Farrāj. 40 vols. Kuwait.

III. Poetry Collections

ʿAbīd b. al-Abraṣ. 1994. *Dīwān ʿAbīd b. al-Abraṣ*. Ed. ʿU. F. al-Ṭabbāʿ. Beirut.

Abu Dhuʾayb al-Hudhalī. 1998. *Dīwān Abī Dhuʾayb*. Ed. S. al-Miṣrī. Beirut.

ʿAmr b. Qamīʾa. 1919. *The Poems of ʿAmr Son of Qamīʾah*. Ed. and trans. C. Lyall. Cambridge.

Dhu ʾl-Rumma. 1995. *Dīwān shiʿr Dhi ʾl-Rumma*. Ed. Z. Fatḥ Allāh. Beirut.

Hesiod. 1978. *Works and Days*. Ed. M. L. West. Oxford.

Labīd b. Rabīʿa. 1962. *Sharḥ dīwān Labīd b. Rabīʿa al-ʿĀmirī*. Ed. I. ʿAbbās. Kuwait.

al-Nābigha al-Dhubyānī. 1963. *Dīwān al-Nābigha al-Dhubyānī*. Ed. K. al-Bustānī. Beirut.

al-Zawzanī, Abū ʿAbd Allāh al-Ḥusayn. 1972. *Sharḥ al-Muʿallaqāt al-sabʿ*. Beirut.

IV. Secondary Sources

Ali, A. 1990. *Al-Qurʾān: A Contemporary Translation*. Princeton.

Collins, D. 2002. "Reading the Birds: Oiônomanteia in Early Epic." *Colby Quarterly* 38:1:17–41.

Fahd, T. 1966. *La divination arabe: Études religieuses, sociologiques et folkloriques sur le milieu natif de l'Islam*. Leiden.

al-Fayyūmī, M. I. 1979. *Fi ʾl-fikr al-dīnī al-Jāhilī*. Cairo.

Fontenrose, J. 1978. *The Delphic Oracle: Its Responses and Operations. with a Catalogue of Responses*. Berkeley.

Foucault, M. 1977. *Language, Counter-memory, Practice: Selected Essays and Interviews by Michel Foucault*. Ed. and trans. D. F. Bouchard and S. Simon. Ithaca.

Frolov, D. 2002. *Classical Arabic Verse: History and Theory of ʿArūḍ*. Leiden.

Heidegger, M. 1984. *Early Greek Thinking: The Dawn of Western Philosophy*. Ed. and trans. D. F. Krell and F. A. Capuzzi. San Francisco.

Izutsu, T. 1964. *God and Man in the Koran: Semantics of the Koranic Weltanschauung*. Tokyo.

Jeffery, A. 1938. *Foreign Vocabulary of the Qurʾan*. Baroda, India.

Jones, A. 1994. "The Language of the Qurʾān." *The Arabist: Budapest Studies in Arabic* 6/7:29–48.

Keller, C. A. 1946. *Das Wort OTH als "Offenbarungszeichen Gottes": Eine philologisch-theologische Begriffsuntersuchung zum Alten Testament*. Basel.

Mohammed, Kh. 2002. Review of A. Ali, *Al-Qurʾān: A Contemporary Translation* (Princeton 1990). *Middle East Studies Association Bulletin* 36:1:47.

Momen, M. 1985. *An Introduction to Shiʿi Islam: The History and Doctrines of Twelver Shiʿism*. New Haven.

Nagy, G. 1990a. *Greek Mythology and Poetics*. Ithaca.

——. 1990b. *Pindar's Homer: The Lyric Possession of an Epic Past*. Baltimore.

——. 2002. "The Language of Heroes as Mantic Poetry: *Hypokrisis* in Homer." *Epea Pteroenta, Beiträge zur Homerforschung: Festschrift für Wolfgang Kullmann zum 75. Geburtstag* (eds. M. Reichel and A. Rengakos) 141–150. Stuttgart.

Nicholson, R. A. 1930. *A Literary History of the Arabs*. Cambridge.

Peirce, C. S. 1955. *Philosophical Writings of Peirce*. Ed. J. Buchler, J. New York.

Sebeok, T. 1976. *Contributions to the Doctrine of Signs*. Bloomington, IN.

Thompson, S., ed. 1989. *Motif-Index of Folk-Literature*. 6 vols. Revised and enlarged. Bloomington, IN.

Torczyner, H., et al. 1938–1958. *Lachish (Tell ed Duweir)*. 4 vols. London.

Vernant, J.-P. 1991. *Mortals and Immortals: Collected Essays*. Trans. F. Zeitlin et al. Princeton.

Wellhausen, J. 1897. *Reste Arabischen Heidentums*. ed. 2. Berlin.

Wright, W., ed. and trans. 1967. *A Grammar of the Arabic Language, Translated from the German of Caspari and edited with numerous additions and corrections*. 2 vols. in 1. ed. 3, revised. Cambridge.

Zwettler, M. 1978. *The Oral Tradition of Classical Arabic Poetry: Its Character and Implications*. Columbus, OH.

——. 1990. "A Mantic Manifesto: The Sūra of 'The Poets' and the Qur'ānic Foundations of Prophetic Authority." *Poetry and Prophecy: The Beginnings of a Literary Tradition* (ed. J. L. Kugel) 75–119. Ithaca.

2

Theoclymenus and the Poetics of Disbelief: Prophecy and Its Audience in the *Odyssey*

Jack Mitchell

In this essay I will reconsider the role of Theoclymenus, soothsayer (*mantis*) of the *Odyssey*, in the light of current ideas about performance in Homer. I hope to retrieve Theoclymenus from relative obscurity by showing that he functions, at the heart of the *Odyssey* and especially at a crucial juncture, as the bridge between the very practice of formal performance that underlies Homeric poetry and the theme of *atasthalia* 'wantonness'. A proper understanding of Theoclymenus should lead to a better appreciation of how epic itself depicts the relationship between the performing poet and his audience. We will also see that, on the sole occasion when that relationship breaks down, the breakdown is condemned in the harshest terms by the *Odyssey* itself.

Let us follow Theoclymenus through the tale. He appears out of nowhere in Book 15 (xv 223), on the run from murder charges, a *mantis*, heralded by a veritable Homeric fanfare: thirty lines of biographical introduction and genealogy (225–255). In itself, this is remarkably lengthy; but it is the apparent discrepancy between the grandeur of Theoclymenus' introduction and his subsequent role that used to provoke Analyst disdain.[1] Yet the genealogy is "still typically Homeric in that it only provides information that is relevant for the role Theoclymenus is to play" (de Jong 2001:372). We may go further: while Theoclymenus' great-grandfather Melampus is the only ancestor to enjoy a full ring-composition (226–242), further adventures both of his second cousin, Amphiaraus (the best *mantis* of his day [252–253] who "died in Thebes

1 See the bibliography at Fenik 1974:233n1. Most disdainful is Page 1955:86–88, whose arguments Fenik refutes one by one. Here both argument and counterargument, framed in terms of character motivation and intention, remind us how much has been gained from the integration of the concept of cultural poetics into Homeric scholarship. My own approach agrees with that of Derek Collins (2002), who identifies "rhetorics of divination" and notes that "divination relies on a discourse not between the gods and the diviner . . . but between the diviner and his audience" (20). The present essay may be read as an analysis of how the *Odyssey* employs Theoclymenus in the cultural context described by Collins.

on account of presents to a woman" [247]), and of his uncle, Cleiton (whom "golden-throned Dawn seized on account of his beauty, so that he might be among the immortals" [250–251]), are hinted at. Amphiaraus stars in Pindar's *Pythian* 8, while Gregory Nagy has shown that the "rapt by the Dawn" motif, experienced by Cleiton, is widely paralleled (Nagy 1999:190–204). In short, Theoclymenus' biographical introduction features more compression than expansion of potentially fruitful epic material. We may conclude that its length, including the expansion of Melampus' ring-composition, is well calculated; perhaps the parallel of Melampus' plight in "fleeing his fatherland" (228) with the situation of his great-grandson Theoclymenus has prompted the select expansion of the Melampus story. In any case, a legitimate thirty lines point to a more significant role for Theoclymenus than scholars have yet been able to establish. Can he meet these high expectations? The answer can be found through careful examination of his three prophecies.

First Prophecy: Telemachus

Theoclymenus' first prophecy, to Telemachus, gives us our first glimpse of this *mantis* in action, but poses a riddle as to mantic technique.

After the introductory fanfare, Theoclymenus supplicates Telemachus, receives welcome, and sails back to Ithaca with the young prince, who has just learned the minds and cities of at least a few men and is at last on the road to manhood.[2] The narrative then cuts to Eumaeus and Odysseus at dusk; at daybreak (495) we return to Telemachus' ship. The crew breakfasts on a beach on Ithaca; Telemachus, warned by Athena of the suitors' plans to waylay him on return, bids his comrades sail on without him; and Theoclymenus makes his first prophecy.

It will be worthwhile to go through the context and procedure of this prophecy carefully. At 506–507, Telemachus promises his comrades a feast, addressing them with the second-person plural ὑμεῖς twice (503 and 506). Theoclymenus intervenes to ask, essentially, "What about me?"

> πῇ γὰρ ἐγώ, φίλε τέκνον, ἴω; τεῦ δώμαθ' ἵκωμαι
> ἀνδρῶν οἳ κραναὴν Ἰθάκην κάτα κοιρανέουσιν;
> ἦ ἰθὺς σῆς μητρὸς ἴω καὶ σοῖο δόμοιο;

2 Theoclymenus' age is not specified, but he addresses Telemachus as φίλε τέκνον at xv 509; his father, Polypheides, took over as premier *mantis* from his own first cousin once removed, Amphiaraus, who died prematurely amid the pre-Trojan generation's "Seven against Thebes" cycle (xv 246–247); all in all, Theoclymenus is presumably, like Odysseus, middle-aged. Contra, Hoekstra suggests that he is old (Heubeck and Hoekstra 1989 *ad loc.*).

Where shall I go, dear child? Whose house shall I reach
Of the men who hold sway over rocky Ithaca?
Indeed shall I go straight to the house of your mother and to
your halls?[3]

Odyssey xv 509–511

The last line is clearly an attempt to garner an invitation. Telemachus politely remarks that this is impossible in the present dire circumstances at his house (512–517). Remarkably, he next suggests that Theoclymenus should go to the house of Eurymachus, one of the suitors (518–520) and thus his enemy;[4] and though Telemachus does add that he is the best of them (521), he doesn't fail to wish that they may be destroyed by Zeus before marriage (524).

At this point the dialogue is interrupted by the narrator, who produces a bird of good omen (δεξιὸς ὄρνις, a 'right-hand bird') in the form of a hawk tearing a pigeon apart in its claws (525–527). Theoclymenus calls Telemachus over to speak to him privately (529), and then prophesies. His speech is four lines long. The first two lines affirm that the bird in question is a bird of omen indicating a god's will,[5] and the last two contain the "message" of the prophecy. As to the affirmation that a bird of omen has flown past, it is notable that Theoclymenus characterizes the bird to Telemachus in just the same terms as the narrator has done to us: thus Telemachus is evidently unaware of anything unusual until Theoclymenus takes him aside. Certainly no one else notices the bird, in contrast to a previous bird of omen at Sparta earlier in Book 15, at whose apparition "those looking on rejoiced, and everybody's heart was glad" (xv 164–165). Here Theoclymenus' interpretation is very straightforward:

ὑμετέρου δ' οὐκ ἔστι γένος βασιλεύτερον ἄλλο
ἐν δήμῳ Ἰθάκης, ἀλλ' ὑμεῖς καρτεροὶ αἰεί.

There is no race more kingly than yours (pl.)
In the land of Ithaca; rather you (pl.) [are / will be] always
powerful.

Odyssey xv 533–534

3 Translations are my own throughout.

4 See Page's Analyst objections at Page 1955:98n5.

5 The narrator has already described it as δεξιὸς ὄρνις / κίρκος, Ἀπόλλωνος ταχὺς ἄγγελος, which leaves some doubt as to whether it is meant that all falcons are swift messengers of Apollo, that this particular falcon is one, or that "right-hand birds" are (naturally) messengers of the god of prophecy.

It is interesting that verb, and thus tense, are omitted from the last half-line.[6] To this Telemachus replies,

> αἲ γὰρ τοῦτο, ξεῖνε, ἔπος τετελεσμένον εἴη·
> τῷ κε τάχα γνοίης φιλότητά τε πολλά τε δῶρα
> ἐξ ἐμεῦ, ὡς ἄν τίς σε συναντόμενος μακαρίζοι.
>
> Ah, stranger, may that word come to pass!
> Then you would swiftly know friendship and get many presents
> From me, so that whoever met you would call you blessed.
>
> *Odyssey* xv 536–538

He immediately calls to his trusty companion Peiraeus and addresses him (540–543), first characterizing him as his most loyal comrade (540–541) and then telling him to take Theoclymenus to his own house and "be hearty friends with him and honor him 'til I come" (ἐνδυκέως φιλέειν καὶ τιέμεν εἰς ὅ κεν ἔλθω), to which Peiraeus consents (544–546).

Let us review what has happened here. Theoclymenus invites himself to Telemachus' house (509–511). Telemachus counters, not without a hint of self-pity, that this is impossible (513–517) and tells him to go to the house of one of his enemies (518–524). A bird flies by. Theoclymenus takes the young man aside and tells him forcefully that a god-sent bird of omen has appeared, and that his lineage is unbeatable. Telemachus says, "May it come to pass," and he immediately sends the soothsayer to his best friend's house.

Clearly the whole scene revolves around the question of where Theoclymenus is to stay in Ithaca. Since the prophecy lies squarely between the initial, shoddy invitation and the subsequent, hospitable invitation, the question is not whether Theoclymenus has made use of his prophetic ability for his own advantage, but how, and why it should be so effective. In order to answer this riddle, we must explore the relationship of mantic prophecy and archaic epic.

Rhapsodes and *Manteis* in Panhellenic Greece

Although "ordinary" people in the *Odyssey* make prophecies and interpret omens (Mentor/Athena, Helen, the disguised Odysseus) and, on one occasion, try but fail to do so (Menelaus), Theoclymenus differs from them in being a professional.[7] The *Odyssey* classes the profession of *mantis* with those of *iêtêr* 'healer', *tektôn* 'carpenter', and *aoidos* 'singer of tales' as being *demioergoi* or

6 On the fluidity of temporal boundaries in epic prophecy, see Collins 2002:22.

7 On non-professional bird interpretation, see Collins 2002:27–29.

'workers for the *dêmos*', that is, itinerant craftsmen (xvii 382–386; see Nagy 1990a:56–57). As we have seen from his biographical introduction, however, Theoclymenus' professionalism is not one he has taught himself, as has the *aoidos* Phemius (xxii 347); rather, it runs in the family: his father (Polypheides), grandfather (Mantius), and second cousin (Ampharaus) were all *manteis.*

This reminds us of that most famous professional lineage, the *Homêridai*, or "descendents of Homer," the title used by Chian rhapsodes whose claim to possess the authoritative Homeric tradition depended on at least a notional descent from the archetypal epic poet (Nagy 1990a:74–75). Within the rhapsodic tradition's representation of poetic and prophetic function, however, the parallel is not primarily with Homer but with Hesiod, a major figure in the rhapsodic repertoire (Athenaeus XIV 620c), whom the Muses provide with an αὐδὴν / θέσπιν, ἵνα κλείοιμι τά τ' ἐσσόμενα πρό τ' ἐόντα (a voice / Divine, so that I might give renown [*kleos*] to what is to be and what has been before; Hesiod *Theogony* 31–32). In the same manner, the *mantis* Calchas is described as one ὃς ᾔδη τά τ' ἐόντα τά τ' ἐσσόμενα πρό τ' ἐόντα (who knew and/or saw what is, what is to be, and what has been before; *Iliad* I 70).

To describe the *mantis* as a "prophet" in the modern sense of one who foretells the future, is thus misleading, since he functions with regard to present, future, and past alike: indeed, Theoclymenus' three prophecies, the latter two of which are specifically described with the verb *manteuomai* (*Odyssey* xvii 154, xx 380), all concern present events. It is also significant, as we will see, that Calchas' mantic relationship to present, future, and past is described by means of the verb *oida*, which in Homeric Greek signifies, equally and simultaneously, both 'know' and 'see'.[8] Rather than defining mantic activity in terms of temporal relationships, we should look to the *mantis*'s source of inspiration, Apollo: the *mantis* taps into the omniscience of the god (θεοπροπίας ἀναφαίνεις: *Iliad* I 87) and declares divine knowledge publicly,[9] just as the omniscient Muses (*Iliad* II 485) and also apparently Apollo as well (*Odyssey* viii 488) inspire the *aoidos*, the rhapsode, and the praise-poet in performance.[10]

8 For an analysis of the visualizing epistemology of *oida* in Homer, see Onians 1951:15–18.

9 On the use of φαίνω in the visualizing poetics of mantic interpretation, see Nagy 2003:25–36.

10 Nagy 1990a:163n82 offers a suggestion on the relationship between *mantis* and Muses: "The very form *Mousa/Moisa* (from ***mont-ia*; possibly **month-ia*) may well be revived from the same root **men-* as in *mania*. This possibility, along with others, is discussed by Chantraine 1968:716. If this etymology is correct, then the very word for 'Muse' reflects an earlier stage where not only the one who is inspired and the one who speaks the words of inspiration are the same, but even, further, the type of mental state marked by *mania* is not yet differentiated from the type of mental state marked by formations with **men-t-* and **men-h2* 'remember, have the mind connected with', which of course is the source of the 'mant' in *mantis*.

Theoclymenus' own name is archetypal in this respect, meaning "he who listens to the god."[11]

These links both with the Homeric and Hesiod poetry of the rhapsodic repertoire and with the representation of epic poetry in Homer via the *aoidos* Demodocus prompt us to ask what relationship may obtain between a *mantis* like Theoclymenus inside Homer and *manteis* outside Homer in Panhellenic culture. Certainly it is clear, as Nagy has shown, that the representation of epic by epic is subject to a process he terms *diachronic skewing* (Nagy 1990a:21–24), whereby the depiction of occasional, lyre-accompanied performances by Demodocus and Phemius belies the attested reality of rhapsodic practice while nonetheless insisting on key elements of real rhapsodic poetry, such as the invocation of the Muse or the subject-matter of *nostoi* (*Odyssey* i 326). How then does the depiction of Theoclymenus correspond to the reality of prophecy in the archaic period?[12]

The obvious starting point is Delphi. There the *mantis* of *manteis*, the Pythia, delivered inspired utterances (χρῆσμοι) direct from Apollo that were formulated as hexameter verse by a *prophêtês*[13] and delivered back and presented to the secular community by a *theôros* 'sacred emissary', three stages that may be termed "oracular utterance," "oracular formulation," and "oracular performance."[14] Nevertheless, in *Pindar's Homer* Nagy notes, first, that in the *Odyssey* the distinction between the *mantis* (concerned with the oracular utterance) and the *prophêtês* (concerned with the oracular formulation) can be blurred, in that "the figure of Teiresias represents a stage where the *prophêtês is* the *mantis*" (Nagy 1990a:163). He goes on to note, secondly, that we find in Theognis an appropriation of the term *theôros* by the Theognidean poet himself, who, being concerned with the crafting of verse, would more naturally fall into the category of *pro-*

11 Cf. Nagy 1990a:422, on *kluô*: "Homeric poetry . . . is marked by the privileging of the auditory metaphor, at the expense of the visual: the inability of the poet to *see* is a guarantee of his ability to go beyond personal experience and thus to *hear* the true message of the Muses, which is the *kleos* 'glory' (from verb *kluo* 'hear') of Homeric poetry (*Iliad* II 486)."

12 The following discussion draws largely on Nagy's discussions (1990a) of the diachronic relationship between rhapsodes and soothsayers. For a succinct recapitulation of these ideas, see Nagy 1990b.

13 Nagy 1990a:162, drawing on Plato *Timaeus* 72a, ὅθεν δὴ καὶ τὸ τῶν προφητῶν γένος ἐπὶ ταῖς ἐνθέοις μαντείαις κριτὰς ἐπικαθιστάναι νόμος for the *prophetes* and *Timaeus* 72b, τῆς δι' αἰνιγμῶν οὗτοι φήμης καὶ φαντάσεως ὑποκριταί for the meaning of *hupokritai*. The parallel of a 'lineage' (γένος) of *prophêteis* with the inherited authority of the Homeridai, as with the mantic forebears of Theoclymenus, is noteworthy.

14 For a discussion of public performance in the consulting city as the consummation of fifth-century oracles, see Maurizio 1997.

phêtês.[15] In other words, just as the representation of an occasional, lyre-strumming *aoidos* like Demodocus harks back, via diachronic skewing, to a stage in which lyre-players and rhapsodes were as yet undifferentiated,[16] so too the representation of a *mantis* who hears a god's voice and presents it to the community all by himself represents a diachronically skewed mantic tradition that will later be differentiated into oracular utterance, oracular formulation, and oracular performance as a result of the centralizing effects of Panhellenic oracular centers, chiefly Delphi.[17] Essentially, Theoclymenus is to the oracular tradition of Delphi as Demodocus is to the rhapsodic tradition of Homer, each an extension of Panhellenic realities into the fabulous realm of epic.

Since Theoclymenus, as an itinerant *mantis*, thus subsumes both oracular utterance (by his very name) and oracular performance (by his activity in the *Odyssey*) in a historical context of retrojection, we are on firmer ground in considering his role in oracular formulation. If Homer represents Theoclymenus as participating in a tradition of soothsaying that extended to contemporary times,[18] and if that tradition was integrated into a broader pattern of divinely inspired performance whose contemporary medium was the dactylic hexameter, what could be more natural than to suppose that Theoclymenus' medium for oracular formulation while wearing his *prophêtês* hat should be the regularly metered verse of Delphi and the rhapsodes, if not the dactylic hexameter itself?

In support of such a hypothesis, I turn to Egbert Bakker's analysis of the nature of the hexameter in *Poetry in Speech: Orality and Homeric Discourse*,[19] though I can do no more here than summarize his principal argument. Bakker has shown that the "paratactic" style of hexameter poetry closely corresponds to the way we verbally reactivate visual memory "piece by piece" in telling stories, in which "the intonation unit is the linguistic equivalent of the focus of consciousness, the amount of information that is active at any

15 Further, for a study of Hesiod's status as the outsider whose authority depends on his "otherness," see Martin 1992.

16 We may suppose, too, that, whether historically or notionally (or both), such undifferentiated performers would have been practitioners of composition-in-performance; Collins (2002:36) identifies the apparent spontaneity with which Homeric characters interpret bird omens as parallel to such bardic composition-in-performance.

17 Signs of oracular centralization, whereby the public comes to the *mantis* instead of the *mantis* going to the public, can be seen in the description of the *mantis* Polypheides, Theoclymenus' father, ὅς ῥ' Ὑπερησίηνδ' ἀπενάσσατο πατρὶ χολωθείς / ἔνθ' ὅ γε ναιετάων μαντεύετο πᾶσι βροτοῖσι, which must represent something like a "private" oracle. See further Nagy 2003, chapter 1, on the interpenetration of mantic, oracular, and epic poetry.

18 For surveys of the mantis figure, see Roth 1982 and Parker 1999.

19 See Bakker 1997, esp. chaps. 3–5.

one time in a speaker's consciousness" (Bakker 1997:48). The "segmentation of spoken discourse into intonation units," whereby "each unit represents a single focus of consciousness" corresponds to the segmentation of Homeric verse by means of particles such as (most commonly) δέ, καί, δή, and ἄρα. The result is a "syntax of movement" by means of which the storyteller chooses a sequence of details, each expressed in a single intonation unit and momentarily filling the consciousness of the audience, and thus guides his listeners' thoughts in precisely the direction he wishes. Although the interaction of intonation units and the hexameter's metrical cola cannot be reduced to a simple formula, patterns are evident, chief among them the division of the line at the medial caesura into two balanced halves; each of these typically represents a single focus of consciousness, as in the following verses. I have taken them at random, inserting the symbol | to indicate the correspondence of meter with "syntax of movement," and included a literal translation.

> ἔκ ῥ' ἀσαμίνθων βάντες | ἐπὶ κλισμοῖσι καθῖζον,
> χέρνιβα δ' ἀμφίπολος | προχόῳ ἐπέχευε φέρουσα
> καλῇ χρυσείῃ | ὑπὲρ ἀργυρέοιο λέβητος
>
> Now getting out of the bath | they sat down on the chairs
> And hand-washing water, the maidservant, | she poured it into the bowl, having brought it,
> And lovely and golden the bowl was, | poured the water over the silver basin.
>
> *Odyssey* xvii 90–92

We may compare it to the style of spoken discourse we encounter every day; for example: "Those ballplayers, and the steroid question, all those boutique drugs they've got these days, well, I don't want to prejudge it—the damage to the sport, to the fabric of it, it could be substantial. But let me tell you, if my own son had that advantage, well, a boy like that could go far, no question about it."

One obvious difference between a sports-bar conversation and Homeric performance is that of dignity; another is that of regular meter. As Nietzsche noted, "above all, [in employing verse] men desired the utility of the elemental and overpowering effect that we experience in ourselves as we listen to music: rhythm is a compulsion; it engenders an unconquerable urge to yield and join in; not only our feet follow the beat but our soul does too" (Nietzsche 1974:84). The effect of a large dose of regularly metered verse on an audience is above all one of mild hypnosis,[20] an effect that leads Homeric poetry to describe itself as *thelkteria* 'bewitchments'.[21] This mild hypnosis is a channel for *visualizing* communication, so that what the poet sees in his "mind's eye" is transferred, image by image, to the "mind's eye" of his audience. Bakker writes:

> [The linguist Wallace] Chafe has drawn attention to the capacity of the human mind to be activated not only by sensory input from the immediate environment, but also by what is not in the here and now. In the latter case, which Chafe calls "displacement" (as opposed to the "immediacy" of our physical environment), the speech-producing consciousness receives its input, by way of remembering or imagining, from another consciousness that is either the speaker's own or belongs to someone else. This remote consciousness is located in another time and/or place in which it does the actual seeing. The human mind appears to have a natural inclination to turn away from the physical present and to create a mental here and now, either by producing speech or listening to it. The obvious sign of this imaging potential in human discourse is the ubiquitous deployment of evidentiality markers and other linguistic devices pertaining to the here and now—the pretence is that what is remembered or imagined is actually *seen*, and the devices are deployed *on the assumption that the listener is willing to play along with the pretence.*
>
> Bakker 1997:77–78; emphasis added

Communication between poet and audience is thus fundamentally *visual*, despite the aural medium of verse;[22] and as we will see, the fact that the mechanics of hexameter communication depend on willing audience participation will prove important during Theoclymenus' third prophecy.[23]

20 In the course of performing a 1000-line poem in English dozens of times, I have myself verified this effect on the audience. But one need only consider the experience of seeing a Shakespeare play acted: the first five minutes are difficult and require close concentration, but soon we are hypnotized by iambic pentameter and follow readily.

21 Penelope to Phemius in Book 1: Φήμιε, πολλὰ γὰρ ἄλλα βροτῶν θελκτήρια οἶδας (i 337) besides his woeful *nostoi* songs.

22 See n11 above.

23 Similarly, in comparing archaic bird interpretation with contemporary African divinatory practice, Collins reports that "divination shifts the cognitive processes involved to what has been called a nonnormal or nonordinary mode" (Collins 2002:20) whereby "even when participants may acquiesce in shifting to a nonnormal mode of cognition, it is in the processes of mediation and synthesis" (what I have termed 'oracular utterance,' 'oracular formulation,' and 'oracular performance' above) "where we find the vested structures of power that must

In the meantime, however, I can now suggest why Theoclymenus' first prophecy was so effective in convincing Telemachus to send him to Peiraeus' house instead of to Eurymachus'. If, within the overall world of the dactylic hexameter in which the Odyssey unfolds and in which every speech-act,[24] no matter the genre, is performed, Theoclymenus is privileged to employ, by virtue of his status as professional *mantis*, formal and consciousness-manipulative speech, probably in verse, and most likely the oracular dactylic hexameter itself, we can see that in four lines he wrests control of his audience's psyche and bends it to his own ends. The first two lines,

> Τηλέμαχ' οὔ τοι ἄνευ θεοῦ ἔπτατο δεξιὸς ὄρνις·
> ἔγνων γάρ μιν ἐσάντα ἰδὼν οἰωνὸν ἐόντα
>
> Telemachus, not without a god has a right-hand bird flown past
> And I understood, beholding it face-to-face, that it was a bird of omen
>
> *Odyssey* xv 531–532

assert his authority through the bird, while the last two, quoted earlier, redirect the authority onto Telemachus' lineage. Since this newly conferred authority depends on the intermediary of the *mantis*, Theoclymenus has impressed his own status on the young prince in the most forceful way possible: by verse-based magical performance, or forcing his solitary audience to *see* his own kingliness.

Second Prophecy: Penelope

Theoclymenus' second prophecy, to Penelope, takes place at Odysseus' house, in Book 17. Here we discover a different sort of reaction to mantic performance than applied in the case of Telemachus, and a second riddle to consider regarding audience response.

To recap: the prince, having encountered his father at the swineherd's hut, proceeds to town; being a good son, he must visit his mother. She asks him about his trip (xvii 44); but he fobs her off (46–51) and, remarkably, says that he must go fetch Theoclymenus immediately (52–56)—so strong is his new bond with the soothsayer as a result of the first prophecy. He then brings Theoclymenus back to his house (from which the suitors are absent) and gives

be present to authorize the oracular reading. Without collective subscription to those structures, as constituted both in general and at the given moment, the interpretation will fail to persuade" (Collins 2002:21).

24 See Martin 1989:1–42 on the Homeric designation of authoritative speech acts as *muthoi*.

him the full *xenia* 'hospitality' treatment (84–95), incidentally showing up the initial excuse that prompted the first prophecy (xv 513–517). Penelope arrives and again asks Telemachus if he has heard of his father; he recounts his adventures (xvii 107–149), including Menelaus' second-hand report that Odysseus is on Calypso's island (140–147). Of course, Telemachus is by now aware that his father is on Ithaca, sowing doom; in restricting his account to Menelaus' report, he is being economical with the truth. The news that Penelope's husband may be alive "rouses the heart in her breast" in a whole-line formula used to indicate an emotional reaction.[25]

At this point Theoclymenus breaks in suddenly and prophesies.

> ὦ γύναι αἰδοίη Λαερτιάδεω Ὀδυσῆος
> ἦ τοι ὅ γ' οὐ σάφα οἶδεν, ἐμεῖο δὲ σύνθεο μῦθον·
> ἀτρεκέως γάρ τοι μαντεύσομαι οὐδ' ἐπικεύσω.
> ἴστω νῦν Ζεὺς πρῶτα θεῶν ξενίη τε τράπεζα
> ἱστίη τ' Ὀδυσῆος ἀμύμονος, ἣν ἀφικάνω,
> ὡς ἦ τοι Ὀδυσεὺς ἤδη ἐν πατρίδι γαίηι,
> ἥμενος ἢ ἕρπων, τάδε πευθόμενος κακὰ ἔργα,
> ἔστιν, ἀτὰρ μνηστῆρσι κακὸν πάντεσσι φυτεύει·
> οἷον ἐγὼν οἰωνὸν ἐυσέλμου ἐπὶ νηὸς
> ἥμενος ἐφρασάμην καὶ Τηλεμάχῳ ἐγεγώνευν.
>
> O reverend wife of Laertes' son Odysseus,
> Indeed he[26] does not know/see clearly; listen to my speech [*muthos*],[27]
> For I will prophesy [*manteusomai*] to you precisely and not hide anything.
> Let Zeus first among the gods bear witness, and this hospitable [*xenios*] table too,
> And the hearth of the blameless Odysseus at which I have arrived,
> That indeed Odysseus is already in his native land,
> Sitting or approaching, and learning of these evil acts,
> But he is sowing evil for the suitors one and all:
> Such was the bird of omen that, while upon the well-benched ship
> I was sitting, I pointed out and described to Telemachus.
>
> *Odyssey* xvii 152–161

25 For example, iv 366, xiv 361, xv 486, xvii 47 (especially), and xvii 216.

26 The pronoun refers to either Telemachus or Menelaus; for arguments supporting Menelaus see Russo, Fernandez-Galiano, and Heubeck 1992 *ad loc.*

27 See n24 above.

We learn from the scholia that this passage was a point of discrepancy in ancient editions: the χαριέστεροι[28] (lit. "more gratifying") versions of Homer athetized the last two lines (160–161), while the κοινότεροι (lit. "more universalizing") athetized the whole speech, together with Penelope's reply. As to the χαριέστεροι, their objection to the last two lines must be that Theoclymenus was *not* sitting on the well-benched ship when he made his first prophecy, according to Book 15: the crew had just been breakfasting on the shore (xv 499–500). What is more interesting for my purposes is that the message reported from the bird of omen in Book 15 was nothing like what Theoclymenus is now saying it was. There, the lineage of Odysseus was kingly and powerful forever; now the lineage is forgotten and Odysseus is on the prowl. This more serious inconsistency has prompted the κοινότεροι, though not the χαριέστεροι, to doubt the whole passage.

Fortunately we are now more familiar than were ancient scholars with the idea of *reperformance*. Gregory Nagy has been chiefly responsible for the application of this concept, which lies at the root of oral tradition, to archaic Greek poetics. In a recent formulation:

> The notional "sameness" of a Homeric response on each occasion when Homeric poetry is being performed is part of an overlap mentality of unchangeability in Homeric performance itself. Such a mentality . . . is revealed by the Homeric contexts of *hupokrinesthai* [the verb used for the interpretation of omens]. In other words, Homeric poetry presents itself as the same thing each time it is performed, just as the words of heroes (and gods) that are quoted by the poetry are imagined to be the exact same words on each occasion of each new performance.
>
> Nagy 2003:22

Gregory Nagy has produced a model for the evolution of the textual status of Homer,[29] one in which this "notional sameness" gradually results in the degree of real textual fixation we are familiar with, and Homeric poetry gradually sheds its *aoidos*-esque occasionality. Mantic performance, however, is by its very nature occasional, depending on flashes of lightning or the flight of birds, difficult to replicate at, say, a competition at the Panathenaea. As a result, when the occasion arises to articulate the will of the gods in a context

28 See G. Nagy's 2002 Sather lectures (in the forthcoming *Homer the Classic*) for a full account of this history of χαριέστεροι and κοινότεροι versions of Homer in Alexandria, as attested in the *scholia maiora*.

29 Nagy 1996, as well as the forthcoming 2002 Sather lectures.

in which these mantic *accoutrements* are not available to the speaker, reference must be made to *prior* mantic interpretations, which are then reperformed, notionally identical to the original interpretation but in fact as fixed in the context of performance as Homeric poetry. Thus in *Iliad* II, Odysseus "reperforms" Calchas' vision of a snake devouring birds and being turned to stone, a vision that he reinterprets to suit present circumstances and to inspire the Achaean troops (II 299–330). In this context, whether or not Odysseus has correctly quoted Calchas, or even described the vision correctly, is irrelevant: the point is that he has borrowed Calchas' authority as *mantis* for the duration of his performance.

If Odysseus was forced to reperform Calchas' omen because, as a non-*mantis*, he lacked the authority to appropriate the will of the gods without recourse to past performances, Theoclymenus in his second prophecy has been forced to fall back on his prior bird of omen for a simple enough reason: there are no birds inside the secular space of Odysseus' house. Nor would his principal audience, Penelope, be aware of a contradiction with his first prophecy: the occasionality of reperformance triggers the reinterpretation of the bird of omen, but the suitability of the performance itself remains the only criterion of authenticity.[30]

But how does Penelope react? We can suppose that Theoclymenus has deployed the same "consciousness-shifting" technique that was so effective with her son; indeed, the speech to Penelope is even more formalized. He begins (line 152) with a full line of address; the next line discredits other sources of authority; the third defines the terms of his speech-act, and he deploys the professional verb *manteuomai*. The next two lines are an oath that draws especially on the theme of *xenia* 'hospitality' that Theoclymenus is linked with throughout. We may note that the "message" of the prophecy that follows again describes a situation in present time; even the intimation of future action (that Odysseus is "sowing evil for the suitors") follows from a present tense verb. Interestingly, the touchstone for this mantic performance is now placed at the end of the speech; if it followed the order of the first prophecy (touchstone, then message), the last couplet would fit between lines 154 ("I will prophesy") and 155 (the oath).

Nevertheless, despite the elaboration of this speech, Penelope's reaction differs markedly from that of her son—although she replies with precisely the same words, remarking,

30 Cf. Collins 2002:22: "The 'truth' of divination . . . refers to its performative, and performable, efficacy."

> αἲ γὰρ τοῦτο, ξεῖνε, ἔπος τετελεσμένον εἴη·
> τῷ κε τάχα γνοίης φιλότητά τε πολλά τε δῶρα
> ἐξ ἐμεῦ, ὡς ἄν τίς σε συναντόμενος μακαρίζοι.
>
> Ah, stranger, may that word come to pass!
> Then you would swiftly know friendship and get presents
> From me, so that whoever met you would call you blessed.
>
> *Odyssey* xvii 163–165 (= xv 536–538)

This speech is followed directly by a change of scene as we cut to the suitors outside the house; the line in question is the well-known scene-ending marker, ὣς οἱ μὲν τοιαῦτα πρὸς ἀλλήλους ἀγόρευον ("Thus they conversed with one another in that manner"; *Odyssey* xvii 166). In other words, Penelope does not react in any concrete way whatsoever to Theoclymenus' second prophecy, and the scene initially appears anticlimactic. I will argue, however, that more can be understood from Penelope's reply than first meets the eye.

Her three-line response, which I will call the "may it come to pass" triplet, also appears at a critical juncture for psychological assessments of Penelope, namely her first interview with the disguised Odysseus in Book 19. Traditionally she has been considered a "naïve Penelope" unaware of vengeance-related goings-on until her reunion with Odysseus in Book 23; in 1950, P. W. Harsh first promulgated a "sly Penelope" who recognizes the beggar's true identity quite early on in Book 19 (Harsh 1950:1–21). My own view is that a middle course is more sensible: Penelope achieves gradual recognition of the disguised stranger—or rather, gradual recognition that the stranger is disguised.

It will be helpful now to summarize Odysseus' speeches and Penelope's reactions to them in their first interview in Book 19. The case for a "sly Penelope," or at least a Penelope skilled in the rhetorical arts, starts strong: after she begins with the typical *Odyssey* "Who are you?" couplet (104–105), Odysseus deploys an elaborate compliment to her before refusing to answer on account of his woefulness (107–118). Penelope counters by implying that she perceives his compliment as such but that his flattery is inappropriate in light of her own woeful situation in her husband's absence (124–163); the theme of her speech is *dolos* 'trickery' (137). In the last two lines she repeats her request that he identify himself (162–163), and we understand that, rhetorically, her woeful narrative constitutes a rebuttal to Odysseus' excuse that he is too woeful to describe himself: "Don't talk about woe to me!" is the implication. He replies with his third "Cretan lie," once again misidentifying himself as an old *xenos* 'guest-friend' of Odysseus' from Crete. This speech is an inspired blend of fact and fiction[31] that the narrator describes as "many lies very similar to the truth" (ἴσκε ψεύδεα πολλὰ λέγων ἐτύμοισιν ὁμοῖα; 203) in a line nearly identical to that put into the Muses' own mouths in Hesiod as they describe their essence (ἴδμεν ψεύδεα πολλὰ λέγειν ἐτύμοισιν ὁμοῖα; *Theogony* 27), an unmistakable sign that Odysseus is here appopriating the characteristics of a performing bard. Penelope's emotional reaction to this tale is vividly described with a simile of melting snow (203–208). But she proceeds to declare that she will test the stranger by asking him to describe Odysseus (215–219); when he does so (221–248), her reaction is even more emotional (249) and she remarks that she is now in complete sympathy with the stranger, though she will not see Odysseus again (253–260). Odysseus counters with another blend of fact and fiction, concluding with the announcement that Odysseus will shortly be coming home:

> ἦ μέν τοι τάδε πάντα τελείται ὡς ἀγορεύω·
> τοῦδ' αὐτοῦ λυκάβαντος ἐλεύσεται ἐνθάδ' Ὀδυσσεύς,
> τοῦ μὲν φθίνοντος μηνός, τοῦ δ' ἱσταμένοιο.
>
> Indeed now all these things shall come to pass just as I declare.
> In this very month Odysseus shall come hither,
> While this month is waning or while the next one is rising.
>
> *Odyssey* xix 305–307

To this Penelope replies with the very same "may it come to pass" triplet we encountered in her own and her son's reactions to Theoclymenus' prophecies above.

It is especially noteworthy that in replying to this amateur prophecy of her husband's return she shows no emotion and does not do so for the rest of the interview in Book 19, which features another three speeches by Odysseus; this contrasts with her previously emotional reactions just as her cool reaction to Theoclymenus in Book 17 contrasts with Telemachus' hearty reaction in Book 15.

In looking over the three instances of the "may it come to pass" triplet, two patterns of incongruity emerge. Firstly, the first two instances, those spoken to Theoclymenus, do not fit with the content of his prophesies: specifically, this triplet refers to future action, whereas Theoclymenus has been describing present-tense situations. Secondly, with regard to the trip-

[31] For an analysis of the blend of fact and fiction in this speech, see de Jong 2001:468–469.

let's promise of *xenia*, in the first instance Telemachus' acceptance of Theoclymenus as a *xenos* does not depend on any "fulfillment" of the latter's words, since Telemachus immediately shows him all welcome; in the second instance, Theoclymenus has already received *xenia* from Telemachus (xvii 84–95) by the time Penelope promises it to him (xvii 162–165); in the third instance, Penelope has previously remarked that in requital for the beggar's news of Odysseus he will be welcome and revered in her halls (xix 254), and in any case immediately offers him the bath of welcome (xix 317).

What are we to conclude from these seeming incongruities? Simply that the "may it come to pass" triplet is neither a simple expression of a speaker's personal reaction nor tailored to suit the occasion of utterance. Instead, given that the common denominator of all three instances is that of audience response to a statement of empirically unverifiable facts that the audience is asked to accept on trust, it seems that the "may it come to pass" triplet is no more than Homeric poetry's way of politely reacting to an act of mantic performance. We have seen that Odysseus himself, while no *mantis*, nonetheless shares in the Book 19 scene a line of characterization with the Hesiodic Muses, and I noted earlier the mantic affinities of Hesiod. By expressing solidarity, as it were, with the *mantis*'s statements the audience acknowledges the validity of the performance, if not of the content of the message. Indeed, in the case of Odysseus, Penelope's reaction may be considered as the turning point at which "naïve Penelope" begins to change into "sly Penelope," ceasing to weep, and proceeding to test Odysseus with her dream in the latter half of Book 19: clearly she has her suspicions of the stranger, provoked by her perception that he is lying—or rather performing. The irony in the Book 19 instance of the "may it come to pass" triplet, then, is that Odysseus' lying tale culminates in a prediction of his own imminent return, which is genuine—but we have already met a "lying" or performance-based description of Odysseus' ongoing plans for vengeance in Theoclymenus' second prophecy. Thus, given the parallels between Odysseus' mantic act in the first half of Book 19 and Theoclymenus' in Book 17, what could be more natural than to conclude that Penelope, in deploying the "may it come to pass" triplet with Theoclymenus, communicates her awareness that an act of performative prophecy has taken place?

We should thus be wary of thinking that Penelope simply "disbelieves" Theoclymenus. As we see from her unemotional reaction to his performance (parallel to her noted absence of emotion in reacting to Odysseus' prediction), which contrasts with Telemachus' whole-hearted enthusiasm for the soothsayer after the first prophecy, she has evidently not allowed her consciousness to be affected by Theoclymenus' mantic verse.

Penelope's awareness of performance, then, contrasts with Telemachus', whose consciousness clearly *is* affected. This contrast readily corresponds to our own experience of performance—of opera, for example.[32] While attending an operatic performance, one is conscious of simultaneously being *at* the opera—that is, sitting in a dark opera house surrounded by the rest of the audience and listening to dramatized music—and being *in* the opera, involved in the unfolding story on stage to the extent of following the turn of each musical phrase and feeling the sweep of a soprano's arm. From the arguments I presented earlier, it can be seen that Bakker's "consciousness units" correspond to musical phrases in an aria that affect us—manipulate our consciousness—insofar as we are *in* the opera, while the applause at the end of a moving aria reflects audience awareness that they are *at* the opera, and corresponds to the "may it come to pass" triplet of mantic performance as deployed by Telemachus and Penelope. It is possible, however, to be *at* and *in* the opera in a different way: as an opera singer or an opera connoisseur in the audience. In that case, one's presence *in* the opera instead constitutes an insider's awareness of how the music and production are put together. For the outsider, the entrance of the ghost in *Don Giovanni* is terrifying, since he is in the grip of the plot and of Mozart's chilling melody; for the insider, the entrance of the ghost differs from many another such entrance in other *Don Giovanni* productions and may be evaluated as such. The insider's interest is no less keen—rather the contrary—but his heightened awareness is critical and meets art, as it were, on equal terms.

This review of the rhetorical ability of Penelope on display in Book 19, and particularly in the skillful speech of xix 123–163, which refutes Odysseus' unwillingness to identify himself, has surely demonstrated that she, like her husband, is rhetorically skilled enough to recognize skilled performance when she sees it. In this light, the fact that Theoclymenus' second prophecy leaves her cool, unemotional, but nevertheless polite and engaging (in deploying the "may it come to pass" triplet) reflects a quite different type of audience reaction to mantic performance than the one that resulted from Theoclymenus' first prophecy to her more naïve son: hers is the collaborative "insider's" reaction.

[32] See Nietzsche's (1974:80) interesting analogy between the formal performance of Italian opera and the formal performance of verse. I use the example of opera because our culture is not very familiar with formal performance in narrative verse.

Third Prophecy: The Suitors

Theoclymenus' first two prophecies, to Telemachus and Penelope, constitute mere preludes to his great confrontation as *mantis* with the suitors in Book 20. Here my conclusions as to the nature of mantic performance and of audience reaction can be applied more briefly and with somewhat greater contrast.

Odyssey 20 is an important, though short (394 line), book whose function is to set the stage for the bow contest in Book 21 and the revenge in Book 22. It does so on the levels of plot and theme alike: it brings all the characters together at Odysseus' house, and it showcases the wantonness (ἀτασθαλία) of the suitors. The wantonness gains greater and greater momentum as the book rolls to a climax in Theoclymenus' third prophecy. It is expressed, moreover, through the prolific slaughter and eating of animals, a theme that underlies Theoclymenus' vision and mantic response.

Egbert Bakker has noted that, among Odysseus' adventures, the only one to appear in the *Odyssey*'s proem is that of the slaughter of the Cattle of the Sun (Bakker 2005:15), whereby Odysseus' companions αὐτῶν γὰρ σφετέρῃσιν ἀτασθαλίῃσιν ὄλοντο ("perished as a result of their very own wantonness [*atasthalia*]"; *Odyssey* i 6). Bakker further observes that both this slaughter and the Suitors' depredations are characterized as ἀτασθαλία (Bakker 2005).

Now let us turn to Book 20 and briefly consider the rising tempo of wantonness as the book approaches Theoclymenus' final prophecy. Dawn breaks at line 90. Soon (xx 147–156) Eurycleia rouses Odysseus' household to work, since the suitors are in the habit of showing up early (μαλ' ἦρι νέονται—a present-tense verb, with repeated aspect) and "then there is [always, continuing the sense of habitual activity] a feast for all of them" (155–156). Next, Eumaeus arrives, leading three pigs (162–163), and asks the disguised Odysseus if the suitors are still dishonoring him, to which Odysseus replies,

> αἲ γὰρ δή, Εὔμαιε, θεοὶ τισαίατο λώβην
> ἣν οἵδ' ὑβρίζοντες ἀτάσθαλα μηχανόωνται,
> οἴκῳ ἐν ἀλλοτρίῳ, οὐδ' αἰδοῦς μοῖραν ἔχουσιν
>
> Ah, indeed, Eumaeus, may the gods avenge the outrage,
> the outrage that these men in their arrogance <u>wantonly devise</u>
> in the house of someone else, and they don't show proper respect.
>
> *Odyssey* xx 169–171

(The phrase <u>wantonly devise</u> is formulaic, applied elsewhere to the suitors at iii 207, xvi 93, xvii 143, and, reconfigured, at xxii 47). Next (xx 173) the goatherd arrives, leading goats "to be a banquet for the suitors"; then the cowherd arrives "leading a cow for the suitors" and remarking that the suitors are in the habit of ordering him (κέλονται, another verb with repeated aspect) to "bring cattle for them themselves to eat" (213) and that he would be on the point of fleeing to another land if he didn't still hope for Odysseus' return (222–225). At 241 we find the suitors now planning to kill Telemachus openly; but instead they proceed to Odysseus' house:

> ἐλθόντες ἐς δώματ' Ὀδυσσῆος θείοιο
> χλαίνας μὲν κατέθεντο κατὰ κλισμούς τε θρόνους τε
> οἵ δ' ἱέρευον ὄϊς μεγάλους καὶ πίονας αἶγας,
> ἵρευον δὲ σύας σιάλους καὶ βοῦν ἀγελαίην
>
> Coming to the halls of the godlike Odysseus
> They put down their cloaks upon the chairs and seats
> And they slaughtered great sheep and fat goats
> And they slaughtered shiny pigs and the cow from the herd
> *Odyssey* xx 248–251

Soon they are threatening to "put an end" to Telemachus in his own house (273–274) for his objections to their behavior. At 284–298 a suitor mocks Odysseus and throws a cow's foot at him; soon another is mocking at length the household's hope that Odysseus may yet come home (321–337). When Telemachus then announces that he will consent to his mother's marrying her choice of them, the suitors break out in unquenchable laughter (346). What follows bears quoting in full:

> οἵ δ' ἤδη γναθμοῖσι γελώων ἀλλοτρίοισιν,
> αἱμοφόρυκτα δὲ δὴ κρέα ἤσθιον· ὄσσε δ' ἄρα σφέων
> δακρυόφιν πίμπλαντο, γόον δ' ὠίετο θυμός,
> τοῖσι δὲ καὶ μετέειπε Θεοκλύμενος θεοείδης·
> "ἆ δειλοί, τί κακὸν τόδε πάσχετε; νυκτὶ μὲν ὑμέων
> εἰλύαται κεφαλαί τε πρόσωπά τε νέρθε τε γοῦνα,
> οἰμωγὴ δὲ δέδηε, δεδάκρυνται δὲ παρειαί,
> αἵματι δ' ἐρράδαται τοῖχοι καλαί τε μεσόδμαι,
> εἰδώλων δὲ πλέον πρόθυρον, πλείη δὲ καὶ αὐλή,
> ἱεμένων Ἔρεβόσδε ὑπὸ ζόφον, ἠέλιος δὲ
> οὐρανοῦ ἐξαπόλωλε, κακὴ δ' ἐπιδέδρομεν ἀχλύς.
>
> And they were now laughing with the mouths of different men,
> And now they were eating blood-soaked meat; and look, their eyes,
> They were filled with tears, and the heart was fixed on wailing.

> And among them spoke forth the godlike Theoclymenus,
> "Ah, wretches, why are you suffering this blight? For night
> Has been wrapped around your heads and faces and your limbs beneath.
> A sound of wailing has been kindled, and your cheeks have been covered in tears;
> The walls and the handsome rafters have been spattered with blood,
> And the porch is full of ghosts, and the hall is full of them as well,
> Ghosts longing to go to Hell, in the gloom beneath; and the Sun,
> It has disappeared from the sky, and a blighting mist has fallen.
>
> *Odyssey* xx 347–357

This is Theoclymenus' final prophecy, seven lines long. It is linked with the poem as a whole in two ways: by the narratological device of focalization (with a twist), and by way of the grand theme of *atasthalia*.

To begin with focalization, Theoclymenus' intervention here is altogether sudden: we have not heard mention of him previously in Book 20, in fact not since Book 17. Thus, although it is clear to us *in retrospect* that the three line vision of 347–349—a description fixed in a tableau by means of imperfects (γελώων, ἤσθιον, ᾠίετο)—are "focalized" through the eyes of Theoclymenus (who presents them, with perfect-tense verbs, as *faits accomplis*),[33] they initially appear to be entirely legitimized by the narrator as regular narrative. We have seen that his first prophecy Theoclymenus was obliged to assert that he had seen a bird of omen, and it was not clear whether his audience had also seen it; here it is clear from the suitors' subsequent irony (xx 362) that they do not see this vision, and presumably no one else does.[34] In performance of the *Odyssey*, then, the vision is only subsequently focalized: rather, it is a case of perspectival zeugma,[35] belonging to (and authorized by) the narrator firstly and only subsequently restricted to Theoclymenus. As we have seen from his first two

33 On focalization, see de Jong 1997:29–40.

34 Contra Guidorizzi's view, to my mind highly improbable, that "after [Theoclymenus'] words, the suitors return to their senses and resume their arrogant and violent attitude, evidently forgetting what has just happened" (Guidorizzi 1997:2). I rather agree with the scholiast, who remarks: "No disappearance of the sun occurred: rather Theoclymenus sees such things while prophesying (μαντευόμενος) in some sort of divine inspiration (ἐνθουσιασμοῦ) that the sun disappears on them (αὐτοῖς). The suitors are unconcerned, seeing nothing of the sort" (scholia B *ad loc.*).

35 The rhetorical term *zeugma* ('yoking') refers to the use of a word that carries two distinct meanings simultaneously: see Edwards 2002 for a fruitful analysis of the new resonance of zeugma in the context of oral performance.

prophecies, however, Theoclymenus is more than capable of extracting more performative meaning from his divine inspiration than he was given, and if his subsequent exposition (352–357) includes more details than his focalized vision, we may suspect that he is again, in good faith, more concerned with performance than with reporting precisely what he sees.

Nevertheless, though the narrator and Theoclymenus thus narratologically overlap in this prophecy, they coincide still more in the pattern of thematic reference governing both vision and exposition. Specifically, the supernatural details correspond to those attending the slaughter of the Cattle of the Sun by Odysseus' companions, described in Book 10 but of course highlighted in the *Odyssey*'s proem (i 6–7). Following the slaughter, the gods "presented visual omens (τέραα προύφαινον), and the skins crawled, and the meat on the spits mooed—the meat both raw and cooked—and there came a sound like cattle" (xii 394–396); most importantly, the sun god Helius threatens to "go down to Hades and shine among the dead" (xii 382–383), by implication leaving the earth in perpetual night. *Chez Ulysse*, these details are paralleled in the aural portent of wailing (xx 353), the raw meat the suitors are suddenly eating (xx 348),[36] and most of all by the disappearance of the sun from the sky (xx 357).

The suitors' reaction to all this is not simple disbelief but ridicule. They laugh at Theoclymenus (358); one declares that he is crazy (ἀφραίνει, 360) and zeroes in specifically on the vision of Night (whose cosmic resonance I have just noted) for his mockery. Theoclymenus responds with a proud speech (364–370) in which he defends his sanity, but in which the prophetic note is not struck—the first time we have seen him in secular mode since he beseeched Telemachus for hospitality in Book 15. Interestingly, his last words include the "ἀτάσθαλα μηχανάασθε" formula applied six times elsewhere to the suitors; then "he went back to the house of Peiraeus, who warmly received him": a telling contrast to the violation of *xenia* by the suitors, who finally proceed to "ridicule the guests" (374). They one and all (375) try to provoke Telemachus, slandering the disguised Odysseus and suggesting that both he and Theoclymenus should be sold. As to the unidentified Theoclymenus, the suitors remark, ἄλλος δ' αὖτέ τις οὗτος ἀνέστη μαντεύεσθαι ("And this other fellow, whoever he is, stood up to prophesy"; *Odyssey* xx 380), an activity they couple with begging for bread and wine uselessly, like the disguised Odysseus (377–379).

36 For a view of this detail as a reference to the Dionysiac practice of ὠμοφαγία (the eating of raw meat), see Guidorizzi 1997:4–7.

An evaulation of the suitors' reaction in terms of audience response to performance shows that Theoclymenus' technique of consciousness manipulation has here had no effect at all; or rather, the suitors have not allowed themselves to participate in the performance as an audience must.[37] To continue the operatic analogy, they are rather in the position of someone, or rather a group of people, at the opera who are unable to *hear* the music as more than noise: they are simply *at* the opera and cannot enter *in*; and the natural reaction is laughter and mockery. Otherwise, while perhaps disregarding Theoclymenus' message, as Penelope does, they would at least acknowledge the legitimacy of his performance. As we have seen from line xx 380, however, the fact of Theoclymenus' performance is itself, for them, a subject of irony and ridicule. With that Book 20 ends: following the law of the rising climax, the suitors' arrogance can go no further.

Prophecy and Self-Referentiality

This essay has followed Theoclymenus through his three prophecies in the Odyssey and has tried to explain why a figure seemingly so marginal should enjoy the most prestigious "introductory biography" in all of Homer.

Examining Theoclymenus' first prophecy, to Telemachus, I sought to explain the uncanny power of his words, which successfully reversed Telemachus' decision as to where the soothsayer should stay on Ithaca, by exploring the ways in which the figure of the *mantis* in Homer corresponds to the figure of the *aoidos* on the one hand and to the reality of oracular activity in archaic Greece on the other. I found that the *formality* of mantic performance is analogous to the formality of rhapsodic epic and of Delphic oracular verse. Drawing on Egbert Bakker's understanding of the hexameter as a tool for the manipulation of consciousness, I concluded that Theoclymenus must, in prophesying, be employing a formal device with equal psychological potency, if not the hexameter itself. The conversion of Telemachus—thereafter the soothsayer's warm friend—can thus be understood as partaking of rhapsodic magic.

Coming to Theoclymenus' second prophecy, to Penelope, I reconsidered the question of what it means for an audience to "disbelieve" a *mantis*. We saw that Penelope's reaction constitutes a formal acknowledgement of the fact of performance, achieved through deployment of the "may it come to pass" triplet. With reference to another instance of this triplet in Book 19, which again coincided with a cool, unemotional reaction by a rhetorically skilful woman, I interpreted her "disbelief" as the "insider's" perspective

37 See. p. 57 above.

on performance, one in which the insider is able to remain autonomous by means of an awareness that she is both *in* and *at* the performance—in contrast to Telemachus, the young "outsider," who was wholly *in* to the extent of responding to the performer's will.

In considering Theoclymenus' third prophecy, to the suitors, I found that the suitors, while aware that a mantic performance had taken place, reacted with mockery and sarcasm both to the performance itself and to the very idea of mantic performance. They were definitely not "in" but merely "at"; and Theoclymenus left in a rage, never to be heard from again.

Throughout the investigation of these prophecies, I also noted three types of affinity between Theoclymenus the *mantis* and the poet of the *Odyssey*. First, there is the relationship with the rhapsodic tradition. Delphi and the rhapsodes shared the same meter; the rhapsodic hero Hesiod is described with the same line that characterizes the *mantis* Calchas in the *Iliad*—they know present, future, past. Within the *Odyssey* itself, however, *aoidoi* (representatives of the *Odyssey* poet) share the same source of inspiration with *manteis*, namely Apollo, and they are classed together as *dêmioergoi* (xvii 382–386). Second, beyond the rhapsodic tradition as a whole and its self-representation, I found that Theoclymenus is in collusion with the narrator in two respects: he obviously knows what is going on in the *Odyssey*'s story to a greater extent than anyone but Odysseus, though the source of his knowledge is somewhat ambiguous as he is ready to reinterpret omens to suit his own purposes on the spot; and he is involved in two "perspectival zeugmas" on the narratological level, whereby the narrator discloses information first to the audience *as* the narrator and subsequently makes it clear that his own statements were focalized through the soothsayer: in such situations, narrator and soothsayer blur.[38] Third, however, and most significantly, we have seen how Theoclymenus' final prophecy corresponds to the *Odyssey*'s central theme of *atasthalia* and its discontents, as Theoclymenus' speech to the suitors draws on imagery not seen since the wantonness of Odysseus' companions. As a *xenos* himself, moreover, Theoclymenus embodies both the well-treated guest and the ill-treated guest, receiving welcome from Telemachus and abuse from the suitors.

In the end, then, what is Theoclymenus' role? How is the thirty-line fanfare at his first appearance justified by his subsequent actions? I believe we can conclude, in light of these arguments, that Theoclymenus represents the idea of formal performance in the latter half of the *Odyssey*, as well as

[38] Cf. Martin's suggestion (Martin 1989:234–236) that Achilles and the *Iliad* narrator narratologically overlap.

being the articulator of the *atasthalia* theme. This is a role that cannot suit a rhapsode or an *aoidos* inside the story, since that story is still in the process of unfolding and epic's province is the past. The *mantis*, however, represents the divine will, which is readily identified by epic *with* epic, *inside* epic.[39] The suitors' response to Theoclymenus is clearly contrasted with Telemachus' and Penelope's engagement with mantic performance; but their rejection of formal performance is expressed in a simultaneous rejection of the very theme of the *Odyssey*. Pitilessly enough, this twofold rejection of both epic message and epic medium, effected through the figure of Theoclymenus, is equated in the *Odyssey* with unforgivable folly.

39 Cf. Collins's general conclusion on the representation of bird divination in epic, that "early epic can draw analogies between an internal character's performed bird divination and its own external performative mode" (Collins 2002:35; see generally 35–40).

Bibliography

Bakker, E. 1997. *Poetry in Speech: Orality and Homeric Discourse*. Ithaca.

——. 2005. "Homeric Epic Between Feasting and Fasting." *La poésie épique grecque: Métamorphoses d'un genre littéraire* (eds. F. Montanari and A. Rengakos) 1–30. Entretiens Hardt 52. Geneva.

Chantraine, P. 1968. *Dictionnaire étymologique de la langue greque: Histoire des mots*. Paris.

Collins, Derek. 2002. "Reading the Birds: *Oiônomanteia* in Early Epic." *Colby Quarterly* 38.1:17–41.

Edwards, M. 2002. *Sound, Sense, and Rhythm: Listening to Greek and Latin Poetry*. Princeton.

Fenik, B. 1974. *Studies in the Odyssey*. Wiesbaden.

Guidorizzi, G. 1997. "The Laughter of the Suitors: A Case of Collective Madness in the *Odyssey*." *Poet, Public, and Performance in Ancient Greece* (eds. L. Edmunds and R. W. Wallace) 1–7. Baltimore.

Harsh, P. W. 1950. "Penelope and Odysseus in *Odyssey* 19." *American Journal of Philology* 71:1–21.

Heubeck, A., and Hoekstra, A. 1989. *A Commentary on Homer's Odyssey. Vol. 2: Books 9-16*. Oxford.

de Jong, I. J. F. 1997. "Narrator Language versus Character Language: Some Further Explorations." *Hommage à Milman Parry. Le style formulaire de l'épopée homérique et la théorie de l'oralité poétique* (ed. F. Létoublon) 293–302. Amsterdam.

——. 2001. *A Narratological Commentary on the Odyssey*. New York.

Martin, R. P. 1989. *The Language of Heroes: Speech and Performance in the Iliad*. Ithaca.

——. 1992. "Hesiod's Metanastic Poetics." *Ramus* 21.1:11–33.

Maurizio, L. 1997. "Delphic Oracles as Oral Performances." *Classical Antiquity* 16.2: 308–334.

Nagy, G. 2003. *Homeric Responses*. Austin.

——. 2000. "'Dream of a Shade': Refractions of Epic Vision in Pindar's *Pythian* 8 and Aeschylus' *Seven against Thebes*." *Harvard Studies in Classical Philology* 100:97–118.

——. 1999. *The Best of the Achaeans: Concepts of the Hero in Archaic Greek Poetry*. Rev. ed., Baltimore.

——. 1996. *Poetry as Performance: Homer and Beyond*. Cambridge.

——. 1990a. *Pindar's Homer: The Lyric Possession of an Epic Past*. Baltimore.

——. 1990b. "Ancient Greek Poetry, Prophecy, and Concepts of Theory." *Poetry and Prophecy: The Beginnings of a Literary Tradition* (ed. L. Kugel) 56–65. Ithaca.

Nietzsche, F. 1974. *The Gay Science*. Trans. Walter Kaufmann. New York.

Onians, R. 1951. *The Origins of European Thought*. Cambridge.

Page, D. L. 1955. *The Homeric Odyssey*. Oxford.

Parker, R. 1999. "Through a Glass Darkly: Sophocles and the Divine." *Sophocles Revisited: Essays Presented to Sir Hugh Lloyd-Jones* (ed. J. Griffin) 11–30. Oxford.

Roth, P. A. 1982. "Mantis: The Nature, Function, and Status of a Greek Prophetic Type." Ph.D. diss., Bryn Mawr.

Russo, J., Fernandez-Galiano, M., and Heubeck, A. 1992. *A Commentary on Homer's Odyssey. Volume 3: Books 17–24*. Oxford.

3

The Places of Song in Aristophanes' *Birds*

Dan Sofaer

Birds' Ideal Music between Tradition and Utopia

Scholars of Greek Old Comedy often treat comic lyric in a limited manner: meters are analyzed, the occasional allusion to Anacreon or Pindar is noted, the emotional effect of a song is surmised, but somehow these analyses rarely affect our reading of the play in its larger context. For that, we are advised to make ourselves well-informed about law courts, contemporary political figures, and other prosaic facts, from the dull to the obscene. Such an approach to the lyrics of comedy is, as I will be arguing here, inadequate, largely because music in its various guises was such an important fact of life in Athens, so much so that even the most frivolous-sounding comic song may have had serious overtones by virtue of its intervention in an ongoing discourse about music and society. For recovering this socially charged musical discourse, recent studies of nondramatic lyric could provide alternative approaches, as they emphasize less the personal/confessional (and bare textual) aspect and more the social, religious, and economic aspects of performance occasions.[1] For the Greeks, as these other studies show, a song is more than just words and music: who is singing, who is listening, and where and when and to what instruments a song is sung reveal as much as the song itself. Complications arise when applying these contextual approaches to comic lyric, since it is part of a genre with its own conventions and occasions. Still, taking as our model

I would especially like to thank Mark Griffith for his help with this essay. I am also indebted to D. J. Mastronarde and R. P. Martin for two helpful courses in Aristophanes, and to all those at Berkeley who commented on this paper.

1 See, for instance, Gentili 1988; Calame 1977 (vol. 1 translated into English as Calame 1997); Nagy 1990:9 ("If the occasion [of a song] should ever be lost or removed, then the intent of the utterance is destabilized"); Kurke 1991.

the many later efforts at remembering archaic lyric poets during antiquity, we might try to join in this process and understand the way archaic poetry was remembered in comedy and what this remembrance signifies within the larger cultural framework. A play that suggests itself as a classic example of comedy remembering lyric is Aristophanes' *Birds*.[2] M. S. Silk has lately called into question the inflated praise of earlier scholars,[3] and it is still unclear how these lyrics should be appreciated: the range of Aristophanes' lyric styles is considerable, and the musical structure of entire plays deserves consideration as well.[4] That Aristophanes' relationship to the earlier lyric poets was more than parodic, that he aspired to be taken as an authoritative maker of songs, is suggested by the substantial archaic lyric echoes of two of his parabasis odes.[5] We also face a question: how traditional are Aristophanes' comedies and their music? Anton Bierl, for example, sees Aristophanes as the inheritor of a living chorus culture, while Evanghelos Moutsopoulos sees Aristophanes' music as part of the new ethopoietic tendencies associated with Damon.[6] Can both be

2 See Herington 1985, Kugelmeier 1996. Some scholars now consider it a misnomer to speak of lyric in Athenian drama, but when looking for reflections of archaic lyric songs and occasions in drama, the term remains meaningful despite the fact that dramatic songs were accompanied by the *aulos*.

3 Silk 1980. See also Perkell 1993, Mathews 1997, and Silk 2000 for a response and a more favorable reading of the Hoopoe's song.

4 My approach to musical design is a slightly complicated one: I assume, unlike Bernhard Zimmermann (see n10 below), that the lyrics of *Birds* are somewhat independent from the surrounding dialogue and interact more with one another and with lyric traditions than with the prosaic language and action of the rest of the play. This separate appreciation of a play's music I take to be a prerequisite for a subsequent investigation of the relationship of a play's music to the music and culture surrounding it. For a discussion of metrical design, see Parker 1994.

5 See Fraenkel 1962:191–215 (on parabasis odes) and Bremer 1991. For Kugelmeier (1996:2), "reflex" is a wider category than parody or paratragedy and can include direct quotation, altered quotation, lost quotation, and reflections of poets as personalities. An example of a lyric reflection is *Peace* 796–801: "With such music must the skillful poet hymn public hymns [δαμώματα] of the pretty-haired Graces / When the spring swallow makes a full-voiced noise, perching / But let not Morsimos be granted a chorus," reflecting Stesichorus PMG 212: "With such music must we hymn public hymns of the pretty-haired Graces, luxuriously discovering a Phrygian note / when spring is coming." Compare Corinna PMG 690. Kugelmeier considers the self-reference "skillful poet" to be typical of comic reflection of lyric. The meter of the added phrase is the typically comic ithyphallic. Some other lyric reflections (discussed by Kugelmeier): PMG 851 and *Acharnians* 263–279 reflect a similar tradition; Pindar fr. 76 is reflected in *Acharnians* 636–640, fr. 89a in *Knights* 1264–1273.

6 Bierl (2001:19) studies the chorus in immediate relation to the Athenian audience instead of as an ideal spectator of the action: "Dieser *communis opinio* stellen wir ein dynamisches, offenes und transversales Modell entgegen: der dramatische Chor kann aus dem inneren Plot heraus die aüsere Kommunikationsebene übergreifen, ohne die Dimension des Fiktionalen ganz aufzugeben." Bierl's approach may lend itself more to *Thesmophoriazusae*, which he mainly treats, than to *Birds*. On the ethopoietic approach see Moutsopoulos 2000:59–82.

correct? Yet this would present a problem, since two disparate aspects of the same poet and culture would be treated in incommensurable terms, at least if Moutsopoulos's "ethopoietic" approach implies a level of artistic autonomy incompatible with the inheritance and management of a chorus culture.

Without pretending to resolve this issue, I hope that an investigation of *Birds*, written in the midst of Aristophanes' career and at a transitional point in Athenian musical practice,[7] may help us further address it. To make a start, let us imagine that *Birds* might do for lyric what *Frogs* does for tragedy: place it under scrutiny, through the citing and enacting of positive and negative examples. This represents lyric's encounter with Aristophanes as a critic, but since he had to try to please his audience as well, we can also see it as lyric's encounter with the Athenian public. As Richard Martin points out, "in *Birds*, it seems that the lyric . . . is always tugging against the social" (Martin 1999:198). Aristophanes evaluates lyric through performance, and thus the judgments expressed must be seen in the context of the production, comic conventions, and plot. But we also need to take into account the larger contexts evoked by the music. In the end, as I hope to show, comedy does take song seriously,[8] both by producing exemplary music and by responding to contemporary musical and cultural issues. The musical teaching that results may not be as coherent and explicitly propositional as that of a philosopher like Plato (and for this we may perhaps be grateful), but it is likely to be more practical and dynamic, since it comes from an actual musical practitioner.

A final general consideration: *Birds* is a utopia of sorts. Scholars are divided on how the Athenian public would have received the utopian vision of Cloud-cuckoo-land. The old discussion of political allegory versus escapist fantasy has developed into a disagreement mostly to do with Peisetairos'

7 Wilson 2000 argues convincingly that the robustness of the choregic institution well into the fourth century makes it impossible to speak of "choral decline" in any overall sense, as had Kranz's *Stasimon*. Aristophanes' own practice does reveal some changes, however. McEvilley 1970 notes the greater proportion of lyrics not found in the typical comic song positions (such as the parodos, parabasis, etc.) in the later plays. See also Nagy 1990:108: "the point remains that the old traditions of lyric are obsolescent by the time of Aristophanes, and in fact . . . *Birds* is the last attested comedy of Aristophanes that mentions or parodies the compositions of Pindar." I will have more to say about the "Pindaric poet" below. For two different accounts of changing Athenian choral/musical practice, compare C. Segal in *CHCL* 1:242–244 ("By the last quarter of the century the festivals which provided the occasion for song were losing their religious basis") and Kurke 2000:85–87, stressing more musical professionalization, the competing performances of the law courts and assembly, and changes in education.

8 See Herington 1985:106: "'The craft' is referred to with enormous respect by all parties [of the *Clouds' agon*]. It, alone, escapes any kind of mockery in this play, and indeed in Aristophanes' work generally."

acquisition of power over the cosmos.[9] Utopia, however, may be the best place from which to take our bearings: the play constructs a world in which songs both old and new play a large part. We therefore must try to discern how that music sounds against the play's fantastic world-building. Attention to the graceful music of the play could make us more tolerant of Peisetairos' lust for power. Or perhaps the total control of music in Cloud-cuckoo-land should remind us of Plato's harsher reforms. In either case, I take as my goal to try to extricate the play's lyric ideals from the rest of *Birds*' imaginary cosmos, keeping in mind its complicated, possibly contentious relationship to the Athenian musical culture of which it was part.

Song vs. Speech

As a starting point for gaining a sense of *Birds*' comic lyric, and how it relates to its surroundings, it is helpful to refer to Old Comedy's distinctive juxtaposition of song and speech. The comic *agon* and parabasis contain songs and speeches in alternation,"epirrhematic syzygy," but these syzygies represent only a part of the mediation that takes place over a whole comedy between song and speech. A thorough review of the various song types and their dramatic contexts on the scale of Bernhard Zimmermann's cannot be undertaken here,[10] but we can focus instead on a still more basic structural principle, namely, the performance and avoidance of song. In *Wasps*, for example, the pattern is striking: several hundred lines of relatively prosaic subject matter (1–216, 471–1008) are followed by an explosion of song language and song-oriented action (217–221, 1224–1246, 1450–1473). This alternating pattern does not always correspond to the sung and spoken meters of the play and

9 Several of the chapters in Dobrov 1997 portray Peisetairos as a sophist at odds with Athenian democratic norms; Nan Dunbar has argued that some of these readings depend on a scrutiny of the play available more to scholars than the Athenian audience; see Dunbar 1996. MacDowell 1995:224 also rejects the picture of Peisetairos as sophist: "There is a fundamental reason why all interpretations of this type must be rejected. The spectators are encouraged to identify themselves with Peisetairos and to side with him against his opponents throughout the play, and at the end he is triumphantly successful." I agree with MacDowell about Peisetairos, but I also agree with Gilbert Murray's emphasis on poetry in the play. MacDowell seems less justified in saying (227): "it will not do to call Cloudcuckooland the land of poetry; poetry is the only profession of which Peisetairos expels not just one but two practitioners." These practitioners may be excluded so as to include other musical practice. A play about music need not be merely an escapist fantasy on that account.

10 Zimmermann (1985–1987), in his important analysis of song types, focuses on the relationship between song and plot in a way that can reduce song to a function of the plot. But the songs can also be seen as semi-independent units more in relation to each other and to other traditions than to the immediately surrounding action.

the traditionally recognized comic structures, but instead reflects the shifting content of a given comedy, the dramatic fate and social status of its characters, and many other more-than-aesthetic factors. This alternation of song and speech may only finally be comprehensible in terms of comedy's claim to mediate song's relation to speech for the culture it serves.[11]

In *Birds* the place of song and speech is first addressed in the following lines:

> οἱ μὲν γὰρ οὖν τέττιγες ἕνα μῆν' ἢ δύο
> ἐπὶ τῶν κραδῶν ᾄδουσ', Ἀθηναῖοι δ' ἀεὶ
> ἐπὶ τῶν δικῶν ᾄδουσι πάντα τὸν βίον.
>
> As you know, cicadas sing for just a month or two
> out on their branches, Athenians sing constantly at court cases
> their whole lives long.
>
> *Birds* 39–41

These lines refer primarily to Athenian litigiousness, but the song metaphor is not accidental. It prepares us for the notion that the lost Athenians on stage may find a place where singing has its natural place.

Throughout the play, song and speech are brought into confrontation, with Peisetairos representing the powers of speech and the Bird chorus representing the powers of song. Peisetairos, λεπτὸς λογιστής that he is (317: 'subtle reckoner'), devotes lines 462–626 to the amazing attributes of birds without mentioning the beauty or expressiveness of their songs, apart from the rooster's not very lyrical wake-up call (489).[12] The play's speeches have

[11] Nagy 1990:36 stresses this opposition: "We cannot say that the iambic trimeter of Athenian tragedy and comedy is *lyric* for the simple reason that it is patently recited as opposed to sung. As for what is sung, we call that *lyric* by opposition to what is recited. . . . Thus the opposition of song and poetry in tragedy not only recapitulates diachronically an earlier opposition of SONG and speech, it also imitates synchronically the actual opposition of song and speech in real life." In *Wasps*, singing in court is seen as a problem by Bdelycleon, at least, and he wins the *agon* by directing his father's attention to prosaic facts. Philocleon is, on the other hand, an accomplished singer, storyteller, and revelrous trouble-maker, whatever his limitations as an aristocratic symposiast. A fragment of *Farmers* (fr. 101 K-A) runs "the old men in session still say, when a poor defense speech is given, 'you're singing'" (ἔτι γὰρ λέγουσ' οἱ πρεσβύτεροι καθήμενοι / ὅταν κακῶς τις ἀπολογῆται τὴν δίκην / ᾄδεις). See also Hall 1995:39–58, and 2002:7: "in [tragic] iambics people constantly use such verbs as *legein* and *phrazein* in reference to their own speech and that of their interlocutors, whereas the semantic range referring to lyric utterance, which includes *melpein* and *aidein*, is quite different." See also Dunbar 1995 *ad Birds* 39–41, where she compares the French expression '*chansons!*' meaning 'nonsense!'

[12] Contrast Democritus B 154 D-K, where birds' song is their most useful product for man, along with house-building: "We are pupils of the animals in the most important things: the spider for

little to say about bird song; that is left for the Bird chorus to demonstrate when Peisetairos has left the stage. Peisetairos later copes with several human singers, striving to keep *their* song in its place. Finally, he himself joins in the singing (1743). We could imagine a different comedy in which a tuneful Papageno engaged in lyric dialogue with nature's songsters from the start, but Peisetairos' preference for *logoi* is constantly in evidence: "now I will wing you by speaking," he says to the sycophant (1437: νῦν τοι λέγων πτερῶ σε), and at the end, "I enjoy these hymns, I enjoy these songs, and I *admire* their *logoi*" (1744: ἄγαμαι δὲ λόγων).[13]

The *logoi* of the play, its rhetorical, discursive tours de force, its constative speech, leave at least three major windows for birds and singing: the Hoopoe's song and the two parabases. Elsewhere, *logoi* predominate, especially during the crucial negotiations with the enraged chorus: "what *logos*?"(314); "don't fear the *logos*" (323); "there is a further *logos*" (336); "It's sensible first to hear the *logoi*" (381–382); "what *logoi* do they speak?" (416). The chorus finally says, λόγων ἀνεπτέρωμαι (433), applying a typical song metaphor (with erotic connotations as well) to song's opposite.[14] Peisetairos then readies his *logos*, switching to a baking metaphor: "one *logos* is kneaded and ready" (462). Some near-synonyms of *logos* and *legein* also contribute to Peisetairos' persuasive discourse, such as *phrazô*, *didaskô*,[15] and the *peithô* of his name, and his speeches include the picture of the polis as a *polos* (178–193), the use of *tekmeria* (482–521) and fable (471–475), all of which can perhaps be understood as different kinds

spinning and mending, the swallow for building, and the songsters, swan and nightingale, for singing, by way of imitation" (trans. Kathleen Freeman).

13 Calame 2004:179 takes these *logoi* to be "words of praise" close in sense to *muthoi* as used by Xenophanes and Pindar. See Xenophanes 1.14 Gentili/Prato.

14 431–433: "command him to speak, to speak / for I am all aflutter / hearing the speeches you're speaking about." Note also 461. Admittedly, ἀναπτερόω (433) is also a prose word; for its elevated usage, Aeschylus *Libation Bearers* 228. Confrontation of song and speech might also be discerned in Zethus and Amphion's dispute over the best life in Euripides' *Antiope*. Zethus says to his brother (188N): "stop melodizing [but Kannicht in TGF prints Wilamowitz's ματᾴζων instead of Nauck's μελῳδῶν] and cultivate the *eumousia* of wars." At some point Amphion says (202N): "Well, I would sing *and* speak something wise" (ἐγὼ μὲν οὖν ᾄδοιμι καὶ λέγοιμί τι / σοφόν). This can be understood as a typical Greek polarity meaning something like "all language acts," but comedy plays on the potential tension in this polarity (see n10 above).

15 Slater 1997:79–80 portrays Peisetairos as a *chorodidaskalos*: "The teaching role is then assumed by Peisetairos . . . a process which describes equally well the chorodidaskalos' task and the process of political persuasion." The audience might also have noticed his distance as a speaker of *logoi* from a chorus of singing animals. Note also the unusual use of διδάσκω at 548, 550, with Dunbar's paraphrase *ad loc.*, "I instruct you to do x, which would not have occurred to you." See Pickard-Cambridge 1968:55, on this verb in inscriptions as indicating the play was produced in person by the poet, and Pickard-Cambridge 1968:71 on διδασκαλία as the word for the dramatic poet's training of the chorus.

of *logoi*. But, as the man-bird confrontation appears to suggest, the explicit term *logos* occupies an extreme position on a spectrum with *aoidê* at the other extreme. Thus, the right relationship of song and speech is not only part of the comic medium in general; it may also be a utopian goal this particular comedy conjures up by bringing men and birds on stage and attempting their reconciliation through a dynamic juxtaposition of song and speech.

The Bird Chorus

If the Birds represent song in this play, we might also ask (before going on to look at the lyrics themselves): what, musically and culturally, is involved in bringing on stage a chorus of birds? With what expectations would a chorus of birds be viewed by an Athenian audience? The bird chorus traditions of Old Comedy would be the first place to look for an answer, but we don't know much about them.[16] Admittedly, birds are never solely lyrical creatures, either in this play or elsewhere in Greek tradition. Nan Dunbar's commentary is full of other aspects of bird life, and elsewhere she suggests that Aristophanes learned about birds from eating them.[17] Another important aspect of birds for Greeks is their aggressive behavior and appearance in competitive games: cock-fights and quail-tapping are attested throughout the centuries, and from the "Getty Birds" and some of the earlier representations of bird choruses on vase paintings, one can guess that roosterlike aggressiveness played a large part in earlier bird choruses.[18] But Aristophanes, without excluding these

16 See Dunbar 1995:228, and in general, for discussion and illustrations, Sifakis 1971. Aristophanes later wrote a play called *Storks*. Magnes had already written a play called *Birds* (scholium on *Knights* 522), and we hear of another in the *Suda* (K 2340). Kantharos later wrote a *Nightingales*. Since Hesiod and Bacchylides refer to poets as songbirds (*Works and Days* 208; Bacchylides 3.98), one is tempted to suppose a link between these plays and plays with choruses related to (though not necessarily consisting entirely of) poets: *Archilochoi*, *Hesiodoi*, *Cleoboulinai*. Aristophanes' *Gerytades* featured contemporary poets as well (though not a chorus of poets) conversing in Hades. But useful as such a connection between birds, choruses, and poets would be for reading *Birds*, there is no evidence for these themes being brought together in early Old Comedy so far as I know.

17 See Dunbar 1994:113–129. The juxtaposition of the lyrical birds 3–5 of the chorus *penelops*, *alkuon*, and *keirulos* is suggestive, but they only make up one-eighth of the twenty-four-person chorus. Birds in edible guise appear frequently in comedy (*Acharnians* 1007; *Clouds* 339; *Peace* 1149, 1197).

18 For quail-fights and quail-tapping, cf. *Birds* 1299, with Dunbar's note (1995 *ad loc.*), Chrysippus SVF 3.167, and Marcus Aurelius I 6 (which should probably read καὶ τὸ μὴ ὀρτυγοκοπεῖν). The aggressive aspects of birds are discussed by Green 1985:2:95–118. Green 1985 also argues for a uniform chorus resembling the ithyphallic rooster-men on the vase. The vase may be connected to the production, but it is hard to believe it actually represents the chorus. A few

aspects, appears to have emphasized especially lyric, epic, and even religious symbolism for his chorus. So without going so far as to use *Birds* as evidence of forgotten bird cult (with the *drukolaptes* starring as a Greek relative to King Picus),[19] we are entitled to focus on the traditional, musical associations of the Bird chorus as comprising a key theme of the play, exceptional as they may be for extant Old Comedy.

We are doubtless dealing with many layers of significance, and the following list of considerations is not meant to be exhaustive: 1) from the reactions of the protagonists it is clear that birds are potentially fearful creatures, especially man-sized semi-birds like Tereus. Not only are humans scared at the prospect of encountering the Hoopoe,[20] but throughout the play, humor is interspersed with strangeness; the Birds confront humans with their mortality at the Homeric opening of the parabasis (685–687): "Come, men of short life, like the generation of leaves." There is sometimes the sense, along with all the exuberant fantasy, that we are far from the safety of the city. From what we know about the significance of birds elsewhere in Greek tradition, this sense of the uncanny about the chorus need not surprise us. As Ovid went on to exploit, many myths resulted in the transformation of humans into birds, and many species were therefore associated with these partly terrible, partly merciful outcomes. 2) The seemingly effortless improvisations of many species, especially the nightingale, served as a model for oral performance in general, and for Alcman's choral poems in particular.[21] 3) The ability to fly is represented in

other negative connotations of birds are pomposity (as with Lamachus' feather plume) and a lightweight mentality (as at Plato *Timaeus* 91d6, Sophocles *Antigone* 342–343).

19 Harrison 1927:94–117 remains a stimulating discussion of birds in Greek life. See also Forbes Irving 1990, especially 96–127 on bird metamorphoses.

20 On the "mortal terror" of Tereus, see Gelzer 1996:194–215. Note also the frequent and not wholly ironical use of δεινός (13, 27, 63). The motif of a journey out of Athens and into an archaic world was also explored in *Amphiaraus*, in which a father and son visit that hero's cave. Gilbert Murray suggested that this play was written in the interval before *Birds* and that both are "plays of regeneration" (1933:138). The meter of the following fragment of *Amphiaraus* (fr. 30 K-A) indicates it was probably part of the parabasis and hence may have been a message straight from Aristophanes: "I know I'm doing something old-fashioned, I'm aware of what I'm doing" (οἶδα μὲν ἀρχαῖόν τι δρῶν, κοὐχι λέληθ' ἐμαυτόν). Moulton 1996 emphasizes the novelty of Aristophanes' myth-making in *Birds*, but this novelty is interwoven with archaism. Take, for example, the reference to Athens as *Kranaoi* (123). The word ἀρχαῖος is also the key to the Birds' claim to power (469). Admittedly, much of the archaic language is in the first place paratragic, as is Tereus himself (Sophocles had recently staged a *Tereus*), but paratragedy has an added force in the quasi-archaic world of *Birds*. The play may contain archaizing music as well, as I will try to show.

21 Many cultures imitate birds, and this need not exclude serious content. For a description of a bird-song cycle that fuses bird mimesis, emergence, and home-finding myth and comedy in California among the Cahuilla (a tribe of the San Joaquin valley in and around Palm Springs),

one of the most ubiquitous of metaphors, "winged words" and its many variants. A wing seemed a power, analogous to a sail or an oar, or to the songs that spread the fame of heroes, athletes, or beautiful youths.[22] 4) On the divine level, wings belong to gods that carry messages and are most directly involved in the human world: Hermes, Eros, Iris, Athena Nike. In Homer, Athena may change into an ἀνόπαια, if such be a bird (*Odyssey* i 320). At least one scholar has connected this and a few other Homeric god-into-bird transformations and similes with the possible epiphantic status of bird images in Minoan and Mycenean cult.[23] 5) Although less commonly found in the historical period than the reading of entrails, the mantic significance of bird flight is preserved in Homer, and Hesiod's *Works and Days* probably led straight into a discussion of birds and mantic matters (see M. L. West's edition of *Works and Days*, 364–365). Therefore, to sum up, although a bird cannot actually assume the godhead without a comic effect, we can see them ensconced at almost any other level of religious and poetic practice: they or their wings adorn, herald, reveal, symbolize power and immortality, while they above all sing as model singers.

---

see Apodaca 1999:152. See also Felds 1990 on the Kaluli of New Guinea and their bird mimesis. Compare also Calame 1983:480 on Alcman fr. 140 = 40 Page, and 91 = 39 Page for the idea of learning song from birds as connected to oral performance. Birds are also at least twice evoked in Alcman's longest extant choral fragment (1.60–63, 100–101 Page). Why does Alcman have his young dancers compare themselves to birds? Calame's explanation (1977 2:72–82) is compelling whether or not one accepts his view of the poem as an initiatory rite: the dancers compare themselves to birds so as to include themselves in a heavenly–earthly scheme in which they are subordinate to the Sirens (cf. the rhetorical force of fr. 1.98 Page: σιαὶ γάρ). *Birds* contains no such theme of earthly subordination . The comparison with Alcman thus must also be made a contrast. Lyric poetry may have freed itself of any obvious paedogogical responsibilities in this play. The fact that lines 250–251 probably echo Alcman (among a covey of other birds and meters) only drives this difference home. The metrical difference is worth noting: Aristophanes has lightened his meter, including only two dactylic metra per line instead of the three of the original poem, if this is an allusion to the original poem.

22 See especially Theognis 237–254: σοὶ μὲν ἐγὼ πτέρ' ἔδωκα, κτλ.—as well as Pindar *Pythian* 8.34, *Nemean* 6.48–49, *Nemean* 7.22; see also Euripides *Helen* 147 for the wings/sails metaphor and LSJ s.v. πτερόν III 1. In tragedy and in other emotionally charged situations, according to Padel 1992:96–97: "when people are mad, very afraid, drunk, angry, youthfully reckless, or much in love, their soul, *thumos* or *nous* 'flies.'" For a wing as having a "power," see Plato *Phaedrus* 246d6: πέφυκεν ἡ πτεροῦ δύναμις τὸ ἐμβριθὲς ἄγειν ἄνω.

23 Nilsson 1950:330–340, 491–496. In Homer, the gods sometimes change themselves into birds, but never into other animals: *Odyssey* i 320, iii 372, xxii 240; *Iliad* V 778, VII 59. One should not speculate that Aristophanes is unconsciously expressing vestiges of belief, but that he and his audience might have encountered the same imagery in what was to them already archaic art and felt a similar puzzlement to ours, without, perhaps, the same comfortable distance. For a more recent discussion of bird epiphany in ancestor cult, and some parallel evidence concerning the Ugaritic and Phoenician *marzeah*, see Carter 1995:285–312.

This inherited bird conglomerate, associated with the divine but not itself authoritative, combined with Old Comedy's own tendency to make a place for song as a separate focus, makes it probable that the lyrics of the play would have had a special resonance and would have been taken as more than parody. Other scholars have noted the serious voice of the Bird chorus and its religious overtones, including its similarity to some tragic lyrics, and these approaches deserve further elaboration.[24] Recently, however, Andrew Barker has argued that the nightingale's role is probably a risqué spoof on certain aspects of the New Music (Barker 2004:185–204). How should this affect our view of the chorus and its singing? Especially given that the nightingale is the most prominently lyrical bird in the play, the question must be addressed. It might be said in response to Barker that such a joke could become tedious if it were to dominate the whole play. I make the following working assumption: the Hoopoe's prelude may well be, as Barker maintains, a pastiche of genres (192), and the nightingale may at times be portrayed as an immodest *auletris* representing the prostitution of music; nonetheless, the chorus could eventually achieve a kind of authority by performing one or more types of music meant to be exemplary, and in some sense utopian, despite the raunchy humor. Though it is often very hard to point to where exactly in the text one begins and the other leaves off, parody and positive example can be seen as two edges of the same musical-critical attack, in which Aristophanes could present both negative and positive views, in both parodic and serious moods, resulting in this comedy's particular brand of *spoudaiogeloion*.

The opening lyrics have been much discussed.[25] For our purposes, it is best to think of them as a kind of overture to the lyrics sung by the Birds

24 Perkell 1993:2–5, though she concludes this quality is ultimately delusive. Mathews 1997 calls attention to significant repetitions and compares the style to that of Sophocles' *Oedipus at Colonus*, 668–678.

25 References in n3 above. See also Nagy 1996:41n7 on ἰτώ/ἴτω. Representing birds in this and other passages leads to some striking metrical features. "Twittering, especially at moments of emotion, is mimicked by resolution" (Parker 1997:240–241). Torrents of short syllables can give the impression of metrical chaos. Compare Pratinas' hyporchema's opening lines as discussed by Anderson 1966:47. Some other observations on the play's meter: "It is a unique feature of *Birds* that dochmiacs are also found interspersed in passages where the singer or singers show no signs of extraordinary excitement"; "The repeated use of certain rhythms with structural and thematic functions, which is so common a feature of Aristophanes' plays, is absent here . . . the chief metrical characteristic of the play is diversity: every major type of meter found in Attic drama is represented" (Parker 1997:297). However, within this diversity there may be a progression toward order, from the extreme diversity of the Hoopoe's song, to the pathetic dactylo-epitrite of the Birds' pledge of allegiance to Peisetairos (451–459), to the quiet majesty of the dactylo-trochaic parabasis odes, and finally, to the still more majestic fifty-one consecutive long syllables (technically anapaests) of the second parabasis. Admittedly, this progression

themselves. Compared to Aristophanes' other extant plays, the choral entry, sometimes itself a lyrical moment, even for the speaking characters of the early plays, is greatly expanded.[26] This expansion, however, does not emphasize the force of the chorus or its cohesion; it is accomplished at the price of the chorus's unity. Musical roles are assigned to several figures: the aulete, the Hoopoe, the Nightingale. The birds are a messy chorus at first, and here we should remind ourselves that the positive symbolic potential of birds referred to above may apply more to individual birds and species: once a large group of different species is assembled together, we have more what one of the protagonists calls a κακὸν ὀρνέων (294–295)—a potentially annoying, if also exciting, crowd of birds.[27] The diversity and strangeness of the chorus is worth considering in the light of the unity and social cohesiveness we usually associate with Athenian choruses. The civic themes of the play, including its utopian city-building, are in tension with this chaotic arrival. But for the comic χορευταί, a guise of diversity (and, one imagines, maybe even preening in response to all the attention) will be exchanged for a more cohesive dance and song, first in hostility and then in submission to Peisetairos' new plan. Accordingly, the catalogue of meters of the Hoopoe's song is replaced by some agitated dochmiacs in their first songs (327–335, 343–351), and then, in response to the Hoopoe's and Peisetairos' persuasions, the music is elevated to a more stable and impressive-sounding pair of songs in dactylo-epitrite. The first reads:

> Man was born always and in every way a tricky thing.
> Tell me, though—for you might reveal something fine and
> noble—
> What you see at hand, some greater power neglected
> By my mind devoid of understanding.
> Whatever you see, tell the public. For whatever good you
> provide
> Will be held in common by all.
>
> *Birds* 451–459

does not account for all the lyric of the play, but includes nearly all the high points. For the problems involved in discussing the structure of a whole play, see Parker 1994.

26 The lines of early plays showing the convention of heralding the chorus raise audience expectations, sometimes in lyrical language: *Wasps* 218–221, *Knights* 225–227, *Acharnians* 179–181, *Peace* 289–300. These passages show the transition from speech to song to be both deliberate and exciting.

27 For birds as an annoyance (in this case eagle, swan, and "strange bird"), see Euripides *Ion* 154–183.

Zimmermann observes that the contrast between excited singers and stately dactylo-epitrite might have a comic effect (Zimmermann 1985–1987, 2:108). The first line, however, with its gnomic pessimism reminiscent of Simonides,[28] does have a disconcerting force of its own, which may have carried through the whole stanza, despite its otherwise colloquial, demagogic language. The whimsical incongruity of a gnomic utterance about "human nature" (implied by the verb πέφυκεν) coming from a chorus of birds bemoaning the effects of human trickery, and referring to their own proverbial stupidity, does not exclude a serious commitment to listen and obey if persuaded. The traditionally choral meter, rare for comedy,[29] contributes to this effect of a performed commitment and gives the chorus itself a new, more unified shape on stage.

Once they have been persuaded to found a city together with humans and to seize control of the known world, the next major task of the Birds is to provide the music for that world (737–751, 769–783; 1058–1070, 1088–1100).[30] The chorus do not bid the actors farewell, and this may give the *kommation*'s opening a certain abruptness.[31] The ithyphallic meter and some of the language are reminiscent of the Rhodean swallow song (PMG 848), but ἦλθες can also express joy at being reunited with one's *philoi*.[32] There is also a reference at lines 682–683 to a well-known poem about the *aulos* (PMG 947b):

O dearest of all birds.
Fellow singer of my hymns.
Nightingale, fellow nurseling.
You've come, you've come. You've appeared
producing a song that is sweet to me

28 PMG 520, 1–2: ἀνθρώπων ὀλίγον μέν / κάρτος. . . . Cf. also PMG 525, 527, Semonides 1.3–4 West: νοῦς δ' οὐκ ἐπ' ἀνθρώποισιν ἀλλ' ἐπήμεροι / ἃ δὴ βοτὰ ζόουσιν, οὐδὲν εἰδότες. Admittedly, the Birds' attack on man as 'tricky' is slightly off-beat from these graver expressions of pessimism.

29 *Clouds* 457–475 and *Assembly Women* 571–580 are two other examples, as well as *Knights* 1264ff. and *Peace* 775ff., which reflect earlier poetry (see n5 above). See Parker 1997:89–90, comparing the Birds' use of dactylo-epitrite here to Stesichorus, especially because of the "long dactylic sequences which sometimes open with [two shorts]."

30 I anticipate the objection that the parabasis's music is solely for the Athenian public (thus Bremer 1991:159 takes the wail of the Muses and Graces as built-in applause), that the illusion is wholly broken and hence the lyrics are not strictly relevant to the world being built; but a) the parabasis of *Birds* does not include the usual intrusion of the poet's voice speaking directly to the public, and b) the lyrics in particular develop meter and language used earlier in the play. So the parabasis does seem more inwardly referential than most.

31 MacDowell 1995, commenting on *Wasps* 1009, notes the fixed convention ἴτε χαίροντες vel sim., in the first five comedies.

32 Cf. *Odyssey* xvi 23: ἦλθες, Τηλέμαχε, γλυκερὸν φάος. Also Sappho 1.5, 1.25, Euripides *Ion* 887, Theocritus 12.1, Catullus 9.5 (venisti. O mihi nuntii beati). Trygaios welcomes Opora with a similar Sapphic echo: ὦ φιλτάτη, δεῦρ' ἐλθὲ καὶ δός μοι κύσαι (*Peace* 709).

> ... as you play the
> Fine-sounding aulos, amidst spring noises.
>
> *Birds* 677–683

Despite the raucous fun that Barker and others point to in this scene, this lyric prepares us for the parabasis odes by sounding a springlike note. As with the Hoopoe's song, we can take some of the aesthetic pressure off if we conceive of it as a prelude or *ouverture*.

It is important for my reading that in the parabasis odes, the Birds sing of themselves not merely as birds, but as fellow-creatures with others in a landscape that is enchanted by their song and where the songs and dances they sing and perform for Pan and the Mountain Mother are sacred songs and dances: νόμους ἱερούς and σεμνὰ χορεύματα (745–746).[33] They also derive this sacred, musical authority from a very particular source: Phrynichus, one of the first tragedians. His presence as a once-productive bee may imply that comedy now produces the kinds of songs the tragedians produced in the good old days, when a tragic poet appears to have been an intriguing hybrid of lyric poet and actor-tragedian.[34]

> Muse of the thicket—tio tio tio tio tiotinx—variegated Muse
> With you I make numinous, lyrical hymns to Pan
> Through my vibrant cheek
> While perched in the leafy mannah ash—tio tio tio tinx
> In glens and on mountain tops—tio tio tio tio
> And sacred dances for the Mountain Mother—tototo tototo toto-
> totinx

33 I have settled for the translation 'numinous' for *hieros*, thinking of the Latin phrase *numen inest* said by Ovid of a grove upon entering it (*Fasti* III 295–296).

34 Phrynichus, unlike the strictly lyric poets, was native to Athens, and this makes him a natural predecessor. In no other Aristophanic reference does he so clearly serve as a poetic model. "It may be that . . . Ar. is at least partially echoing a song by [Phrynichus]"; Dunbar 1995 *ad loc.* Note Φρύνιχος ὡσπερεί μέλιττα and compare *Wasps* 1490, where Phrynichus crouches, ὥς τις ἀλέκτωρ. These similar-sounding words used in connection to Phrynichus may imply the "as if" of play-acting as well as simile. The surviving, mostly Aristophanean, reminiscences of Phrynichus form a fascinating composite. We hear of him as a writer of a steamy love song quoted by Sophocles for the benefit of a youth (Ion of Chios FGH 392 6); as a lyric poet whom Aristophanes' Aeschylus dared not try to rival (*Frogs* 1299–1300), as well-dressed and closely juxtaposed with Ibycus and Anacreon at *Thesmophoriazusae* 161–165, and as the favorite poet of the old jurors in *Wasps* 200 who sing ἀρχαιομελισιδωνοφρυνιχήματα ("honey-sweet-Pete-Seeger-Guantanamera-songs-of-old"). Phrynichus was one of the first actor-dramatists (*hypokritai*), who had the ability to affect the city all-too-powerfully with his personifications (Herodotus VI 21). He was also said to have taught dance (TGF 1 Thespis 10). A strikingly similar picture of poets "carrying" the sweetness of song from gardens to human beings is found at Plato *Ion* 534a–b.

> Whence also once Phrynichus . . . often found nourishment
> Of lasting melody bringing sweet song—tio tio tio tinx.
>
> *Birds* 737–752

This rather convoluted lyric suggests several overlapping spaces: first, the thicket, as home of the local Muse.[35] Then, in a relative clause (it is a mark of high style to connect relative and vocative), μεθ' ἧς ἐγώ, the song connects this place with other places known for birdsong: glens and mountaintops. Then, after another relative, ἔνθεν, Phrynichus is seen to occupy yet another space and time (the tense is switched to the imperfect). Each of these relatives are best taken as referring back to the Muse at the beginning of the stanza. The language of the ode is highly organized, as can be seen in the humming repetition of the *mu* sound and the syllable *mel-*, which connects 'Muse' to 'bee', 'ash tree', and 'song (limb)'. Yet there is also variation within the stanza, and departure from traditional forms. The poetic locutions "on mountain tops" and "perched" are very close to Homer and archaic lyric yet not exact borrowings.[36] ἀναφαίνω with reference to sound is unusual (compare Aeschylus *Suppliants* 829), but must have accorded well with the simultaneously verbal and visual song and dance. The combination of dactyls and trochees is also unusual. But the mannah ash (μελία) is the right choice of tree, solid and Homeric, and possibly chosen as a tree of origins.[37] Thus, the lyric

35 Bremer 1991:146–147 discusses Aristophanes' unusual use of "driving" his Muses and "using" them. Muses in Aristophanes (*Acharnians* 665; *Wasps* 1022, 1028; *Peace* 816; *Lysistrata* 1295; *Frogs* 229, 674) often have a local, and sometimes a rustic character.

36 The use of the adjectival ὄρειος, rare in archaic verse, may make the song sound a little more up-to-date than the noun constructions usually employed. Compare κορυφαῖς ἐν ὀρείαις (740) with ἐν κορυφαῖς ὀρέων of Alcman (PMG 56); the two words are also juxtaposed in Homer (*Odyssey* ix 121; and *Iliad* II 456: οὔρεος ἐν κορυφῇς). See Calame 1983:521. See also Anacreon (PMG 357): ὑψηλὰς ὀρέων κορυφάς. For "perched," a verb almost inseperable from the representation of birds in archaic poetry, cf. *Odyssey* xix 520: καθεζομένη (of the nightingale); also Ibycus PMG 317 (Wilamowitz's conjecture): ἰζάνοισι (of the *penelops* and *halkuon*). Cf. also Hesychius ἰζίνες· οἰωνοί. The *penelops* is represented by Ibycus as perching, despite the fact that it was, according to the scholiast, a ducklike creature. Dunbar 1995 (*ad* 98) says this could be poetic license, but if so, what motivates it? The audience expected to hear about perching when birds were sung about. 'Bird' requires 'tree'. This is no merely verbal formula but has to do with the evocation of place. Once you have a bird, a tree, and a rock, a place can constitute a grove. See Burkert 1985:84–87. For an interpretation of the *penelops* as a bird of lament, associated with Penelope and the *halkuon*, see Levaniouk 1999.

37 Used for spear shafts, and tree nymphs were said to be born from it (see Hesiod *Theogony* 187, with West's commentary). A tradition existed that mankind were born from it as well (see Hesychius, LSJ suppl. s.v. μελία: μελίας καρπός· τὸ τῶν ἀνθρώπων γένος). Kakridis (*ad loc.*) says the poet mentions this tree for the wordplay alone, but its physical characteristics may be important as well.

has more of solidity and rootedness than one would expect from a chorus of Birds.

When approaching the antode's whooping swans and awe-struck gods, we do need to keep a sharp eye out for parody. Kenneth Dover points out that the very language of this ode reappears in *Thesmophoriazusae* to the response *bombax*! (45; see Dover 1972:147–148). Still, the immediately preceding ode is probably the more important referent, and the links between the odes are subtle: the swans 'occupy' the river bank (774: ὄχθῳ ἐφεζόμενοι) just as the singer 'perched' on the mannah-ash (742: ἑζόμενος μελίας ἔπι φυλλοκόμου). Bremer and Sommerstein argue that Alcaeus' *Hymn to Apollo* is specifically invoked here, but the legendary song of the swan is well-known from Homer to Callimachus and is found in a fragment of Aristophanes, so the exclusively Alcaean reference seems uncertain.[38] The song also strives for the stunned effect of some Homeric similes, in which the night sky is illuminated by Zeus' thunderbolt, or simply by the breaking of αἰθήρ through the clouds (*Iliad* VIII 555–558, XVI 297–300). The language is high and has archaic elements, but so did much of the new lyric.[39] The stretching of linguistic convention in such a phrase as 'wailed a song' (μέλος . . . ἐπωλόλυξαν) could be parodic or sincere. Given this difficulty, it may be helpful to ask a more basic question: what is the myth of Apollo's birth and chariot-ride doing in the stanza and how has it been transformed? The answer is less parodic than profoundly comic: the swans, from the very start of the stanza, have assumed a position in the myth in keeping with the recent promotion of birds to rulers of the cosmos: their whooping at Apollo's birth is recalled as an event that foreshadowed the age of bird rule. The myth is now really about the contributions of swans to a divine music for which Apollo was once the sounding board. Thus they occupy the prominent position in the stanza, and the god is a direct object, never hymnically addressed (ἴακχον Ἀπόλλω). Since this is such a clear departure from any known hymn to Apollo, it seems likely that the parabasis stretches its initial seriousness to the breaking point. The ode to the Muse of the Thicket had

38 Sommerstein (*ad* 769–784) points out the switch to a past tense at 772, referring to a mythic occasion. See Campbell's *Greek Lyric Poetry* (Loeb) for Terpander 1 = Alcman 12A (P.Oxy. 2737 = Aristophanes fr. 590 K.-A). "The swan [sings] something of the kind to the accompaniment of its wings" (κύκνος ὑπὸ πρεγύγων τοιόνδε). The attribution of this fragment to no less than four poets by Alexandrian scholars shows the difficulty in looking exclusively to Alcaeus. In the shorter Hymn to Apollo (21), consisting of five lines, the singer (ἀοιδός) "always sings of Apollo while holding his shrill lyre," while the swans sing in the present tense, at the bank of the river Peneios. Kugelmeier 1996:218 prefers to see a reworking of Alcmanic material (cf. PMG 56, 89) and meter.

39 See, for example, Hordern 2002:36: "Despite Timotheus' reputation for innovation, his phraseology and vocabulary are at times highly traditional."

shown the sacredness and originality of comic song, but the swans, while in a sense partaking in this sacred song, could be said to overextend themselves by taking comic song to a realm of hymn where it might not comfortably belong.

In the second parabasis, a still more comprehensive perspective is taken, with the Birds replacing Zeus as all-seeing deities and protectors of the earth's produce:

> Any moment now, all mortals
> Will sacrifice to me, all-seeing and all-ruling,
> And pray sincerely. For I observe the whole earth,
> And I preserve the flourishing grains and fruits
> By killing all species of the insect race.
>
> *Birds* 1058–1064

The repetition of the word 'all' and a series of fifty-one consecutive long syllables produce an effect of comprehensive grandiosity.[40] A panoptic[41] view of the seasons is taken, with the birds effortlessly enduring them. Archaic poets were greatly interested in the seasons (e.g. Alcman 20 Page, Hesiod's *Works and Days*), but this picture of birds equally content in all seasons bespeaks an enlightened optimism not found in earlier poetry.[42] Yet by including a certain number of harsh-sounding phrases for the birds' insecticide—"killing all kinds of beasts," "I kill whoever hatefully outrages fragrant gardens," "they perish beneath the murders of my wing"—the poet keeps the language from being too flowery and otiose, and some traditional/choral bird aggression is preserved. Similarly, the cicada, now assuming its honorary epithet ἀχέτας,[43] makes a sharp, song-like noise (ὀξὺ μέλος . . . βοᾷ), and the comic cretics also cut through the more splendid long syllables. Thus, the overall effect is of a tranquility that is also piercing. The nightingale's thicket is not without its solid branches and thorns. The traditional resonances of this ode, however, are not so easily pinned down. Probably no one poet is referred to; rather, the verses follow the evocations of place that Homer, Sappho, Alcman, Pindar, and Sophocles all exhibit, shorn of the sometimes fearful specificity of divine encounters in

40 This meter was associated with Terpander (PMG 698: Ζεῦ πάντων ἀρχά, πάντων ἀγήτωρ . . .) and is also used by Euripides at *Iphigineia in Tauris* 123–129, a run of forty-four consecutive long syllables.

41 παντότης is found at Aeschylus *Suppliants* 139, referring to Zeus, the "all-seeing father," and similarly at *Eumenides* 1045, emphatically ending the *Oresteia* trilogy.

42 Compare Xenophon *Memorabilia* IV 3 (thought by some to be spurious).

43 *Birds* 1095–1096. Applied by Euripides to the swan at *Electra* 151 and by [Aeschylus] to the shepherd's pipe at *Prometheus* 574–575.

natural landscapes, not to speak of the obligations of prayer, processions, and sacrifice.[44]

Finally, to hazard a guess, the style of *aulos*-playing that accompanied these lyrics may have been associated with spring and called "Phrygian" in a recondite, archaic sense.[45] The point of this playing, whatever name we assign it (and we can actually hear an echo of it, thanks to the τιὸ τιὸ τιό of the chorus, which presumably would have somehow matched the playing), was probably to induce a kind of tranquility. This musical clue helps assure that the Bird chorus was meant as a serious evocation of auletic/lyric traditions despite the spoofs on contemporary music and musicians throughout. Recent studies of the *aulos* as an energizing and even threatening instrument provide a neat contrast to this utopian *aulos*-playing. Plato would remove the *aulos* from his utopia (leaving, suggestively, a syrinx for herdsmen—399d8),

44 In archaic poetry, a garden or grove is often a place for a seduction or rape: *Iliad* XIV 347–349; *Hymn to Demeter*; Archilochus 196a.42–44W; Anacreon PMG 346, 408 (image of a fawn in a wood), 417.6 (νῦν δὲ λειμῶνάς τε βόσκεαι). Erotic overtones are hard to find in the lyrics of *Birds* (except perhaps 1097–1101 where the chorus envisions sporting with mountain nymphs). The nightingale is elsewhere subject to some subtle and not so subtle attentions, but they are not expressed in song. Has nature here been de-eroticized for the sake of tranquility? Whatever erotic associations birds might have in the play, there is little sense of an erotic encounter. Arrowsmith 1973:119–167 connects the lust for power with sexual lust and would treat the tranquility of the play as ironic. Another attitude to nature found in archaic poetry is the appreciation of fertile soil (and in an inverse trope the affirmation of one's homeland despite the lack of fertile soil). This is closer to the attitude of the Birds to the earth they oversee, as protectors of its fertility against insects (ἀνθηρός in 1093 is close to Sappho's ἀνθεμώδης at 96.14 Lobel-Page, for example). See Le Meur 1988:20–22.

45 The idea of a mild or gentle Phrygian style may sound surprising, but see Anderson 1996:46, based largely on PMG 56 (Apollo as *aulos* player), Alcaeus' hymn 307 I (b), Alcman PMG 126, and Stesichorus PMG 212 ("having gently [ἁβρῶς] discovered a Phrygian tune with spring on its way," a lyric Aristophanes recalls in *Peace* [see n5 above]). Not all *auloi* are loud and threatening: PMG 375 (Anacreon spoke of tender half-*auloi* for use in festivities more than competitions). For later antiquity, West cites Plutarch *Moralia* 713a: "The *aulos* is not to be kept from the table; libations call for it, along with the wreath, and it sounds a divine note to accompany a paean . . . pouring out a sweet sound that brings calm [γαλήνη] deep in the soul." The springlike note is reinforced by mentions of spring in the play: 682–683 (κρέκουσ' αὐλὸν φθέγμασιν ἠρινοῖς), 1099. To appreciate how exceptional this tranquilizing use of the *aulos* might be for theater, compare Wilson 1999 and Martin 2003, who rightly see the *aulos* as energizing, wild, and in tension with male civic identity. But adjectives like σύναυλος, ἔναυλος (which also means 'of the farm'), and φίλαυλος of the dolphin (Euripides *Electra* 435), also imply harmony, tranquility. Compare *Anacreontea* 60.10. See also West 1992:181: "There was ritual *aulos* music in the Phrygian mode attributed to Olympus, including some used in the cult of the Mother of the Gods," citing PMG 810 (Telestes). "These were perhaps the pieces of Olympus that Plato and Aristotle admired as having the power to arouse and inspire, and as revealing those who stand in need of the gods. . . . If so, it goes some way towards explaining Plato's hospitality towards Phrygian." It may be that Aristophanes was similarly hospitable to *aulos*-playing in an archaically tinged Phrygian mode.

but Aristophanes was in a position to refine and archaize his *aulos* in practice. Implicitly, then, the parodies of New Music and recovery of an older, simpler music[46] are compatible.

Lyrical Interruptions: Literary Criticism in Cloud-Cuckoo-Land?

More can be discovered about *Birds*' ideal music by looking at the non-ideal music of the intruder scenes.[47] These intruders are rejected both on aesthetic grounds and for the social roles they claim. Their language is made up of clichés about flying and poorly-digested quotations, but, equally importantly, the genres they bring, encomiastic ode and dithyramb, are too embedded in demanding cultural practices to be acceptable in Cloud-cuckoo-land, where birds are to provide the music gratis.

The play has already targeted some poets and promoted others, and this is one of Aristophanes' constant themes,[48] but in no other extant intruder scenes (such as *Acharnians* and *Peace*) do poets and music figure so prominently. This is partly explained by the musical influence already exerted by the Birds: Athens has gone bird-mad and this means everyone is singing (1300–1303). But a begging poet—the first real intruder—arrives before singing has become the rage:

> *Poet*: Muse, call the Land of the Cloud and Cuckoo blissful
> In your songs of hymn.
> *Peisetairos*: Where did this business come from? Hey, who are you?
> *Poet*: I am a nimble follower of the Muses, for I sing a song of
> sweet-tongued words according to Homer . . .
> *Peisetairos*: Well, you're certainly wearing a hole-y little cloak. But,
> poet, why have you made your damned way here?

46 At least one other poet/musician was known for archaizing (we do not know when he lived): Pankrates. [Plutarch] *Moralia* 1137f: ἐζήλου γοῦν, ὡς αὐτὸς ἔφη, τὸν Πινδάρειόν τε καὶ Σιμωνίδειον τρόπον καὶ καθόλου τὸ ἀρχαῖον καλούμενον ὑπὸ τῶν νῦν. See Kugelmeier 1996: 112n203.

47 For the technique of teaching music by negative example, see Plutarch *Demetrius* 1.6, of a music teacher who takes his student out to a theater to hear how music should *not* be played. See Bélis 1999:30–31.

48 G. Murray 1933: 156: "At least eleven poets and musicians come in for some chaff," only a slight exaggeration. Poets already probably mocked: Akestor (31), Sophocles (through the parody of his *Tereus*), Melanthios (151), and Diagoras of Melos (1073), who is probably the poet of PMG 738–739. However, Dunbar 1995 (*ad* 766) finds the theory that Meles was Cinesias' father "improbable."

> *Poet:* I've made songs for your Nephelokokkugia, lots of nice
> dithyrambs,[49] songs for young women, and à la Simonides.
> *Birds* 904–910, 915–919

In his poverty, the beggar-poet is eager to offer any genre for any occasion, but also seems dimly aware that foundation songs are called for. There follow several Pindaric quotes that some have taken as an oblique criticism of Pindar's obscurity. However, from his costume and begging, the audience would have immediately been able to distinguish this *bettelpoet*, as Kugelmeier calls him, from the wealthy Theban. There is other evidence that Aristophanes admired Pindar (see n4 above). Still, the fact that the poet limits his quotations to Pindar is striking. The joke is apparently that, despite the various goods he has promised, Pindar's poems are what he has memorized and he *will* recite Pindar in all circumstances. And it makes for a comic effect to have the poet beg for basic necessities in high-flown, *Pindareia epea*. But the reference to Hieron may also throw a sidelight on the colonial enterprise of Cloud-cuckoo-land. The quote runs: "but [there is] some swift rumour of the Muses, like the rapid sparkle of horses. You, dear founder of Aetna, named after holy places, give us whatever you gladly wish to give, you your very self [τεᾷ κεφαλᾷ]" (924–930). As is clear from his response, "*this* guy is just gonna cause us a lot of problems" (τουτὶ παρέξει τὸ κακὸν ἡμῖν πράγματα), this is not the kind of attention Peisetairos wants, despite his self-proclamation as city-founder. What would the Athenian audience have made of this reference to Pindar and Hieron and its rejection? Is it simply a famous and appropriate poem to quote? Or were they meant to think about it in connection to the colonizing themes of the play? At first glance, these themes might seem remote to an Athenian audience, but if we keep in mind the intense involvement of Athens with colonies in Southern Italy and Sicily, especially in 415, then maybe we should reconsider the assumption that the Athenians only attended plays to hear about themselves.[50] The play had already contained many references to colonies, and the audience would have been readied for this perspective.[51] Thus, mocking

49 πολλὰ καὶ καλά. Kugelmeier 1996: 109: "Sowie das marktschreierisch klingende Angebot. . . ."

50 If this passage is focused on Pindar specifically as a poet for colonies, then it cannot be used to indicate declining comprehension of Pindar's encomia in general. (Hamilton 2003: 17–23 is exaggerated, using such terms as "irrelevant," and "expired worldview.") We do not know the context or speaker of Eupolis' fragment (398 K.-A.) on the silencing of Pindar, or of the fragment about the lyric poets (148 K.-A.), so it is also difficult to draw conclusions on this basis. Plato's references to Pindar show that Pindar's verse was part of the education of late-fifth-century upper-class Athenians (Kurke 1991: 5n17).

51 How is *Birds* a play about colonization? It seems strategically to confuse us: the protagonists set out on foot instead of building ships (cf. *Iliad* II 664 for this as a typical stage in founding

a relationship between colonial founder and poet belonging to a bygone age might have dramatized the novelty of *Birds*' colonial enterprise.

Pindaric style is not wholly rejected in the play, as for instance in the lyric dialogue at 1313–1322, in which a few Pindaric notes are sounded and interrupted, and high lyric style and bustle are combined in a striking way:

> *Chorus*: Soon someone will call this city most populous.
> *Peisetairos*: Just let that be our luck!
> *Chorus*: Desires prevail over my city.
> *Peisetairos*: Hey, carry faster.
> *Chorus*: What noble thing is lacking for a man to live with?
> Wisdom, longing, immortal graces, and the face of serene and gentle peace of mind.
>
> *Birds* 1313–1322

The meter here is anapaestic, a meter closely related to the dactylic parabasis ode, but now comic interruption has been included in the high style. The epithet πολυάνωρ, 'abundant in men', is a rare one, but the idea is familiar to the lyric tradition, especially if we think of the near-synonyms εὔανδρος and εὐανδρία.[52] Dunbar rightly sees an ironic contrast between the wing-carrying and the "peace of mind" (Dunbar 1995:649). But despite the irony, these Pindaric concepts are seen positively enough to motivate the enterprise and flurry. Thus, on the whole, it may be a mistake to see a criticism of Pindar in *Birds.*

The next poet-intruder is Kinesias the dithyrambist. He is not offering his poetry but has come demanding wings with the next wave of intruders. His singing represents Athenian bird-madness within the illusion of the drama,

a colony): τόνδε τὸν βάδον βαδίζομεν (42). The items they have with them may or may not be for a foundation ceremony, and they speak ambiguously of their purposes: καθιδρυθέντε διαγενοίμεθ' ἄν (45). The stem *hidru* is suggestive of foundations, but διαγίγνομαι, 'live one's life', does not sound like the rigorous planning required in a new colony. Their bird guides, whom they bought instead of encountering, are on their wrists instead of leading them from above. What sort of oracle is Tereus? Above all, they lack the piety required of colonial founders, cf. Malkin 1987:183. Malkin's treatment of Lampon in this play relies on late sources, but his general portrait of changing trends in colonization in the fifth century is highly relevant: colonies were breaking away from their mother cities (Thucydides VII 57), new colonies were no longer led by individuals with Delphic authority but by delegates, and even by Hieron's time Sicily was no longer a frontier and his colonization of Aetna was seen by some as a selfish effort to gain founder's honors (Diodorus Siculus XI 66.4). See Asheri in CAH. While *Birds*, it is now agreed, is no allegory for the Sicilian expedition, its colonial chaos may reflect some of these Sicilian realities.

52 πολυάνωρ: Euripides *Iphigenia in Taurus* 1281; *IG* 4.1^2 129.12: σώιζετε τόνδ' Ἐπιδαύρου ναὸν ἐν εὐνομίαι πολυάνορι. εὔανδρος: PMG 856; ἄγετ' ὦ Σπάρτας εὐάνδρου are warlike anapaests a little like these (but with one fewer foot per line) and once attributed to Tyrtaeus. Admittedly, εὐανδρία has an added connotation of manly courage that is absent from πολυάνωρ.

where everyone is singing (1300: ᾖδον δ' ὑπὸ φιλορνιθίας πάντες μέλη) but also leads to a confrontation between comedy and dithyramb as competing Athenian cultural institutions. Kinesias' personal attributes may also have a few literary-critical ramifications. For instance, Peisetairos welcomes him as φιλύρινος Κινεσίας (1378). Lime wood is a light and flimsy wood, and the implication may be that his verse is λεπτός in a negative sense.[53] It may not be an accident that the birds, despite their own partly aethereal nature, are associated with more solid woods, holm-oak (615—as are the Acharnians at *Acharnains* 180) and mannah ash (742). Is his 'bandy-leggedness" (1379: πόδα . . . κυλλὸν . . . κυκλεῖς) meant to reflect his clumsy handling of metrical feet? To make a contrast, Kinesias and his diction are cloudy, the birds are connected to the thicket, to marshes, gardens, fields, the sea (230–254); Kinesias wishes he could fly (1383: βούλομαι μετάρσιος κτλ.), while the Birds can fly; Kinesias borrows from other lyric poets (especially from Anacreon), but the Birds do not borrow as much as one would expect; Kinesias' poetry is represented as polymetric and artificial (Dunbar 1995:662), with alliteration and repetition (1395–1396). The songs of the Birds are mostly solid blocks made up of one or two meters (since they do not sing the opening catalogue). But the contrast may extend further: for Kinesias, a social/artistic role is comically suggested and rejected. Peisetairos cracks a revealing joke: "Well, would you be willing to stay here and take on a chorus of shrikes?"[54] Kinesias wants nothing to do with a bird chorus. "You gotta be kidding me," he replies (καταγελᾷς μου, δῆλος εἶ). Kinesias, as a dithyrambist, depends on a choregic system that operates according to *phyle*. Slater has already pointed out that there may be a metatheatrical reference to the playful rivalry between dramatic recruitment of choruses (according to deme) and dithyrambic recruitment (see Slater 1997:90n40). Perhaps, in this archaizing utopia, the word φυλή ('tribe') has been linked to the related word φῦλον, used by Alcman as a synonym of animal genus (compare 251: φῦλα μετ' ἀλκυόνεσσι ποτῆται, as well as 1088–1089: εὔδαιμον φῦλον . . . οἰονῶν, with Alcman 89.6, 106 Page), and Peisetairos' offer of a bird φυλή should be taken as a mocking pun. In any case, the joke reveals that dithyramb does not belong in Cloud-cuckoo-land because human choruses do not belong, and the heroic/mythic subjects of dithyramb do not belong either, as we have seen from the birds' lyrics.

53 Not always with positive associations. See Cameron 1995:488–493. Cf. also Aristophanes *Gerytades* 156 K-A, with Athenaeus' comment (XII 551a): "he lambasts them as λεπτοί, having them sent as ambassadors to the [older] poets in Hades."

54 Dunbar 1995 accepts the emendation (at 1407) Κρεκοπίδα (as humorously derived from an unidentified bird species, κρεκίς, which I have translated 'shrike') for the manuscript reading Κεκροπίδα. A scribe ignorant of the bird κρεκίς may have altered the text to match the φυλή name, missing the pun.

Epilogue: In the Basket of Muses

Taken together, then, the lyrics and the intruder scenes of *Birds* embody a musical policy: that only songs in relatively simple yet lively meters be performed, with sweet yet sharp language, accompanied by a gentle, spring-like *aulos*, alluding to birds and poets of old, but avoiding myth and foundation legend, polymetry and ecstatic passions. Would any Athenian have wanted to live in such a place? Perhaps not. But what might such a fantasy have meant to its audience? How might they have placed it? Such questions are always hazardous, and I can only offer a suggestion: *Birds*' musical fantasy expresses a late-fifth-century aspiration, which existed alongside political and cultic realities, and of which birds were one of the emblems. What aspiration? Precisely the aspirations of a life according to music, free of the obligations of the polis. This does not, I should add, mean a life without any obligations at all, for within the world-building program of the drama plenty of musical discipline is necessary. But it does mean a departure from the more warm-blooded, demanding deities of the Athenian calendar, from jury- to trireme-service.[55] This comes across most clearly at the end of the *agon* (especially at 611–626 and 723–725), where it is agreed by both parties that birds are going to be more serviceable deities than the Olympians with their temples to build and festivals to celebrate and pay for all year round. Birds can be worshiped in bushes at no expense, and trips to Delphi and Ammon will no longer be necessary:

> *Euelpides*: Hey-o, won't these birds be much better for us as rulers?
> *Peisetairos*: Hell yeah. First of all, we won't have to build them
> stone temples, provided with golden doors, but instead
> they'll live under bushes and holm oak. Yes, an olive tree
> will do for the holiest of them.
>
> *Birds* 610–618

These immanent deities will never run off and hide in the clouds like Zeus (726–728). The play's frequent representation of the birds as Muses (724: ἕξετε χρῆσθαι μάντεσι Μούσας, 737: Μοῦσα λοχμαῖα), or as accompanying Muses

55 Note the lack of references to Dionysus in this play, and of his κίσσος (mentioned only at 238), which is usually frequent in descriptions of natural scenery, as at Sophocles' *Oedipus at Colonus* 674. Is this because birds, wings, etc., are foreign to Dionysus' symbolic realm? One notes, however, the presence of a winged man (below the handle of neck amphora Oxford 1965.126, reproduced in the plate following p. 289 in Sourvinou-Inwood 2003 and discussed at 111–112) in a scene representing the welcoming of Dionysus to Attica. This shows that bird costume and Dionysus belong together from very early in Attic visual traditions.

(782–784: Μοῦσαί τ' ἐπωλόλυξαν. τιὸ τιὸ τιοτίγξ), or as themselves 'musical' (1332: μουσικά, of songbirds), as well as the more mysterious epithet μουσόμαντις (276), and, finally, the prominence of music in the play altogether, leads us to suspect that the Muses (along with Apollo, their musical director) are its most significant deities, and in a sense it is really they who have replaced the Olympians as objects of worship.

The semantics of Muses and music are very much alive and contested in this period, and not a fixed convention (see, in general, Murray and Wilson 2004). Although the word μουσεῖον never actually appears in the text, it may be a word that corresponds in some sense to Cloud-cuckoo-land. Pieria,[56] on the north slope of Olympus, which Euripides calls a μούσειος ἕδρα (*Bacchae* 410), or Helicon, where, by the following centuries at least, a μουσεῖον would house Hesiod's writings (Pausanius IX 31.4 with Strabo IX 2.25) and where musical competitions (Athenaeus XIV 629a) would be overseen by the nearby Boeotians, were actual places where music was sacralized. But metaphorically, especially for Euripides, μουσεῖα are 'places of bird-song', though the meaning can be extended to include singing creatures as well (cf. Kannicht on Euripides *Helen* 174 and fr. 88). In Athens, a μουσεῖον (a shrine to the Muses often supplied with running water) often formed part of an association, such as a school, including philosophical schools.[57] A διδασκαλεῖον (the large private space set up by a choregos for choral training) might have been provided with such a shrine to slake the thirst of dancers, and in later usage the two words could be used synonymously (see Wilson 2000:72, 338, and *Scholia ad Aeschines* 1.10). The word's meaning and usage could be a matter of debate: Aristotle (*Rhetoric* 1406a24) censures Alcidamas' phrase "Nature's school of the Muses had he inherited," presumably as an ineffective, overly complicated metaphor. Alcidamas also had named his book Μουσεῖον and was probably thinking along the same lines as Aristophanes when he appealed to the Muses as patrons, but his association of rhetoric and the Muses was rare and in keeping, perhaps, with his insistence on improvisation and performance. At any rate, seeing *Birds* in terms of these synchronic struggles over music would help us contextualize the chorus' debt to diachronic lyric traditions.

Within the play, alongside Peisetairos' world-encompassing ambition, there are desires expressed for a simple, leisurely lifestyle of wedding feasts and hanging around gymnasia (128–142). Even the Hoopoe, charmingly, speaks

56 Already used as a metaphor for poetry by Sappho (55.3) and Pindar (*Olympian* 9.27, 6.42) on which see Le Meur 1988:37–38.

57 Wilamowitz argued that this indicated that the schools were really *thiasoi*, but cf. Lynch 1972:108–134.

like a cultured Athenian, using litotes and the fashionable term τριβή: "Life among the birds? Really not a bad way to spend your time" (156: οὐκ ἄχαρις εἰς τὴν τριβήν). As many scholars have noted, the play does not maintain this peaceful thread, but explodes into political fantasy. The lyrics do, however, keep the desires expressed at the beginning for a simpler life alive throughout the play. What these Athenians are partially looking for, and what the lyrics deliver, is the sense of a disciplined cultural association, freer than political/legal bodies, with their fines (38), their endless jury duty, their hassles and dangers of ostracism and war. Having set out to get as far away from Athens as possible, in reality, I would suggest, the play's music travels about as far away as Socrates and Phaedrus on their walk along the Ilisos, or as far as Plato himself when he founded the Academy at nightingale-haunted Colonus.

Perhaps the Muses never quite had belonged to the city. From Hesiod's encounter onward, they owe their authority to a certain removal from the negotiations of the agora. Thus Plutarch remarks, "They established μουσεῖα at the farthest places from the cities" (*Moralia* 521d).[58] That is what our play's music has done—it has set out for a kind of cultural sanctuary. It is part of Aristophanes' complexity that a serious, sanctified musical discourse can be extricated from the midst of what is otherwise a mocking, irreverent confrontation with the polis.

Indeed, the musically significant aspects of *Birds* I have been pointing to may have been better appreciated by the poet-scholars of Alexandria than by more recent scholars. *Birds* may have been read by the Alexandrians as the obscure handbook of cultural symbols, of poetic know-how, that it perhaps really is. Callimachus' treatise *On Birds* probably purported to discuss all the birds mentioned in the play, and poetry, ornithology, and mantic science appear to have been connected for Callimachus.[59] References to birds played a large part in literary criticism: even if we don't accept Housman's conjecture ἀηδονίδες at *Aetia* fr. 1.16, the same passage contains the wish, "let me

58 See P. Murray 2004:365–389, who emphasizes the opposition between Muses and rhetorical *tekhnê*.

59 For Callimachus' *On Birds*, see Pfeiffer's edition, frs. 414–428, and Dunbar 1995:33. Fr. 428 Pfeiffer concerns the inauspiciousness of the κρέξ for newlyweds, and elsewhere he wrote of ἴυγξ, daughter of Echo (fr. 685), who drugged Zeus, slept with him, and was transformed by Hera into her current state. Judging from some archaic lyric fragments, this interest in specific birds and their attributes went back to the late archaic period, and the preservation of these quotations by Alexandrian scholarship suggests that the Alexandrian poets regarded the earlier poets as shrewd in these matters. Cf. PMG 606 (Tzetzes), "the swallow is called κωτίλη by Simonides and Anacreon for its garrulousness"; PMG 538 (*Etymologicum Magnum*), "All larks must naturally have a crest"; PMG 586 (ἀηδόνες πολυκώτιλοι); PMG 437, calling the κόκκυξ "a spring bird like a ἱέραξ or a most pitiful bird."

be the winged one [πτερόεις, of the cicada]," and the noun 'nightingale' was soon made a synonym for poetry itself, as for example at Callimachus *Epigrams* 2.5 Pfeiffer, "your poetry lives on" (τεαὶ ἀηδόνες). This meaning can be traced back to fr. 74 of Phrynichus Comicus, a contemporary of Aristophanes, where a bad poet is called Μουσῶν σκελετός, ἀηδόνων ἠπίαλος, ὕμνος Ἅιδου "Muses' cadaver, nightingales' nightmare, hymn of death." As has recently been discovered, it was left to Posidippus to revive Homeric mantic language, integrating it with more recent tales about birds in significant flight (see Baumbach and Trampedach 2004). Finally, the library of Alexandria itself, with its associated μουσεῖον (equipped with walkways and trees) was called a Μουσέων τάλαρος. It has recently been maintained that Timon of Phlius here refers to no bookworm cage at all, but to a very pleasant, open basket full of warblers (Cameron 1995:31–32; see also Mineur 1985:383–387). In any case, the phrase suggests an ensemble of birdlike humans, a little like the cast of *Birds*, utterly devoted to cultural pursuits. Basket or cage, the library would be outlived by the nightingale, who sang on, as Gregory Nagy has shown, through the troubadours to Thomas Hardy (Nagy 1996:212): "the song of the nightingale is the very opposite of an ad hoc invention: it is a song of continuity, . . . that cannot end with the death of the songbird."

Bibliography

Anderson, W. S. 1966. *Ethos and Education in Greek Music.* Cambridge, MA.

Apodaca, Paul. 1999. "Tradition, Myth, and Performance of Cahuilla Bird Songs." Ph.D. diss., UCLA.

Arrowsmith, William. 1973. "Aristophanes' Birds: The Fantasy Politics of Eros." *Arion* 1.1:119–167.

Barker, Andrew. 2004. "Transforming the Nightingale." In Murray and Wilson 2004:185–204.

Baumbach, M., and Rampedach, K. 2004. "Winged Words: Poetry and Divination in Posidippus' *Oiônoskopika.*" *Labored in Papyrus Leaves: Perspectives on an Epigram Collection Attributed to Posidippus (P.Mil.Vogl.VIII 309)* (ed. Benjamin Acosta-Hughes et al.) 123–160. Hellenic Studies 2. Washington, DC.

Bélis, Annie. 1999. *Les musiciens dans l'antiquité.* Paris.

Bierl, Anton. 2001. *Der Chor in Der Alten Komödie.* Beiträge zur Altertumskunde 126. Liepzig.

Bonnafé, Annie. 1987. *Poésie, nature, et sacré.* Vol. 2, *L'âge archaïque.* Paris.

Bremer, Jan. 1991. "Aristophanes on His Own Poetry." *Entretiens Hardt* 38:125–165.

Burkert, Walter. 1985. *Greek Religion.* Cambridge, MA.

Calame, Claude. 1977. *Les choeurs de jeunes filles en Gréce archaïque.* Rome.

——. 1983. *Alcman.* Rome.

——. 1997. *Choruses of Young Women in Ancient Greece.* Lanham, MD.

——. 2001. "Quelque formes chorales chez Aristophane: Addresses aux dieux, mimesis dramatique et 'performance' musicale." *Chanter les dieux* (ed. Brule Vendries) 115–140. Rennes. English version in Murray and Wilson 2004:157–184.

Cameron, Alan. 1995. *Callimachus and His Critics.* Princeton.

Carter, Jane B. 1995. "Ancestor Cult and the Occasion of Homeric Performance." *The Ages of Homer: A Tribute to Emily Townsend* (eds. Jane B. Carter and Sarah P. Morris) 285–313. Austin.

Dobrov, Geoffrey W., ed. 1997. *The City as Comedy: Society and Representation in Athenian Drama.* Chapel Hill, NC.

Dover, K. J. 1972. *Aristophanic Comedy.* Berkeley.

Dunbar, Nan. 1994. "Aristophane, Ornithophile et Ornithophage." In Thiercy and Manu 1994:113–129.

——. 1995. *Aristophanes' Birds.* Oxford.

——. 1996. "Sophia in Aristophanes' *Birds.*" *Scripta Classica Israelica* 15:61–71.

Easterling, Pat, and Hall, Edith, eds. 2002. *Greek and Roman Actors: Aspects of an Ancient Profession.* Cambridge.

Feld, Steven. 1990. *Sound and Sentiment: Birds, Weeping, Poetics, and Song in Kaluli Expression.* Philadelphia.

Forbes Irving, P. M. C. 1990. *Metamorphosis in Greek Myths.* Oxford.

Fraenkel, Eduard. 1962. *Beobachtungen zu Aristophanes.* Rome.

Gelzer, Thomas. 1996. "Some Aspects of Aristophanes' Dramatic Art in the Birds." In Segal 1996:194–215.

Gentili, Bruno. 1988. *Poetry and Its Public in Ancient Greece: From Homer to the Fifth Century.* Baltimore.

Green, J. R. 1985. "A Representation of the Birds of Aristophanes." *Greek Vases in the J. Paul Getty Museum* (ed. Jiri Frel) 2:95–118. Malibu, CA.

Hall, Edith. 1995. "Lawcourt Dramas: The Power of Performance in Forensic Oratory." *Bulletin of the Institute for Classical Studies* 40:39–58.

——. 2002. "The Singing Actors of Antiquity." In Easterling and Hall 2002:3–38.

Hamilton, John T. 2003. *Soliciting Darkness: Pindar, Obscurity, and the Classical Tradition.* Cambridge, MA.

Harrison, Jane. 1927. *Themis: A Study of the Social Origins of Greek Religion.* Cambridge.

Herington, John. 1985. *Poetry into Drama: Early Tragedy and the Greek Poetic Tradition.* Berkeley.

Hordern, J. H. 2002. *The Fragments of Timotheus of Miletus.* Oxford.

Kakridis, Ph. 1974. *ΑΡΙΣΤΟΦΑΝΟΥΣ ΟΡΝΙΘΕΣ.* Athens.

Kugelmeier, Christoff. 1996. *Reflexe früher und zeitgenossischer Lyrik in der alten attischen Komödie.* Stuttgart.

Kurke, Leslie. 1991. *The Traffic in Praise: Pindar and the Poetics of Social Economy.* Ithaca.

——. 2000. "The Strangeness of 'Song Culture': Archaic Greek Poetry." In Taplin 2000: 58–87.

Le Meur, Nadine. 1988. "Paysage et poésie dans la lyrique grecque." *Paysage et milieux naturels dans la literature antique* (ed. Christine Mauduit) 19–38. Lyons.

Levaniouk, Olga. 1999. "Penelope and the *Pēnelops.*" *Nine Essays on Homer* (ed. Miriam Carlisle and Olga Levaniouk) 95–136. Lanham, MD.

Lynch, John Patrick. 1972. *Aristotle's School: A Study of a Greek Educational Institution.* Berkeley.

MacDowell, Douglas M. 1995. *Aristophanes and Athens: An Introduction to the Plays.* Oxford.

Malkin, Irad. 1987. *Religion and Colonization in Ancient Greece.* Leiden.

Martin, Richard P. 1999. "Translator's Preface [to the *Birds*]." *Aristophanes, 3: The Suits, Clouds, Birds* (eds. David R. Slavitt and Palmer Bovie) 195–201. Philadelphia.

——. 2003. "The Pipes are Brawling: Conceptualizing Musical Performance in Athens." *The Cultures within Greek Culture* (eds. Carol Dougherty and Leslie Kurke) 153–180. Cambridge.

Mathews, Gary. 1997. "Aristophanes' 'High' Lyrics Reconsidered." *Maia* 49:1–42.

McEvilley, Thomas. 1970. "Development in the Lyrics of Aristophanes." *American Journal of Philology* 91:257–276.

Mineur, W. H. 1985. "From Book-Worms to Reed Warblers." *Mnemosyne* 38:383–387.

Moulton, Carroll. 1994. "Comic Myth-Making and Aristophanes' Originality in *Birds*." In Segal 1996:216–228.

Moutsopoulos, Evanghelos. 2000. "La musique dans l'oeuvre d'Aristophane." *Le théâtre grec antique: La Comedie. Actes du 10ème colloque de la Villa Kerylos à Beaulieu-sur-Mer les 1er & 2 octobre 1999* (eds. J. Leclant and J. Jouanna) 59–82. Paris.

Murray, Gilbert. 1933. *Aristophanes: A Study.* Oxford.

Murray, Penelope and Wilson, Peter, eds. 2004. *Music and the Muses: The Culture of 'Mousike' in the Classical Athenian City.* Oxford.

Nagy, Gregory. 1990. *Pindar's Homer: The Lyric Possession of an Epic Past.* Baltimore.

——. 1996. *Poetry as Performance: Homer and Beyond.* Cambridge.

Nilsson, Martin P. 1950. *The Minoan-Mycenean Religion and Its Survival in Greek Religion.* Lund.

Padel, Ruth. 1992. *In and Out of the Mind.* Princeton.

Parker, L. P. E. 1994. "Ce qui nous manque: mètre et effet dramatique chez Aristophane." In Thiercy and Manu 2004:73–85.

——. 1997. *The Songs of Aristophanes.* Oxford.

Perkell, Christine. 1993. "On the Two Voices of the Birds in *Birds*." *Ramus* 22:1–18.

Pickard-Cambridge, Arthur. 1968. *The Dramatic Festivals of Athens.* Oxford.

Segal, E., ed. 1996. *Oxford Readings in Aristophanes.* Oxford.

Sifakis, Gregory Michael. 1971. *Parabasis and Animal Choruses: A Contribution to the Study of Attic Comedy.* London.

Silk, Michael. 1980. "Aristophanes as Lyric Poet." *Yale Classical Studies* 26:99–151.

——. 2000. *Aristophanes and the Definition of Comedy.* Oxford.

Slater, Niall. 1997. "Performing the City in *Birds*." In Dobrov 1997:75–94.

Sommerstein, Alan. 1995. *Birds: With Introduction and Commentary.* Oxford.

Sourvinou-Inwood, Christiane. 2003. *Tragedy and Athenian Religion.* Lanham, MD.

Taplin, Oliver, ed. 2000. *Literature in the Greek and Roman Worlds.* Oxford.

Thiercy, Pascal, and Manu, Michel, eds. 1994. *Aristophane: la langue, la scène, la cité (Actes du colloque de Toulouse 17–19 Mars 1994).* Bari.

West, M. L. 1992. *Ancient Greek Music.* Oxford.

Wilson, Peter. 1999. "The *Aulos* in Athens." *Performance Culture and Athenian Democracy* (eds. Simon Goldhill and Robin Osborne) 58–95. Cambridge.

——. 2000. *The Athenian Institution of the Khoregia: The Chorus, the City, and the Stage.* Cambridge.

Zimmermann, Bernhard. 1985–1987. *Untersuchungen zur Form und dramatischen Technik der Aristophanischen Komödien.* Beiträge zur Klassischen Philologie 154, 166, 178. Königstein.

4

Some Refractions of Homeric Anger in Athenian Drama

T. R. Walsh

Think of institutions and customs which have created . . . out of the enjoyment of anger perpetual vengeance.

Nietzsche 1997:27

In Aeschylus' *Suppliants*, a particular kind of anger is identified through formulaic language that directly continues Homeric usage. In this play, the noun κότος ('anger'), when it indicates the anger of Zeus, is always accompanied by a term denoting suppliancy, a central theme of the play. A clear example of the relationship between κότος and the institution that is central to Aeschylus' *Suppliants* comes early in the drama, at the very point when the chorus tries to persuade Pelasgus, the King of Argos, to accept its supplication.

To argue for asylum, the chorus members insist on their genealogical relation to the Argives (308–324). After sketching out their genealogy in order to claim kinship with Pelasgus, the Danaids provide reasons why he should grant them asylum (329–346). In the course of this explanation they invoke δίκη (343) and the relation of the political to the sacred (346). Both parts of their presentation come to a close with a reference to Zeus and, most importantly, to his anger (347), a specific kind of anger: βαρύς γε μέντοι <u>Ζηνὸς ἱκεσίου κότος</u> ("Heavy indeed is <u>the anger of Zeus of the suppliants</u>"). Coming as it does at the end of a lengthy stichomythic passage, and thereby capping a series of arguments that are dramatically and rhetorically presented so as to acquire Pelasgus' assistance, the chorus's reference to Zeus and his κότος is worth our attention. I suggest that this reference to the κότος of Zeus is meant to focus the king's attention on a crucial aspect of Zeus' power, one that he dare not ignore as he weighs whether or not to help the suppliants.

I dedicate what may be good in this essay to the fond memory of a dear friend, Laura Lei Collins. *Ave atque vale.*

The significance of this reference to Zeus' κότος is underscored by three more citations of the Olympian's κότος later in the play. These four instances, when taken together, present a formulaic phrase consisting of the anger word (κότος) followed by a genitive phrase consisting of the name of Zeus accompanied by a qualifying element (ἱκταίου, 385; ἱκεσίου, 347 and 616; ἱκτῆρος, 478) specifying Zeus' role as the protector of suppliants. Whether one sees such formulaic features as an imitation of the Homeric banquet's oral-traditional style or as responding to the immediate demands of Greek tragic poetics, these repetitions lead us to to ask why κότος—precisely this kind of anger—is selected as the emotional driving force for the king of the gods.[1]

One way to answer this question regarding κότος in Aeschylus' *Suppliants* is to inquire about how formulaic these four phrases from *Suppliants* actually are. Further, we must ask if κότος in Aeschylean poetic style functions in a way similar to or different from Homeric poetic style, with respect to either usage or semantics. Consider the four relevant formulaic phrases:

Ζηνὸς ἱκταίου κότος (385)
Ζηνὸς αἰδεῖσθαι κότον / ἱκτῆρος (478–479)
Ζηνὸς ἱκεσίου κότος (347)
Ζηνὸς ἱκεσίου κότον (616)

As formulas these lines exhibit *variatio* in selecting for their focus one particular aspect of Zeus, with different adjectival forms based on the root ἱκ-. Such variation is part of dramatic choral style, especially that of Aeschylus, but *variatio* itself is not unknown in Homeric poetic style.[2] This Aeschylean variation establishes a kind of declension for the relationship between Zeus and the suppliants. Two things remain consistent in this poetic variation: the name of

1 Other words for anger occur in this play, but this formula is consistent only with κότος. Cf., for contrast, μῆνις μάστειρ' (163), μηνιταῖ' ἄχη (206); ὠμῇ ξὺν ὀργῇ (187), ὀργάς (763); and μένει (dative of μένος, 756). On the word μῆνις, see Muellner 1996. I note in passing that, metrically, χόλος is the exact equivalent of κότος and so could be used in any of these passages. As I argued in Walsh 2005, chapter 1, a consistent use of one word instead of the other in distinctive verbal contexts indicates that these words are not synonymous in Aeschylus any more than they are in Homer. In this light, it is understandable that the scholiast at 385–386, perhaps long separated from the linguistic context that kept the formally identical words κότος and χόλος functionally distinct, silently refers us to the χόλος of Zeus as he explicates Aeschylus' Ζηνὸς . . . κότος (Friis Johansen 1970:160). So too Harris collapses κότος with the other anger words in his brief discussion of this play (Harris 2001:161n10). This confusion reflects the history of the word, for which Dindorf long ago noted "nusquam hoc vocabulo usus est Sophocles, semel legitur apud Euripidem *Rhes.* 827 . . . *saepissime apud Aeschylum*" (Dindorf 1876:186). The Homeric context of the passage from the *Rhesus* should be flagged. In a fuller study of the post-Homeric uses of κότος, I will suggest that in later literature it is one indicator of an archaizing style.

2 On stylistic variation in Homeric style, see Muellner 1976:25.

the god (in the genitive) and the word for anger (κότος/-ν). Since the word can easily be changed for another anger word (notably χόλος) with no change in meter, I suggest that something special is meant by κότος indicating that it is the anger word appropriate for the wrath associated with Zeus' relationship to the traditional rights of suppliancy.

In Aeschylus' *Suppliants*, the phrase Ζηνὸς . . . κότος (/-ν) (4×), it turns out, is always accompanied by a word indicating suppliancy, formed from ἱκ-, occurring in all three possible metrical locations for that term: inserted within the formula, following the formula, or preceding it (the forms being ἱκεσίου, ἱκταίου, ἱκτῆρος, respectively). Thus every possibility for the placement of the term referring to suppliancy is accounted for. This full presentation of the κότος of Zeus suggests that this kind of anger is not merely a generic term for anger in Aeschylus' *Suppliants*. After discussing just what this significance is, I will go on to suggest that these findings can be applied to other Aeschylean plays where κότος is used. How Aeschylus uses κότος, it will be clear, continues the meaning of κότος in Homer. Those observations will find support for the idea that Homeric usage in this instance is refracted through Aeschylean theater.[3]

It is not only generic items at the level of narrative that are refracted as textual matter moves through time. The cultural capital provided by a culture's key-terms (see Wierzbicka 1997) is also subject to such change, modification, and reception. So too for the notion of anger, we should keep in mind that radical change can alter semantics. A different kind of analysis suggests continuity instead of transformation. I am thinking here of Harris 2001, a thorough review of the ideology of anger, in the light of "restraint," in Greco-Roman antiquity. This ambitious work grounds its analysis in how the restraint of anger came to be encoded in the classical world, especially as a topic of philosophical interest. The result is a long-needed encyclopedic study of "anger-control" as it developed from Greece to Rome, with a special focus on how philosophical discourse about restraining the passions developed in the West.[4]

My approach has a different purpose, since, as I argue elsewhere (Walsh 2005: Part 1), κότος is a kind of enabling anger, not one to be restrained but rather, and emphatically, one to be deployed in response to violations that lead to long-term retaliation, such as, for example, the Trojan War. Indeed,

3 I have borrowed the term "refracted" from Gregory Nagy, who uses it to accommodate the complexities of the relationships between genres as they utilize the store of culture in differing but intrinsically related ways. For an exemplary use of the concept of refraction to track the differing ways in which traditional material is handled across epic, drama, and lyric, see Nagy 2000.

4 I regret that I was not able to use Konstan's important 2006 book on Greek emotions for this article.

we have already seen that the Danaids encourage the κότος of Zeus; far from restraining it, they desire to engage the aspect of Zeus that mobilizes anger in response to violated supplication.[5] In order to examine closely how this kind of anger works, I resist producing an encyclopedic overview of anger; rather, my approach in this essay is deductive, focusing on what Aeschylus means by using κότος in these passages.

Now Harris's chapter on anger in the polis (Harris 2001: chapter 8) in fact presents a brief discussion of Aeschylus' *Suppliants*, where divine anger is identified as a preserver and creator of order: "It was maintained earlier that an old Greek tradition did sometimes array divine anger on the side of moral rules, and that is its role here. This anger is therefore presented in a wholly positive way" (Harris 2001:161). What needs to be added to this formulation is that one word especially singles out such a "positive" form of wrath, and that word is κότος.[6]

That is to say, for me, the requirements of the texts precede any examination of concepts, a difference in method that I hope makes my work complementary to and not competitive with those who find the emotions displayed in archaic literature worth pursuing. I believe the examination of Aeschylus' use of κότος in the following pages will demonstrate the value of a focus grounded in particular texts.

Κότος in *Suppliants*

Aeschylus' usage of κότος in *Suppliants* continues Homeric style, where, among the Homeric words for anger, there is one word associated with the social institution of the "feud."[7] In a book devoted in part to this word, *Fighting Words*

5 Harris assigns this kind of anger to an "old Greek tradition" (Harris 2001:161; see 137).

6 For a brief review of the data, see Sidaras 1971:32, where Aeschylus' special use of the term is noted; I think more is involved than whether one word or another is a "favorite word" of Aeschylus. For Homeric usage, see Garson 1985. Cairns in Braund and Most 2003:31 thoughtfully refers to my work; I regret that my argument was not available for his use in this important article.

7 See Walsh 2005:97–104. On feuding in a Greek context see Cohen 1995:87–118. Miller (1990: 178–220) presents insights into the way a society (here Old Norse) constructs itself around its institutions of feuding, vengeance, and the law. It is common to suggest that feuding is not relevant to the early Greeks: e.g. Harris 2001:135. Yet, it is possible for feuding structures to be "refracted" into a state-based legal system; see Cohen 1995:87–118. We in classics are still far from a thorough analysis of the way feuding-structures survive into archaic and classical cultural contexts, despite the fact that weighty historical issues such as the relationship between gender and violence are implicated in such relationships. Once again, Old Norse studies present an exemplary model; cf., besides Miller, Anderson 2002, Clover 1993, Byock 1982. The institution of the feud and the concept of vengeance need to be distinguished; see

and Feuding Words (2005), the heuristic method I adopted was to study the folk-definition of Calchas in *Iliad* I 74–83 in order to compare that definition against the evidence of the Homeric texts, the *Iliad* and the *Odyssey*. In his definition, Calchas contrasts two kinds of anger by specifying their constituent features. The Homeric data, I argue in *Fighting Words*, supports Calchas' definition. To clarify these matters for Athenian tragedy, I need to begin by reviewing my earlier findings regarding κότος.

In *Fighting Words*, I argue that the internal evidence of Homeric diction pointed to a focused understanding of two words, κότος and χόλος. These two words are crucial to understanding the role of conflict and emotion in Homeric narrative; they are also significant elements for the plots of the *Iliad* and the *Odyssey*. I set Calchas' definition in his speech at *Iliad* I 74–83 against the instances of κότος (and χόλος) in the *Iliad* and the *Odyssey* (see the introduction to Walsh 2005). The result is a confirmation of Calchas' folk-definition. Also important for the method is the value given to "key terms" in a particular cultural context (Wierzbecka 1997). One conclusion that emerges is that κότος is connected with the type of social aggression identified as "feuding," because that form of violence lasts over time, with a resolution found—at least ideologically—outside human political activity. Furthermore, in Homeric narrative κότος tends to be directed to the most dramatic and central events—for example, the fall of Troy. Moreover, κότος is associated with the early vocabulary of Greek ethics. For a Homeric example of this association between anger and ethics see *Iliad* XVI 386, where the κότος of Zeus is punishing an entire community for σκολιὰς θέμιστας (Walsh 2005, chapter 5).

Since I am arguing that the meaning of κότος depends on its Homeric significance, I will briefly review the "definition" of Calchas. The fundamental terms underlying this distinction are drawn by the prophet Calchas (*Iliad* I 78–82):

> ἦ γὰρ ὀΐομαι ἄνδρα χολωσέμεν, ὃς μέγα πάντων
> Ἀργείων κρατέει καί οἱ πείθονται Ἀχαιοί.
> κρείσσων γὰρ βασιλεύς, ὅτε χώσεται ἀνδρὶ χέρηϊ·
> εἴ περ γάρ τε χόλον γε καὶ αὐτῆμαρ καταπέψῃ,
> ἀλλά τε καὶ μετόπισθεν ἔχει κότον, ὄφρα τελέσσῃ.

on vengeance de Romilly 1970 for Aeschylus, and Saïd 1984 for the tragedy of vengeance, along with Svenbro 1984, both in Verdier 1980–1984, a four-volume collection of articles on vengeance. I distinguish vengeance from "the feud," since the feud is an institution that emerges under specific social circumstances (such as warfare), whereas vengeance emerges as a response to human conditions in varying social circumstances.

> I expect to anger the man who rules powerfully over all the Argives and the Achaeans obey him. For a king is the more angry, when he rages against a lesser man; for if he swallow down his χόλος in a day, yet he will continue κότος into the future, until it is accomplished.

As I argued in *Fighting Words* (Part I), a distinction is drawn here between χόλος and κότος based on the categories that can be examined across both the *Iliad* and the *Odyssey*. Those categories include a) time; b) power; and c) the body—such that, for a βασιλεύς [= power], κότος lasts into the future (μετόπισθεν) [= time], though χόλος is dealt with in short order (αὐτῆμαρ) [= time], and, finally, χόλος is associated with a bodily states such as digestion (καταπέψῃ) [= the body], in contrast to the end of κότος, labeled as belonging to concepts such as τέλος (ὄφρα τελέσσῃ) [= time].

In short, a binary distinction is established between a concrete form of anger, χόλος, and a kind of abstract anger such as κότος. Though there is nothing in itself remarkable in establishing a distinction between the abstract and the concrete, it is crucial that we notice how the difference between these two forms of anger underlies the ideology of Homeric anger. Each word represents one part of a set of binaries, whose boundaries are marked by categories such as *time*, *power*, and *the body*. Finally, it is also crucial that the distinction here argued for is explicated by Calchas.[8]

The author in whose work κότος is best attested after Homer is Aeschylus.[9] Aeschylus not only continues the Homeric usage of κότος as defined by Calchas, but, importantly, the surviving dramas from Aeschylean theater are centrally focused on this specific kind of conflict associated with κότος, namely the social conflict called the feud. In literary terms, κότος is thematic for Aeschylean drama.[10]

The thematic focus of κότος emerges early in Aeschylus' *Suppliants*, where King Pelasgus draws a distinction similar to the very one drawn by Calchas in *Iliad* I 74–83. That is to say that the distinction between χόλος and κότος points to a special meaning that highlights a vast depth of social conflict in the following passage from Aeschylus' *Suppliants*.

8 Again, see Walsh 2005 for a full discussion of these two terms, and see the introduction to that book for further argumentation. On key-words as a useful tool for cultural analysis, see Wierzbicka 1997, and see the discussion of the "folk-definition" in Walsh 2005:14.

9 Already noticed in Dindorf 1876, s.v. κότος. See also Franklin 1895:49.

10 The *Iliad*, in contrast, tends not to focus on feuding vengeance, as it sees issues of violence and aggression through a warrior's eyes; the *Odyssey* associates the vengeance of Odysseus with the feud whenever possible in order to justify Odysseus' revenge on the suitors. On the issue of Odysseus, anger, and vengeance, see Walsh 2005:85 and Svenbro 1984.

When the suppliants approach King Pelasgus, he askes them why they have come (*Suppliants* 333–336):

> Βα. τί φῂς ἱκνεῖσθαι τῶνδ' ἀγωνίων θεῶν,
> λευκοστεφεῖς ἔχουσα νεοδρέπτους κλάδους;
> Χο. ὡς μὴ γένωμαι δμωὶς Αἰγύπτου γένει.
> Βα. πότερα κατ' ἔχθραν, ἢ τὸ μὴ θέμις λέγεις;

> *King*: Why do you claim suppliancy of these gods of the assembly,
> with these newly-cut, white-wreathed branches?
> *Chorus*: That I not become a slave to the line of Aegyptus.
> *King*: Which is it: do you refer to something having to do with hatred or to something unlawful?

The distinction is drawn between an instance of hatred and a violation of something deeper, here called *themis*. King Pelasgus sees a difference between a request from someone who has a particular grievance against Aegyptus (κατ' ἔχθραν, 336), and a request from one asking to maintain a higher level of law (τὸ μὴ θέμις, 336) by accepting them as suppliants.

For a parallel to this situation, I refer to Chryses' appeal for his daughter in *Iliad* I 11–32, where the priest asks that Agamemnon release his daughter (30), supporting his authority for the request through his position as priest of Apollo. The outward manifestation of this authority is clear from the presence of the fillets of the god (14) and the σκῆπτρον (15) paralleled by Aeschylus in the suppliant women's λευκοστεφεῖς . . . νεοδρέπτους κλάδους; (334). That Agamemnon fails to acknowledge the role of the priest in representing Apollo is a crucial part of his refusal of the priest's request.

This refusal of the request of Chryses in his role as a priest has consequences too well-known to review here.[11] It is prudent, then, that in *Suppliants* 333–336, Pelasgus tests the source of the suppliants' complaint, and hence the authority behind it, before he makes a decision. If their claim refers the king to a personal hatred, it is not a claim he, as king, need pursue. But something that is τὸ μὴ θέμις—well, that is another matter indeed: its claim is beyond the personal sphere because it reaches into the social and religious sphere. It is the Danaids' task to convince him that their request depends on his allegiance to Zeus, and to what is indeed θέμις.

It is just this kind of distinction that marks the difference between κότος and other forms of anger. Indeed, I am encouraged in pursuing this ethical

[11] It may be significant that οἱ ἀγώνιοι θεοί include Apollo, beside Zeus, Hermes, and Poseidon; see LSJ s.v. ἀγώνιος.

meaning for Aeschylean κότος by a summation of the ethical focus of *Suppliants* offered by Friis Johanssen : "Throughout [the Danaids] express their aversion to the marriage . . . and also to the Aegyptids . . .; they further represent both as characterized by ὕβρις (30, 81, 104, 426, 528, 817, 845), Aegyptids as possessed by ἄτη (106–111), and the marriage as impious (9–10), contrary to θέμις (37), to αἶσα and to δίκη (82)" (Friis Johansen 1970:30). This flurry of ethical terms like ὕβρις, ἄτη, and θέμις brings to the fore the primary ethical concern of *Suppliants*. It will turn out that κότος is the kind of anger appropriate, given these ethical concerns, to the violations feared by the Danaids.

To review, forms of κότος are used in *Suppliants*[12] that involve a formula that indicates the wrath of Zeus, god of suppliants, a wrath that has to do with how well he protects their interests. Indeed, at the very beginning of this play, as the chorus is attempting to persuade the king to accept their suppliancy, Pelasgus counters that he must hesitate to enter into a risky war, with the result that the supplicants come to make their strongest argument for their plea, an argument from δίκη (343–344):

Χο. ἀλλ' ἡ δίκη γε συμμάχων ὑπερστατεῖ·
Βα. εἴπερ γ' ἀπ' ἀρχῆς πραγμάτων κοινωνὸς ἦν

Chorus: But it is justice that stands as an ally protecting you.
King: Only if it had a share of the deeds from the start.

An argument from justice (δίκη) can only win the day if the action is from its origin (ἀπ' ἀρχῆς) just. In this context, to cap the argument that Pelasgus should accept their suppliancy, the chorus advises him, in a line discussed above, who their ally is: βαρὺς γε μέντοι Ζηνὸς ἱκεσίου κότος ("Yes, heavy is the κότος of Zeus of the suppliants," 347). Κότος is used here in conjunction with δίκη (343) in order to secure the allegiance of Pelasgus. As I hope was made clear above, and as Pelasgus is about to assert in expressing his worry, it is not a private house in which the suppliants are seeking refuge (365–368). Because of the public nature of this circumstance, it is no ordinary wrath—not even an "ordinary" divine wrath—that the chorus must introduce, if they are to persuade the king to grant them asylum.[13] The wrath in question must have a secure anchor in public life.

12 Including παλίγκοτος at 376; κότον occurs at 427, with κότῳ at 744; the remaining instances are at 347 and 385 (nominative); 67 (genitive); 478 and 616 (accusative).

13 Winnington-Ingram strikingly links the wrath of violated suppliancy and that of violated guest-friendship: "'Heavy is the wrath of Zeus Hikesios, said the chorus leader in *Supplices* [347]. No less heavy is the wrath of Zeus Xenios; and it is this wrath, together with an intolerable pollution, which Danaus will have brought upon himself and upon his daughters.

This usage of κότος, consistent with what occurs in Homer, is further underscored in the stasimon following the stichomythy that we have just seen capped by the reference to Zeus' κότος. In this stasimon, the king's worries, as presented in the stichomythic passage, are probed further for their consequences. After the king explains his concern that a conflict (νεῖκος, 358) might arise were he to receive them, the suppliant women once again invoke a higher power, this time Θέμις (360), linked to suppliancy (ἱκεσία Θέμις, 360). But Pelasgus points out that his public responsibility requires that he avoid doing anything that may bring pollution to his polis (365–369). While he considers this pollution, and as the chorus admonishes him that he might incur such pollution by *not* helping them (370–375), the issue of κότος comes up again in the following way.

After the chorus warns Pelasgus that he himself needs to beware of pollution (ἄγος φυλάσσου, 375), he turns the sentiment around (376): ἄγος μὲν εἴη τοῖς ἐμοῖς παλιγκότοις ("would that my παλιγκότοι have pollution"), in which most translators give "enemies" for παλιγκότοι.[14] That translation is adequate only if it is remembered how deep the enmity is.[15] Now κότος, because this specific anger lasts over time until it reaches a τέλος, is bad enough when it involves two mortal enemies, but it spells real trouble when divine anger is at issue. Thus, the stakes are higher when the chorus, in referring to divine anger, specifically identifies the κότος of Zeus in order to emphasize how crucial it is for Pelasgus to come to their aid. Indeed, they advise him to look to Zeus, the one who helps those who are not being given their due by their neighbors (381–385). Δίκας (384), too, carries a threat that the κότος of Zeus awaits those unwilling to heed a plaintiff's laments (385–386):

But he will also have brought it upon the city of which he is now king" (Winnington-Ingram 1983:64). Moreover, the wrath that links suppliancy, guest-friendship, and the political consequences of their violation continues to have the same name for Aeschylus as it had for Homer, and that name is κότος. On the dilemma posed by violence and the wrath of Zeus see also Lloyd-Jones 1990:274: "Pelasgus is simply a good and conscientious king, confronted with a grim dilemma: either he must receive the suppliants, thus risking war with all its horrors, or he must bring down on himself and his people the wrath of Zeus, protector of suppliants."

14 For a discussion of this derivative and its use in lyric and drama, as well as its remarkable survival in the Greek medical terminology of Hippocrates and Galen, see Aly 1906:48–49.

15 On κότος and its relation to the concept of the enemy see Aly 1906:48–49, where it is clear that the notion of a longstanding wrath and enmity are continued in this compound long after κότος the noun falls away from use as a typical word for anger. The lemma meaning "enemy" also resonates with the Sanskrit cognate of Greek κότος, *śatru*, 'enemy' (Walsh 2005:90; cf. 91; for the (Cuneiform) Luwian cognate *kattawatnalli* as an "attribute of the word for enemy," see Walsh 2005:92).

μένει τοι Ζηνὸς ἱκταίου κότος
δυσπαραθέλκτος παθόντος οἴκτοις.

The κότος of Zeus of the suppliants keeps its watch,
difficult to be charmed by the laments of one who suffers.

If the word οἴκτοις ("laments") here refers to prayers, then the κότος of Zeus, like Hades itself (see *Iliad* IX 158), is unreachable by petition. In such a case, the κότος of Zeus is paramount in its alliance with a claim for justice (cf. δίκαν, 395) and it is a major factor for Pelasgus to consider as he weighs his choices regarding the Danaids' suppliancy.[16]

It emerges from this review that Aeschylus is using κότος every bit as much as terms such as δίκη and θέμις, in order to build the Danaids' case for suppliancy. Κότος is designed to bear such a strong weight, precisely because it comes from Zeus, and because it seems to be the mechanism of enforcement for the justice of Zeus, the "or else" behind Ζεὺς . . . ἀφίκτωρ (*Suppliants* 1).[17]

No passage in early Greek literature more clearly shows the complexity of κότος as does the very next choral sequence of *Suppliants* (418–437), since the ethical vocabulary in which κότος is implicated comes here to be laid out in classic ring-structure form. I quote the passage at length, since so much of it is directly relevant to establishing the sense of κότος in this drama.

Now the Danaids make their strongest plea to persuade the king to do the right thing (418–437):[18]

Χο. φρόντισον καὶ γενοῦ
πανδίκως εὐσεβὴς πρόξενος·
τὰν φυγάδα μὴ προδῷς,
τὰν ἕκαθεν ἐκβολαῖς
δυσθέοις ὀρομέναν·

Take thought and be, in all justice, our revered ally.
Do not betray this refugee,
one driven from afar by impious blows

μηδ' ἴδῃς μ' ἐξ ἑδρᾶν
πολυθέων ῥυσιασθεῖσαν, ὦ

16 δυσπαράθελκτος is Schütz's conjecture, for M's ὦ δυσπαραθέλκτοις. Page prints the conjecture, which is consistent with the meaning developed here, as does West 1990. On μένει in 385, see line 435, discussed below.

17 On force as integral to Zeus's justice, see Cohen 1993.

18 The textual problems in this ode do not affect the argument.

πᾶν κράτος ἔχων χθονός·
γνῶθι δ' ὕβριν ἀνέρων
καὶ φύλαξαι κότον.

Do not watch as I come to be driven as plunder from out of these holy seats,
O you who have all the power of the land. Know mortals' hubris and keep a
watch out for κότος.

μή τι τλᾶις τὰν ἱκέτιν εἰσιδεῖν
ἀπὸ βρετέων βίαι δίκας ἀγομέναν
ἱππαδὸν ἀμπύκων,
πολυμίτων πέπλων τ' ἐπιλαβὰς ἐμῶν.

Do not endure to merely look at the suppliant dragged from the gods' images
in violation of justice, dragged like a horse by the bridle, nor merely to look at
the assaults on my many-threaded robes.

ἴσθι γάρ, παισὶ τάδε καὶ δόμοις,
ὁπότερ' ἂν κτίσῃς, μένει Ἄρει 'κτίνειν
ὁμοίαν θέμιν.
τάδε φράσαι δίκαια Διόθεν κράτη.

Now take thought, these things remain for your children and your household,
in whatever way you act, to pay in recompense that is the equal of θέμις.
Consider these things to be the just power of Zeus.

Here I have underlined, besides κότος, words that are associated with the ethical field in which κότος can be found. Structurally, κότος is positioned at the exact center of this stasimon: that is to say, it is the center of a ring structure. That structure is framed with two verbs of knowing in the first and last stanza (φρόντισον and ἴσθι). The singular importance of κότος is secured with a cue from the stylistics of ring composition—that the center of the text contains the main point, namely to guard against the perfidy of mortals and to guard against divine κότος (γνῶθι δ' ὕβριν ἀνέρων / καὶ φύλαξαι κότον, 426–427). Moreover, the notion of "guarding" against κότος associates this kind of anger with the notion of pollution cited above (for example, ἄγος φυλάσσου, 375).

This message is supported by assertive claims regarding justice, in the first strophe, for the one who saves the refugees (γενοῦ πανδίκως . . . πρόξενος, 418), and in the concluding antistrophe for Zeus (δίκαια Διόθεν κράτη, 437). With respect to the thematics of κότος, Aeschylus emphasizes both the length of time it takes to bring conflict to an end (434–435), and the price that the children will pay with the phrase μένει ἐκτίνειν (435), which resonates strongly with the earlier phrase μένει τοι . . . κότος (385).

In a sense, I have been reviewing the rhetoric of the term κότος in Aeschylus' *Suppliants* because Aeschylus' concern with conflict, aggression, and retribution makes his discourse contemplative (or perhaps "philosophical") about the meaning of such terms. Aeschylus, that is, seems ready to explore the significance of ethical terms. Moreover, the force of κότος argued for here lends itself to such philosophical exploration. I will return to this matter at the end of this essay.

For this play, such exploration leads to a profound climax, when Pelasgus capitulates as he agrees to help the Danaids attain their asylum, even though he is still in the throes of the dilemma that faces him, namely, the expected attack of the sons of Aegyptus in response to that asylum (474–477).

> εἰ δ' αὖθ' ὁμαίμοις παισὶν Αἰγύπτου σέθεν
> σταθεὶς πρὸ τειχέων διὰ μάχης ἥξω τέλους,
> πῶς οὐχὶ τἀνάλωμα γίγνεται πικρόν,
> ἄνδρας γυναικῶν οὕνεχ' αἱμάξαι πέδον;

> But if, against your blood-kin and on your behalf, I have taken a stand before
> the city-walls to engage in battle against the sons of Aegyptus, how is there
> not a bitter price to pay, since men bloody the earth for women?

The anger of Zeus, that anger that persuades Pelasgus to assent to the Danaids' request, is precisely the institution that makes vengeance out of anger. I also refer this passage to Homer, where it can be shown that κότος implicates the flight of Helen with Paris, the consequence of which is the war at Troy. The Achaeans fighting against the Trojans are parallel, with respect to κότος, to the sons of Aegyptus fighting against the Argives.[19]

19 And note that the terms are reversed. Homer presents the violation of Helen leading to a κότος

But it is κότος that forces Pelasgus to play his hand, after the Danaids' winning argument (*Suppliants* 478–479):

> ὅμως δ' ἀνάγκη Ζηνὸς αἰδεῖσθαι κότον
> ἱκτῆρος· ὕψιστος γὰρ ἐν βροτοῖς φόβος.
>
> Nonetheless, it is necessary to honor the κότος of Zeus the god of suppliancy. For this fear is the most profound among mortals.

These words alone should give us pause. The greatest fear (ὕψιστος . . . φόβος, 479) has as its basis the κότος of Zeus. Under such circumstances, κότος persuades Pelasgus, ultimately, to receive the Danaids.

The following passage of *Suppliants* presents Danaus' report of Pelasgus' speech to his people, asking them to support his decision (*Suppliants* 615–618):

> τοιάνδ' ἔπειθε ῥῆσιν ἀμφ' ἡμῶν λέγων
> ἄναξ Πελασγῶν, ἱκεσίου Ζηνὸς κότον
> μέγαν προφωνῶν μήποτ' εἰσόπιν χρόνου
> πόλιν παχῦναι . . .
>
> Such a speech did the King of the Pelasgians use in persuading them on our behalf, that the city should not magnify hereafter the wrath of Zeus of the Suppliants . . .

This kind of reasoning makes best sense if there is a special relationship between enmity and the kind of resentment indicated by κότος, and this relationship is part of the thematics of this drama. In this case, Pelasgus presents to a voting citizenry the case for not provoking κότος. This is an anachronism, since an archaic concept is put in the heart of a democratic process.[20] Nonetheless, just as the Eumenides at the end of the *Oresteia* will need to be accommodated, so too will κότος here need its accomodations.[21]

It is clear then that κότος belongs closely with the other terms proper to the ethical world of tragedy: δίκη, ὕβρις, θέμις are all part of its semantic

---

that sends armies against Troy. Here Pelasgus' position seems more like Priam's, in that his acceptance of the fleeing women, as he avoids the κότος of Zeus, leads to the attack of an invasion force. For a good examination of the way the idea of the "feud" can explicate Athenian practice, see Cohen 1995, especially chapter 5; and Walsh 2005, chapters 3–6. It is exactly the reciprocal nature of feuding that makes κότος so potent as an argument on either side of the feuding relationship. For comparative and cross-cultural overviews of vengeance see Verdier 1980 and 1984.

20 See Lloyd-Jones 1990:264–265 for a discussion of the supposed political anachronisms in the play.

21 For a probing of the issues involved in these kinds of tensions in Aeschylean artistry, see Griffith 1995.

field. Moreover, kingship has to do with κότος, especially as regards the power wielded by the king. The scholiast associates the κότος of 427 with Zeus (τὸν τοῦ Διός), and this interpretation is consistent, certainly, with what we have seen elsewhere in this play. But it is more important to note that, as in Homer, a relationship partaking of κότος can either be described from the point of view of the god involved or from that of either of the human antagonists. Such a relationship is reciprocal, but nonetheless, it often has to do with the power of a dominant party and a subordinate, as in the relation of suppliancy or kingship.[22]

This stasimon both in its high poetic artistry and its dramatic importance shows, I repeat, the centrality of κότος for Aeschylus' conceptualization of conflict and emotion. Because of this centrality, I am encouraged to think that the importance of κότος that I argued for in *Fighting Words* is verified. In the rest of this essay, I hope to show that, in fact, Aeschylus' drama is concerned even more than epic with highlighting the role of κότος and that later drama drops this concern. The result is from a diachronic point of view a refraction of Homeric κότος.[23]

Before turning to the *Oresteia*, where Aeschylus' concern with the anger of the feud is inescapable, one further passage in *Suppliants* shows κότος as it functions to heighten the climax of the play, where the Danaids see the approach of the suitors (*Suppliants* 743–745):

> δοριπαγεῖς δ' ἔχοντες κυανώπιδας
> νῆας ἔπλευσαν ὧδ' <u>ἐπιτυχεῖ κότῳ</u>[24]
> πολεῖ μελαγχίμῳ σὺν στρατῷ.
>
> With dark-prowed thick-timbered ships they have sailed thus accompanied by a <u>wrath that hits its mark</u>, along with a great dark army.

Though the textual problems in this passage are serious, no one disputes that κότος is to be associated with the expedition of the Aegyptids.This is a pivotal moment in the trilogy, no doubt pointing to the conflict that arises when allying

22 On reciprocity and anger see Watkins 1977[1994] and Muellner 1996.

23 See n3 above.

24 I am translating here in accordance with a conjecture that itself "hits the mark," so far as κότος is concerned. I follow Turnebus' ἐπιτυχεῖ at 744 instead of M.'s ἐπεὶ τάχει, the text leading to Page's reading, which I reject. Turnebus' reading is strikingly consistent with the meaning of κότος that I have been arguing for, namely, that κότος lasts until it reaches its τέλος. On the importance of τέλος in this play see Zeitlin 1992:222.

oneself with κότος.[25] For this kind of anger is reciprocal, so that its very power is liable to be unleashed in return at those who claim that Zeus' κότος is on their side. It is thus far from a contradiction for the play to point to the unerring κότος of the Aegyptids. This situation is more like the dueling scene in book 3 of the *Iliad*, where Menelaos and Paris face off κοτέοντε (*Iliad* III 345). The dual says it all: κότος, this daunting force allied with justice, right and the power of Zeus, is also managed by one's enemy. Far from a solution, κότος is, in fact, the problem.

And it is a problem, to return to my epigraph from Nietzsche, rooted in the human capacity for enabling cultural continuity. Not only politically, through its mobilization of allegiance and coherence, as well as of force and destruction, but also poetically, in its long-lived productivity through formulaic language and poetic tradition, κότος is an instance of what a culture can do in the face of the seeming evanescence of existence. For it is the cultural memory, and those institutions that support it, that the suppliants in this play rely upon, so that by invoking the κότος of Zeus the characters make utterly clear how great the stakes really are.

Κότος in the *Oresteia*

Although *Suppliants* gives a tightly focused perspective on the meaning of κότος, in the *Oresteia* Aeschylus makes the most extensive use of the semantics of κότος. The trilogy shows clearly how the term fits into the ethical vocabulary of the archaic and late-archaic ethical universe that we have been examining. See, for example, the first use of κότος in the trilogy, which occurs in a gnomic statement occurring after the chorus laments the destruction wrought by the Trojan War (*Agamemnon* 456–457):

> βαρεῖα δ' ἀστῶν φάτις σὺν <u>κότῳ</u>,
> <u>δημοκράντου</u> δ' ἀρᾶς τίνει <u>χρέος</u>.
>
> Heavy is the voice of the citizens accompanied by <u>κότος</u>, and it pays the <u>debt</u> of a curse <u>validated by the people</u>.[26]

[25] Note here that the κότος is that of the suitors. Just as Paris and Menelaus, in the depths of their κότος, are said to be engaged κοτέοντε (*Iliad* III 345), so too here κότος is reciprocal. These questions reach deeply into the issues of the play. For our immediate purposes it need only be acknowledged that κότος here involves fundamental questions of the narrative, and that those questions include issues of δίκη, etc. See Walsh 2005:24–25.

[26] After Fraenkel's translation: "Dangerous is the people's talk, with anger in it; it pays the debt arising out of a curse pronounced by the people." For the meaning of δημοκράντου see Fraenkel 1950 ad 369, with Page 1957: 110–111. I thank Timothy Pepper for encouraging me to clarify the difficulties presented by this passage.

As with the examples noted above, the anger of κότος is appropriate to a publically ratified (δημοκράντου) curse and the duty (χρέος) that is attendant upon it; that is to say, it has to do with power. Consistent with the terms of Calchas' definition, this passage shows that κότος involves the enforcement of public standards across time. What Fraenkel says about the compound δημοκράντου has explanatory power for κότος as well: "The κραίνειν-element brings out the idea that the curses are to be regarded as valid utterances, that they carry with them the *guarantee of fulfilment*. This is in fact an essential characteristic of ἀραί, so that they can be regarded in the light of *legally binding obligations*" (Fraenkel *ad* 457; emphasis added).

By now the themes typical of passages featuring κότος have become familiar. Here the notion of the binding fulfillment of a curse recalls *Iliad* I 82, ὄφρα τελέσσῃ). In addition, immediately following the passage just quoted, Aeschylus highlights the long time that must pass in awaiting this fulfillment (μένει, 459, and χρόνοι, 463); moreover, παλιντυχεῖ (465) calls to mind the πάλιν of παλίγκοτος (*Suppliants* 376). Finally, these lines, as in other κότος passages, clearly focus on δίκη (464), thus continuing the association of κότος with the early Greek ethical lexicon.

Given these features of κότος, one can happily agree when Fraenkel correctly retains κότον in as vexed a passage as *Agamemnon* 767, where the notion of ὕβρις, persistence, and so forth are brought to bear on the ethical center of the play's action (*Agamemnon* 763–771; translation and text after Fraenkel):

> φιλεῖ δὲ τίκτειν ὕβρις μὲν παλαι-
> ά νεάζουσαν ἐν κακοῖς βροτῶν
> ὕβριν, τότ' ἢ τόθ' †ὅτανt τὸ κύριον μόλῃ
> †νεαρὰ φάος† κότον
> δαίμονά †τε τὸν† ἄμαχον ἀπόλεμον, ἀνίερον
> θράσος, μέλαιναν μελάθροισιν Ἄταν,
> εἰδομέναν τοκεῦσιν.

> An old *hubris* loves to engender a young *hubris* among the ills of mortals,
> right then when the appointed day has come, [?] a κότος, a *daimon*, a
> boldness not to be battled, not to be warred against, unholy, a dark *Atē*, in the
> likeness of her parents.

Once again, the textual problems should not blind us to the significance of this passage for understanding the term κότος. It would be odd, were κότος merely one synonym among many for "anger," to have it so exalted among terms like ὕβρις and ἄτη, even to the extent perhaps of being itself a *daimon*. We have already seen in *Suppliants* that it is closely associated with ὕβρις; indeed it is here nearly identified as being the offspring of the aged ὕβρις. The fact that it is not susceptible to war, and that it crosses generations, also confirms the validity of the Homeric meaning of κότος within an Aeschylean context; this passage displays the notion of stability over time through a genealogical metaphor, with a striking emphasis on ἄτη and θράσος, ultimately to center—literally—on κότος. That κότος occupies the exact center of this stanza, once again, carries weight in the light of my earlier analysis of the choral ode at *Suppliants* 418–437.

The other relevant passages in the *Agamemnon* also suggest the semantic force of κότος. Thus the herald is asked by the chorus to recount the storm at sea in terms of the κότος of the gods (*Agamemnon* 634–635): πῶς γὰρ λέγεις χείμονα ναύτικῳ στράτῳ / ἔλθειν τελευτῆσαί τε δαιμόνων κότῳ ("How do you say the storm arrived at the naval host and how did it come to reach completion by the κότος of the gods?").[27] That storms can be associated with κότος is easily seen in a crucial passage in the *Iliad*, where we find a storm simile foregrounding the notion of κότος (*Iliad* XVI 383–393).[28] In sum, the notion of κότος is reinforced by τελευτῆσαι, the storm context, and the direct punishment meted out by the gods.

Κότος occurs also in *Agamemnon* 1211, where the anger of Apollo at Cassandra is styled Λοχίου κότῳ. Apollo's anger is divine and affects Cassandra's prophetic powers, so we could judge this to be an anger both numinous and intransigent. This passage amounts to an explicit reference to the ethical universe of ὕβρις or δίκη that often accompanies κότος.[29]

In *Libation Bearers*, the nature of κότος continues the meanings just reviewed, especially in regard to the relation of κότος to δίκη and the ability of

27 The translation follows Fraenkel's note to 635, though Fraenkel's point about the "addition" of τελευτῆσαι needs to be modified now that we know that forms of τέλος are thematically linked to κότος. The chorus is asking about the "whole story" from beginning to end, a good proöimial gesture. Moreover, as Fraenkel stresses in his note to 634, γάρ is "a reference to a point farther back" in time. Note that the herald picks up the wrath theme with μῆνις at 649.

28 See Walsh 2005, chapter 5. And note the expected association with *díkē* in the Homeric passage.

29 Both remaining instances of κότος in the *Agamemnon* (1261, 1641) engage textual problems that do not affect the present argument.

κότος to endure over time. For example, its semantic thrust can be seen in the following passage (*Libation Bearers* 32–41):

τορὸς γὰρ ὀρθόθριξ δόμων
ὀνειρόμαντις, ἐξ ὕπνου κότον πνέων,
ἀωρόνυκτον ἀμβόαμα
μυχόθεν ἔλακε περὶ φόβῳ
γυναικείοισιν ἐν δώμασιν βαρὺς πίτνων,
κριταί <τε> τῶνδε' ὀνειράτων
θεόθεν ἔλακον ὑπέγγυοι
μέμφεσθαι τοὺς γᾶς νέρθεν περιθύμως
τοῖς κτανοῦσί τ' ἐγκοτεῖν.

The shrill, hair-raising dream-prophet of the house,
breathing κότος in her sleep, would cry out from the innermost
parts
of the house a cry in the night out of fear,
falling heavily on the women's quarters,
and the judges of those dreams
from the gods cried out, guaranteeing
that those beneath the earth aggressively blame and have κότος
against the killers.

I take the ὀνειρόμαντις to be Clytemnestra,[30] whose actions have stirred the underworld deities to have κότος. Indeed, it is not her anger at Agamemnon that is a κότος, since in fact her complaints are resolved through action. The nature of κότος is such that it must be brought to a conclusion, and only extra-human entities can manage this.[31] In this passage, the long-lasting and reciprocal nature of κότος is emphasized by the repetition of the word κότος, framing the passage at line 23, with ἐγκότειν at line 31.

The first stasimon of the play uses storm imagery (yet another passage to be referred to *Iliad* XVI 383–393), and in so doing displays a use of κότος appropriate for an ode that will conclude with Δίκη and subsequent punishment. In the first case, after κότος is used in the storm image (593), it should now not surprise us that in the third stasimon the chorus should associate the arrival of Δίκη with κότος (*Libation Bearers* 946–952):

30 Though others maintain it is ambiguous, see Garvie *ad loc.* Here the reference is to the same cry of Clytemnestra as mentioned at 535 (see Lloyd-Jones 1979:12).

31 Such as the ὀνειρόμαντις and τοὺς γᾶς νέρθεν. See Walsh 2005, chapter 5.

ἔμολε δ' ᾧ μέλει κρυπταδίου μάχας
δολιόφρων ποινά,
ἔθιγε δ' ἐν μάχᾳ χερὸς ἐτήτυμος
Διὸς κόρα—Δίκαν δέ νιν
προσαγορεύομεν
βροτοὶ τυχόντες καλῶς—
ὀλέθριον πνέουσ' ἐν ἐχθροῖς κότον.

And he has arrived, the one concerned for the crafty vengeance of a treacherous battle; and she touched his hand surely in battle, did the daughter of Zeus—and *Dikē* is what we mortals aiming rightly call her—breathing as she does a fatal κότος among the enemy.

This stasimon is a victory song describing the result of the action that Orestes is performing, the murder of Aegisthus and Clytemnestra. By citing κότος as the "anger" that accompanies the movement of Δίκη towards this action, Aeschylus draws our attention not only to the deceit involved in this particular act of revenge (δολιόφρων ποινά, 947), but also to the motivating force rooted in the anger of feud.

Nor is this relationship between δίκη and κότος adventitious, as can be shown from the striking evidence of fr. 148 (Smyth 1971):

τῷ μήτε χαίρειν μήτε λυπεῖσθαι φθιτούς.
ἡμῶν γε μέντοι Νέμεσίς ἐσθ' ὑπερτέρα,
καὶ τοῦ θανόντος ἡ Δίκη πράσσει κότον.

The dead neither rejoice nor suffer.
It's for us that Nemesis has the greater weight,
and Δίκη accomplishes the κότος of the dead man.

This fragment, from the lost *Ransom of Hector*, is anchored to the oldest meaning of κότος, namely the wrath associated with the institution of the feud. In such a context, the wrath can live beyond the lifetime of the one who claims to have been injured. For Aeschylus, following Homer, κότος is not a personal emotion, to be acted upon by a living person, but more like a social drive, which can affect the world by means of a force like ἡ Δίκη. In these words, then, this play re-asserts Calchas' implied point that κότος is most dangerous precisely because it reaches its τέλος even beyond death.

It is no wonder then that κότος should pose a particular problem for Orestes as the *Oresteia* progresses. For it is precisely that κότος lacks a τέλος until it finds satisfaction that dogs him through to the end of the trilogy. The importance of a correct understanding of κότος becomes clear when we try to interpret Orestes' dilemma at *Libation Bearers* 1024–1026: πρὸς δὲ καρδίᾳ φόβος / ᾄδειν ἕτοιμος ἠδ' ὑπορχεῖσθαι κότῳ ("At my heart fear is ready to sing and dance with κότος"). This grim metaphor anticipates the part played by the drama's enforcers of κότος, the Furies. Thus, the victory revel that should accompany his "defeat" of Aegisthus and Clytemnestra cannot be performed, because of the logic of the feud that is moving through the drama. It is no wonder that his defense consists of declaring that it is οὐκ ἄνευ δίκης (1027) that he acted. This is a desperate assertion that he needs in order to ground his act in some kind of ethical universe.

Indeed, κότος is the anger of the Furies, as Apollo asserts. Here he insists that the Furies have overlooked Clytemnestra's crime but not that of Orestes (*Eumenides* 219–224):

> εἰ τοῖσιν οὖν κτείνουσιν ἀλλήλους χαλᾷς
> τὸ μὴ τίνεσθαι μηδ' <u>ἐποπτεύειν</u> <u>κότῳ</u>,
> οὔ φημ' Ὀρέστην σ' <u>ἐνδίκως</u> ἀνδρηλατεῖν.
> τὰ μὲν γὰρ οἶδα κάρτα σ' ἐνθυμουμένην,
> τὰ δ' ἐμφανῶς πράσσουσαν ἡσυχαίτερα.
> <u>δίκας</u> δὲ Παλλὰς τῶνδ' <u>ἐποπτεύσει</u> θεά.

> If, therefore, you are so lenient at those who kill one another that you do not punish or <u>keep watch over them with κότος</u>,[32] I deny that you hunt Orestes <u>justly</u>. For I know that you are very engaged in the one case, while you are acting quite clearly at ease otherwise. The goddess Pallas will <u>watch over</u> the process of justice in these matters.

The contrast between the Furies and Athena is built on the kind of justice each one is seeking. In the one case, Apollo claims that κότος does not attend their action toward Clytemnestra and Aegisthus, while in the case of Orestes, their anger is an unswerving κότος. The parallelism (ἐποπτεύειν, ἐποπτεύσει; ἐνδίκως, δίκας) is clear; even clearer is the association of κότος with retribution and the oversight of the Furies (220).

32 LSJ gives "punish" for ἐποπτεύειν here, citing only this passage in that meaning (I 2). The sense of κότῳ is perfectly consistent with the usual meaning of 'oversee' or 'watch over' (I 1), where the dative shows the means by which the Furies guard their prey. This sense is also in play below at line 224, δίκας δὲ Παλλὰς τῶνδ' ἐποπτεύσει θεά, where the contrast in manner of overseeing could not be more stark. It is precisely κότος that will mark the difference between the watchfulness of Athena and Apollo and that of the Furies.

The dilemma is put even more starkly when Athena and the Eumenides engage in this exchange (*Eumenides* 425–426):

Χο. φονεὺς γὰρ εἶναι μητρὸς ἠξιώσατο.
Αθ. ἀλλ' ἦ 'ξ ἀνάγκης, ἤ τινος τρέων κότον;

Chorus: Yes, for he has deemed it worthy to be the murderer of his mother.
Athena: But was it out of necessity or fearing someone's κότος?

Passages like these show what is at stake in the close study of κότος. For now that we know that κότος is not merely an old word for anger, but one that carries with it a heavy cultural charge, it is clear that Athena's question to the Eumenides is crucial. This kind of κότος has a complex relationship with necessity, as was evident already in Calchas' definition. This kind of anger, having been identified with that of the Furies against Orestes, is now called into service to defend him as well. It is possible for it to play this double role, since, as in the *Iliad*, κότος lies at the heart of the ethical point of the trilogy, and here that point has to do with the institution that drives the curse of the house of Atreus: the feud.

This survey of Aeschylus' use of κότος has affirmed the high value that Homer's prophet, Calchas, placed on this form of anger and shows that its force extends beyond the Homeric epics. Κότος is, in fact, associated with the most powerful of terms in the early Greek lexicon of power and ethics: ὕβρις, ἀνάγκη, and δίκη, Fundamentally it is located, as an ethical construct, not with ordinary conflict and ordinary violence, but with something the early Greeks were very much concerned with: intractable violence that could extend across generations; it can be associated with either side of the feuding parties, and, to end, it must reach some kind of τέλος.

I conclude this review of the relevant passages in Aeschylus with one that highlights even more the cultural power of κότος: it plays a vital role in a society's view of itself as stable and orderly.[33] When the Eumenides see that things are not going to end as they had wished, they threaten to put an end to κότος itself (*Eumenides* 499–501):

οὐδὲ γὰρ βροτοσκόπων
μαινάδων τῶνδ' ἐφέρ-

[33] I cite here the title of the classic study of the feud by J. Black-Michaud, *Cohesive Force* (1975). The point is that in a feuding culture the acts surrounding feuding violence provide a social cohesion that is otherwise lacking. In other words, such violence is not seen as a negative but a positive thing. See my discussion in Walsh 2005, chapter 5.

ψει κότος τις ἐργμάτων.

For from the maenads that keep watch over mortals, no κότος at all stemming from deeds will approach.

The threat signifies the end, not so much of anger, but of the force that moves retribution and justice.[34] This threat targets culture itself.[35]

Other Tragedy

A word needs to be said about the virtual absence of κότος from the rest of the surviving corpus of Athenian theater. Aeschylus, because of his concern with δίκη, draws out clearly what we suspected in the *Iliad*: the anger styled κότος has more to do with deeply rooted cultural matters than with immediate emotional reaction to a violation of a personal kind.

While it would be facile to say that the relationship of δίκη to human action in the rest of Athenian tragedy is wholly different in Sophocles and Euripides, it remains a fact that κότος all but entirely drops from their poetic lexicon, in both lyric and non-lyric passages. Thus in Sophocles, we only find one-word fragments, ἐνεκότουν (fr. 1042 Pearson), and another, ἐπίκοτα (fr. 428 Pearson).

In the Euripidean corpus, there is only one instance of κότος (*Rhesus* 827–829). In this solitary case, Euripides continues the meaning of κότος delineated in *Iliad* I.82–83; it is sufficient to say that the context is Homeric, and that using this word is a poetic brushstroke giving the play an archaic color. For both Sophocles and Euripides, κότος has ceased to function as an independent term for anger; for these tragedians—insofar as we can tell—κότος takes on nothing like the elegant structure that Aeschylus crafted for it. That movement from its central place in Aeschylus (following Homer) to its peripheral fate in the other major tragedians marks a pivotal stage in the history of

34 Note the parallel to this formulation at *Eumenides* 314, where the Furies claim that to someone with clean hands, their μῆνις will not approach (ἐφέρπει); see μηδ'... ἐφερπέτω νόσος, at 942.

35 A few passages have been left out of this discussion. I have omitted *Prometheus*, given the current consensus as to its authorship, though the relevant passages are consistent with my findings: *Prometheus* 163 (100–167 choral—Zeus' anger keeping the οὐρανίαν γένναν [165–66] in subjugation), and 602, referring to Hera's κότος. The other instances of Aeschylean κότος—*Eumenides* 800 (Athena warning the Eumenides not to let their κότος free upon Athens) and (similarly) 889—are all also in keeping with Calchas' definition. Moreover, the Eumenides' threat to end κότος mirrors Achilles' wish that χόλος die (*Iliad* XVIII 107–110). Here κότος is linked only to its own destruction, while in Achilles' wish, the end of a different kind of anger (χόλος, *Iliad* XVIII 108, linked to ἔρις, *Iliad* XVIII 107) is tied, powerfully, to Achilles' wish for his own death (*Iliad* XVIII 98). See Walsh 2005:217–219.

this word. By the end of the fifth century the numinous concept of κότος had disappeared from the productive poetic lexicon of ancient Greek tragedy.[36]

Observing the history of a word is one way to drive home that human culture in all its manifestations, perhaps especially in the ubiquitous institution of language, is in a state of flux. Cultural permanence is but a fiction with which members of ephemeral human groups console themselves and tease their subjects.[37] Yet the shimmering and insecure ideas promoted by human discourse have all too real consequences, whether they be styled good or bad. Nietzsche's point in the epigraph that I set at the beginning of this essay is directed at this idea. I close this essay by quoting the context for his assertion about anger:

> Think of institutions and customs which have created out of the fiery abandonment of the moment perpetual fidelity, out of the enjoyment of anger perpetual vengeance, out of despair perpetual mourning, out of a single and unpremeditated word perpetual obligation. This transformation has each time introduced a very great deal of hypocrisy and lying into the world: but each time too, and at this cost, it has introduced a new suprahuman concept which elevates mankind.
>
> Nietzsche 1997:27

For the early Greeks, the understanding of anger as "perpetual," as taking its place among the obligations and loyalties that appear fundamental to human experience, participates both in the fictiveness of human culture and in its "elevation." We do well to acknowledge the specific words that mark these "institutions and customs."

36 For a parody of Aeschylean usage see *Frogs* 844 and Stanford's note. Note the pun in *Frogs* 846.

37 Yes, I am resisting, somewhat reluctantly, Nietzsche's evaluation of cultural permanence as "hypocrisy and lying."

Bibliography

Aly, W. 1906. *De Aeschyli Copia Verborum Capita Selecta.* Berlin.

Anderson, C. 2002. "No Fixed Point: Gender and Blood Feuds in Njals's Saga." *Philological Quarterly* 81:421–440.

Black-Michaud, J. 1975. *Cohesive Force.* Oxford.

Bowie, A. M. 1993. "Religion and Politics in Aeschylus' *Oresteia*." *Classical Quarterly* 43:10–31.

Braund, S. and Most, Glenn. 2003. *Ancient Anger: Perspectives from Homer to Galen. Yale Classical Studies* 32. Cambridge.

Byock, J. 1982. *Feud in Icelandic Saga.* Berkeley.

Clover, C. 1993. "Regardless of Sex: Men, Women, and Power in Early Northern Europe." *Speculum* 68:363–387.

Cohen, David. 1993. "The Theodicy of Aeschylus: Justice and Tyranny in the *Oresteia*." *Greek Tragedy* (ed. Ian McAuslan and Peter Walcot) 45–57. Oxford. Originally published in *Greece and Rome* 33 (1986): 129–140.

——. 1995. *Law, Violence, and Community in Classical Athens.* Cambridge.

de Romilly, Jacqueline. 1970. "Vengeance humaine et vengeance divine: Remarques sure l' Orestie d'Eschyle." *Altertum und jedes neue Gute für Wolfgang Schadewalt* (ed. Konrad Gaiser) 65–77. Stuttgart.

Dindorf, W. 1876. *Lexicon Aeschyleum.* Leipzig.

Fraenkel, E. 1950. *Aeschylus: Agamemnon.* 3 vols. Oxford.

Franklin, S. B. 1895. *Traces of Epic Influence in the Tragedies of Aeschylus.* Baltimore.

Friis Johansen, H. 1970. *Aeschylus: The Suppliants.* Copenhagen.

Garson, R. W. 1985. "Aspects of Homeric Usages." *Phoenix* 39:1–5.

Garvie, A. F. 1969. *Aeschylus' Supplices: Play and Trilogy.* Cambridge.

Gould, J. 1973. "HIKETEIA." *Journal of Hellenic Studies* 93:74–103.

Griffith, Mark. 1995. "Brilliant Dynasts: Power and Politics in the *Oresteia*." *Classical Antiquity* 14:62–129.

Harris, William V. 2001. *Restraining Rage: The Ideology of Anger Control in Classical Antiquity.* Cambridge, MA.

Konstan, D. 2006. *The Emotions of the Ancient Greeks: Studies in Aristotle and Classical Literature.* Toronto.

Lloyd-Jones, H. 1979. *The Libation Bearers by Aeschylus.* Englewood Cliffs, NJ.

——. 1990. "The *Supplices* of Aeschylus: New Date and Old Problems." *Greek Epic, Lyric, and Tragedy: The Academic Papers of Sir Hugh Lloyd-Jones,* 274–275. Oxford.

Miller, I. M. 1990. *Bloodtaking and Peacemaking: Feud, Law, and Society in Saga Iceland.* Chicago.

Muellner, L. C. 1976. *The Meaning of Homeric εὔχομαι through Its Formulas.* Innsbruck.

——. 1996. *The Anger of Achilles: mēnis in Greek Epic.* Ithaca.

Nagy, Gregory. 2000. "'Dream of a Shade': Refractions of Epic Vision in Pindar's *Pythian* 8 and Aeschylus' *Seven against Thebes.*" *Harvard Studies in Classical Philology* 100:97–118.

Nietzsche, F. W. 1997. *Daybreak: Thoughts on the Prejudices of Morality.* Trans. R. J. Hollingdale. Cambridge.

Page, D. L. 1957. *Aeschylus: Agamemnon.* Oxford.

Pearson, A. C. 1917. *The Fragments of Sophocles.* Cambridge.

Podlecki, A. J. 1986. *The Political Background of Aeschylean Tragedy.* Ann Arbor.

Saïd, Suzanne. 1984. "La tragédie de la vengeance." In Verdier 1984:4.47–90.

Sidaras, A. 1971. *Aeschylus Homericus.* Göttingen.

Smyth, H. W. 1971. *Aeschylus.* Vol. 2. Cambridge, MA.

Stanford, W. B. 1983. *Greek Tragedy and the Emotions.* London.

Sullivan, Shirley Darcus. 1997. *Aeschylus' Use of Psychological Terminology: Traditional and New.* Montreal.

Svenbro, Jesper. 1984. "Vengeance et société en Grèce archaïque. A propos de la fin de l'Odyssée." In Verdier 1984:3.47–64.

Thalmann, William G. 1986. "Aeschylus' Physiology of the Emotions." *American Journal of Philology* 107:489–511.

——. 2004. "'The Most Divinely Approved and Political Discord': Thinking about Conflict in the Developing Polis'." *Classical Antiquity* 23:359–99.

Verdier, Raymond. 1980–1984. *La Vengeance: Études d'ethnologie, d'histoire et de philosophie.* 4 vols. Paris.

Walsh, Thomas R. 2005. *Fighting Words and Feuding Words.* Lanham, MD.

Wilson, D. F. 2002. *Ransom, Revenge, and Heroic Identity in the Iliad.* Cambridge.

Watkins, C. 1977. "A propos de μῆνις." *Bulletin de la Société de Linguistique de Paris* 72: 187–209. Reprinted in *Selected Writings* (Innsbruck, 1980) 565–87. Innsbrucker Beiträge zur Sprachwissenschaft 80.

West, M. L. 1990. *Aeschyli Tragoediae.* Stuttgart.

Wierzbicka, Anna. 1997. *Understanding Cultures through Their Key Words.* Oxford.

Winnington-Ingram, R. P. 1983. "The Danaid Trilogy." *Studies in Aeschylus* 55–72. Cambridge. Updated version of "The Danaid Trilogy of Aeschylus," *Journal of Hellenic Studies* 81 (1961): 141–152.

Zeitlin, F. 1992. "The Politics of Eros in the Danaid Trilogy of Aeschylus." *Innovations of Antiquity* (eds. R. Hexter and D. Selden) 203–252. New York.

5

Language about Achilles: Linguistic Frame Theory and the Formula in Homeric Poetics

Charles Stocking

The Formula: Some Theoretical Considerations

Few if any scholars today can deny that the formula is an essential feature of Homeric verse. G. S. Kirk says in the preface to his *Iliad* commentary:

> The whole question of the formular, conventional or traditional component in the Homeric language is extremely important for the exact appreciation of any particular passage, and of course of the whole poem. Something of a reaction is detectable at present from the extreme claims and inconclusive statistics that proliferated after the Milman Parry revolution, but it remains true, nevertheless, that the deployment of a partly fixed phraseology is a fundamental aspect of Homer's style and technique—one that shaped his view of life almost. One can well ignore Homer's "use of phrases" as an ordinary poet's "use of words."
>
> Kirk 1985:xxiii

Kirk rightly asserts that to understand Homer, one must understand his use of the formula. And yet, Kirk also seems to hint that formula studies are in a state of *aporia* with the "extreme claims and inconclusive statistics that proliferated after the Milman Parry revolution."[1] One may wonder to what extent one can have an "exact appreciation of any particular passage" without an *exact* understanding of what the formula is and what it does. One of the major diffi-

I would like to thank Greg Nagy, Paul Kiparsky, Thomas Walsh, and Richard Martin for all their help and input on this project.

1 Parry had originally defined the formula as "a group of words regularly employed under the same metrical conditions to express a given essential idea" (M. Parry 1971:13). The popularity of the formula in Homeric studies may be attributed to the central role the formula played in Milman Parry's oral formulaic theory (for the history of influence and development of which see Foley 1985). Parry's definition has undergone many changes, but no consensus has ever been reached by the scholarly world.

culties in understanding the formula and its function, I think, can be attributed to the implicit assumption of many Homeric scholars that the formula is somehow unique to Homer, or at least to his genre, oral poetry. Some recent and not-so-recent studies in the field of linguistics, however, would indicate that Homer's use of formulae may not be so different from an everyday speaker's use of natural language. At a 1976 conference on statistical linguistics, C. J. Fillmore says about natural language, "an enormously large amount of natural language is formulaic, automatic, and rehearsed rather than propositional, creative, or freely generated" (Fillmore 1976:9). His comments suggest that something similar to the Homeric formula exists as an aspect of language in general, with as much significance as one attributes to the phenomenon in Homeric poetry. Thus a linguistic analysis of the formula, with the aim of gaining some new insights as to how the formula operates in Homer and to what end, seems worthwhile. Fillmore proposed a theory to account for the enormously large amount of formulaic natural language, known today as frame theory semantics. This essay will apply frame theory to the Homeric formula. As we will see, not only is the theory consistent with the way the formula operates within Homer, but I believe it will make for a useful tool in the interpretation of Homeric poetry, as I hope to demonstrate with an analysis of a speech by Achilles at XVI 200–209.

The groundwork for a linguistic frame theory analysis of the formula was first laid out in 1974, at the Ann Arbor Conference in Michigan, by Paul Kiparsky, prior to Fillmore's own work on formulaic language. At the conference, Kiparsky equated formulae in Homeric poetry with the *bound expressions* of ordinary language. Bound expressions are of two types, fixed and relatively bound, which correspond nicely to Hainsworth's (1968) fixed and flexible formulae. Bound utterances are considered to have at least one of three properties: *non-compositional semantics*, *arbitrarily limited distribution*, and *frozen syntax*. In terms of a generative grammar, fixed phrases are ready-made surface structures that can be considered as entries in a lexicon, whereas flexible phrases are defined by co-occurrence, insofar as there is a restriction between lexical items. This is the principle of *non-compositional semantics*, which would call for Homeric formulae not to be entered as individual words, but as formulae, when fixed, or with reference to their co-occurring words when flexible. Cunliffe's lexicon of the Homeric dialect does reflect this principle with regard to word co-occurrences, though fixed formulae themselves have yet to be entered separately.[2] An example of *arbitrarily limited distribution* in English would be the

2 We see this principle in effect with dictionaries of slang. For example in an internet Rap dictionary (www.Rapdict.org) you can find entries such as *around the way* (adj.), defined

phrase *livelong day*, which has no corresponding **livelong night*. An example in Homer of arbitrarily limited distribution is θυμὸς ἀγήνωρ, where ἀγήνωρ is limited only to the term θυμός, in the *Iliad*, and only once used predicatively, even though as an adjective it could theoretically be applied to any number of nouns.[3] The equivalent property of *limited distribution* in flexible expressions in English would be *kick the (blank)*, which may be filled in with more than one word, but limited only to a few. An example of flexible limited distribution in Homer can be found in the phrase (blank) ἔμπεσε θυμῷ, which may be filled in with χόλος or δέος. An example of *frozen syntax* in English would be *foregone conclusion*, the syntax of which would not allow a phrase such as **foregone though the conclusion may be*. The formula θυμὸς ἀγήνωρ also demonstrates relatively *frozen syntax* because it appears almost always in the nominative case at line end, and only once in the dative at *Iliad* XXIV 42, ἀγήνορι θυμῷ. Kiparsky's analysis of the formula as bound expression has two major conclusions. First, Parry's insight about the formula as a means for improvisation in metrical verse may be reconsidered as a special utilization of the formula, not its cause.[4] And ultimately Kiparsky concludes that "the language of oral literature does not differ qualitatively from ordinary language."[5]

Thus, Kiparsky provides us with the first step in our attempt to rethink the formula in terms of language universals. Nevertheless, his account provides us with only a partial understanding of the formula. We are able to classify and identify formulae as bound expressions, based on formulae having

as "From the neighbourhood. *From around the way*—Beastie Boys (No sleep till Brooklyn [1986])." And *being [down] with something* (v.): "Favouring something, thinking the same way. *Howie Tee, are you down with me?*—The Real Roxanne and Howie Tee ((Bang zoom) let's gogo)."

3 This example of arbitrarily limited distribution weakens Visser's nuclear-semantics approach to the formula (1988). While it most definitely seems the case that there are functionally semantic units in Homeric phrases, and prosodic elements as well, it does not seem right to argue that those semantic units must be individual words. In the case of θυμῷ ἀγήνορι, Visser would have to argue that θυμός is the semantically functional unit and ἀγήνορι the prosodic, as he does with the Noun-Epithet formulae. Or he could argue the other way as well. However, there is a case (at *Iliad* XXIV 42) where this formula is used in a violation of Hermann's Bridge. The usage is a clear example of a two-word phrase that is a semantically functional unit, so much so that it is able to violate one of Homer's own prosodic tendencies.

4 Kiparsky 1974:88. As we have seen in the case of the formula θυμὸς ἀγήνωρ, the difference in prosodic shape corresponds to a difference in syntax, and, because of its relation to semantics, syntax outweighs prosody for formulaic variation. Nagy 1974a comes to a similar conclusion about the secondary significance of meter in Homeric poetry, but from a diachronic perspective.

5 Ibid. Bakker 1997 comes to a similar conclusion, though his is based more on stylistic features of ordinary language than on the formal linguistic features that Kiparsky addresses. Fillmore's suggestions would indicate that there may not even be a quantitative difference between oral literature and natural language with respect to the formula.

any one of the three properties listed above. But when Kiparsky discounts ease of versification as the primary cause of the formula, we are left with the question "What motivates the formula?"[6] Following in Kiparsky's footsteps, I suggest we look toward the study of bound expressions and their motivation in the field of linguistics for an answer.

Kiefer provides a general framework that we may use for our "formulaic question," through a pragmatic-semantic approach to bound expressions. Kiefer understands bound expressions to be "stereotypical utterances, which are automatically evoked by certain speech situations" (Kiefer 1996:575). To better define and elucidate this notion, he employs Fillmore's frame theory semantics. The notion of the *frame* was first introduced in the field of artificial intelligence by Minsky, whose original working definition is perhaps the easiest to understand:

> When one encounters a new situation (or makes a substantial change in one's view of the present problem) one selects from memory a structure called *frame*. This is a remembered framework to be adapted to fit reality by changing details as necessary. A *frame* is a data structure for representing a stereotyped situation, like being in a certain kind of living room or going to a child's birthday party. Attached to each frame are several kinds of information"
>
> Minsky 1975:212

Fillmore applies this notion of frame to lexical semantics, arguing that in place of semantic markers,[7] frames should mark all lexical items. He states that "if a language has a lexical item, a part of our understanding of a text containing it is an understanding of the culture or world in which the classifications the word implies are sensible."[8]

According to Kiefer, every general frame has any number of specialized sub-frames, which are defined by a set of subevents, known as a *script*. The script is also a notion that began in cognitive science, an outgrowth of artificial-intellingence studies. A script is a socially stabilized order of events that is derived from a person's experiences (see Shank and Abelson 1977). Kiefer provides the following example of a frame and script:

6 Kiparsky's account of syntactic motivation explains only why variations of particular formulae are used, not why formulae are used instead of propositional phrases.

7 According to semantic markers theory, originally outlined by Katz and Fodor 1964, lexical meaning is comprised of a series of atomic features, such as +Male, +Adult, and -Animate.

8 Fillmore 1976:27. While Kiefer does not entirely subscribe to Fillmore's argument, he does believe frames can be productively applied to the lexical treatment of bound utterances.

Frame: Commercial Transaction
  Sub-frame: Commercial Transaction at the flea market
    script: (A is the buyer, B the seller)
    e1) A stops in front of the stand.
    e2) B makes an offer.
    e3) (i) A is not interested in the offer.
      (ii) A is interested in the offer and asks for the price
    e4) B answers A's question.
    e5) A thinks the price is too high and offers a lower price.
    e6) B makes a counteroffer
    e7) A thinks the price is still too high and offers a price slightly lower than B's last price.
    e8) B agrees
    e9) A pays
    e10) B hands over the merchandise
    e11) A thanks and says goodbye
    e12) B thanks and says goodbye.

Kiefer notes that each subevent may (and some must) be accompanied by one or more bound utterances. More often than not, he argues, bound utterances associated with particular subevents of a frame are semantically transparent, although they often can become shortened and opaque, and can be semantically demotivated.[9] Kiefer also interprets degrees of boundedness, not according to grammatical features but according to the *events* in which bound expressions occur. There are three possibilities for the boundedness of an expression in relation to an event.

1) Bound Expression (Ui) ←→ Event (i)
Here there is a 1:1 correspondence between bound expression and subevent of a given script. In this case, Ui always points to E(i) and hence to the respective frame of E(i). And E(i) always prompts Ui. For example the bound expression "Paper or plastic?" has a one-to-one correspondence with a particular event at a supermarket, where the bag-boy asks which type of bag the customer would like his groceries in. Any use of that phrase in a different event would somehow be making a reference to the event at the supermarket.

[9] This in many ways responds to Watkins's objection to Kiparsky's argument at the Ann Arbor conference that most formulae in Homer are not idioms such as "addled eggs" (Watkins 1974:108–109). Idioms are one subfield of bound expressions, and they share in the three properties of those types of expressions.

2) Ui ←→ {E(i)}

In this case the utterance is associated with a large number of events. And the larger the set {E(i)} the less bound the phrase, and the more restricted the set of events, the more bound the phrase. An example of this relation can be seen in the relatively bound phrase of hip-hop slang, "being down X" which has several manifestations related to different events. The phrase can appear with any subject and in any tense, but when it is "down with that" or "down for that," it is in a situation where the speaker expresses his consent to participate in an activity. Whereas when the phrase is "down with him, her, you, etc." the speaker is making claim to those with whom he relates and associates himself. Hence the less bound a phrase the more events there are to which it may refer.

3) E(i) → {Ui}

Here the event cannot be recovered by the phrase, simply because there are free expressions in a script as well as bound expressions. Ultimately, we may come to understand bound expressions as those utterances that facilitate the fulfillment of a sequence of events according to an individual's cognitive frames.

Frame theory semantics and its application to bound expressions as presented by Kiefer will provide a useful model for understanding the function and motivation of the formula in Homeric poetry. What we see from Kiefer's study is that the central motivation of bound expressions is their ability to reference particular frames. A speaker will use a bound expression to place a person into a particular frame, and the person hearing the bound expression will know what frame he is to be thinking in and with. The same holds true, I believe, for the Homeric formula. In fact, application of this theory unifies several observations and approaches to Homeric language into a single cohesive model.[10]

Let us begin with the notion of the *frame* as it relates to Homeric poetry. Our definition of a frame, to restate, is a data structure for representing a stereotyped situation. This linguistic notion can be found in the term *theme* as it is used in the scholarship of oral poetry. Lord has defined theme as "the groups of ideas regularly used in telling a tale in the formulaic style of traditional song" (1960:68). Gregory Nagy, in *Homeric Questions* (1996), provides a working definition following Lord (1960) of theme as "a basic unit of content." At the Ann Arbor Conference, Nagy also stated that "the theme is the key to all other levels of fixity in oral poetry—including both the formulaic and

10 Both Russo and Edwards in Morris and Powell 1997 hint at what was an impending moratorium in the study of Homeric poetics at the level of formulae. I hope to bring the formula back into view and demonstrate in what ways it is relevant to the more recent studies that have moved past the "formulaic question."

the metrical levels" (Nagy 1974b:274). Calvert Watkins suggests something along the same lines when he writes that formulae are "set phrases which are vehicles of themes. The totality of themes may be thought of as the culture of the given society" (Watkins 1977:9). In Watkins's quote, we see the formula working in the precise same manner as a bound expression, as a vehicle of the theme or frame. Watkins also indicates why themes are significant: because the totality of themes of a given society are equivalent to its culture. Yet perhaps, with an understanding of frames as a *cognitive* phenomenon, we may correct this equation slightly. Themes would not constitute culture for the archaeologist, who is looking at a society's material properties. And so it may be more appropriate to say that the totality of themes may equal the *experience* of a given culture. Thus, a frame may be understood not only as an individual's data structure for an event, but a cultural data structure.[11] These various treatments of theme all stress its significance for poetic composition as a basic thought structure for the poet to work with. That is to say, a stereotyped situation must be represented in the mind of the oral poet for him to perform the poem. We also see in these notions of theme how the formula is in the service of theme. It places the audience within the experience of a culture.

Because a frame is as much a part of culture as it is a part of individuals within that culture, we can have a linguistic understanding of John Miles Foley's appropriation of *receptionalism* (Foley 1985:39–60). Receptionalist theory is a theory of literature in which the role of the "reader" is considered essential to the meaning of a "text," and thus a major factor in its production as well.[12] Foley applies this model to oral literature, where reader becomes audience. As a result he must modify the theory slightly: "We may say that all members of the audience interpret the text according to a shared body of knowledge that is their inheritance" (Foley 1985:45, emphasis added). We may understand this inheritance of the audience to be its *cultural* inheritance. And

11 Watkins's suggestion concerning the oral-poetic theme as constituting culture and its relation to frame theory, I believe, provides a mechanics of "cultural poetics" as it is defined by Leslie Kurke and Carol Dougherty. As they explain, "In a sense, this concept of art as necessarily and profoundly interactive with its social 'frame' inverts (and thereby compliments) Geertz's theoretical model. Geertz teaches us to read ritual as art; the New Historicist would have us see art as ritual," first noting that "archaic texts are often scripts for ritual performance" (Dougherty and Kurke 1998:6). It is not a coincidence that in defining cultural poetics, Kurke and Dougherty employ both terms, "script" and "frame," metaphorically. The metaphors become substantive within frame theory proper. The social "frame," I would suggest, is fundamentally related to the more technical cognitive frame, such that the praxis of art and ritual stem from the same cognitive source. Throughout this essay I will employ the term "cultural poetic frame" as an extension of Kurke and Dougherty's original concept in light of the research in cognitive science and its relations to both art and ritual.

12 For receptionalist theory proper, see Iser 1974.

later Foley uses an analogy from E. H. Gombrich's *Art and Illusion* (1960) to say of the embodiment of this inheritance that "these stereotypes comprise not simply a convenient method of representation but a set of cognitive categories. If the interpretive contract signed by painter and viewer alike is adhered to, both participants are perceiving according to these categories" (Foley 1985:50, emphasis added). Foley draws this conclusion based on the fact that, according to Gombrich, there is an agreement that a pictorial representation of reality is "a transposition, not a copy" (Foley 1985:49). What matters for a person viewing a painting, then, is the internal logic of a painter's work and how well that logic may be understood by the viewer. It is because painting is meant to portray a *virtual* reality that one must employ cognitive categories for representation. And yet even in everyday speech, as Kiefer and Fillmore argue, these cognitive categories are employed. It is not a special feature of art alone, but a basic fact of communication. Frame theory thus accounts for the cognitive categories shared by poet and audience, and it also accounts for the cultural aspect of these cognitive categories. Thus, in the utilization of bound expressions, the poet's aim is to cause his audience to employ particular cognitive categories, which we may better understand as frames. Foley, I think, is exactly correct in his understanding of *how* oral poetry works. However, his model may be difficult to follow because of the twofold appropriation of theories foreign to an oral medium, and thus may lead to unnecessary complications in working out the details. Frame theory does not change Foley's model, but rather streamlines it, and is perhaps a more appropriate conception insofar as it functions within the same sphere as oral poetry, that is, the sphere of verbal communication.

Thus we see how the linguistic *frame* and the oral-poetic *theme* are conceptual equivalents. As Kiefer demonstrated, frames rely on scripts. I turn to Thomas Walsh's work on χόλος to demonstrate how an oral-poetic theme functions like a frame in its utilization of scripts. Walsh states, "This word χόλος is the technical term in the oral poet's vocabulary for the story of the withdrawn hero, who refuses to fight, seeks refuge with a companion, and returns only too late" (Walsh 2005:192) Thus, Walsh argues that the term χόλος does more than make reference to notions of anger, it is conceived of as representing an entire set of subevents. In other words, the term χόλος contains within it a potential script.[13] Fillmore explains that frames and scripts are

13 Walsh also argues that χόλος is the genre of the *Iliad*, as νόστος is the genre of the Odyssey. I will be working with the theme of χόλος and Walsh's suggestion about the *Iliad's* genre later in this essay. It is important to note that the events of a χόλος theme are implied, and are not predetermined. As Walsh himself argues, χόλος, unlike κότος, has no immediate *telos*, though

useful not only for the interpretation of groups of words; often the interpretation of abstract nouns requires a particular script. Fillmore offers the example of *charity*: "We have a schema in which one person gives something to another under the following conditions. The giver is under no obligation to make the gift, the receiver is put under no obligation to the giver as a result of receiving the gift, and the giver believes that his gift will benefit the receiver" (Fillmore 1976:17). The theory thus accounts not only for formulae, but for culturally charged individual words as well.[14]

Whereas Walsh's work demonstrates an implicit application of scripts, Elizabeth Minchin makes a formal application, and she also realizes the cultural implications of the cognitive script:

> I suggest that these so-called themes have been laid down, as scripts, in the memories of aspiring singers long before their apprenticeship. Homer, along with other singers and all members of their audience, would have acquired them in the normal course of living, either through his experience of life in the real world, or through listening to the stories of others. These units are not particular to the repertoire of the singer; they are part of everyone's repertoire.
>
> Minchin 2001:39

Minchin points out that the scripts the poet employs will be just as familiar to the audience as to himself. The aspects of Homeric poetry to which she applies scripts are type-scenes, lists and catalogues, descriptive segments, similes, and

---

it is thought to be short-lived. χόλος has a potentiality, which makes it worthy of an *Iliad*-sized epic (Walsh 2005:197–201).

14 As in the flea-market transaction, the χόλος script is a generalized sequence of events and not the instantiation of any particular sequence. Nagler outlined a similar concept of an arranged, but abstract, order of events, which he called a *motif*: "The pattern . . . identified by these key notions, or elements, is not meant to represent a rigid type-scene, in the original sense of the term; it is a kind of ideal configuration intermediate in abstraction between a much more general impulse (a branch of the 'family,' or subset of the Gestalt) and any particular exemplar" (Nagler 1974:68). He distinguishes his understanding of motif as different from the type-scenes that Fenik 1968 and Arend 1933 describe. Nagler himself also understood a problem with the Gestalt or sphota as being too "mystical." But he prefers to be over-general rather than to "maintain that an *Iliad* was created with a finite number of well-defined formula systems undergoing a limited number of predictable transformations" (14). The notion of frame avoids the potentially infelicitous rigidity of such a formulaic system, which Nagler too was attempting to avoid. But the frame also avoids the imprecision of the "mysticism" involved with ideas of a Gestalt. To return to Nagy's definition of theme, theme is a basic unit of content, and I would add that, as frame, it is the most basic *culturally meaningful* unit. Anything more generalized than the cultural frame would place oral poetry outside of poetry's functional sphere of influence. The notion of frame reflects the basic understanding that oral poetry is culturally anchored.

invocations. In other words, her treatment of the cognitive script deals with the narrative aspects in Homeric poetry. The script by itself, after all, is only conducive to the interpretation of narrative, since the subject matter is the sequencing of events.

Yet scripts are equally applicable to the speeches of Homeric poetry, through the function of the formula as a means of referencing a given script and frame. The notion of formulae as reference is also addressed by Foley, in what he calls the *metonymy* and *traditional referentiality* of the formula: "Traditional referentiality, then, entails the invoking of a context that is enormously larger and more echoic than the text or work itself," and he also states, "Such a process of generating meaning I call *metonymy*, designating a mode of signification wherein the part stands for the whole" (Foley 1985:7). Foley accurately describes the function of bound expressions as they relate to frames, without any reference to frame theory semantics. And yet he deals only with the interaction between poet and audience, and the same may also be said of Minchin. Is it the audience alone that hears the echoic signification of formulae? Frame theory semantics, as a theory of communication, tells us that is not the case, for bound expressions do more than make reference to frames, they help facilitate action.[15]

This relation between speech and action is specifically dealt with by Richard Martin in his taxonomy of speech terminology in Homer, distinguishing ἔπος from μῦθος, the latter term characterizing what may be understood as speech-acts.[16] Martin argues that the individual characters are performers in their own right, through their individual speech acts, and that the whole of the *Iliad* is a speech act of memory. Martin's work on speech-acts has important ramifications for the application of frame theory to Homeric poetry,[17] as it suggests that the general signification of formulae will be the

15 When the person bagging your groceries at the supermarket asks "Paper or plastic?" he is doing more than helping you to situate yourself within a grocery store, he is attempting to carry out the action of bagging your groceries.

16 Martin 1989, chap. 1. Speech-acts are considered to be those statements that simultaneously communicate something and perform an action, beyond the act of communication. For speech-act theory proper see Austin 1962.

17 We see traces of the beginnings of a theory of frames and scripts in J. L. Austin's work on speech-acts. When discussing the possible infelicities of speech-acts, he states, "There must exist an accepted conventional procedure having a certain conventional effect, that procedure to include the uttering of certain words by certain persons in certain circumstances" (Austin 1962:14, emphasis added). The flea-market transaction presented by Kiefer is basically an example of the very phenomenon that Austin describes. That the procedure is *accepted*, according to Austin, indicates its cognitive aspects, and that it is *conventional* indicates its cultural aspects.

same for both the characters within Homeric poetry and the audience hearing the performance. For the audience, the speech-acts of Homer, as the realization of the poetic performance, function as a bond between the generalized subevents of a frame/theme and the surface formulae, which occur within the speech-acts. That is to say, the speech-acts mark major points in the narrative of the Homeric poems, and formulae thus tell the audience what the relation and significance of those speech-acts to the narrative is, by referencing the frame/theme. And within the poem, that same referentiality of formulae to their respective frames is also occurring, but with the primary motive of facilitating some immediate action.[18] As we saw earlier, Minchin observes that the poet's repertoire is the audience's repertoire as well. We may add that such a repertoire also belongs to the characters within the poem.

Thus, I believe frame theory is the model that accounts for the formula most accurately. Not only is the theory native to the medium of oral poetry, but it systematizes and codifies the work of many scholars into a productive model. We may schematize frame theory in relation to oral poetry:

Cognitive Understanding	*Poetic Product*
1) *Frame/Theme*	
2) *Sub-Frame:*	
3) *Script*	
E1	4) ←Speech act → {formulae X/Y/Z . . .}
E2	"
E3	"
E4	"
. . .	. . .

The Formula Sets X, Y, Z . . . may have correspondence in a 1:1 ratio to events in a theme, or they may correspond to multiple events but still only in application to one theme, or to multiple events in various themes. As Kiefer suggested, the number of events to which a formula may apply depends on that formula's degree of boundedness, and Kiparsky's three criteria can be used to determine

18 I realize that this last suggestion may appear to be overreaching. And yet it follows when one considers the nature of semantic meaning applied to works of fiction. If I am watching a movie about a fast food restaurant, and a character working at the restaurant asks "Do you want fries with that?", I will understand the phrase in the same manner as the character placing his order. But that bound expression will have an effect on the character, whereas it will not affect me. And perhaps fries will have a larger significance in the movie, which I will be able to recognize, but the character won't. Nevertheless, basic semantic meaning and the frame to which "Do you want fries with that?" refers will be the same for both the character and the viewer. In narratological terms, we may say that formulae have a strong focalizing effect. What formulae focalize are the virtual experiences of a given culture (see Watkins 1977:9 and Foley 1985:45).

the degree of boundedness. It is important to note that this is not a descriptive model of the formula, but a cognitive model. A frame is a generalized culturally bound notion of an event and others like it. As such, frame theory is able to give an account of both the composition and reception of oral poetry. From Nagy, Watkins, Lord, and others, we see that theme motivates formula; according to Foley, every occurrence of a formula also invokes all other occurrences for an audience. Thus the audience may have a model, like that of the poet, so that for the audience, we may say that formula motivates theme.

A version of frame theory has been applied to Homeric studies before; D. Gary Miller (1982 and 1985) employed cognitive science to formulate a new model of oral composition. Miller primarily relies on the notion of a *schema*, which is more or less equivalent to what Kiefer identifies as a frame. Miller gives a grid, which is very much like the model provided above.

```
                         Schema
Subschema                 //\\
                      /////\\\\\
Formula
```

However, what Miller fails to achieve is the precise relation of formulae to scripts and frames. The last level of his chart, the level of formulae, is the most nondescript. Kiefer's work on the bound utterance allows us to begin where Miller left off. Miller's model, though deeply involved with cognitive science, is still only a model of composition, and the formula has no role greater than as result of compositional need, for Miller seems to understand the formula only in terms of the cognitive processes of composition, rather than in terms of their linguistic manifestation in speech.[19] He argues that the primary function of the formula is ease of versification (Miller 1982:42), and for this reason he objects to Kiparsky's theory. If we understand the formula by the three properties of bound expressions mentioned earlier, then the formula cannot simply be an aid in versification, because what formulae signify is different from what individual words signify. In other words, formulae have special semantic features, which are what cause the poet to utilize them in verse (more so than individual words). Miller claims that "the matter of meaning is 'automatically' incorporated into formulae by virtue of the fact that any

19 Miller 1985:360. Miller understands "formula" to cover any number of "conventions of usage," which include freezes, collocations, etc. One might wonder how productive the term *formula* is under these circumstances. Clearly there would not be any singularly understood function to a formula in this respect. My project is an attempt to understand the formula in relation to speech. And the formula as bound expression seems most useful in that area.

phrase (bound or otherwise) necessarily has a semantic representation" (Miller 1982:40). While this is true, Fillmore shows that there is a difference between the semantic representation of a bound utterance and a regular phrase. Compare for example, the two bound phrases cited by Fillmore:

> "He was *on land* briefly this afternoon."
> "He was *on the ground* briefly this afternoon."

Fillmore explains that "on land" is part of a frame whose other member is "at sea," and "on the ground" is part of a frame whose other member is "in the air" (Fillmore 1976:15). And so we see that bound utterances are specifically related to cultural frames, so that they signify events, facilitate actions, and add cultural value more easily than the equivalent propositional arguments with individual words. In a sense, ease of versification does motivate the use of formulae, but it is a secondary motivation, compared with the cultural-semantic motivation.[20]

The speech of Achilles at *Iliad* XVI 200–209, I believe, provides a unique opportunity for demonstrating how the proposed linguistic frame theory model of the formula works, and that its unique status as a conveyor of cultural-semantics allows it to be a useful tool in the interpretation of Homeric poetry. Like any piece of speech or narrative in the Homeric epics, Achilles' speech contains both formulaic and non-formulaic elements. However, the formulaic elements in Achilles speech appear markedly so, and would indicate that Achilles is aware of both formulaic language and the implications of that language according to frame-theory semantics.[21]

Linguistic Frame Theory Applied: A Language about Achilles

> Μυρμιδόνες μή τίς μοι ἀπειλάων λελαθέσθω,
> ἃς ἐπὶ νηυσὶ θοῇσιν ἀπειλεῖτε Τρώεσσι
> πάνθ' ὑπὸ μηνιθμόν, καί μ' ᾐτιάασθε ἕκαστος·
> σχέτλιε Πηλέος υἱὲ χόλῳ ἄρα σ' ἔτρεφε μήτηρ,
> νηλεές, ὃς παρὰ νηυσὶν ἔχεις ἀέκοντας ἑταίρους·

[20] Is a phrase such as "on land" for the sake of *ease* in speaking about the location of a person who had been, but no longer is "at sea"? It seems first and foremost to be the culturally established way to talk about such a situation, and only because of that fact is it more readily available for speakers.

[21] In other words, Achilles' awareness of the Homeric language indicates not merely that frame theory semantics is applicable to Homeric language (any passage would do for such a demonstration), but that the Homeric poet is aware that Homeric language works as such. Achilles' awareness points to the poet's own awareness, as would be logically consistent with the nature of frame theory semantics.

οἴκαδέ περ σὺν νηυσὶ νεώμεθα ποντοπόροισιν
αὖτις, ἐπεί ῥά τοι ὧδε κακὸς χόλος ἔμπεσε θυμῷ.
ταῦτά μ' ἀγειρόμενοι θάμ' ἐβάζετε· νῦν δὲ πέφανται
φυλόπιδος μέγα ἔργον, ἕης τὸ πρίν γ' ἐράασθε.
ἔνθά τις ἄλκιμον ἦτορ ἔχων Τρώεσσι μαχέσθω.

"Myrmidons, let no one forget the threats directed at me, you, which you made against the Trojans during the whole period of my μῆνις, and each one of you would accuse me, 'Stubborn one, son of Peleus, your mother reared you on χόλος, hard one, you, who hold your companions by the ships though they are unwilling. Let's just go back home again with the sea-faring ships, since evil χόλος has fallen upon your heart.' These things would you say to me thick and fast, gathering together. But now the great work of war shows itself, which you desired before. So let each man fight against the Trojans with a brave heart!"

Iliad XVI 200–209

What makes this speech particularly relevant for a frame theory model of the formula is the fictive quotation Achilles delivers at lines 203–206. We know that this is not an attempt at verbatim quotation because of its generalizing quality. The catalogue of Myrmidons has just been completed and Achilles is giving the rallying cry to his men, allowing them to go to war. Part of his strategy is to recall their previous threats and claims. Mentioning previous threats, as Achilles does, is not an unheard-of rhetorical move in the speeches of the *Iliad*. At VII 96, Nestor rebukes the Achaeans and addresses them as ἀπειλητῆρες. At XIII 219–220, Poseidon, in the form of Thoas, asks Idomeneus, Ἰδομενεῦ Κρητῶν βουληφόρε ποῦ τοι ἀπειλαὶ / οἴχονται, τὰς Τρωσὶν ἀπείλεον υἷες Ἀχαιῶν; ("Idomeneus, council bearer of the Cretans, where do the threats go, which the sons of Achaeans threatened against the Trojans?"), and the same formula of XIII 219 is used at XX 83, where Achilles addresses Aeneas. When Akamas has killed Promachus, he boasts at XIV 479, Ἀργεῖοι ἰόμωροι ἀπειλάων ἀκόρητοι ("Argive Bowmen, untiring in threats"). There are two speech-acts in which the mention of threats or boasts appear, either in rebukes or directives calling for action; the two can but do not have to coincide. Thus Achilles is keeping with traditionally scripted behavior in mentioning threats. However, the threats themselves intended for the Trojans appear to be directed at Achilles, because the Myrmidons are not actually fighting, hence the dative at XVI 200. Coupled with those threats is the complaint quoted at XVI 203–206. The very fact that the verb indicating the quote has ἕκαστος as the subject means that the quotation itself is different in nature from other *Iliad* quotations, such as we find when Odysseus quotes Peleus at IX 254–258.[22] Nestor also uses the same quote technique as Odysseus, when speaking to Patroclus, at XI 786–789. The purpose of these quotations appears to be to add vividness in re-activating the memory of the addressee, or at least that is the rhetorical strategy, for both Odysseus and Nestor, after delivering the quote, say, ὣς ἐπέτελλ' ὁ γέρων, σὺ δὲ λήθεαι ("Thus the old man enjoined upon you, but you forget."). Both quotations appear in directives, where the addressee is not behaving in accordance with the speaker's desires—desires that the speaker demonstrates are rooted in the addressee's own upbringing vis-à-vis quoting the father. Achilles' quotation would seems to have a similar function, to vivify the memory of the Myrmidons' threat. However, what Achilles quotes is not the threat itself, but the attendant complaint to Achilles. In addition to this odd choice of quotation, the quotation itself cannot have the semblance of an actual quotation if it is to be what 'each man' has said.

Unreal quotation is characteristic of one particular speaker in the *Iliad*, Achilles' antagonist, Hector, and yet to a different end. At VI 459–461: καί ποτέ τις εἴπῃσιν ἰδὼν κατὰ δάκρυ χέουσαν·/ Ἕκτορος ἥδε γυνὴ ὃς ἀριστεύεσκε μάχεσθαι / Τρώων ἱπποδάμων ὅτε Ἴλιον ἀμφεμάχοντο ("And someone seeing you pouring forth tears may say, 'This is the wife of Hector, who was best at fighting among the horse-taming Trojans, when they fought around Troy.'"). And at XXII 106–108: μή ποτέ τις εἴπῃσι κακώτερος ἄλλος ἐμεῖο·/ Ἕκτωρ ἧφι βίηφι πιθήσας ὤλεσε λαόν. / ὣς ἐρέουσιν ("Lest a man worse than me should say, 'Hector, persuaded by his own might, destroyed his people.' Thus they will speak."). Since the situations Hector imagines are those of either praise (Book 6) or blame (Book 22) both of which are executed verbally, giving a quotation demonstrates those potential genres of discourse being realized.[23] And yet, unlike Hector's speech, which expresses a potential, Achilles' quotation expresses something in the past.

Achilles' quotation is similar in tense and aspect to the formula used in narrative, τις εἴπεσκεν, of which Hector's quotations are the future-tense version. However, the formula τις εἴπεσκεν is often used with a partitive genitive, "of Achaeans and Trojans." Hence the subject, τις, is a collective pronoun, whereas ἕκαστος is distributive, so that the speech-event, which Achilles

22 Odysseus' quotation also has occurrences of elision absent from Achilles' quotation (IX 255): δώσουσ' αἴ κ' ἐθέλωσι, σὺ δὲ μεγαλήτορα θυμὸν. Including what is an actual linguistic phenomenon of Greek speech makes Odysseus' quote seem all the more plausible. The stylistic elements of Achilles' speech will be discussed shortly.

23 Agamemnon gives a similar boast quotation at IV 178–182.

"quotes," is distributed among all the Myrmidons. In addition, the verb introducing the unreal quotation, ἠτιάασθε, is in the imperfect tense. The distributive subject, coupled with the imperfect verb, indicates that Achilles conceives of the situation as an iterated speech-event, in much the same way as one would conceive of a generic speech act in relation to its script.[24] Because Achilles' quotation is not simply repeating what has been said, nor projecting what will be, it must be re-presenting what has been said, as a projection of speech into the past. Achilles' quotation is a poetic mimesis. As the scholia *ad loc.* reads, ἀπέστροφε τὸν λόγον ἀπὸ τοῦ διηγηματικοῦ ἐπὶ τὸ μιμητικόν. From a stylistic analysis of the quotation, we will see that Achilles' mimesis is filled with conventional formulaic language, part of which is involved with the cultural poetic frame of χόλος, with the result that Achilles is positioning this speech-event within that frame. It is by virtue of the speech's attachment to this frame that it is able to be conceived of as an iterated speech-event in the first place.

> σχέτλιε / Πηλέος υἱὲ / χόλῳ / ἄρα / σ' ἔτρεφε / μήτηρ,
> νηλεές, / ὃς / παρὰ νηυσὶν / ἔχεις / ἀέκοντας / ἑταίρους·
> οἴκαδέ περ σὺν νηυσὶ / νεώμεθα / ποντοπόροισιν
> αὖτις, / ἐπεί / ῥά / τοι / ὧδε / κακὸς / χόλος ἔμπεσε θυμῷ.[25]
>
> *Iliad* XVI 203–206

σχέτλιος

This word is one that contains within it an implicit scripted series of events, which is referenced every time the term is used. σχέτλιος occurs in the first foot of a line twelve of the thirteen times it appears. The word is defined as 'obstinate' (coming from **sche-thlios*; see Chantraine 1968–1980, s.v.) and

24 Tzvetan Todorov speaks of just such a phenomenon; he discusses three types of narratives in relation to the phenomenon of frequency: *singulative narrative*, *repetitive narrative*, and *iterative discourse*. Iterative discourse, he says, is a single discourse which 'evokes a plurality of events" (Todorov 1981:31). Such is the discourse involved in scripts. Todorov comments on the role of iterative discourse in classical literature, but nevertheless undermines its significance.

25 The notation is an adaptation of Richard Martin's notation for his analysis of Achilles' speech in Book 9 (Martin 1989:166–171). Martin had identified two types of formulae, syntagmatic and paradigmatic; syntagmatic formulae consist of metrically fixed and flexible formulae, and paradigmatic formulae are those individal words that frequent a given metrical slot. According to frame theory, there is a need to distinguish between fixed and flexible formulae because flexible formulae may apply to more than one frame, whereas that is not the case for fixed expressions. Thus flexible formulae have a single underline, fixed formulae a double underline, and metrically frequent individual words a dotted underline.

appears only in speech.[26] There are three basic ways in which it is used. First, in conjunction with a relative clause, σχέτλιος ὅς, as part of a characterization or name-calling based on a particular action, where the relative clause contains the action that is the driving force of the speech about the person. In II 112, Agamemnon gives a false directive to go home, calling Zeus σχέτλιος, ὃς πρὶν μέν μοι ὑπέσχετο καὶ κατένευσεν.[27] Agamemnon mentions Zeus, presenting the following logic to his men: "Zeus promised that we'd win, but we're going to lose, so go home." The same exact lines are used at IX 19, where this time Agamemnon is not secretly trying to rally the troops but is sincere about his directive. In fact, II 111–119 are exactly identical to XIX 18–25, the first half of Agamemnon's speech. σχέτλιος is used the same way at V 403, when Dione tries to console Aphrodite and speaks of Diomedes as σχέτλιος ὀβριμοεργὸς ὃς οὐκ ὄθετ' αἴσυλα ῥέζων. And it is used again in a similar manner at VIII 361, although without the relative clause, when Athena complains to Zeus, σχέτλιος, αἰὲν ἀλιτρός, ἐμῶν μενέων ἀπερωεύς. These uses occur toward the middle of a speech.

The second way in which σχέτλιος is used is in direct abuse, rather than for the sake of introducing some other main action. This occurs when Helen has enraged Aphrodite, and Aphrodite responds, μή μ' ἔρεθε σχετλίη, μὴ χωσαμένη σε μεθείω (III 414). And in Book 10, Diomedes rebukes Nestor for having woken him up: σχέτλιός ἐσσι γεραιέ· σὺ μὲν πόνου οὔ ποτε λήγεις (X 164). Lastly, Apollo rebukes the gods for not rescuing Hector's body from Achilles: σχέτλιοί ἐστε θεοί, δηλήμονες· οὔ νύ ποθ' ὑμῖν / Ἕκτωρ μηρί' ἔκηε βοῶν αἰγῶν τε τελείων; (XXIV 33–34).

The third use may be classified under *metri causa*, although it serves stylistic ends as well. In our first group, σχέτλιος introduced an action or characterization essential to the speech, in the second group, σχέτλιος is purely a term of rebuke. In our third type of usage, we find σχέτλιος wedged in between two complete thoughts, where σχέτλιος is structurally and semantically unnecessary to the preceding or following lines. Ajax speaks about Achilles, saying, Ἀχιλλεὺς / ἄγριον ἐν στήθεσσι θέτο μεγαλήτορα θυμὸν / σχέτλιος, οὐδὲ

26 As far as I can tell, this reconstruction is slightly odd, because according to Grassman's law, deaspiration usually occurs with the first of two aspirated consonants. While there are exceptions, they are based on particular consonant clusters, and C + l is not one of them. Still, deaspiration of the second element may be a result of the aspiration in the first element being more semantically and pragmatically significant, as in the case of the aorist passive imperative ending, *-θηθι > θητι, where the aorist passive element is the more salient feature. This may also hold true for σχέτλιος, where retention of the initial aspirate makes it more semantically transparent than would be *σκέθλιος.

27 Agamemnon's speech presents us with a *figura etymologica*, between σχέτλιε and ὑπέσχετο.

μετατρέπεται φιλότητος ἑταίρων (*Iliad* IX 628–630). Here we see a complete thought phrase before σχέτλιος and another directly after. The same occurs when Glaukos rebukes Hector: πῶς κε σὺ χείρονα φῶτα σαώσειας μεθ' ὅμιλον / σχέτλι', ἐπεὶ Σαρπηδόν' ἅμα ξεῖνον καὶ ἑταῖρον (XVII 149–151). From a propositional perspective, removal of σχέτλιος would only cause the meter to suffer. But the enjambed name-calling after a statement seems to add an emotive effect.[28] Achilles says of Patroclus, ἦ μάλα δὴ τέθνηκε Μενοιτίου ἄλκιμος υἱὸς / σχέτλιος· ἦ τ' ἐκέλευον ἀπωσάμενον δήϊον πῦρ / ἂψ ἐπὶ νῆας ἴμεν, μηδ' Ἕκτορι ἶφι μάχεσθαι (XVIII 12–14). Priam also addresses Hector, Πηλεΐωνι δαμείς, ἐπεὶ ἦ πολὺ φέρτερός ἐστι / σχέτλιος· αἴθε θεοῖσι φίλος τοσσόνδε γένοιτο / ὅσσον ἐμοί (XXII 40–42). And Hecuba addresses Hector right after Priam: τείχεος ἐντὸς ἐών, μὴ δὲ πρόμος ἵστασο τούτῳ / σχέτλιος· εἴ περ γάρ σε κατακτάνῃ, οὔ σ' ἔτ' ἔγωγε / κλαύσομαι ἐν λεχέεσσι φίλον θάλος, ὃν τέκον αὐτή (XXII 85–88).

At the most mechanical level, σχέτλιος is merely a means of starting a new line. And yet, the form of address is not void of meaning. It is not socially relevant nomenclature, since mortals apply it to immortals (Agamemnon to Zeus), immortals to mortals (Dione to Diomedes), parent to child (Priam and Hecuba) and comrade to comrade (Ajax, Glaucon, Achilles). Rather, I would suggest that σχέτλιος is a term applied in a particular script. It may be used simply as the first foot of a line for emotive effect, or it may be syntactically connected to whatever thought is being expressed. But it is always used in the same scripted series of events: when someone delivers a directive/rebuke (as a result of not carrying out a directive) because the person in question is behaving contrary to expectation, and this leads to frustration on the speaker's behalf. Achilles' use of the term in the quotation is consistent with its other uses. However, in the case of Book 16, it is the first word of the quotation, which occurs only once else (Book 24). By positioning σχέτλιος as the first word of a mimetic quote, Achilles takes what is a common element of rebuke-directives and uses it as a typological marker for such speeches. In other words, he is establishing conventional modes of speech through the process of mimesis even as the epic progresses.

28 Devine and Stephens, in their discussion of hyperbaton, cite Russian, which can classify sentences as emotive or non-emotive, based on word-order and prosody. "It is natural to associate the high frequency of hyperbaton in the orators with a more emotive style that makes greater use of pragmatically marked word order, and the lower frequency in the historians with a preference for a more detached and analytical style" (Devine and Stephens 2000:59). The position of σχέτλιος does not change within the verse line, however. We see in this third group that it is an interjection and is not syntactically connected to either the preceding or following phrases. Thus, we may say that in these instances of σχέτλιος there is only a pragmatic, and hence emotive, function.

Achilles represents this particular speech type, a σχέτλιε speech, in connection with speeches directed at himself, through the use of the vocative, Πηλέος υἱέ. David Shive considers the string σχέτλιε Πηλέος υἱέ as a single, unique formulaic unit of address (Shive 1987:116). We have already seen that σχέτλιε often occupies the first foot of the hexameter line. Πηλέος υἱέ beginning the second foot occurs as a formula five times in the *Iliad*, three in speech, one in narrative, and one in direct address. Shive mentions three of the examples to demonstrate Homer's favoring a creative rather than economical approach to formulae ending at the feminine penthemimeral caesura: XVIII 18, ὤ μοι Πηλέος υἱὲ δαΐφρονος ἦ μάλα λυγρῆς, where ὤ μοι adds emotion; XX 2, ἀμφὶ σὲ Πηλέος υἱὲ μάχης ἀκόρητον Ἀχαιοί, where he argues the prepositional phrase is unnecessary; and XXII 8, τίπτέ με Πηλέος υἱὲ ποσὶν ταχέεσσι διώκεις, where τίπτε breaks regular word order (although on what grounds he does not make clear). Shive's notes on these three passages are part of his attack on Parry's idea of Homer's "traditional" language. Shive's mistake is the need to consider σχέτλιε Πηλέος υἱέ as a single formulaic unit. Who is to say that the formula Πηλέος υἱέ did not have that very purpose of freeing up the first foot and the rest of the line following the caesura after it, as a boundary marker of sorts? It is significant that Shive notices the first hemistich of XVI 203 as a unique formula; it does seem to have formulaic status. What he failed to notice was the context of this unique formulaic unit. Achilles has constructed the first hemistich of XVI 203 from a scripted lexical item, the significance of which we have seen above, in conjunction with a formulaic form of address for Achilles. In connecting the lexical item and its implied script with the name of Achilles, Achilles connects the generic speech type with speeches addressed to himself, thus suggesting that the speeches addressed to Achilles are part of a certain generic script.[29] That script is part of the χόλος frame.

χόλος

Like the initial address, the first phrase of Achilles' mimetic quotation lacks any degree of boundedness and is comprised of individual lexical items: χόλῳ ἄρα σ' ἔτρεφε μήτηρ. Thematically, Achilles' quote is a speech about χόλος, given that it is used twice in the course of four lines. In fact, the majority of occurrences of the noun are in the two metrical slots that it occupies in this speech, after the feminine penthemimeral caesura and the hephthemimeral caesura, the two most common caesuras in the *Iliad*. A word such as χόλος has

29 It should be noted that all occurrences of this vocative are after Book 16, again making it impossible to suggest that Achilles is simply repeating speech.

a large amount of metrical dexterity; it could appear in almost any spot, and does. However, Tom Walsh has demonstrated the poetic importance of χόλος. The fact that occurrences of χόλος cluster around the caesuras would indicate a confluence of meter and content in the poet's composition of his lines.

The form is unique following the feminine penthemimeral caesura. The only forms found are χόλος and χόλον, both of which are metrically equivalent to χόλῳ, short-long, if followed by a word beginning with a consonant. In this metrical slot, there are only two fixed phrases using χόλος or χόλον: χόλος λάβειν before a bucolic diaeresis at I 387 and VI 166, and χόλον θυμαλγέα πέσσει at IV 513, with variant πέσσων at IX 565. The other seven occurrences of noun forms of χολ- in this spot are individual lexical items, usually filling the rest of the fourth foot with particles such as δέ τε or δέ μιν, or verbs. Achilles' construction following the first hemistich is not unusual as far as formulae and metrics are concerned. But nowhere is it used as a dative of instrument. χόλῳ occupies a primary spot in the line, after a caesura, and is also the first element of the phrase, and so it stresses the innovation of the statement—that he was weaned on bile, as opposed to milk (cf. scholia A: ὑπερβολικῶς οὐ γάλακτι, ἀλλὰ χολῇ). This exceptional form of the noun anticipates how we are to render the verb. Forms of the verb occupy the fifth foot following the bucolic diaeresis only once. Hector speaks about Paris at VI 282: μέγα γάρ μιν Ὀλύμπιος ἔτρεφε πῆμα ("For the Olympian has nursed him as a great pain"). The same grouping of 'pain' and 'nursing' occurs at XXII 421; this time Priam speaks about Achilles: Πηλεύς, ὅς μιν ἔτικτε καὶ ἔτρεφε πῆμα γενέσθαι. In this second example we have a Hainsworth-type formula, a "repeated word group" (Hainsworth 1968:35), or a relatively bound phrase. This flexible phrase, which shares the same metrical placement of the verb, is also similar in sense to Achilles' phrase at XVI 203 and may have had some influence on the construction of that phrase. We see from these other two examples that 'rearing' can have negative connotations, best expressed by Thetis' words to Achilles at I 414: ὤ μοι τέκνον ἐμόν, τί νύ σ' ἔτρεφον αἰνὰ τεκοῦσα; ("My dear child, why did I raise you, bearing you bitterly?"). The last word of the first line of the quotation is a metrically fixed lexical item in the *Iliad*, occurring 42 of 63 times in the final foot, usually in the formula πότνια μήτηρ, τέκε μήτηρ, γείνατο μήτηρ, or otherwise.

And so the elements of this first phrase are attested elsewhere in the *Iliad*. What is significant is that all three major elements, χόλος, τρέφω, and μήτηρ, are associated with Achilles. The majority of the occurrences of χόλος in noun form pertain to Achilles or are used by him. χόλος relates to Achilles 25 of the 49 times that it appears, just over 50 percent, while the other uses are distributed among the gods and some heroes. Cunliffe understands χόλος here to stand for χολή, 'bile', but this does not preclude character association with Achilles. And Thomas Walsh has demonstrated that the term χόλος indicates more than anger, but rather the anger associated with a particular series of events. To restate, Walsh defines χόλος as "the technical term in the oral poet's vocabulary for the story of the withdrawn hero, who refuses to fight, seeks refuge with a companion, and returns only too late" (Walsh 2005:192). And he defines three locations or contexts for this type of anger: 1) contest and challenge (168–171); 2) dispute and quarrel, or νεῖκος (171–175); and 3) the death of a φίλος (175–182). Achilles uses that very same poetically charged word here in a nonconventional manner as far as the *Iliad* is concerned, in connection with his own mother and his raising. In addition, the whole line lacks any degree of boundedness. In this way, Achilles gives a representation of the reworking of a generic poetic frame specifically in light of himself. It appears that Achilles is representing the Myrmidons as seeing Achilles fundamentally linked to this poetic script and frame. If Achilles is being reared on a particularly poetic and culturally significant form of anger, we may ask whose anger. Without a doubt it would be the χόλος of Thetis, the context of which would be Walsh's site three, the death of a φίλος, namely her own son.[30] It is as though the poetic frame of χόλος has been genetically passed on to Achilles, so that Thetis' χόλος becomes Achilles' χόλος and informs the basic plot of the Iliad.[31] Thus, in the first line of Achilles' mimesis, the beginning address, σχέτλιε Πηλέος υἱέ, provides information about the general form of what is said to him. They are directive rebukes. The phrase that follows is unique from a formulaic perspective, but again with elements common in speaking about Achilles, which still reference a particular frame. In his commentary on this quotation, Janko (1992:345) mentions Achilles' sensitivity to Patroclus' charge of savageness, which includes discussion of his mother at XVI 33–35:

> νηλεές, οὐκ ἄρα σοί γε πατὴρ ἦν ἱππότα Πηλεύς,
> οὐδὲ Θέτις μήτηρ γλαυκὴ δέ σε τίκτε θάλασσα
> πέτραι τ' ἠλίβατοι, ὅτι τοι νόος ἐστὶν ἀπηνής

30 For Thetis is forced to marry a mortal and bear a mortal child. For the potential anger and power of Thetis, see Slatkin 1991. Most interestingly, Thetis' χόλος, alluded to only here, is the result of the νεῖκος between Zeus and Poseidon, site 2 of χόλος! The progression of themes from νεῖκος to death of a φίλος in the Thetis story exactly mirrors the progression of νεῖκος between Achilles and Agamemnon to the death of a φίλος with Patroclus. The confrontation between Zeus and Poseidon in Book 15 also has the same formulaic language as Achilles' language in Book 16 concerning his dispute with Agamemnon.

31 Achilles' matrilineal connection and its tragic implications are emphasized most in Hera's response to Apollo in Book 24.

> "Hard one, your father was not the horseman Peleus, nor Thetis your mother, but the gray sea bore you, and the steep rocks, because your mind is unbending."

Janko mentions the accusation of savageness only as the point of comparison, but there is at least one linguistic connection as well.

νηλεές

At XVI 204, Achilles uses the term of address νηλεές. Popularly, the term is an epithet of χαλκός, occurring eleven times as such in the *Iliad*. Most likely based on its use as an epithet, it also applies to ὕπνος, ἦμαρ, ἦτορ, and θυμός. Seldom does the word occur as a term of address by itself, except in Patroclus' speech (above) and Ajax's at IX 632 with hyphaeresis, νηλής. Both these occurrences are in the first foot of the line, and the only other occurrence in the first foot is in Phoenix's speech in IX 497: νηλεές ἦτορ ἔχειν. And so we have the less regular usage and metrical occurrence of νηλεές occurring in other speeches about Achilles and also by speeches from actual Myrmidons, and Ajax as well. The use of νηλεές may be accounted for compositionally because of its earlier occurrence in Patroclus' speech in Book 16 and so would be fresh in the mouth of the poet and in the ears of the potential listeners, a result of D. Miller's "memory chunks" phenomenon. But it seems beyond chance that the other two metrical fits are also in speeches directed at Achilles. In light of its use here, and by Ajax, Phoenix, and Patroclus,[32] we may begin to create a formula set for the χόλος frame, although this is an extension of the proper frame for νηλεές as an epithet of bronze in battle scenes.[33]

XVI 204

The rest of XVI 204 does not have language that is markedly connected to Achilles, but does contain conventional elements. The first is the formula παρὰ νηυσί(ν). It occurs 36 of 49 times before the feminine penthemimeral caesura. There are several other formulae, which include παρὰ νηυσί(ν). One line of particular interest from a compositional view is II 391–393, Agamemnon's threat,

32 Walsh (2002, chap. 10) discusses the three embassy speeches of Book 9 in light of the χόλος. Patroclus' speech in Book 16 is also very much involved with the χόλος theme, as he says at line 30. Many of the formulaic and lexical and formulaic elements of Achilles' quote are common to those speeches. σχέτλιος, for example, is also in Ajax's speech in Book 9.

33 The use of the lexical item in Achilles' quote demonstrates how Homeric language can be creative through its employment of traditional frames.

ὃν δέ κ' ἐγὼν ἀπάνευθε μάχης ἐθέλοντα νοήσω
μιμνάζειν παρὰ νηυσὶ κορωνίσιν, οὔ οἱ ἔπειτα
ἄρκιον ἐσσεῖται φυγέειν κύνας ἠδ' οἰωνούς.

"Whomever I see having gone far from battle, remaining beside the curved ships, for him it will not be possible to escape the dogs and birds."

The phrase μιμνάζειν παρὰ νηυσὶ κορωνίσιν occurs nowhere else, although μιμνάζειν παρὰ νηυσὶ occurs at X 549, about Nestor, and παρὰ νηυσὶ κορωνίσιν occurs at II 297, IX 609, XIX 44, XX 1, XXII 508, XXIV 115, and XXIV 136. Here is a case of a complex formula, composed of two separate formulae but acting as a single constituent.[34] The phrase παρὰ νηυσί(ν) is the kernel of a series of formulae, where the base form is used at XVI 204 as part of a constructed speech. παρὰ νηυσί(ν) also occurs a total of 32 times in speech. Use in speech more than narrative is significant, because in narrative the formula could simply be locating a particular act, and have a purely descriptive function. But within speech, such as in Agamemnon's threat, παρὰ νηυσί(ν) often seems to have an implied antonymy, meaning not 'on the battle field' and not 'at the walls of Troy': ἀπάνευθε μάχης. Thus the phrase παρὰ νηυσί(ν), when used in speech, implies a script much like Fillmore's "on land" vs. "at sea" example. And far from mere description, this small prepositional phrase contains within it the heroic ethic of action. We see this in Thetis' wish that Achilles remain by the ships at I 416, where she speaks of Achilles as αἶσα μίνυνθα, and in Hector's boast at VIII 180–183:

ἀλλ' ὅτε κεν δὴ νηυσὶν ἔπι γλαφυρῇσι γένωμαι,
μνημοσύνη τις ἔπειτα πυρὸς δηΐοιο γενέσθω,
ὡς πυρὶ νῆας ἐνιπρήσω, κτείνω δὲ καὶ αὐτοὺς
Ἀργείους παρὰ νηυσὶν ἀτυζομένους ὑπὸ καπνοῦ.

"But when I am at the hollow ships, let there be some remembrance of the destructive fire, when I burn the ships with fire, and I will kill the Argives beside the ships panic stricken because of the smoke."

The implied script of παρὰ νηυσίν explains why Achilles' companions are presented as ἀέκοντας ἑταίρους; they want to fight.

34 This is a common feature of Homeric formulae, which we can also see in a formula such as κραδίη καὶ θυμὸς ἀγήνωρ, composed of κραδίη καὶ θυμός, which is used in emotive situations as patients, and θυμὸς ἀγήνωρ, which is used as an agent. Both meanings are combined in Ajax's use in his speech to Achilles at IX 635, for he is discussing what action (agentive aspect) one would take who is bereaved of someone near and dear (patient aspect).

Both ἀέκοντας and ἑταίρους frequent their respective metrical slots in XVI 204, but never occur together as such. The oblique cases of the adjective ἀέκων primarily occur in the bound phrase referring to horses, τὼ δ' οὐκ ἀέκοντε πετέσθην, eight of the thirteen times that it occurs in the metrical slot of XVI 204. ἑταῖρος as an individual lexical item here does not so clearly derive from a bound expression. The various forms of ἑταῖρος (excluding the four-syllable dative plural) occur at line end 98 of the 121 times that the noun occurs in the *Iliad*. Nor is the noun attached to any particular formula. There are some formulae in which forms of ἐσθλός, ἔθνος, πίστος are attached to the noun to complete a line after the bucolic diaeresis, but these are few compared to the number of different lines that occur with ἑταιρ- at line end, most of which lack a bucolic diaeresis. The status of ἑταῖρος and its almost invariable position would indicate that the metrical fixity of individual lexical items in a line is not always derived from formulae, as above. Rather, it can have independent status and perhaps be a major keystone in the process of composition.[35] XVI 204 is the only line of Achilles' mimetic speech that does not contain a bucolic diaeresis, and yet what appears to be a stylistic irregularity is in keeping with the conventions of the *Iliad*.

XVI 205

The conventional character of Achilles' mimetic speech comes through most clearly at XVI 205: οἴκαδέ περ σὺν νηυσὶ νεώμεθα ποντοπόροισιν. This line presents overlapping bound formulae centered around the verb. νεώμεθα occurs at II 236, III 283, VII 335, XIV 505, and XXII 392, all in the metrical position of XVI 205, most likely because it allows for a bucolic diaeresis. At II 235–236, Thersites rebukes the Achaeans: ὦ πέπονες κάκ' ἐλέγχε' Ἀχαιΐδες οὐκέτ' Ἀχαιοὶ / οἴκαδέ περ σὺν νηυσὶ νεώμεθα, τόνδε δ' ἐῶμεν ("Oh weaklings, evil reproachable Achaean women, no longer Achaean men, let's go back home with the ships"). Similarly, Agamemnon at III 283, praying to Zeus before the duel of Menelaos and Paris, says ἡμεῖς δ' ἐν νήεσσι νεώμεθα ποντοπόροισιν ("Let us go back in the sea-faring ships)." Achilles does not seem to be referring to either of these speeches, in the way that he may be making reference with νηλεές to speeches about himself. Thersites is most likely using conventional language, especially since Nestor at VII 96 reproaches the Achaeans with the exact same phrase, Ἀχαιΐδες οὐκέτ' Ἀχαιοί.[36] Also at VII 335, Nestor says οἴκαδ'

35 A good example of single words having thematic and compositional significance is the use of ἄνδρα in the *Odyssey*, on which see Kahane 1994. It is also a good example of Richard Martin's paradigmatic formulae (1989).

36 It is interesting that Nestor, the best speaker, and Thersites, αἴσχιστος δὲ ἀνὴρ ὑπὸ Ἴλιον

ἄγῃ ὅτ' ἂν αὖτε νεώμεθα πατρίδα γαῖαν, which contains elements of XVI 205. In fact all the elements of these two formulae occur in a number of combinations with each other. XVI 205 compresses those combinations into a single line. Returning home is also a common theme in the speeches of the *Iliad* as a threat—Agamemnon in Book 2, Thersites in Book 2—and also as a positive sign of release from fighting—Agamemnon in Book 3, Nestor Book 7, the latter most likely the inspiration for the former.

XVI 206

> αὖτις, ἐπεί ῥά τοι ὧδε κακὸς χόλος ἔμπεσε θυμῷ.

The last line of Achilles' quotation has in part the same influence as νηλεές. αὖτις occurs occasionally in the first foot, although it also frequents the second and third feet, which would indicate that its positional appearance is variable and not fixed. What is interesting in this particular line is the fact that αὖτις is enjambed (which occurs nowhere else that it begins a line). Milman Parry discusses three ways in which one verse may relate to a following verse (M. Parry 1971:253). First, a sentence may end with the line, and a new sentence may begin the next line. The second type is when a thought is complete by verse end, but the sentence continues the next verse by adding free ideas through new word groups. This he refers to as unperiodic enjambment, a term taken from Dionysus of Halicarnassus. Finally, a verse can end without the thought completed, in which case enjambment is necessary. Carolyn Higbie adds two more types of enjambment to the list, and she also reclassifies Parry's "necessary" as clausal and suggests necessary enjambment to be those instances when the verb is enjambed, since that is the crucial element in a clause (Higbie 1990:49). Her fourth type is violent enjambment, where there is close connection between the elements that verse end divides. The use of αὖτις by Achilles can be classified as this second, unperiodic, or adding type, given that the previous line could easily make a sentence on its own. Furthermore, αὖτις adds nothing semantically to the previous line, since returning home implies going back. At least here, αὖτις seems to have a purely functional status as line filler. The same appears true for the rest of the first half-line up until χόλος. αὖτις, ἐπεί has a strong phonetic similarity to the common line beginning αὐτὰρ ἔπειτα. Furthermore, the only cases in the quotation of the metrical

ἦλθε (II 216), would use the same formula. This suggests that it is not the content of Thersites' langage that is the problem. As Martin remarks, "Thersites' style deserves no respect because he does not have the heroic martial performance record needed to back up his words" (Martin 1989:111).

phenomena of hiatus and correption occur at the first half of this line with τοι ὧδε. It is significant that there has not been hiatus or correption up until this point. Parry gives an account of hiatus as the desire to express a thought being stronger than the need for metrical regularity (M. Parry 1971:191–196). We may exclude from Parry's generalization any such phrases that originally included a digamma, although that is not the case here. Thus far Achilles has been demonstrating conventional language, what "everyone" says, and so there has been no need to express a thought that has not already been manifested in formula. This first half-line does not seem to express any thought significant enough to require hiatus either. And yet, αὖτις, ἐπεί ῥά seems like a formulaic echoing already. The strain in the conventional language appears to be a result of Achilles' efforts to get to the main concern of this line, the fixed formula χόλος ἔμπεσε θυμῷ.

All three elements χόλος, ἔμπεσε, θυμῷ occur in their metrical slots as individual lexical items, but it is their status as bound phrase that is most important at XVI 206. The entire phrase is used by Phoenix in Book 9: βάλλεαι, οὐδέ τι πάμπαν ἀμύνειν νηυσὶ θοῇσι / πῦρ ἐθέλεις ἀΐδηλον, ἐπεὶ χόλος ἔμπεσε θυμῷ (435–436). It may be the case that Achilles is referring to Phoenix's speech at this point. The formula occurs in a line that Achilles himself heard. However, the formula occurs in various forms throughout the *Iliad*. At XI 155, we have a Hainsworthian word-expectancy formula with the same mention of fire that is in Phoenix's speech: ὡς δ' ὅτε πῦρ ἀΐδηλον ἐν ἀξύλῳ ἐμπέσῃ ὕλῃ. More important are the occurrences of the entire formula in Book 14. First, at XIV 206–207, Hera requests that Aphrodite give her φιλότητα καὶ ἵμερον (198) under the pretext that she is going to resolve the dispute between Oceanu and Tethys: ἤδη γὰρ δηρὸν χρόνον ἀλλήλων ἀπέχονται / εὐνῆς καὶ φιλότητος, ἐπεὶ χόλος ἔμπεσε θυμῷ. And that portion of her speech is repeated when she speaks to Zeus at XIV 300. So the formula broadly applies to all situations where strife is intended to be resolved.[37] While we do not know if the formula is Achilles-specific, it does apply to him and the situation, and Achilles is most likely aware of both these facts. Walsh identifies this formula as "a narrative marker, to indicate the exact moment at which the present situation came to be" (Walsh 2005:133). Thus the two occurrences of χόλος in this mimesis indicate the transfer of this poetically charged anger from mother to son, from past to present. Based on the information presented thus far, the

37 Furthermore, at IV 32 Zeus speaks to Hera with the formula ἀσπερχὲς μενεαίνεις, which Apollo uses toward Achilles at XXII 10. The situation in Books 4 and 22 are similar, since both deal with the sacking of Troy, and as a result there are similar frames involved and hence similar formulae are showing up.

conventional character of Achilles' mimesis is clear. I would suggest even further that Achilles means to employ conventional language about himself. This is evident from the fact that many of the conventional elements, though not all, come from three major characters and their speeches to Achilles: Patroclus, Phoenix, and Ajax. The use of νηλεές suggests most strongly that the mimesis presents more than just formulaic language; it presents formulaic language about Achilles, because as a term of address, it is not the normal usage in the *Iliad*, except as it applies to Achilles. The Achilles-specific conventions are combined with mere conventional formulaic elements, such as line 205, and there are other aspects that are part of both categories, such as the term σχέτλιος and the last formula, χόλος ἔμπεσε θυμῷ. Through his employment of conventional elements in conjunction with his two mentions of χόλος, he achieves two ends. In the first place, we have a mimesis of a generic speech-act, a χόλος speech (which Achilles seems to identify by the term σχέτλιε). Ostensibly, this is a mimesis of the Myrmidons, but this analysis reveals that the language of Achilles' quotation has more similarities with the speeches involved with the χόλος frame than with any specifically Myrmidonic language. The conventional language in Achilles' mimesis reflects a phenomenon of formulae clustering as result of thematic motives, otherwise known as frames. And the fact of mimesis presented within the poem gives us the added bonus of character awareness in such an operation. The second achievement of this mimesis is the intimate connection of this generic speech-act with Achilles' own character, as the address σχέτλιε Πηλέος υἱέ indicates, as well as the phrase χόλῳ ἄρα σ' ἔτρεφε μήτηρ. In presenting the mimesis of an iterated speech-event, of which Achilles is the subject, and the frame of which is χόλος, we see Achilles become a part of the traditional frame. Still, we may wonder and even doubt whether there is any difference between the conventional character of Achilles' mimesis and the conventional character of any other speech in the *Iliad*. One might consider it to be simply a good imitation of speech, without having to draw conclusions about Achilles' special knowledge of how epic language works. This might very well be the case, were it not for the fact that the conventional character of Achilles' mimetic quotation is offset by Achilles' own non-conventional and self-reflexive language in the rest of the passage.

The Language of Achilles, Revisited

The very first line of Achilles' speech, XVI 200, gives us a typological introduction to the activity and quality of this particular speech. As I noted earlier, it is common in speeches to begin by mentioning previous boasts. In fact, there is one other occurrence of ἀπειλάων in its position here: Ἀργεῖοι ἰόμωροι ἀπειλάων ἀκόρητοι (XIV 479). But the conventionality of Achilles' first line stops there. Chantraine notes that nowhere else in the *Iliad* and only once elsewhere in the *Odyssey*, xvi 303, is there a third-person aorist imperative prohibition (Chantraine 1953:231). Achilles is thus in one respect "generating grammar." The aorist imperative prohibition is necessary in achieving the generic subject, μή τις . . . ἕκαστος, which will be the object of his mimesis. The verb that takes this unprecedented form is λανθάνω. Although the form of the verb is unattested elsewhere, forms of λανθάνω do occur in the last foot and a half of the hexameter line, such as λανθάνοντο (IV 127), and ἐκλελαθέσθαι (VI 285). The verb is especially apropos to the mimesis that follows. λανθάνω is a rhetorical device regularly employed when calling someone to action. And we see the rhetorical use of the verb as a result of what appears to be a deep-structure connection between action and forgetting.[38] For forgetting may also be the pointed effect of blame speech acts, as Hector claims at XXII 281–282: ἀλλά τις ἀρτιεπὴς καὶ ἐπίκλοπος ἔπλεο μύθων, / ὄφρά σ' ὑποδείσας μένεος ἀλκῆς τε λάθωμαι. And forgetfulness is the effect that death ultimately brings, as the description of the dead Cebriones indicates at XVI 775–776. While forgetting and fighting seem to be fundamentally linked within the action of the poem, forgetting and speech are also fundamentally linked, as we see with Nestor's speech from XI 786–789 (above).[39] The work of Miller and Minchin has shown the importance of memory in frame theory and how this may apply to composition, through the abstract frame and cognitive script (Miller 1985:354–371; Minchin 2001:11–31). In light of the linguistic application of frame theory, I think we can account for the two classes of objects that λανθάνω takes in Homer.[40] Kiefer demonstrates that there is a correspondence between speech-acts and events in a script. Thus, by metonymy, forgetting a particular speech, as Achilles does (Book 9) and as Patroclus does (Book 11), entails the forgetting of an entire script, which, in a

38 Collins 1998 traces this relationship between action and forgetting in light of ἀλκή.

39 For Nestor and poetic memory, see Dickson 1995.

40 To my knowledge, a full analysis of the verb λανθάνω, and its subjects and objects, has not been done, though the results I think could tell us very much about the nature of Homeric poetry and its thematic issues.

heroic context, would indicate proper paths of behavior. The cognitive frame as cultural tradition not only helps in the telling of stories, but in the culture depicted within the narrative, particular scripts may have a prescriptive function. Thus, when Cebriones is described as having forgotten his horsemanship, his death marks his disengagement from the culture of which he was a part, and the scripted action in which he participated as a part of that culture. When, in Book 11, Nestor makes that accusation of forgetting to Patroclus, he asserts that Patroclus has gone through the same process of disengagement. The verb λανθάνω, however, appears nowhere else in the *Iliad* with ἀπειλή or its derivatives, though the effect of other speeches may indicate precisely that semantic relationship. Still, the threat itself is something different from strength, or from horsemanship. To warn against forgetting one's threat may be the equivalent of the bound phrase "put your money where your mouth is." But an ἀπειλή is also a genre of discourse itself (Martin 1989:65–77), and as such there are two implications for Achilles' warning not to forget one's threat. First, Achilles is repositioning his men in the proper frame and event to which threat speech-acts belong, battle. And yet to warn against forgetting one's boasts is also to warn against forgetting one's power as a speaker, a power that Achilles then demonstrates.[41]

μῆνις

The cultural-poetic awareness with which Achilles might be operating suggests itself most strongly in the first hemistich of XVI 202, πάνθ' ὑπὸ μηνιθμόν. The phrase is noted by Leaf as yet another "linguistic peculiarity" of the passage, since ὑπό + acc. with a temporal sense is used only at XXII 102 in narrative. Scholia A sees this as one possibility, the other being that μετὰ πάσης μήνιδος καὶ χόλου was meant, although this appears an entirely unheard of use of ὑπό. Eustathius uses the phrase as a temporal referent to situate the narrative, indicating that the rage was sixteen days long. What we may infer from Eustathius' observation is that Achilles' mention of the rage is what ends the time of his rage. The word in question, μηνιθμόν (from the verb μηνίω and cognate with μῆνις),[42] occurs only in Book 16: once at lines 61–62, where Achilles responds to Patroclus: ἀσπερχὲς κεχολῶσθαι ἐνὶ φρεσίν· ἤτοι ἔφην γε / οὐ πρὶν μηνιθμὸν καταπαυσέμεν "([it is not possible] to have unending χόλος in the mind, although I said before, that I would not stop the μηνιθμόν"). And

41 This possible division between event/action and speech shows up later (XVI 626–631).

42 The exact etymology for μῆνις is not clear. Schwyzer 1931 had originally proposed **mnanis*, a derivative from the root **mna-*. Chantraine considers the etymology impossible to ascertain.

again at XVI 281–282; this time the narrator speaks: ἐλπόμενοι παρὰ ναῦφι ποδώκεα Πηλεΐωνα / μηνιθμὸν μὲν ἀπορρῖψαι, φιλότητα δ' ἑλέσθαι ("[The Trojans] expecting that the son of Peleus had left his anger beside the ship, and taken up friendship)." Leonard Muellner cites these examples in Book 16 as the "polar opposite of Achilles' withdrawal" (Muellner 1996:135) in Book 1. Achilles' use at XVI 61 seems to be an overt reference to his response to Ajax at IX 650–655, but in language that echoes IX 517–518, where Phoenix says, οὐκ ἂν ἔγωγέ σε μῆνιν ἀπορρίψαντα κελοίμην / Ἀργείοισιν ἀμυνέμεναι χατέουσί περ ἔμπης.[43] While μῆνις is not exclusive to Achilles,[44] μηνιθμόν and its associations with the μῆνις of Book 9 are specifically Achillean. The thematic character and connection of μηνιθμόν and μῆνις to Achilles are what allow for it to be an adverbial time marker. The infix *-mo-* of μηνιθμόν, according to Chantraine (1968:137), has an IE origin and is used in nouns indicating action derived from a verb, in this case μηνίω. Because the action form of the noun μηνιθμόν only applies to Achilles, the action has certain entailments, namely the withdrawal of Achilles in Book 1, mentioned by Muellner. The relation of μῆνις to action indicates that it functions as a frame, much like χόλος. Nagy was the first to suggest that μῆνις was the name of a theme in oral poetry (Nagy 1979:72–73). Muellner takes up Nagy's suggestion with an in-depth analysis to understand the narrative "action" that the theme implies; as he says, μῆνις "is not separate from the action it entails."[45] μῆνις through its reference to narrative action functions in the precise same manner as a frame. This narrative action to which μῆνις refers is linguistically included in the form μηνιθμόν and refers specifically to Achilles' own action, although it is without a possessive, thus indicating the strong, and in this case exclusive, connection between cultural poetic frames and the figure of Achilles. At XVI 202, Achilles is not simply referring to his previous claim in Book 9, nor is this a formulaic or grammatically regular use of μῆνις/μηνιθμόν, but it appears that Achilles has the same formal understanding of *his* rage as does the poet.[46]

43 Watkins 1977 cites this example of μῆνις as the only example of the word spoken by a mortal. The uses of its cognate in Book 16 he considers as intentional avoidance of the actual word.

44 Following a long debate about to whom μῆνις may refer, Muellner says that "only gods and heroes have μῆνις" (Muellner 1996:127n69).

45 Muellner 1996:8. Many of Muellner's observations on μῆνις work within the same sphere as χόλος, and there might not be a clear-cut distinction between the two even to the Homeric poet. In Achilles' response to Patroclus (XVI 61), he uses variant forms of both χόλος and μῆνις.

46 Achilles' use of μηνιθμόν demonstrates the confluence of primary and secondary focalizers within the *Iliad*, a phenomenon that Richard Martin recognized in his analysis of Achilles' speech in Book 9: "The similarity [between Achilles and poet] arises because Homer, when he

XVI 207

After Achilles has delivered his mimetic speech, he concludes with ταῦτά μ' ἀγειρόμενοι θάμ' ἐβάζετε. Both the form and position of ἐβάζετε are entirely irregular. *Baz-* appears as βάζεις twice and βάζειν once, and only at verse end. To even talk about the unprecedented mimetic speech act, Achilles must use unprecedented language. The adverb θάμα also reveals Achilles' implicit accusation of 'each man's' conventional speech. The adverb itself is related to the adjective θαμέες which Cunliffe glosses as 1) "standing close together"; 2) "flying, falling coming thick and fast"; 3) "occuring at short intervals over a space." The adjective always refers to some concrete object: pyres, arrows, people, etc. The adverb appears only once elsewhere in the *Iliad*, at XV 470, and even there it is in reference to arrows: ὄφρ' ἀνέχοιτο θαμὰ θρῴσκοντας ὀϊστούς. The uses here are in the same metrical slot, but Achilles' use of the adverb to refer to speech, rather than some physical object, is entirely innovative in our text. The metaphorical extension of this adverb is consistent with Cunliffe's third definition, "occurring at short intervals," since he imagines an iterated speech event. By depicting the Myrmidons' language as an iterated speech event, and one with markedly conventional language, it appears that Achilles is making an argument for their conventional-formulaic language, and by extension, their conventional thought (given that language relates to cultural frames). We may ask: why doesn't Achilles just come out and say, "you speak so conventionally about me"? Is he straining for words that the Homeric world cannot provide?[47] Perhaps this is the case. But the lack of abstract language provides an added bonus. Because we are dealing with speech, the demonstration is far more powerful than an abstract claim. Not only does Achilles make the argument, but he backs it up with his own verbal prowess.

XVI 208–209

As the next few lines show, however, the agonistic poetics implicit within the passage are not the major purpose of the speech. Our attention is focused

constructs Achilles by means of language, employs all his poetic resources and stretches the limits of his formulaic art to make the hero as large a figure as possible. In short, the monumental poem demands a monumental hero; the language of epic, pressed to provide speech for such a man, becomes the 'language of Achilles'" (Martin 1989:223). The crossover in language from poet to character, which is all the more plausible when formulae are considered cultural mechanisms of communication, will necessarily conflate the two worlds, actual and represented, in performance.

47 This is Adam Parry's argument in his famous essay "The Language of Achilles" (1956), reprinted in A. Parry 1989:1–7.

away from the speech back to the present with the phrase νῦν δὲ πέφανται, which follows a bucolic diaeresis. From this point on, the speech is more or less conventional in its formulae, coinciding with the conventionality of the speech act, a call to battle. Still, the formulaic oddities are not entirely eliminated. πέφανται occurs three other times after a bucolic diaeresis, all in speeches calling troops to battle. At II 122 Agamemnon calls them to battle by feigning a desire to return, and at V 531 and XV 563 Ajax rallies the troops: αἰδομένων δ' ἀνδρῶν πλέονες σόοι ἠὲ πέφανται. *Fain-* + μέγα ἔργον in the next line is a relatively bound formula. The phrase appears at XI 734 (ἀλλά σφι προπάροιθε φάνη μέγα ἔργον Ἄρηος), and at XII 416 (τείχεος ἔντοσθεν, μέγα δέ σφισι φαίνετο ἔργον). Both other uses have a narrative context: in the former, it is Nestor narrating his adventure, in the latter, it is simply the narrator. Thus, there are formulaic and metrically regular lexical elements up until the first hemistich of XVI 208.

After the hemistich, linguistic irregularities arise again. As Achilles mentions his men's speech, it appears as though the conventional language fails. As Janko's commentary tells us, ἕης is an artificial form for ἧς, by analogy with ὅου (from *ὅο) and the possessive ἕος / ὅς. The only motivation for such an analogy would be metrical fit. Furthermore, ἐράασθε appears to be an improvised thematic form of the older athematic ἔραμαι. Here it seems that Achilles (or the poet, as the distinction blurs in this passage) analogizes from other words ending the verse, such as ἀγοράασθε (II 337), ἠγοράασθε (VIII 230), μητιάασθε (XXII 174), and εἰσοράασθε (XXIII 495), which are four of the five thematic uncontracted second-person plural mediopassive endings in the entire *Iliad*, outside of this speech. The diectasis represents the older form, when the contacted theme vowel becomes opaque. Such a form would be in mind given that the suffix shows up just a few lines above, in ἠτιάασθε at XVI 202. Finally, the last line of Achilles' speech, ἔνθά τις ἄλκιμον ἦτορ ἔχων Τρώεσσι μαχέσθω, is comprised of entirely formualic elements. As would be expected, a common event necessarily has certain attendant bound expressions. This is the call to battle, upon which everything else in Achilles' speech is predicated.

And so we see the conventional character of Achilles' mimetic speech, which includes part of a formula set for the χόλος frame, and on the whole Achilles conscientiously refers to that frame, as the source for the Myrmidon's conventional language. And this is offset by his own nonconventional language within the speech. Yet typologically the speech is entirely conventional, as the last line, the culmination of the speech, indicates. Why then is the mimetic speech present? To characterize Achilles? It most definitely does show him to be on a verbal par with the poet(s) of the *Iliad*. And yet characterization would not explain why the mimesis appears where it does. To answer this question, we need to think in terms of the narrative. In Book 16, Patroclus essentially presents us with the Second Embassy. Achilles abandoned the Argives; Agamemnon, inspired by Nestor, sends an embassy to bring him back; Achilles wholly rejects them; Nestor inspires Patroclus to get Achilles to join; Achilles agrees to send Patroclus in his place: a partial acceptance. And as we have seen, an overwhelming majority of the formulae involved in this speech point us back toward Book 9, but are fundamentally linked to the traditional, cultural poetic χόλος frame. Because of the metonymic connection these formulae have to the larger frame, by way of speech-acts, the speeches themselves, when employing traditional formulae, help in performing traditional scripts. The speeches themselves become a means of acting in accordance with tradition. This, I think, is what Adam Parry was attempting to explain in his famous article "The Language of Achilles," when he discusses "the common language." He says, "The unity of experience is thus made manifest to us by a common language. Men say the same things about the same things, and so the world to them, from its most concrete to its most metaphysical parts, is one." And later he adds, "For the language of society is the way society makes things seem" (A. Parry 1989:4–5). Martin correctly demonstrates that there is not necessarily a 1:1 ratio between signifier and signified (Martin 1989:152). That connection is only made possible in speech through the cultural frame and the bound expressions or formulae, which are mechanisms for cultural frames. And so characters participate in the younger Parry's notion of a "unified world," what we may call the *Iliad's* representation of Tradition, through their employment of frames. Achilles, on the other hand, imitates that very participation. For Achilles, the mimesis of his men's conventional speech-behavior allows him to go through the motions, to take part in their traditionality, to accede to it, while still keeping himself at one degree of separation.

But why is he so recalcitrant in simply giving over to the traditional script, which has become so intimately connected with him through the speeches of various characters? Unlike any other heroic figure who might participate in the same script, Achilles' return determines his death, as he explains to Odysseus at IX 412–413. This choice is particular to the character of Achilles and not part of the generic χόλος frame. Achilles' separation, as it is presented through the eyes of various characters within this frame, has particular significance for him, because his separation keeps him alive. From an audience perspective, the figure of Achilles raises the stakes in the χόλος frame. But from the perspective of Achilles and other characters, the application of this generic frame downplays his unique status and situation. Characters such as Ajax, Odysseus, Phoenix, and Apollo view Achilles in a traditional and generic cultural poetic frame, and while the frame applies to Achilles, it is *not* who he *is*.[48] This other side, the Achilles who exists outside the generic cultural poetic frame, is only brought to attention by Hera in her response to Apollo's attack on Achilles (XXIV 56–63). In Achilles' defense, she mentions two "facts": that Achilles, unlike Hector, is part immortal, and that Apollo himself was present at the wedding of Thetis and Peleus. Laura Slatkin has demonstrated the true significance of Thetis' marriage to a mortal (Slatkin 1991). She brings to bear the story of Thetis in Pindar *Isthmian* 8.29–38, which tells how Zeus and Poseidon wanted to marry Thetis, but Themis reported that the son of Thetis would be stronger than his father. With this knowledge, Zeus exclaims:

> . . . ‘ἀλλὰ τὰ μέν
> παύσατε· βροτέων δὲ λεχέων τυχοῖσα
> υἱὸν εἰσιδέτω θανόντ’ ἐν πολέμῳ,
> χεῖρας Ἄρεΐ <τ’> ἐν-
> αλίγκιον στεροπαῖσί τ’ ἀκμὰν ποδῶν.’
>
> "But stop these things, let her have a mortal marriage bed and watch her son die in war, with Ares-like hands, and feet like lightning flashes."
>
> Pindar *Isthmian* 8.35a–37

Thus, it is in his connection to Thetis that Achilles has a heightened status, outside of the traditional χόλος frame and script. Nevertheless, he must accede to the culturally scripted series of events, as he states in XVI 60–62:

> οὐδ’ ἄρα πως ἦν
> ἀσπερχὲς κεχολῶσθαι ἐνὶ φρεσίν· ἤτοι ἔφην γε
> οὐ πρὶν μηνιθμὸν καταπαυσέμεν . . .
>
> Indeed, it was not at all possible to have raged endlessly in my heart, although I said I would not stop my anger . . .

In the course of two lines he refers to the two most poetically charged words of the *Iliad*, both of which exist as cultural scripts, in reference to his own activity and the impossibility of maintaining separation. Examination of the "embassy speeches," which I consider to be more than simply those of Book 9, will make clear Achilles' gradual accession to this traditional script.

48 Although the poetic mimesis says as much when it claims, "your mother reared you on χόλος."

Walsh, I think, is correct to see χόλος as the genre of the *Iliad*. Recalling the script that this word entails one last time, it is "the story of the withdrawn hero, who refuses to fight, seeks refuge with a companion, and returns only too late" (Walsh 2005:192). In this respect, the embassy is not a necessary feature of the story, and therefore is a means by which to expand the story. I consider an embassy speech to be any speech that employs the same formulae (some of which appear in Achilles' mimesis, although there are more parallelisms in the Book 9 speeches), intended for the same effect, to have Achilles behave in accordance with the Achaean society's expectations.[49] As I see it, there are in fact three sets of embassy speeches in the *Iliad*. The first set is in Book 9, the second set is Nestor's speech to Patroclus and Patroclus' subsequent speech to Achilles, and the third set is Apollo's speech to the gods, which results in Thetis carrying Zeus' orders to Achilles.[50] And we can see that Achilles' responses to each speech and set of speeches is progressively shorter and more accommodating. In Book 16, the middle set of embassy speeches, we see him halfway between total refusal to accept and complete acquiescence, and the mimetic speech reflects this position through his quasi-participation in the traditional scripts of the Achaean society. By Book 24, he must give in entirely, though reluctantly, to the traditional cultural frames of the *Iliad*, and none other than his own mother, the reason for his unique existence, is the one to deliver this news. In Achilles' response to Thetis, there is no sign of their intimate connection, only two impersonal lines:

> τῇδ' εἴη· ὃς ἄποινα φέροι καὶ νεκρὸν ἄγοιτο,
> εἰ δὴ πρόφρονι θυμῷ Ὀλύμπιος αὐτὸς ἀνώγει.
>
> "So be it, may he who brings the ransom, take away the corpse, if the Olympian himself, by his own urging commands."
>
> *Iliad* XXIV 139–140

It is only with Achilles' acceptance of the traditionally scripted behavior that the *Iliad* is able to come to its conclusion.[51]

49 Donna Wilson employs Bourdieu's term "symbolic violence" in discussing the embassy of Book 9, and she explains,"The embassy speeches recast Agamemnon's ἄποινα typologically, bringing them into exchanges conventional among φίλοι" (Wilson 1999:143).

50 There are a great number of formulaic parallels between the Ajax and Apollo speeches, one of which is the term σχέτλιος, also seen in Achilles' mimetic speech.

51 Donna Wilson suggests that the mention of ἄποινα here evokes his initial rejection of that offered initially by Agamemnon (Wilson 2002:128). Achilles' indifference thus marks a defeat of his larger purpose. As Wilson says, "What Achilleus had wanted, that is, to identify with his divine self and to attain universal dominance, has been unequivocally denied him" (130).

Formulaic studies have ceased to occupy Homeric scholars' central interest, but I maintain that the formula is just as significant to Homeric poetry as Milman Parry had originally argued, only on different grounds. As we have seen, Kiparsky established that the formula is a linguistic phenomenon akin to *bound expressions*. Understanding the formula in this light requires a complete hermeneutic methodology, which we find in frame theory semantics, as it has been defined by Fillmore and refined by Kiefer. Frame theory is able to combine the work of a number of Homeric scholars into a single cohesive model, which can produce fruitful results for the reading and interpretation of Homeric language. Achilles' mimetic quotation and the prevalence of χόλος within that quotation provide excellent evidence for frame theory as operative within Homeric poetry. What we see at work within the *Iliad* is a particular traditional cultural poetic frame becoming intimately connected with the figure of Achilles, so much so that he becomes a generic element in the frame. Thus a frame theory model of the formula allows us to see a "language about Achilles" developing in the *Iliad*.

Bibliography

Austin, J. L. 1962. *How to Do Things With Words*. Oxford.

Bakker, E. 1997. *Poetry in Speech*. Ithaca.

Chantraine, P. 1953. *Grammaire homerique*. Paris.

——. 1968. *La formation des noms en grec ancien*. Paris.

——. 1968–1980. *Dictionnaire étymologique de la langue greque*. Paris.

Collins, Derek. 1998. *Immortal Armor: The Concept of Alke in Archaic Greek Poetry*. Lanham, MD.

Cunliffe, R. A. 1963 [1924]. *Lexicon of the Homeric Dialect*. Norman, OK.

Devine, Andrew, and Stephens, Laurence. 2000. *Discontinuous Syntax: Hyperbaton in Greek*. New York.

Dickson, K. 1995. *Nestor: Poetic Memory in Greek Epic*. New York.

Dougherty, Carol, and Kurke, Leslie. 1998. "Introduction." *Cultural Poetics in Archaic Greece: Cult, Performance, Politics* (eds. Carol Dougherty and Leslie Kurke) 1–14. Oxford.

Fillmore, C. J. 1976. "The Need for a Frame Semantics within Linguistics." *Statistical Methods in Linguistics* (ed. Hans Karlgren) 5–29. Stockholm.

Foley, J. M. 1985. *Oral Formulaic Theory and Research*. New York.

——. 1991. *Immanent Art*. Bloomington, IN.

Gombrich, E. 1960. *Art and Illusion*. New York.

Hainsworth, J. B. 1968. *The Flexibility of the Homeric Formula*. Oxford.

Higbie, C. 1990. *Measure and Music*. Oxford.

Hymes, D. 1962. "The Ethnography of Speaking." *Anthropology and Human Behavior (eds. Thomas Gladwin and William C. Sturtevant)* 13–53. Washington.

Iser, W. 1974. *The Implied Reader*. Baltimore.

Janko, R. 1992. *The Iliad: A Commentary*. Vol. 4. Cambridge.

Kahane, A. 1994. *The Interpretation of Order*. Oxford.

Kiefer, F. 1996. "Bound Utterances." *Language Sciences* 18.1–2:575–597.

Kiparsky, P. 1974. "Oral Poetry: Some Linguistic and Typological Considerations." *Oral Literature and the Formula* (eds. Benjamin A. Stolz and Richard S. Shannon III) 73–106. Ann Arbor.

Kirk, G. S. 1985. *The Iliad: A Commentary*. Vol. 1. Cambridge.

Lord, A. B. 2000. *The Singer of Tales*. Cambridge, MA.

Martin R. P. 1989. *The Language of Heroes*. Ithaca.

Miller, D. G. 1982. *Homer and the Ionian Epic Tradition*. Innsbruck.

——. 1985. "Towards a New Model of Formulaic Composition." *Comparative Research on Oral Traditions* (ed. J. M. Foley) 351–393. Columbus, OH.

Minchin, E. 2001. *Homer and the Resources of Memory*. New York.

Morris, Ian, and Powell, Barry, eds. 1997. *A New Companion to Homer*. Leiden.

Muellner, L. 1996. *The Anger of Achilles*. Ithaca.

Nagler, M. 1974. *Spontaneity and Tradition*. Berkeley.

Nagy, G. 1974a. *Comparative Studies in Greek and Indic Meter.* Cambridge, MA.

———. 1974b. "Formula and Meter." *Oral Literature and the Formula* (eds. Benjamin A. Stolz and Richard S. Shannon III) 239–260. Ann Arbor.

———. 1979. *The Best of the Achaeans*. Baltimore.

Parry, A. 1989. *The Language of Achilles and other Papers*. Ed. H. Lloyd-Jones. Oxford.

Parry, M. 1971. *The Making of Homeric Verse: The Collected Papers of Milman Parry*. Ed. A. Parry. Oxford.

Shank, Roger, and Abelson, Robert. 1977. *Scripts, Plans, Goals and Understanding: An Inquiry into Human Knowledge Structures*. Hillsdale, NJ.

Shive, D. 1987. *Naming Achilles*. Oxford.

Slatkin, L. 1991. *The Power of Thetis*. Berkeley.

Todorov, Tzvetan. 1981. *Introduction to Poetics*. Trans. Richard Howard. Minneapolis.

Visser, E. 1988. "Formulae or Single Words? Towards a new Theory of Homeric Verse Making." *Wurzburger Jahrbucher fur die Alterumswissenschaft* 14:21–37.

Walsh, T. R. 2005. *Feuding Words and Fighting Words: Anger and the Homeric Poems*. Lanham, MD.

Watkins, C. 1974. "Response to Kiparsky." *Oral Literature and the Formula* (eds. Benjamin A. Stolz and Richard S. Shannon III) 107–111. Ann Arbor.

———. 1977. "Apropos *Menis*." *Bulletin de la Societe Linguistique de Paris* 72:187–209.

———. 1995. *How to Kill a Dragon: Aspects of Indo-European Poetics*. Oxford.

Wilson, Donna F. 1999. "Symbolic Violence in *Iliad* Book 9." *Classical World* 93.2:131–147.

———. 2002. *Ransom, Revenge, and Heroic Identity in the Iliad*. Cambridge.

6

Skillful Symposia: *Odyssey* ix, Archilochus Fr. 2 West, and the Οἶνος Ἰσμαρικός

Timothy Pepper

The Origins of Objects

Though the names and origins of characters tend to receive much attention, the identities and origins of named objects often do not. A good case in point is οἶνος Ἰσμαρικός, 'Ismaric wine', which is mentioned by name only twice in extant ancient literature before the first century BCE—in *Odyssey* ix and Archilochus fr. 2 West.[1] In the second of these two, commentators seem to be interested more in the grammatical relation of the wine to ἐν δορί or to the presumed mechanics of hoisting it in a knapsack than in the reasons for its being identified as "Ismaric." The rubric of "allusion"—of Archilochus alluding to Homer—has usually been used as sufficient justification to pass over the issue with little comment, though we have absolutely no evidence that Archilochus had a *text* of Homer to consult rather than a familiarity with a more fluid tradition.[2] Even if we insist on textual links, however, we can benefit by building up a network of cultural associations around both these texts, for even an intertext can admit more than a simple tip of the hat to a predecessor. Perhaps then we will have a better idea of why *Ismaric* wine specifically is mentioned in these two passages, and only there.

My warmest thanks to Mark Griffith, Jonathan L. Ready, Margaret Foster, Nathan Arrington, and Leslie Kurke for their invaluable feedback on earlier versions of this paper, and to Greg Nagy for his indefatigable help and encouragement.

1 The next specific attestation of Ismaric wine occurs in Virgil (*Georgics* II 37), though in Euripides *Cyclops* 141 Odysseus identifies the wine he carries as "the draught Maron gave me." See below for Maron's association with Ismaric wine.

2 Athenaeus' citation of Archilochus fr. 2 West (I 30f [epitome]) even hints that no strong textual link exists. The quotation immediately follows on the assertion that Archilochus "compared Naxian wine to nectar"—if there were a strong connection between fr. 2 West and *Odyssey* ix, we would expect that Ismaric wine would be included there as well, since the Cyclops himself makes such a comparison (in ix 359; see below).

Local Wines, Panhellenic Reputations

To understand the importance of particular types of wine in aristocratic Greek culture, it is first necessary to travel to the sands of Egypt—or rather, nowadays, to the vaults of the British Museum. The cultural importance of the names of wine and the need to differentiate between them are most apparent in a rather simple letter (published as P.Lond. VII 1948) written by a man named Glaucias to his superior Apollonios, finance minister of Ptolemy II Philadelphus, on May 5, 257 BCE. Glaucias had been sent to inspect an estate under the management of a certain Melas in Bethanath in the Galilee, and he concludes the description of his visit in the following way (lines 8–9): ἔγευσεν δέ με καὶ τοῦ οἴνου, ὃν οὐ διέγνων πότερον Χῖός ἐστιν ἢ ἐπιχώριος. καλῶς οὖν ποιεῖς εὐκληρῶν κατὰ πάντα ("He gave me a taste of the wine too, and I could not discern whether it was Chian or local.[3] You're doing well, then, fortunate in everything"). We see that the origin of a wine could conjure up specific associations, as the Chian here is associated with a standard of excellence against which the Galilean wine measures in taste.[4] In case we are ready to discount the associations with certain wines as the product of Alexandrian labeling and canonization, we need only look to an Athenian stele from 414/3 BCE, chronicling the auction of the property of the profaners of the mysteries of 415, among whom most famously was Alcibiades. One of the items listed is ἀμφορε͂[ς] . . . Χῖο[ι] ("Chian amphoras")[5]—and it is difficult to doubt the good taste of Alcibiades and his companions.[6]

3 Elsewhere in the Zenon papyri, an account of importation expenses (P.Cair. Zen. I 59012.17–19, 22–24; May–June 259 BCE) and two porterage accounts (P.Cair. Zen. I 59013.2, 5; 59014.2; both after May–June 259 BCE) record earlier shipments of Chian and Thasian wine to Apollonios. We can thus justly assume that Glaucias is evaluating the wine for Apollonios, and not merely expressing some rhetorical trope.

4 In *Vita W* of the *Life of Aesop* (no earlier than the first century CE), Aesop compares his lowly appearance and sharp intellect to a jar of wine: οὐδ' εἰς τὴν ἀρετὴν τῶν κεραμίων σκοπεῖν δεῖ, ἀλλ' εἰς τὴν ἔνδοθεν τοῦ οἴνου γεῦσιν ("one must not look at the excellence of the jars, but to the taste of the wine in them" [88]—there are similar sentiments at 26 and 88 in *Vita G*, though in 88 a πίθος is used as for comparison instead of the smaller κεράμιον). Despite Aesop's emphasis on taste as the standard (perhaps related to the sort of wine counterfeiting that Pliny describes in *Natural History* XIV 16–17 [18–20]?), the fact that his companions needed correcting suggests that the origin of a jar was important to the majority of Greeks, as we will see further below.

5 IG I[3] 422.18–20 = Pritchett 1953:250, Stele II, column I, lines 18–20.

6 For other examples of Chian's supremacy among wines, see also Hermippus fr. 77 K-A (mid to late fifth century BCE, from Athenaeus I 29e [epitome]): τοῦτον ἐγὼ κρίνω πολὺ πάντων εἶναι ἄριστον / τῶν ἄλλων οἴνων μετ' ἀμύμονα Χῖον ἄλυπον ("this [Thasian] I judge the best of all wines by far after blameless, painless Chian"—thanks to Margaret Foster for the reference), Aristophanes fr. 225.3 K-A (as the drink of choice of the dissolute brother in the *Banqueters*,

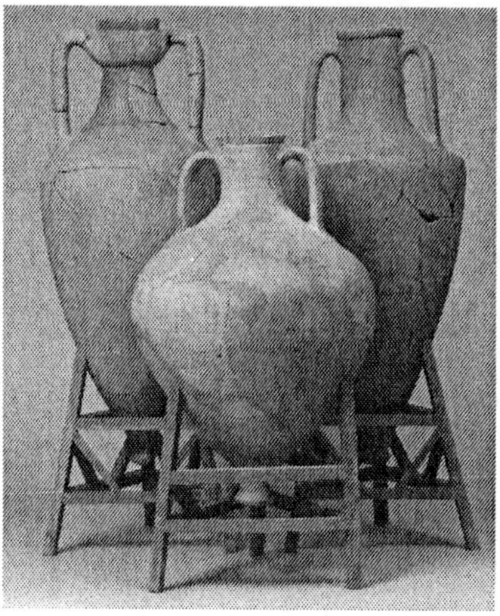

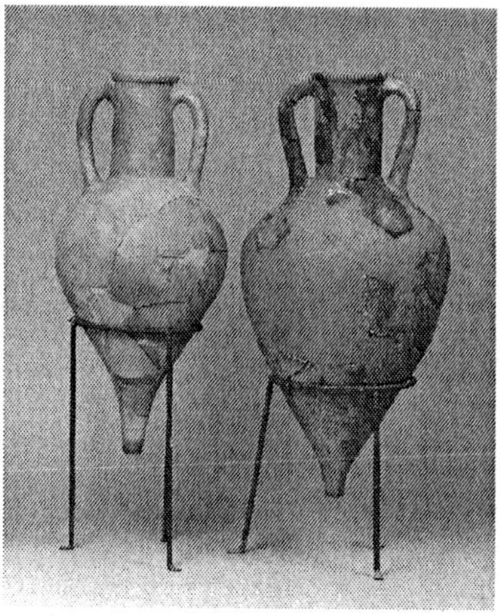

Figure 1 (*left*). Mendean (*front*) and Chian amphoras. The Chian amphora on the left represents the last phase of bulbous-necked amphoras from Chios; the one on the right, the first of the straight-necked ones. Courtesy of the Trustees of the American School of Classical Studies at Athens, after Grace 1961: fig. 43.

Figure 2 (*right*). Jars from Lesbos from the early and late fifth century BCE. Courtesy of the Trustees of the American School of Classical Studies at Athens, after Grace 1961: fig. 52.

Making an association between a wine and a trait is dependent on its being differentiated from other wines from other localities. Archeological evidence confirms that wines could be differentiated by jar design, although uncertainties about the proportion of jars used and reused for different commodities make modern identification of wine jars in the absence of residue analysis somewhat tentative. Nevertheless, jars found in excavations can be placed by locality from shape and color, for variations in local clay would result in distinctive coloration in the firing process. Figures 1 and 2 illustrate

from Athenaeus XI 484f and XII 527c) and fr. 334.2 K-A (one of two wines forbidden by the women in the second version of the *Thesmophoriazusae*, from Athenaeus I 29A [epitome]), and Machon 266 with Gow *ad loc.* (Chian wine, along with Thasian, among items brought by Diphilus as a generous contribution to a dinner and symposium held at the house of the *hetaira* Gnathaena). Unfortunately, IG I^3 422 is broken where the price of the amphoras would be given. Plutarch's pricing of an amphora of Chian wine in fifth-century Athens at the fabulously high price of one mina (*Moralia* 470f) may very well be an exaggeration, as it is reported in the complaint of one of Socrates' associates about high prices there. Lawall 2000, in his survey of graffiti on amphoras from the Athenian Agora, finds prices for Chian wine ranging from possibly 14 drachmas on the low end up to 28 or perhaps 52 drachmas per amphora (15, 31, 33, 42, 52). He notes, however, that price marks are relatively scarce and most likely from wholesale transactions outside of Athens, though the strong representation of Chian jars among those with graffiti argues for frequent decantings from them and consequently for their popularity (80–81).

a few ancient amphoras whose variation in size, shape, and color is so distinctive that we can identify their origin even without looking at the potter's stamp. Further, political changes could influence amphora design: wine jars of Knidian shape were overlaid with a white slip to mimic Rhodian forms or even fired from Rhodian clay during Rhodes' occupation of Knidos in 188–167 BCE,[7] evidence that political power could have an effect. Why would wine jars be made differently when the political situation changed? What is so important about a wine jar?

We find a clue in a scholion attributed to Aristotle, in which he discusses why Menelaus is said to have many women captives yet is never portrayed as sleeping with them (Aristotle fr. 144 Rose). Aristotle explains the potential difficulty in the *Iliad*'s representation of Menelaus' continued acquisition of these unused captive women by means of a comparison: ἐπεὶ οὐδὲ τὸν πολὺν οἶνον εἰς τὸ μεθύειν παρεσκευάσατο ("since neither had he kept at hand the large amount of wine for getting drunk").[8] He formulates the concept as εἰς γέρας, as opposed to εἰς χρῆσιν, terms perhaps best translated here as "symbolic capital" and "productive capital," respectively (οὐκ εἰκός . . . εἰς χρῆσιν εἶναι τὸ πλῆθος τῶν γυναικῶν, ἀλλ' εἰς γέρας; "it is not reasonable that the large number of women were productive capital, but instead [they were] symbolic capital").[9] In other words, the captive women's status as Menelaus' symbolic capital is made clear by analogy with wine's place as a carrier of social prestige and political value. Aristotle considers wine's value as a signifier of social capital obvious enough that it can be used as the primary example and need not be explained to his audience. The container, the wine jar, would be the natural place to indicate the cachet of the wine within it—but what exactly could a simple jar say about its owner?

Strangely enough, an anecdote relates how a wine jar could mold the identity of a polis. According to Athenaeus (XI 784c), when the Macedonian King Cassander founded the eponymous colony of Cassandreia, the sculptor Lysippus created a new type of wine jar by comparing a wide range of other

7 Grace and Savvatianou-Pétropoulakou 1970:319. Lawall 2002:308–309 has questioned Grace's interpretation of the amphora stamps as evidence of Rhodian occupation of Knidos. Even if such is the case, the production of these Rhodian-like amphoras, along with an autonomous mint that produced coins adapted to replace light Rhodian coinage (Reger 1999:89n47), instantiates the close political cooperation between the cities (see Lawall 2002:308nn82–83 for references).

8 Fr. 144 Rose (from Athenaeus XIII 556e); attributed to Aristotle's *Homeric Questions*.

9 Ibid. For the slippage of these two categories in Aeschylus' *Agamemnon* (formulated by Wohl as the "economy of commodities" and the "economy of *agalmata*") through the use of Helen as "universal equivalent," see Wohl 1998:83–91, with 85 and 229n12, which connect the place of Helen in the symbolic economy with her status as prize in *agōnes*.

Figure 3. Chian jar stamp (a) and coin (b), third quarter of fifth century BCE. Courtesy of the Trustees of the American School of Classical Studies at Athens , after Grace 1934: pl. I.1, and Grace 1961: fig. 49.

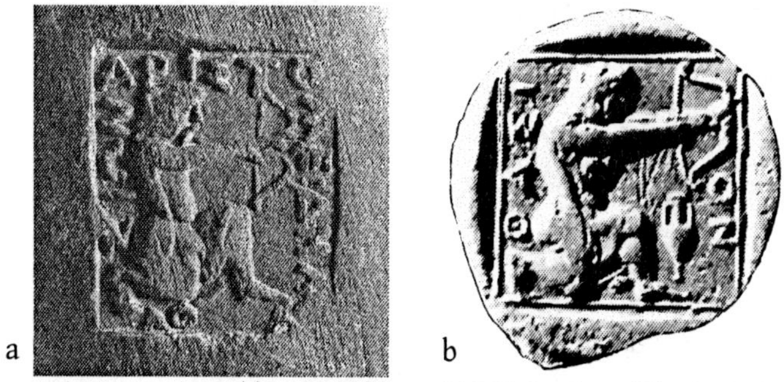

Figure 4. Thasian jar stamp (a) and coin (b), ca. 400 BCE. Courtesy of the Trustees of the American School of Classical Studies at Athens, after Grace 1961: figs. 27 and 28.

cities' jars and copying elements from all, creating a "Pan-Hellenic" jar for the popular Mendaean wine that was being exported from there. In fact, the wine jars of many cities have seals bearing the same iconography as the local coinage. More important, these seals are in relief rather than inset from pressing a coin into wet clay, and therefore were made from special stamps that often appear to have been made by a craftsman, perhaps working from the same seal that provided the model for coin dies (figs. 3, 4, and 5).

These coinlike stamps on wine jars are more explicable if we consider a passage from Aristotle's *Rhetoric* (1375b7). There, a juror is likened to a "tester of silver" (ἀργυρογνώμων) who distinguishes "true justice" (τὸ ἀληθὲς [δίκαιον]), and coinage is equated with "the unchanging and eternal principle of equity, nature, and authenticity" (Kurke 1999:318–319). If we look to the changes in wine measures (see fig. 6) and coins on the island of Chios in the 430s BCE, we can see that this association between coinage and authenticity could both legitimate wine jars and in turn be legitimated by them.

Figure 5. Rhodian jar stamps (a, b) and coins (c), third century BCE. Images courtesy of the Trustees of the American School of Classical Studies at Athens, after Grace 1961: figs. 23–25.

The final types of Chian bulbous-necked amphoras (fig. 6, lower right) had an increased capacity as an adjustment to the Attic khous unit, but turned out to be commercially unviable and were replaced in the late 430s with a long, thin jar of different shape but the same capacity (see fig. 1). The stamps on the earliest of the new jars were modeled after Chian didrachm coinage. However, when the didrachm coinage of Chios itself was replaced by tetradrachms and drachms (before 429/8), the new straight-necked jar on the new drachm coinage simultaneously replaced the bulbous-necked jar portrayed on the didrachms (Mattingly 1981:78–80). The fact that coinage and amphora design could authenticate each other suggests the importance of authentic wine to the identity of the polis, protected in places like Thasos by laws such as one that prohibited the importation of foreign wine in Thasian amphoras to a section of the mainland and even the sale of small amounts of wine from large vessels (see IG XII Supp. 347 and Osborne 1987:105).

This equation of polis-identity with wine appears in one case to have been used as a convenient shorthand, if we believe a story from Aulus Gellius (XIII 5). When Aristotle had to choose a successor between Theophrastus of Lesbos and Eudemus of Rhodes, he asked the students to procure a Lesbian and a Rhodian wine. When it came time to taste these wines, he remarked, "utrumque

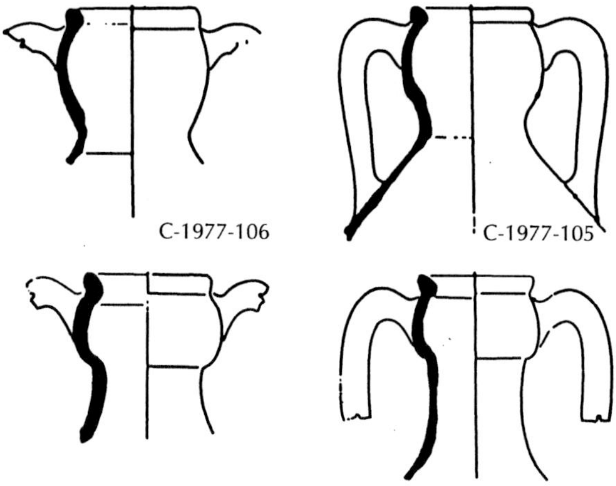

Figure 6. Cross-sections of Chian amphoras from the fifth century BCE. Images courtesy of the Trustees of the American School of Classical Studies at Athens, after Williams 1978:18, fig. 5.

oppido bonum, sed ἡδίων ὁ Λέσβιος" ("both are really good, but the Lesbian is sweeter"). Gellius explains, "id ubi dixit, nemini fuit dubium quin lepide simul et verecunde successorem illa voce sibi, non vinum delegisset" ("when he said that, no one doubted that with those words he had agreeably and tactfully chosen his successor, not his wine"). What, then, can the οἶνος Ἰσμαρικός mean for Homer and Archilochus?

In the Cave of the Cyclops

The Ismaric wine makes its first appearance in a digression in Odysseus' story of his adventures on the Island of the Cyclopes in Book 9 of the *Odyssey*. In exchange for Odysseus' protection during the raid against the Ciconians (related earlier in lines 39–61), Maron, identified as the son of Euanthes and a priest of Apollo, gives οἶνον ἐν ἀμφιφορεῦσι δυώδεκα ("wine in twelve jars," ix 204). Not only does the number of jars match the number of ships that set out with Odysseus on his *nostos*, but Telemachus too orders his nurse to fill twelve jars of the wine second only to that reserved for Odysseus' homecoming (ii 349–353) when he sets out to find his father. As in Telemachus' case, where the filling of the jars is known only to him and the nurse (ii 356), knowledge of Maron's wine is also restricted to only certain important members of the household (ix 206–207). This is real *nostos*-wine, for it incapacitates the Cyclops and allows Odysseus to blind him, and Odysseus wryly indexes its powers when he explains his reason for letting the Cyclops taste his wine: εἴ μ' ἐλεήσας / οἴκαδε πέμψειας ("in case you might pity me and send me home"; 349–350). Odysseus' use of Maron's wine here, however, is not just a simple trick on a nature-demon figure, as Walter Burkert (1991:12) suggests, but a proto-sympotic exchange of sorts.

> Ὣς ἐφάμην, ὁ δὲ δέκτο καὶ ἔκπιεν· ἥσατο δ' αἰνῶς
> ἡδὺ ποτὸν πίνων καὶ μ' ᾔτεε δεύτερον αὖτις·
> "Δός μοι ἔτι πρόφρων, καί μοι τεὸν οὔνομα εἰπὲ
> αὐτίκα νῦν, ἵνα τοι δῶ ξείνιον, ᾧ κε σὺ χαίρῃς·
> καὶ γὰρ Κυκλώπεσσι φέρει ζείδωρος ἄρουρα
> οἶνον ἐριστάφυλον, καί σφιν Διὸς ὄμβρος ἀέξει·
> ἀλλὰ τόδ' ἀμβροσίης καὶ νέκταρός ἐστιν ἀπορρώξ."
> Ὣς ἔφάτ', αὐτάρ οἱ αὖτις πόρον αἴθοπα οἶνον.
> τρὶς μὲν ἔδωκα φέρων, τρὶς δ' ἔκπιεν ἀφραδίῃσιν.
> αὐτὰρ ἐπεὶ Κύκλωπα περὶ φρένας ἤλυθεν οἶνος,
> καὶ τότε δή μιν ἔπεσσι προσηύδων μειλιχίοισι·
> "Κύκλωψ, εἰρωτᾷς μ' ὄνομα κλυτόν; αὐτὰρ ἐγώ τοι
> ἐξερέω· σὺ δέ μοι δὸς ξείνιον, ὥς περ ὑπέστης.
> Οὖτις ἐμοί γ' ὄνομα· Οὖτιν δέ με κικλήσκουσι
> μήτηρ ἠδὲ πατὴρ ἠδ' ἄλλοι πάντες ἑταῖροι."
> Ὣς ἐφάμην, ὁ δέ μ' αὐτίκ' ἀμείβετο νηλέϊ θυμῷ·
> "Οὖτιν' ἐγὼ πύματον ἔδομαι μετὰ οἷς ἑτάροισι,
> τοὺς δ' ἄλλους πρόσθεν· τὸ δέ τοι ξεινήϊον ἔσται."
> Ἦ καὶ ἀνακλινθεὶς πέσεν ὕπτιος . . .

[353] When I had spoken, he took the cup and drank. He was extremely delighted with drinking the sweet wine, and he begged me for yet another cup. "Be so kind," he said, "as to give me some more, and tell me your name at once, so I may give you a guest-gift that you will be glad to have. To the Cyclopes too the fruitful earth bears fine wine, which the shower of Zeus nourishes, but this is a distillation of nectar and ambrosia!" [360] I then gave him another cup of sparkling wine; three times did I give it to him, and three times he drank it down without thought; then, when the wine had got to his head, I said to him with soothing words: "Cyclops, do you ask my glorious name? I will tell it to you, then; but give me, then, the present as you promised. My name is Nobody; Nobody my father and mother and all my friends have always called me." [368] As soon as I had spoken, he answered with an unpitying heart, "Then I will

eat the others beforehand, and will keep Nobody after his friends for the last. This will be your parting gift." [371] Then a deep sleep took hold upon him as he fell back . . .

Odyssey ix 353–371

Odysseus' gift of wine is couched in the language of the proper order of offerings later formalized from drinking ritual in the Classical symposium—each of the tastes is offered as a libation (λοιβή), of which there are three (τρίς, 361), as in every well-ordered symposium.[10] According to the scholiast to Pindar *Isthmian* 6 (at 4 and 10a Drachmann), there are customarily three libations: to Zeus (in some cases with Hera), the heroes (sometimes with Earth), and Zeus the Savior.[11] Polyphemus' words further enhance the connection with libation, for he speaks of the Cyclopes' wine coming from the earth (ἄρουρα, 357) and the rain of Zeus (Διὸς ὄμβρος, 358). The third libation, to Zeus the Savior, literally saves Odysseus, for it is that draught that overpowers the Cyclops and pushes him into a deep sleep. Of course, Odysseus behaves rather unusually for a sympotic guest by blinding his host. Yet the events of the encounter (or at least Odysseus' rhetoric in telling it) and logic of the rituals of consumption support him. The libations are consumed by his host rather than going to, among others, Zeus, who is responsible for protecting the guest-host relationship.[12] Further, Polyphemus promises what turns out

10 It is thus more than an "emphatic," "typical number," as is claimed by de Jong 2001:243. While τρὶς μέν . . . τρὶς δέ and similar formulations occur elsewhere in Homer (*Iliad* V 436f., VIII 169f., XI 462f., XVI 702f., XVI 784f., XVIII 228f., XX 445f., XXI 176f., XXIII 817; *Odyssey* vi 154f., xi 206f., xii 105), they are more than some empty poetic formula. With the exception of *Odyssey* vi 154f. (in which the OCT reads τρισμάκαρες . . . τρισμάκαρες), the construction is used of a process that is interrupted by another event (sometimes spelled out as τὸ τέταρτον). The context here, with the requisite libations and the fact that the Cyclops' fall into drunkenness is preceded by a trading of hexameters (arguably representing a precursor to the practice of singing epic hexameters within the symposium), suggests that sympotic associations or at least the practices that developed into the symposium would not have been lost on the audience.

11 Euripides' *Cyclops* 316–346 has the Cyclops mentioning Earth and Zeus repeatedly at a similar point in the narrative; Euripides is also thinking of the Cyclops' violation of proper sympotic behavior and its influence on the events here. ἁγὼ οὔτινι θύω πλὴν ἐμοί, θεοῖσι δ' οὔ, / καὶ τῇ μεγίστῃ, γαστρὶ τῇδε, δαιμόνων. / ὡς τοὐμπιεῖν γε καὶ φαγεῖν τοὐφ' ἡμέραν, / Ζεὺς οὗτος ἀνθρώποισι τοῖσι σώφροσιν / λυπεῖν δὲ μηδὲν αὑτόν ("I sacrifice to no one except myself—not to gods—and to this belly, the greatest of divinities, since, yes, drinking and eating all day long—this is Zeus for sober men—and to feel no pain oneself"; 334–337)—a somewhat more ironic take on the Cyclops' disastrous wrongheadedness in dealing with sympotic ritual.

12 The traditions recorded by Athenaeus report similar libations during the feast, after the first taste of meat. Philochorus FGH 328 F 5b (Athenaeus II 38c–d [epitome]) claims libations of unmixed wine are made to Agathos Theos, while Philonides (Athenaeus XV 675b–c) records that they are to Agathos Daimon, who is said to represent "the one who discovered [wine]" (τὸν εὑρόντα: Dionysus for Philonides). Both record the libation to Zeus the Savior after the

to be an empty guest-friend gift (ξεινήϊον, 370, picking up on ξείνιον in 356), in contrast to the valuable gift that Maron has given to Odysseus and the wine that the Phaeacians will supply when he embarks on his way home (xiii 69). Odysseus' success in controlling and ordering proto-sympotic ritual with the Cyclops stands in marked contrast to his earlier failures in Book 9[13]—his failure to rescue his men from indulging in drink[14] and being unable to flee a subsequent Ciconian attack, and his failure at stopping his men from taking part in the feast of the Lotus-eaters and being unable to leave.[15] Though it would be excessive to call Odysseus' entire interaction with Polyphemus an unmitigated success, his control of this part of their encounter with Maron's wine allows him to avoid the Cyclops' real threat of physical violence. The Ismaric wine, then, is emblematic of the proper ordering of guest-host interactions between Odysseus and Maron. It is the same proper observance that Odysseus, the teller of the tales, conducts with his well-ordered Phaeacian hosts and with the humble Eumaius,[16] and it foreshadows Odysseus' later role in imposing his

meal, with Philochorus maintaining that the same cup used during the meal is also used for this libation. Niafas 2000:466–475 connects both of these anecdotes with the cult of Dionysus Orthos and with correct mixing as "the hallmark of civilized behavior in the symposium" (468). Saïd 1979:13 emphasizes that violations of the rituals and codes of hospitality within guest-host encounters in the *Odyssey* are emblematic of "la tragression des norms socials et religieuses."

13 And to the frame with which the narrative *Odyssey* begins (i 6–10): Odysseus' failure to hold back and thus to save (ἐρρύσατο) his companions (ἑτάρους), who are uncontrollably and transgressively intent on feasting on the cattle of the Sun.

14 The connection between being unable to control the measure of wine and mortal danger is continued when Odysseus meets Elpenor in the underworld (xi 51–83). In a metaphorical/mimetic replay of the Cyclops episode, Elpenor attributes his death to the fact that ἆσέ με δαίμονος αἶσα κακὴ καὶ ἀθέσφατος οἶνος ("an adverse allotment of a god and *immeasurable wine blinded* me"; xi 61). For later historical and poetic parallels to uncontrolled wine as a cause of death, see n39 below.

15 If we accept the cultural partition of food into "bread/grain" (σῖτος) and "sauce" (ὄψον), sketched out in chapter 1 of Davidson 1997, the Lotus-eaters represent a (culturally unacceptable and uncivilized) sauce-based diet (the Lotus), a contrast that is made clear in this episode by Odysseus' men's taking a meal of grain (ix 87) before setting out to learn "what sort of bread-eating men are on the land" (οἵ τινες ἀνέρες εἶεν ἐπὶ χθονὶ σῖτον ἔδοντες, ix 89). Polyphemus, too, is called "not at all like a bread-eating man" (οὐδὲ ἐῴκει / ἀνδρί γε σιτοφάγῳ; ix 190–191). Compare also Odysseus' advocacy of a meal before battle in speeches in the *Iliad* (XIX 155–183 and 216–237) that draw on themes of social reconciliation, contrasted with Achilles rejection of both meal and reconciliation in his speech at XIX 199–214.

16 See xiv 462–467 with Nagy 1999:236–237; Nagy connects the structure of Odysseus' excuse for telling the story of the cloak with "formalistic excuses" for praise in epinician poetry and notes the similar emphasis of the guest-host relationship within epinician and Odysseus' appeal (esp. xiv 505). We should note, moreover, that the consumption of wine and the practices of socialization connected with it are said to motivate Odysseus' *epos*, at least in Odysseus' rhetoric, and that Odysseus' excuse for speaking in xiv 466–467 builds on the idea that wine can lead one to

order on the drunken revelry of the suitors.[17] But what light can this Maron himself throw on his wine?

Maron's abode is given as a "wooded grove" (ἄλσεϊ δενδρήεντι, ix 200), which may lead us to wonder whether a connection to a local hero cult may be suppressed by the text in accordance with the conventions of epic.[18] In fact, Eustathius (*ad Odyssey* ix 30) notes that Strabo records a "hero-shrine" (ἡρῷον) to Maron at Ismaros (said to be either a city near Maroneia, the colony Maron "founded," or identical with it). The evidence for the form of this cult is found in rather late yet informative sources, which appear to preserve local traditions parallel to those of Homeric epic.[19] Philostratus (Heroicus 17.2) says that Maron is "seen by the farmers" (ὁρᾶται τοῖς γεωργοῖς) around Ismaros. Though the detail may at first not seem very helpful, heroes in hero cults are said to make epiphanies, and γεωργεῖν is used of the devotees of Protesilaus at Heroicus 2.8 (see Nagy 2001:xxvi–xxvii). Just as plants "breathe out"

say what is "better left unsaid" (ἄρρητον ἄμεινον).

17 See Mitchell in this volume (pp. 49–74) on *atasthalia* in the *Odyssey*, with his summary of Bakker 2005. For more on Odysseus, Alcinous and Arete, and Menelaus and Helen as masters of order and discretion, see Austen 1975:182–200. The suitors are repeatedly represented as engaging in excessive and disorderly drinking: see Louden 1999:38–40. Moreover, at xx 292–298 Odysseus in his disguise as the beggar-guest is received in a manner that recalls his treatment by Polyphemus, as Segal 1994:160 notes. The widely accepted view that Odysseus is motivated by his belly, most influentially espoused by W. B. Stanford, has been rightly rebutted by Worman 2002:101–102 for ignoring the importance of fair apportionment in the characterization of Odysseus in both epic and drama. But in contrast to Worman's emphasis on Odysseus as apportioner, I believe the salient focus is on his exercise of power in these scenes, whether by force, trickery, or persuasion. His role as the imposer of order is made particularly clear in the exchange just before Odysseus in disguise takes up his bow: the suitor Antinous tries to dissuade him by saying that he is mad from drink (xxi 293–294), and that he should quietly drink his wine (xxi 309b–310). The first suitor to die is Antinous, who is shot through the *throat* as he raises a cup of *wine* to his lips, immediately after Odysseus casts off his rags and reveals himself (xxii 1–20).

18 Maron is the only local priest mentioned in the *Odyssey* (in his case, of Apollo), and the Ismaric wine itself is only one of two local wines mentioned (along with Circe's Pramnian wine at x 235). For Greek epic's suppression and transformation of the religious dimension of hero cult, see Nagy 1999:116.

19 Although the temporal spread of the prose sources on Maron is not ideal for giving an outside perspective on archaic Greek poetry, Maclean and Aitken 2001:lxxi, lxxiv with n103 argue for the reliability of Philostratus' *Heroicus* for preserving local traditions tied to the epic cycle and hero cult. Diodorus Siculus, who claims to have consulted numerous local histories in Alexandria and Rome, and who appears to draw much of the material in his first book from Hecataeus of Abdera, constructs from his sources a universalist narrative of culture heroes, deified in return for their service to humanity (Sacks 1990:55–82). That local hero cult may be the ultimate source of the information about Maron is strongly suggested by his companion in Osiris' contingent—Triptolemus, who had a cult in Eleusis (Pausanias I 38.6). Unfortunately, the only extant archaeological evidence for the hero cult of Maron is from the Roman period; see, for example, Reinach 1884:51.

(ἀναπνεῖν) fragrance in the presence of Protesilaus in Heroicus 3.3, Maron is said to "breathe out" sweetness and the smell of wine in his epiphanies. The fragrance of the hero's presence is possibly adduced at *Odyssey* ix 197, where Maron is said to be the son of Euanthes (Εὐάνθεος υἱός)—literally, "sweet-blooming."[20] Further, Maron holds himself aloof from the monetary economy, keeping his wine buried beneath the earth (κατορωρυγμένον, 1.4)[21] rather than selling it.

Diodorus Siculus offers other testimony for Maron's possible place within cult. He names him as a companion of Osiris skilled in "vine-cultivation" (τῆς μὲν περὶ τὴν ἄμπελον φυτείας; I 18.2). Later we meet him in Thrace, after Osiris has killed the barbarian king Lycurgus, as the "overseer of the plants there" (ἐπιμελητὴν τῶν ἐν ταύτῃ τῇ χώρᾳ φυτευομένων) and the founder of Maroneia (κτίστην . . . τῆς ἐπωνύμου πόλεως; both Diodorus Siculus I 20.2).

Maron's name does not derive merely from the colony[22] he supposedly founded,[23] but ultimately from μάρη, meaning "hand."[24] Maron's name, then, is connected with his attributes as a cultivator of vines and regulator of nature. In addition to his characteristics in Diodorus, Philostratus describes Maron as "planting and pruning" (φυτεύοντά τε καὶ κυκλοῦντα, 17.2), thus creating "sweet wine" (ἡδυοίνους) to enhance the symposium. He is the oppo-

20 The Ismaric wine's sweet smell in ix 210 also reinforces these traits.

21 This word is also used in Demosthenes 27.53 of a hoard of money for an inheritance, and in Herodotus VIII 36.1 for a plan to protect the sacred property at Delphi by burying it. Thus, we can understand that Maron is protecting his wine from circulating in any way other than gift exchange. The description of this burying comes in a question by the Phoenician about whether the vinedresser must be money-loving (φιλοχρήματος), as he has to deal with the monetary realities of agriculture. When the vinedresser gives the answer that he makes all transactions by barter and has never seen a drachma (Heroicus 1.7), the Phoenician describes the arrangement as a χρυσῆν ἀγορὰν . . . καὶ ἡρώων μᾶλλον ἢ ἀνθρώπων ("a golden market . . . and one of heroes rather than of humans"; Heroicus 2.1). For more on the relationship of metals to aristocratic gift exchange, see Kurke 1999:130–171.

22 Ps.-Scymnus of Chios (676–678) makes the claim that Maroneia was colonized by Chios, a connection that perhaps derives from a mythical genealogy. Oenopion, the son of Dionysus and Ariadne (Diodorus Siculus V 79.1, scholia to Aratus 636) and grandfather of Maron (Hesiod fr. 238 West) was said to have founded Chios (Ion fr. 29 West, from Plutarch *Theseus* 20.2), and had a hero shrine and cult there (Pausanias VII 5.13).

23 Contra Heubeck and Hoekstra 1989:197–198.

24 Fick in *RE* 28.1911, s.v. Μάρων, 2; compare Old Norse *mund* ('hand') <**mn̥t*, and Albanian *marr* ('hold') <**mainō* (Frisk 1960–1972:2:175). Maron's name is thus functionally similar to Χείρων, though its precise connotation is unclear because the only attestation of μάρη (Pindar fr. 310 Maehler) comes without a context. Euripides apparently knows of the etymology, as he has Silenus ask whether Maron was ὃν ἐξέθρεψα ταῖσδ' ἐγώ ποτ' ἀγκάλαις ("the one whom I once reared in these arms"; *Cyclops* 142—I thank Mark Griffith for directing my attention to this passage in particular and in general for persuading me to reconsider the value of *Cyclops* as a source).

site of the savage (ἄγριον, *Odyssey* ix 215) Polyphemus, and it is his proper use of cultivation and exchange that allows Odysseus to master his situation. Like the similarly named Chiron the Centaur,[25] Maron is a figure who bridges culture and the natural world by controlling both through a type of expertise. Philostratus sums up that expertise best by calling Maron καλός τε καὶ ἁβρός (17.2). Paired with καλός, ἁβρός is a positive term,[26] and it fills out the picture of a hero whose cultural power is exercised on the level of non-monetary gift-exchange and performed with the paraphernalia of the symposium. Any hero-cult substrate to Philostratus' account would likely predate the entrance of ἁβρός and its compounds into the Greek language (cf. Kurke 1992:93 with n6). Yet we see concepts later attached to the constellation of ἁβροσύνη already in Odysseus' encounter with Polyphemus and in Odysseus' talismanic use of Maron's wine to control an opponent who does not recognize the aristocratic rituals of gift-exchange or of civilized conviviality.

If these attributes—of a hero of cultivation and culture who himself is a colony founder—have not reminded us of a colonization narrative, we need look no further in *Odyssey* ix than the description of the island of the Cyclopes. The island is a place of untamed agriculture just waiting for colonizers to realize its bounty (Dougherty 1993:21), where "they would have made the island a good settlement" (νῆσον ἐϋκτιμένην ἐκάμοντο; ix 130). Polyphemus, then, is a hostile native who is overpowered by Greek ingenuity,[27] in this case through the wine's rectification of the proto-sympotic and guest-friend rights

25 See the previous note for the similar etymology of the two names. For Chiron as a figure who is a ritual and cultural expert, see *Titanomachy* fr. 6 Allen; as a figure who bridges the forces of nature and civilization, see Dougherty 1993:154n25 with references. Like Maron, Chiron exerts a positive influence on a colonization narrative in Pindar *Pythian* 9.39–61 (Dougherty 1993:143–149 and 154n25).

26 See Kurke 1992:91–120 for a full discussion of the later poetic and political implications of the positive and negative uses of the word. Hammer 2004 attacks both Kurke's "cult of *habrosunē*" and Ian Morris's "middling" values (discussed below) for being guided by theoretical structures rather than the evidence. The heart of Hammer's criticism, however, is that the "multi-vocal" coexistence of sometimes shifting and competing ideologies across the poleis of the archaic period precludes the appropriations of these respective terms by "elite" and "middling" aristocrats. As Kurke 1999:18n48 warns, over-reading this ideological opposition, as Hammer does in his criticism of Kurke and Morris, can make the analysis appear arbitrary and schematic. Though Hammer sees structuralist binaries at the root of Kurke's and Morris's readings, a less cherry-picked look at the evidence reveals that reappropriation and negotiation of the ideological terms is frequently the rule, and that the symposium was more often a place to blow off aristocratic steam than a hothouse of rebellion. I agree with Hammer (505) that behavior and habitus are a necessary element for understanding these various contested terms in archaic Greece, but we must not confuse action with discourse.

27 Likewise, in Euripides' *Cyclops* 411–415 it is "Hellas" that is said to be bringing the wine to the land of the Cyclopes, who in this telling (unlike in the *Odyssey*) are ignorant of wine.

he denies to Odysseus. Maron's wine substitutes for the suppressed qualities of its owner-hero as tamer of uncontrolled nature and bringer of cultured, sympotic order.

"I fight sleep"

> ἐν δορὶ μέν μοι μᾶζα μεμαγμένη, ἐν δορὶ δ' οἶνος
> Ἰσμαρικός, πίνω δ' ἐν δορὶ κεκλιμένος.
>
> "In my spear[28] I have (kneaded barley) cake, and in my spear Ismaric wine, and I drink reclining on my spear."
>
> Archilochus fr. 2 West

Unlike the mention of Ismaric wine in the *Odyssey*, Archilochus' attestation survives with little commentary or context. Athenaeus, as we have him, presents the quote with little indication of its place or even completeness: "[Archilochus] says somewhere" (πού φησιν, I 30f [epitome]). The only other attestation of this poem occurs in a letter of Synesius, in which he writes about keeping watch and fighting sleep (ὑπνομαχῶ) during a barbarian siege (130.265c).[29] Though editions place the provenance of the quotation with Athenaeus, it is perhaps more likely that Synesius used a source that was fuller than the offhand reference there, for he appends to his quote, "I don't know whether these were more appropriate for Archilochus to say" (οὐκ οἶδ' εἰ μᾶλλον Ἀρχιλόχῳ προσήκοντα ἦν ταῦτα εἰπεῖν), suggesting by the placing of μᾶλλον with Archilochus' name that he had a fuller idea about the context of the original either directly or mediated through another source.[30] Synesius' implication that these lines have a dramatic setting of constant vigilance against an enemy—so much that all meals have to be taken in armor—accords fairly well with the fighting against the Thracians mentioned in Archilochus fr. 5 West.[31]

28 Or "on my spear" for this and the following clause. See the discussion below, together with nn32–38.

29 Clay 2004:50 with 166n67 asserts that the *Suda*'s quotation of this poem under the lemma ὑπνομαχῶ is evidence that the poem was originally a *skolion*, meant to be capped by an improvised response. The *Suda*'s citation (Υ 441 Adler), however, derives from Synesius' own quotation of the poem, and the external support Clay cites is not sufficient evidence on its own for the completeness of this fragment.

30 Further, μοι is omitted in the manuscripts of Athenaeus (it was restored by Musurus).

31 Synesius quotes this passage much in the way that spending the night on watch is contrasted with the symposium (and especially lying with one's fellow soldiers is contrasted with lying with a male lover), as at Bacchylides 1.75–80 and Sophocles' *Ajax* 1199–1210. However, Archilochus in fr. 2 is *conducting* the symposium rather than longing for it. If anything, the

The anaphora in the repeated ἐν δορί ('on/in my spear') provides much of the structure and grammatical interest in the fragment, and as such this phrase has attracted the most scholarly comment. Between its two occurrences in the hexameter and its reappearance in the pentameter a grammatical shift takes place: the clauses shift from nominal clauses to a clause with the finite verb πίνω.[32] A number of different translations are possible for ἐν δορί, with the preposition being spatial ('on'), metaphorical ('in [the power of]'), instrumental ('with')[33] or referential ('in respect of', i.e. 'on guard duty')[34] in its first two iterations; and with δόρυ itself able to be translated as 'spear', 'ship',[35] or even 'stocks'.[36] The most subscribed-to interpretation of the phrase, suggested by Campbell, connects it with a Mycenaean vase that depicts soldiers carrying small bags or knapsacks on their spears.[37] To claim that Archilochus had any access at all to Mycenaean art is a dangerous assumption, particularly when the soldiers depicted carry shields shaped differently from a hoplite one, whose loss is the focus of fr. 5 West.[38] Such interpretations assume that his lyric poetry is primarily an exposition of personal experience, and that

battle against sleep should recall the Cyclops, whose loss against it (*Odyssey* ix 371, and more blatantly martial in Euripides *Cyclops* 454) has disastrous consequences for him.

32 Clay 2004:51. This change in syntax would argue against the necessity of each instance of ἐν δορί having the same meaning, *contra* Bowra *apud* Davison 1960:1.

33 Campbell 1982:142 notes that Hybrias the Cretan in his thematically related *skolion* (PMG 909 Page, which begins ἐστί μοι πλοῦτος μέγας δόρυ καὶ ξίφος ["I have a shield and a spear as a great source of wealth"]) suggests the preposition should be read as instrumental; a referential reading, however, is also a possibility.

34 Davison 1960:2 notes that this is the sense in which Synesius must understand the preposition.

35 First suggested by Davison 1960:3 and developed by Gentili 1965:129–134.

36 Cf. Anacreon fr. 43.7 Page; it would thus emphasize Archilochus' mix of high and low values (see below). Since Clay 2004:50 makes a compelling case for the appearance of a spear in the Parian Totenmahl relief as being "a quotation of Archilochus in marble," I have decided on the "traditional" interpretation of δόρυ for the purposes of my argument. Any number of other meanings (which certainly play a secondary role in any reading), however, do not seriously change my interpretation of the passage.

37 Campbell 1982:142; the vase to which he refers (the "Seven against Thebes" Vase) is illustrated in fig. 9 of Clay 2004:50.

38 A plausible connection is perhaps possible if we accept that ἐν δορί could be punning on the epic ἐν . . . δοροῖσιν, the leather bags in which barley flour is carried (*Odyssey* ii 354 and 380). These bags are mentioned at the same place in which Telemachus prepares the wine and other provisions for the Telemachia, and thus are part of the provisions for visiting and exchanging in guest-friend visits. Barley itself appears twice in Homer in symposia, when it is sprinkled on the first cup of wine given to guests (*Iliad* XI 640, *Odyssey* x 234–235), and we know from the scholiast to Aristophanes' *Knights* (at 55) that μᾶζα is ground barley made into dough. Archilochus need not have been familiar with a "text" of "Homer" to draw this connection, for the formulae or even situations cited could easily have existed far before and independently of any text in an oral-poetic tradition. Yet such a connection remains tentative and provisional at best.

he reports "events" much like the filings of a war correspondent would.[39] Yet once we remember that the spear is the weapon not only of the Homeric hero, but the hoplite soldier as well, may we realize that this fragment is dealing with a deeper juxtaposition of archaic Greek ideologies.

Given that the Homeric and the hoplite warrior both fight with the spear yet themselves form programmatic points of contrast for Archilochus,[40] we may be tempted to read the μᾶζα μεμαγμένη ("kneaded barley-cake") at the end of the first clause as such a point of juxtaposition of high and pedestrian. The everyday nature of μᾶζα (Amouretti 1986:123–126) would provide an implicit contrast with the heroic stature of the Ismaric wine in the next clause. Though μᾶζα has been commonly thought to be a porridge, like Circe's *kykeon* in *Odyssey* x 234,[41] Aristotle *Problems* 21 929b11 makes it clear that it was an unbaked cake formed from liquid ingredients and ground parched barley, somewhat like the Tibetan *pag* cake made from *tsampa* (parched barley flour). The combination of μᾶζα with the full force of the perfect participle μεμαγμένη, however, is far more significant than may first appear at a casual reading, for Archilochus is engaging with a proverbial phrase. Glosses on μᾶζα μεμαγμένη and the related μεμαγμένον βίον indicate that the phrase is used "for the good things that are ready at hand" or, in the words of the scholiast to Aristophanes' *Knights*, for "accomplishment" (κατόρθωμα).[42] In the *Knights*,

39 See Campbell 1982:136, 142. Hanson 2000:131 implies that Archilochus fr. 2 West is evidence for his assertion that Greek soldiers went into battle "almost" drunk. Despite the astute observations Hanson makes elsewhere in his book, I find this argument completely unconvincing. In the passages he cites as support (Homer *Iliad* XIV 1–8; Xenophon *Hellenica* V 4.40–44, VI 2.5–23, VI 4.8–13; Menander *Aspis* 53–61; Polybius III 72.5–7; Plutarch *Dion* 30.3–31.1), the midday wine drinking always precedes some military disaster. Hanson defends his view by claiming that "when troops have drunk moderately, such activity merits no mention" (245), a dubious argument from silence. Drinking before battle is much more likely to have been a trope of a poorly disciplined army: their lack of success in battle is due to lack of discipline, which is illustrated by their excesses in conducting an improper "army symposium" immediately before battle. For drink as the cause of death being a part of a later tradition of Hellenistic (literary) epitaphs, see Fantuzzi and Hunter 2004:321–322 with 322n128.

40 See fr. 114 West with Morris 2000:177–178 for a discussion of that poem being programmatic for a "middling" ideology set against an "elite" one; chapter 5 of Morris also gives a more general view of Archilochus' place in the Greek cultural contestations between "middling" and "elite." See n26 for a brief sketch of Hammer's criticism of Morris and a few cautions. One could add in this instance that the contradistinction of the "middling" to the "elite" is one of the linchpins of the "middling" ideology here, even if they actually had more overlap in action than they do in discourse.

41 Amouretti 1986:125n22 draws an analogy with the Tunisian and Moroccan wheat *mhamza* porridge, but its being kneaded argues for something much thicker.

42 ἐπὶ τῶν ἑτοίμων ἀγαθῶν: *CPG* I 432 (Appendix III 86); cf. *CPG* II 39 (Diogenianus III 21), I 7 (Zenobius I 21), I 350 (Gregorius Cyprius I 21), *Suda* β 293, 295 Adler; scholiast to Aristophanes' *Knights* 55. The Tibetan *pag* takes considerable skill to knead (Norbu and Harrer 1960:26): if it

the phrase is used to describe the victory that the Paphlagonian Slave (Creon) steals away from Demosthenes at Sphacteria, and Theodorus Metochites uses the expression in a similar way.[43] In this phrasing, then, the μᾶζα μεμαγμένη is anything but humble. Further, note that in each case the preparer of the μᾶζα is different from the person who enjoys it. Though the grammar of the first clause can follow the same pattern, with μοι serving as a dative of possession, its prominent positioning in an alliterative sequence offers the possibility of reading the pronoun as a dative of agent. Much as fr. 114 West upends preconceived notions of military excellence, Archilochus characterizes himself as simultaneously enjoying a place of privilege and creating it for himself. To belabor a proverbial phrase in English, he is having his cake and eating it too.

Beyond μᾶζα's proverbial associations, however, it has important military ones as well, as it is mentioned along with wine as being supplied to the second ship sent after the Mytilenean Debate (Thucydides III 49.3). This pair of consumables was provided when soldiers and sailors did not have the opportunity to prepare their own food, but Archilochus' portrayal of himself within this situation nevertheless draws on language associated with the elite. What he consumes is simultaneously supplies used in pressing need, with even the Ismaric wine being local—according to Harpocration (s.v. Στρύμη), both Philochorus and Archilochus himself report that the Thasians are fighting the inhabitants of *Maroneia*—and items that have strong associations with the elite and the heroic. As we saw in the previous section, the cult figure of Maron is strongly tied to the Ismaric wine, which itself can provide a talisman of the well-ordered, elite symposium. If we look to Athenaeus, he characterizes

provides a good analogue, it may explain the connection between having a ready supply of a certain food and well-being and accomplishment. The proverbial nature of the phrase could also explain the alternate reading of τοι for μοι in the quotation of fr. 2 in *Suda* Υ 441 Adler.

43 Since Campbell 1982:143 gives a misleading partial quotation of this difficult passage, it is worth quoting it more fully here. The chapter is describing the consequences of seeking wealth without limitations: καὶ οὐ φίλοις μόνον ἄχρηστος, ἀλλὰ καὶ πολλῷ πρότερον ἑαυτῷ, ὥστε καὶ τελευτᾶν τῆς κακίστης ἐκείνης σπουδῆς, καὶ τῶν ἐχθίστων ἐρώτων ἀλθλιώτατα . . ., καὶ μάζαν, κατὰ τὴν παροιμίαν, ἑαυτῷ μεμαγμένην ξὺν πολλῷ τῷ πονῷ καὶ ταῖς φροντίσιν ἑτέροις καταλείπειν καὶ παρατίθεσθαι τοῖς πικρὸν ὄμμα καὶ φθονερὸν †τὸν† τὸ ἐπ' αὐτόν τε καὶ τὰ φίλτατα χρήματα διὰ τοὺς αὐτοὺς καὶ παραπλησίους ἴσως ἔρωτας ἐπιβάλλουσι ("[He is] not only useless to his family, but also much before [that] to himself, so as to fulfill the most unhappy consequences of that worst pursuit and the most hateful desires . . ., to leave behind and to furnish the *māza*, as the proverb says, kneaded by him with much toil and cares to others who cast a bitter and envious gaze on both him and his most beloved money from the same and perhaps nearly equal desires"; 85 p. 559 Müller). The proverb is focalized on the envious heirs; for them, the wealth they receive will be provided for them just like the μᾶζα μεμαγμένη.

epic as depicting two entirely separate types of symposia (V 177b): τούτοις δ' ἀντέθηκε [ὁ ποιητὴς] τὰ μὲν [συμπόσια] ἐπὶ στρατιᾶς, τὰ δὲ τὰ πολιτικώτερον τελούμενα σωφρόνως ("To these things [the symposium of the Phaeacians] [the Poet] has contrasted the [symposia] on a military expedition against those conducted more civically in a moderate way"). It becomes apparent that Archilochus is mixing both these symposia within this fragment while juxtaposing the trappings of the elite and the "middling" life.[44] The final clause of the short couplet makes that fusion even stronger.

The last clause of fr. 2 West, πίνω δ' ἐν δορὶ κεκλιμένος ("and I drink reclining on my spear") may at first appear to be simply a serious breach of military discipline, much in the style of the leaving of the shield in fr. 5 West. The Demosthenic *Against Conon* (54.3) provides testimony that drinking on duty could go unpunished in Athens in the fourth century, so it is a dangerous assumption to restrict our commentary to this aspect alone. The key word here is κεκλιμένος, which is used of reclining at a symposium, on a couch or κλίνη (Bowie 1986:18 with n27). The poem on Gyges, King of Lydia, already shows Archilochus engaging with connections between Greece and the East—where the custom of reclining adopted by the Greeks originated, and with which the practices of ἁβροσύνη[45] became closely connected. Just as the criticism there is couched in the persona of Charon the Carpenter,[46] Archilochus' incorporation of sympotic practice is tied to his self-characterization.[47] If we take Clay's suggestion that the archaic Parian Totenmahl relief, depicting a hero seated on a couch with a spear suspended above him, represents "a quotation in marble" of fr. 2 West,[48] we may even posit that Archilochus is to some extent taking for himself, through the references to Ismaric wine and reclining, the heroic position of Maron as the cultivated arbiter of the refined and potentially orientalizing symposium. Ismaric wine may evoke its careful cultivation, but Maron's power must be taken on Archilochus' terms: through rations and

44 P.Oxy. LXIX 4708 represents a more explicit blending of the life of a hoplite soldier with sustained heroic narrative, if one takes Obbink's suggestions (ii) or (iii) about how the fragments could have fit into a larger narrative (P.Oxy. LXIX 4708 introd).

45 Though the etymology of this word itself is disputed (see for instance Frisk 1960:1.4, 3.16; Chantraine 1968:4–5; van Windekens 1986:1), Kurke 1992:93–94 makes a convincing case for its being connected at least in the Greek imagination with Lydia/the East.

46 Aristotle *Rhetoric* III 17 1418b28, with Campbell 1982:148.

47 P.Oxy. LXXIII 4952 preserves a fragmentary ancient commentary on Archilochus, which, after discussing the biographical tradition of his being born of a slave-woman (see n49), has the last two lines of the first column end tantalizingly with Ἀρχιλόχου χαρακτῆρα ("the persona of Archilochus") and πολλοῖς ("for the many").

48 Clay 2004:48–50, with detail of the spear in plate 18 and overall view of the Totenmahl relief in plate 13.

guard-duty, firmly within the frame of hoplite tactics. On Maron's own home turf Archilochus expropriates the elite position of Maron the colony founder for his self-characterization as the colonist moving to a better life—reflected in the biographical tradition of Critias fr. 88 B 44 D-K, which claims that Archilochus left Paros διὰ πενίαν καὶ ἀπορίαν ("on account of poverty and dire straits").[49] Such repurposing of elite sympotic practice is not entirely unattested,[50] but the degree of his appropriation is remarkable. Like Maron, Archilochus can embellish a Greek symposium at the edge of the Greek world with his refined song , and his later veneration in hero cult implies its artistic success.[51]

Maron at the End

Although the Ismaric wine of Maron survives in name only twice in archaic Greek literature, each of these isolated references integrates with a larger civic discourse of wine and its consumption. As a product that was important to political identity, wine was invested with great cultural meaning. In the case of Ismaric wine, the connection with Maron and the founding of a new

49 This information comes from Aelian's report (*Varia Historia* 10.13) of Critias' criticism of Archilochus, which consists of blaming Archilochus for giving too much compromising information about himself. Interestingly enough, the criticism is phrased in terms of knowledge of Archilochus' "low status" (being born of a slave woman, not cultivating friendly ties with the colonists or the Thasians, not speaking any better about friends than enemies, etc.), which Archilochus has needlessly divulged. It concludes that Archilochus has left τοιοῦτον κλέος . . . καὶ τοιαύτην ἑαυτῷ φήμην ("fame of such a quality and repute of such a quality for himself"). Of course, all this "knowledge" (as far as we can triangulate it) comes from supposedly biographical details that could just as well be part of an Archilochean persona that emphasizes "middling" values. See further Rotstein 2007; Rotstein argues that Aelian's summary is ultimately from an invective, probably poetic work by Critias that deals with Archilochus, who by contemporary standards at Athens was a favorite of people whom Critias would have regarded as his political opponents. Rotstein also suggests (152) that Critias' poem could have been delivered at a [suitably counterrevolutionary] symposium!

50 A similar repurposing of ἁβρός can be found in Xenophon's *Symposium*, within a speech of Antisthenes (4.44): καὶ μὴν καὶ τὸ ἁβρότατόν γε κτῆμα, τὴν σχολὴν ἀεὶ ὁρᾶτέ μοι παροῦσαν, ὥστε καὶ θεᾶσθαι τὰ ἀξιοθέατα καὶ ἀκούειν τὰ ἀξιάκουστα καὶ ὃ πλείστου ἐγὼ τιμῶμαι, Σωκράτει σχολάζων συνδιημερεύειν ("And, what's more—and the most ἁβρός possession of all—you see that I always have leisure so as to see things worth seeing, hear things worth hearing, and—what I value most of all—to spend my days at leisure with Socrates"). Since this speech takes place at a symposium, the word ἁβρός as a marker for elite practice plays a role for Socrates here much like the Ismaric wine for Archilochus: as a foil that draws on correct behavior within the symposium yet rejects other values of the "normal" elite symposium. Murray (1991:87–99) describes a similar melding of heroic and hoplite in Spartan elegiac poetry within the historical framework of the extension at Sparta of elite and military rituals of commensality to the civic class of hoplites.

51 For Archilochus in hero cult, see Clay 2004.

polis, the colony, over foreign opposition looms large. Perhaps the placement of Maron's shrine, at one of the ends of the Greek-speaking world, on the edge of Thrace, made it an attractive middle-term for the notional cultivation and exploitation of colonization. Both Odyssey ix and Archilochus' fr. 2 West offer a slightly different take on the usefulness of Ismaric wine, but both keep the essential terms of cultivation in the colonial symposium. As the narrative on the founding of Cassandreia and the "Cassandreian" jar shows, sympotic trappings were not solely a private affair, but important to public life as well. The symposium and the consequent ingredients of wine and song were not only an important sphere for culture, but also an essential staging ground for colonial and polis identity.

Bibliography

Amouretti, Marie-Claire. 1986. *Le pain et l'huile dans la Grèce antique*. Paris.

Austen, Norman. 1975. *Archery at the Dark of the Moon*. Berkeley.

Bakker, Egbert. 2005. "Homeric Epic between Feasting and Fasting." *La poésie épique grecque: Métamorphoses d'un genre littéraire* (eds. F. Montanari and A. Rengakos) 1–30. Entretiens Hardt 52. Geneva.

Bowie, E. L. 1986. "Early Greek Elegy, Symposium, and Public Festival." *Journal of Hellenic Studies* 106:13–35.

Burkert, Walter. 1991. "Oriental Symposia: Contrasts and Parallels." *Dining in a Classical Context* (ed. William J. Slater) 7–24. Ann Arbor.

Campbell, David A., ed. 1982. *Greek Lyric Poetry: A Selection of Early Greek Lyric, Elegiac and Iambic Poetry*. London. New edition.

Chantraine, Pierre. 1968. *Dictionnaire étymologique de la langue grecque: histoire des mots*. Vol. 1. Paris.

Clay, Diskin. 2004. *Archilochos Heros: The Cult of Poets in the Greek Polis*. Hellenic Studies 6. Washington, DC.

Davidson, James N. 1997. *Courtesans & Fishcakes: The Consuming Passions of Classical Athens*. New York.

Davison, J. A. 1960. "Archilochus Fr. 2 Diehl." *Classical Review* NS 10:1–4.

de Jong, Irene. 2001. *A Narratological Commentary on the Odyssey*. Cambridge.

Dougherty, Carol. 1993. *The Poetics of Colonization: From City to Text in Archaic Greece*. Oxford.

Fantuzzi, Marco, and Hunter, Richard. 2004. *Tradition and Innovation in Hellenistic Poetry*. Cambridge.

Frisk, Hjalmar. 1960–1972. *Griechisches etymologisches Worterbuch*. 3 vols. Heidelberg.

Gentili, Bruno. 1965. "Interpretazione di Archiloco Fr. 2D," *Rivista di filologia e di istruzione classica* 93:129–134.

Gow, A. S. F., ed. 1965. *Machon: The Fragments*. Cambridge.

Grace, Virginia R. 1934. "Stamped Amphora Handles Found in 1931–1932." *Hesperia* 3:197–310.

———. 1961. *Amphoras and the Ancient Wine Trade*. Agora Picture Book 6. Princeton.

Grace, Virginia R., and Savvatianou-Pétropoulakou, Maria. 1970. "Les Timbres Amphoriques Grecs." *Exploration archéologique de Délos 27: L'Îlot de la Maison des comédiens* (ed. Philippe Bruneau) 277–386. Paris.

Hammer, Dean. 2004. "Ideology, the Symposium, and Archaic Politics." *American Journal of Philology* 125:479–512.

Hanson, Victor Davis. 2000. *The Western Way of War: Infantry Battle in Classical Greece*. 2nd ed. Berkeley.

Heubeck, Alfred, and Hoekstra, Arie. 1989. *A Commentary on Homer's Odyssey: Volume II, Books IX–XVI*. Oxford.

Kurke, Leslie. 1992. "The Politics of ἁβροσύνη in Archaic Greece." *Classical Antiquity* 11:91–120.

——. 1999. *Coins, Bodies, Games, and Gold: The Politics of Meaning in Archaic Greece*. Princeton.

Lawall, Mark L. 2000. "Graffiti, Wine Selling, and the Reuse of Amphoras in the Athenian Agora, ca. 430 to 400 B.C." *Hesperia* 69.1:3–90.

——. 2002. "Early Excavations at Pergamon and the Chronology of Rhodian Amphora Stamps." *Hesperia* 71.3:295–324.

Louden, Bruce. 1999. *The Odyssey: Structure, Narration, and Meaning*. Baltimore.

Maclean, Jennifer K. Berenson, and Aitken, Ellen Bradshaw. 2001. "Introduction." In Maclean and Aitken 2001: xxxvii–xcii.

——, eds. 2001. *Flavius Philostratus: Heroikos*. Atlanta.

Mattingly, Harold B. 1981. "Coins and Amphoras—Chios, Samos, and Thasos in the Fifth Century B.C." *Journal of Hellenic Studies* 101:78–86.

Morris, Ian. 2000. *Archaeology as Cultural History*. Oxford.

Murray, Oswyn. 1991. "War and the Symposium." *Dining in a Classical Context* (ed. William J. Slater) 83–103. Ann Arbor.

Nagy, Gregory. 1999. *The Best of the Achaeans: Concepts of the Hero in Archaic Greek Poetry*. Rev. ed. Baltimore.

——. 2001. "Prologue." In Maclean and Aitken 2001: xv–xxxvi.

Niafas, Konstantinos. 2000. "Athenaeus and the Cult of Dionysos Orthos." *Athenaeus and His World* (eds. David Braund and John Wilkins) 466–475. Exeter.

Norbu, Thubten Jigme, and Harrer, Heinrich. 1960. *Tibet Is My Country*. London. 2nd edition, 1986.

Osborne, Robin. 1987. *Classical Landscape with Figures: The Ancient Greek City and Its Countryside*. London.

Pritchett, W. Kendrick. 1953. "The Attic Stelai, Part I." *Hesperia* 22.4:225–299.

Reger, Gary. 1999. "The Relations between Rhodes and Caria from 246–167 BC." *Hellenistic Rhodes: Politics, Culture, and Society* (eds. Vincent Gabrielsen et al.) 76–97. Aarhus.

Reinach, S. 1884. "Inscriptions de Maronée." *Bulletin de correspondence hellénique* 8:50–53.

Rotstein, Andrea. 2007. "Critias' Invective Against Archilochus." *Classical Philology* 102:139–154.

Sacks, Kenneth S. 1990. *Diodorus Siculus and the First Century*. Princeton.

Saïd, Suzanne. 1979. "Les crimes des prétendants, la maison d'Ulysse et les festins de l'Odyssée." *Études de littérature ancienne* (eds. Suzanne Saïd et al.) 9–49. Paris.

Segal, Charles. 1994. *Singers, Heroes, and Gods in the Odyssey*. Ithaca.

Stanford, William Bedell. 1963. *The Ulysses Theme: A Study in the Adaptability of a Traditional Hero*. 2nd ed. Oxford.

Theodorus Metochites. 1821. *Miscellanea philosophica et historia graece*. Eds. Christianus Godofredus Müller and Theophilus Kiessling. Amsterdam. Reprint, 1966.

van Windekens, A. J. 1986. *Dictionnaire étymologique complémentaire de la langue grecque*. Leuven.

Williams, C. K., II. 1978. "Corinth, 1977: Forum Southwest." *Hesperia* 47:1–39.

Wohl, Victoria. 1998. *Intimate Commerce: Exchange, Gender, and Subjectivity in Greek Tragedy*. Austin.

7

Homeric Poetics and the *Aeneid*

Curtis Dozier

Everyone has always known that Vergil imitated Homer, but I do not think it is known whether Vergil thought he was imitating, on the one hand, the work of a blind bard who single-handedly recorded the best versions of the sack of Troy and the wandering of Odysseus, or, on the other hand, the result of a centuries-old oral tradition. Hence the question that Gregory Nagy's Sather Seminar at the University of California—Berkeley in the spring of 2002 left me: How much of what *we* know about the way Homeric poetry was created and performed could Virgil have known? Our understanding of the artistry of Virgil's poetry might very well hang on the answer. If Virgil thought he was imitating a single poet, he was (in Nagy's view) wrong—he misunderstood his model in a fundamental way, since the oral nature of Homeric poetry shaped almost all of its features. In this case we need to ask how this misunderstanding conditions Virgil's imitation. But if Virgil knew he was imitating an oral tradition, we must try to understand how a literate poet represents oral poetics. These two issues might be phrased in contrast with each other: How does a poet imitate formulaic language when he does not realize that it is formulaic? And how does a poet imitate formulaic language when he knows that his language is *not* formulaic?

These tantalizing questions lie behind much of the scholarship on Virgil's imitation of Homer, but it may not be possible to divine what Virgil could have understood about formulaic language. In providing a partial answer, I want to sidestep this problem by asserting that, regardless of understanding, Virgil imitated whatever he saw when he read Homer, or whatever he heard when he heard him read.[1] And so I think it is safe to say that to Virgil, the formulaic

[1] I thank Leslie Kurke for hosting a graduate colloquium at which I presented this paper; still more thanks are due to my fellow Berkeley graduate students who attended that event and offered invaluable advice. Will Shearin and Lauri Reitzammer read and improved a much earlier version of this work. I thank Ralph Hexter for discussing with me how (i.e. with what

language of Homer's poetry must have looked repetitive.[2] In this essay I will examine some ways in which Virgil imitated this feature of Homeric language and how it shapes his poetry, and along the way I will propose what I think is a new way of conceptualizing the relationship of Virgil's poem to the Homeric epics.

My discussion of Virgil's language will depend on some aspects of Nagy's view of how Homeric language works, which I summarize briefly here. To Nagy and his followers, formulaic language is not merely repetitive, but, one might say, pregnantly repetitive. That is, despite their formulaic nature, repetitions *mean* something. When Nagy offers the analogy "formula is to form as theme is to content" (Nagy 1996b:18), he is saying that formula is the basic unit of form just as theme is the basic unit of content, but he also means that in an oral tradition, formula and theme are inextricably linked.[3] Verbal repetition *is* thematic repetition. And so each particular formula invokes the other instances of that formula,[4] by which a network of meaning (often very intricate) is created.[5] Generations of unitarians and Nagy's contemporary critics interpret these networks, which are marked by verbal echoes sepa-

technology) Virgil read Homer. He outlined his ideas on this subject at a lecture, still unpublished but in circulation here in Berkeley, at Stanford University some years ago. Also still relevant is Schlunk 1974.

2 I have not made a detailed study of Jeffrey Wills 1996 because his main interest seems to lie in repetitions within a single poetic line, as he indicates at the start of his sections on gemination (46) and on polyptoton (189n1). I am interested in phrases repeated in different sections of a single work. Still, Wills's subtitle shows that he and I are ultimately interested in the same poetic effects. I have probably erred in neglecting for similar reasons Moskalew 1982. Both works have much to teach us, of course.

3 "Formulas do not have a life independent of themes" (Nagy 1996b:24). See further Miller 1982:44: "Formulas attach to and are triggered by the repetition of certain themes (arming, battles, counsel, dining, etc.)." Lord 2000:32 makes a similar point about the relationship of meter and theme: "rhythm and thought are one."

4 Anyone who asserts that the repetitions of formulas are meaningful comes face to face with the Homeric Question: how can there be "intricate verbal parallelism" (as Miller puts it [1982:8]) in an oral poet? "Poets have a plan in their head, and the plan carries numerous thematic repetitions that may or may not be symmetrical, and with the individual themes go certain formulas. It is simply a misrepresentation of the oral art to think in terms of poets 'remembering' words or phrases over a distance of thousands of lines" (Miller 1982:8, with further bibliography). See also Nagy 1999:xi: "My reading of Homer, especially of the passages in *Odyssey* viii and *Iliad* IX, has occasionally been disputed on the grounds that it gives the impression of literary rather than oral poetics." See also the discussion of the phrase ἄριστος Ἀχαιῶν starting at Nagy 1999:26, in which every instance of this phrase is seen as connected.

5 I use this phrase "network of meaning" instead of Nagy's (and others') "cross-reference" because the latter term implies, to me, an allusion between two particular passages. I want to emphasize the way one passage can refer to many different passages, which in turn refer to other passages, and so on.

rated by immense numbers of lines, as proof of a literate, individual composer of the poems,[6] but Nagy sees them as an integral feature of oral poetics.[7] Such networks are an integral feature on the production side of epic poetry because a bard's virtuosity is measured, in part, by how deftly he creates these networks through traditional language, and they are an integral feature of the poetry on the reception side because formulaic language is "hard-wired" in the minds of both performer and audience.[8] This language was omnipresent in their culture; phrases accumulated meaning for all members of the society, and people had heard so many performances, so many retellings of these episodes, that for many of them certain language was inextricably associated with certain narratives.[9] Thus when that language was used in a different context, all those associations came up in the mind of the listeners. They might not remember specific details of the times they had heard that language before, but the associations were still operative on the level of impression—the mood or tone of an episode could be summoned by the artful use of formulaic language to contrast or reinforce the mood of the episode being performed.[10] For the modern literary critic, then, there is no problem of authorial intention: if *you* can think it, then it is reasonable to imagine that some portion of the ancient audience could have thought it as well, more attuned to the language as they were.

The now-classic Structuralist model of *langue* and *parole* is instructive here:[11] the epic Tradition, with a capital T, forms a complete system of expression, the *langue*. All the performers and all the audience members are conversant in this *langue*. Particular instances of a formula in a particular

6 Goold 1977 is a good example of this kind of argument. Nagy attempts to refute Goold's (and others') assumptions about what oral poets are and are not capable of at Nagy 1996b:26.

7 Nagy 1996b:19: "unity . . . is a result of performance tradition, not a cause effected by a composer." See also Nagy 1999:6–7, where he argues for the audience's role in the creation of a poetic whole using as an example the two halves of the hymn to Apollo which indicate a "social fusion of two distinct audiences."

8 In his Sather Seminar, Nagy frequently employed this term "hard-wired"' to describe the degree to which ancient audiences and performers had internalized traditional language. I do not know where, or if, he uses it in his published work.

9 Nagy 1999:15, where he calls tradition "the culmination of perhaps a thousand years of performer-audience interaction."

10 Lord 2000:32–33 on the "unconscious" role form plays in relation to the "conscious" theme. In this passage he describes various possibilities for understanding how traditional language is received: even on the level of the sounds of words connections can be made. See also Nagy 1996b:25.

11 Nagy 1990a:17n2 and Nagy 1996a:1. The terms *langue* and *parole* go back to Saussure in his *Course in General Linguistics* and their application beyond linguistics is usually attributed to Levi-Strauss in *The Structural Study of Myth.*

performance are individual expressions of this system, that is, examples of *parole*. Thus the networks of meaning I have described can be seen as instances of the *parole* invoking the whole *langue*. This relationship is not so cut-and-dried when it comes to networks of meaning within the Homeric corpus, because while the *langue* must be described diachronically, over time, each *parole* exists as a synchronic event.[12] The Homeric corpus we read today is the product of a diachronic process; it describes the *langue* as it ultimately crystalized.[13] What we lack is a synchronic snapshot of this tradition—that is, we lack an example of any particular performance of Homer.[14] This lack of synchronic perspective makes discussing the network of meaning created by any *parole* difficult, because the performance in which that *parole* occurred must remain hypothetical.[15] In response to his critics, Nagy even acknowledges as much, saying that Homeric cross-references must be diachronic in nature (Nagy 1996b:9; Nagy 2000:40).

And so I return to Virgil and his treatment of what to us are Homeric formulas, and to him were repeated lines and phrases. These repetitions in Homer create networks of meaning, and the same is true of Virgilian poetry, which is rife with the same kinds of cross-references that abound in the Homeric corpus. They are unmistakably literary in character; there is no modern analytic debate about the *Aeneid*.[16] And they are not only intra-

12 On the terms "diachronic" and "synchronic" see Nagy 1996b:17, with further bibliography, in particular Nagy 1990b:20–21.

13 Nagy 1996a:108–110 describes this as the "relatively rigid" stage of Homeric transmission in comparison with earlier periods.

14 The vulgate text of Homer, which I described as a description of the diachronic tradition, is, of course, a synchronic artifact as well, but in the context of Nagy's work can hardly be called the record of a particular performance of the Homeric poems.

15 See Clay 1983:243 for a forceful statement of this objection. Her point is that Nagy calls on a tradition that was "so conservative and fixed as to become a text"—that is, to be, for all intents and purposes, a literary, not oral, artifact.

16 I would like to suggest in passing that we might do well to reconsider the several "inconsistencies" in the *Aeneid*; I refer, for example, to the episode in Book 2 in which Aeneas sees Helen watching the sack of Troy from the roofs in apparent contradiction to Deiphobus' claim in Book 6 that she was with him during the sack, the attribution of Celaeno's prophecy from Book 3 to Anchises in Book 7, and Aeneas' reference to an otherwise unknown prophecy that Palinurus would reach Italy safely in Book 6. These inconsistencies seem to me to share something with similar inconsistencies in Homer, which analytic scholars invoke against unitarian arguments, such as the problem of the duals in the embassy of *Iliad* IX. Critics usually explain away such Virgilian contradictions by, like analytic Homeric critics, expunging lines (as in the Helen episode) or by saying that Virgil would have corrected these had he had time to revise the poem. But I wonder if Virgil, having found such inconsistencies in the Homeric epics, might have intentionally included some of his own in the *Aeneid*.

textual[17] but intertextual; indeed, perhaps no other poet has so openly absorbed so many poetic traditions into a single work.[18] But I think it is uncontroversial to say that the most pervasive model for the *Aeneid* were the Homeric poems.[19] Virgil not only imitated Homeric repetitions but imitated the networks of meaning that they created.

In this essay I want to perform an experiment on the *Aeneid*: what if we see it as a *parole* for the Homeric *langue*? Or, to address the problem with Homeric cross-references that I summarized above, what if we take the *Aeneid* as a synchronic snapshot of the Homeric *langue*, as an individual performance of Homeric themes in Homeric language for a particular audience at a particular moment in time? Characterizing the *Aeneid* in this way will allow us to examine cross-references between a specific *parole* and the diachronic *langue*.

This is not just a theoretical way of talking about allusions to Homer in the *Aeneid*, a subject that even the earliest commentators on Virgil studied. I actually want to treat the *Aeneid* as part of the epic cycle[20] for a day, as it were, which means that I will treat Virgilian allusions to Homer as if they were cross-references within a single poetic system. Research on allusion tends to treat it as a one-way street: a later author alludes to a passage in an earlier author. But cross-references within Homer lack this chronological element, for the networks of meaning are diachronic: one passage refers to a second, which refers to three other passages, one of which refers back to the original passage, and so on. Similarly, in this experiment, a Virgilian passage may refer to a Homeric passage, which then invokes another passage in Homer as well as a Virgilian passage. A metaphor of depth may be useful: upon the bedrock of the Homeric *langue* are built the myriad Homeric cross-references; they reach down, like roots, into the *langue* as far as one cares to follow them. The *Aeneid*, I propose, can be placed like a superstructure on these networks, sending down its own roots into the Homeric networks and the Homeric *langue* below.

17 One famous example of an intratextual cross-reference is Virgil's use of the same line for the death of Camilla (*Aeneid* XI 831) as for the death of Turnus (XII 952). Oliensis 2004 offers an intratextual reading of the *Aeneid* with emphasis on the "distresses of the textual condition"—that is, the way in which violent episodes of opening in the *Aeneid* give us "a meditation on the susceptibility of the written text to scattering." Clearly she and I are approaching the poem from different directions, but we do discuss many of the same passages.

18 See Zetzel 1984:109–111 on the blending of genres in the *Aeneid*. Also Kopff 1981:938.

19 The standard, monumental, study is Knauer 1964; I have relied extensively on Knauer's lists of Virgilian citations of Homer. I have also made use of Albrecht 1881:393–444, which lists the repeated lines in Virgil.

20 Kopff 1981:928 rejects the idea that Virgil ranks himself as a cyclic author, but Conte 1994:277 highlights the way the *Aeneid* can be seen as a continuation of the Homeric narrative.

The specific Virgilian network I will consider is that of the phrase *arma virumque,* the first two words of the *Aeneid*.[21] These two words recur together eleven times throughout the poem, and their programmatic significance is often cited by commentators, if not exhaustively analyzed.[22] Here I focus on their intertextual significance—they represent Virgil's relationship to Homer in that *arma* is a metonymic description of the *Iliad* and *virum* is an exact translation of the first word of the *Odyssey*, Ἄνδρα.[23] We are to understand that Virgil will imitate both the general themes and the smallest details of the Homeric epics.[24] Nagy's concept of formulaic poetics can be found in these two little words: verbal *and* thematic allusion together.

21 Part of the appeal of Nagy's approach to formulaic language is that because he views the Homeric corpus as a complete system, *any* line works as well as any other as an example of how formulaic language works. And so when I started this project I let the *sortes Vergilianae* determine which Virgilian passage I would use to study Virgil's treatment of Homeric repetitions—that is, I closed my eyes, opened my OCT of Virgil, and let my finger fall on a random passage. The gods were smiling on me that day, because my finger fell on the death of Cretheus with its striking repetition of *arma virum*. I mention this because one could object that, as the programmatic phrase of the whole poem, *arma virumque* forms something of a special case in Virgilian language and that for this reason the networks of meaning around *arma virum* should not be taken as representative of the networks formed by other phrases. My response is that, by the same token, *arma virumque* is the perfect phrase for this study because its engagement with the Homeric poems is so deep—after all, my purpose is to understand how Virgil represented the kinds of repetitions he found in Homer in his own work, and what role Homeric language itself plays in that representation.

22 I would have thought that this phrase would have attracted more interest, especially from New Critics, but Hardie 1994 on *Aeneid* IX 57 cites only Bloch 1970:206–211 and Norden's commentary on *Aeneid* VI. More recently Oliensis 2004:31 treats the Cretheus episode.

23 Corinne Crawford has pointed out to me that, *pace* the orthodox interpretation, *arma* is not really a very good metonymy for the *Iliad* since it leaves out so many important features of the Homeric poem. And Levitan 1993:14 shows that the first word of the *Iliad*, μῆνιν, is in fact to be found in the *Aeneid*, in the elided opening of Juno's first speech at *Aen.* I 37: *men(e) incepto. . . .*

24 The word *cano* carries significance as well, for while the Homeric proems ask the Muse or Muses to tell their respective stories, Virgil says "*I* sing." This is usually taken as an allusion to the opening line of the cyclic *Little Iliad*: Ἴλιον ἀείδω καὶ Δαρδανίην ἐύπωλον, / ἧς πέρι πόλλ' ἔπαθον Δαναοί, θεράποντες Ἄρηος ("I sing of Ilios, and Dardania with its beautiful colts, over which the Danaans, the servants of Ares, suffered many things"; *Little Iliad* fr. 1 Allen). Space does not permit a discussion of the relationship between the *Aeneid* and the Trojan epic cycle using the *parole* and *langue* model I have proposed here, but see Kopff 1981 for a survey of the parallels. For now it is enough to say that Virgil is further highlighting the completeness of his imitation of Homer—not just the events of the *Iliad* and the *Odyssey* but the whole tradition of epic poetry dealing with the Trojan War. For a recent treatment of the relationship between the Homeric epics and the epic cycle, see Scodel 2004, an article that offers many tempting angles from which to approach Virgil's attitude toward the Trojan Cycle. Hainsworth 1993 on *Iliad* 524–605, Phoenix's telling of the Meleager myth, points out that the Homeric epics frequently show "knowledge" of the other epic cycles (Theban, Aetolian/Elean, Iolkos). These are described by West 1985:137. It would be interesting to determine what knowledge Virgil had of these cycles and how he employed it.

Probably the most striking repetition of *arma virumque* comes in Book 9, when Turnus kills Cretheus:

> amicum Crethea Musis,
> Crethea Musarum comitem, cui carmina semper
> et citharae cordi numerosque intendere nervis,
> semper equos atque arma virum pugnasque canebat.
>
> Cretheus, the Muses' friend and companion, who always loved songs, and the lyre, and to play through the modes on its strings; he was always singing of horses, the arms of men, and battles.
>
> *Aeneid* IX 774–777

A sympathetic connection between this unfortunate poet and Virgil himself has not been missed by many critics (Hardie 1994 on 777): Cretheus sings his own version of the *Aeneid*, a poem whose subject is *arma virum*. Our first network of meaning begins to take shape around this idea, for similar self-conscious references occur several times in the Homeric poems as well. For example, in Book 9 of the *Iliad* the embassy finds Achilles in his tent singing the κλέα ἀνδρῶν, "glorious deeds of men." (*Iliad* IX 189). The *Iliad*, of course, is itself poetry on this subject, especially in Book 9, where the preceding eight books have shown us the *aristeia* of various heroes, Greek and Trojan. The theme of the *Iliad* as stated in its proem is μῆνις, but this rage springs from the culture portrayed in the poem, in which men are valued by the spoils they win by accomplishing the very things Achilles sings of in his tent while he sulks; if anything, κλέα ἀνδρῶν represents more of the *Iliad* than μῆνις does. And we should note that Achilles sings of κλέα ἀνδρῶν because he cannot participate in them, despite his status as the greatest of all ἀνδρῶν. Aeneas too, the *vir* of Virgil's poem, is absent from battle as Cretheus sings, since he is seeking assistance from Evander. Virgil's typology of Aeneas as Achilles is not based solely on similar actions; here we find the connection made through the recurrence of the proem form.

We find a similarly self-referential situation in the *Odyssey*, where two separate rhapsodes sing of νόστοι. In Book 1, the suitors force Phemius to sing for them: ὁ δ' Ἀχαιῶν νόστον ἄειδε / λυγρόν, ὃν ἐκ Τροίης ἐπετείλατο Παλλὰς Ἀθήνη ("He sang of the baleful homecoming of the Achaeans, which Pallas Athena accomplished [for them] after Troy"; *Odyssey* i 326–327). As with Achilles' κλέα ἀνδρῶν, this subject can be taken to represent the subject of the *Odyssey* at least as accurately as its stated subject, ἀνήρ. Demodocus sings songs that combine the above elements in Book 8: Μοῦσ' ἄρ' ἀοιδὸν ἀνῆκεν ἀειδέμεναι κλέα ἀνδρῶν, / οἴμης, τῆς τότ' ἄρα κλέος οὐρανὸν εὐρὺν ἵκανε, / νεῖκος Ὀδυσσῆος καὶ Πηλεΐδεω Ἀχιλῆος ("Then the Muse inspired him to sing of the fame of the men from that song, whose fame then reached the wide heavens, namely of the strife between Odysseus and the son of Peleus, Achilles"; *Odyssey* viii 73–75). This is more the stuff of the *Iliad* than of the *Odyssey*, recalling as it does the poetry of Achilles in his tent, but Book 8 of the *Odyssey* is when Odysseus begins to tell of his adventures, adventures that contribute to his κλέος. Further, the νόστοι of the Greeks were part of the same poetic tradition that told the story of the Trojan War; indeed, they were considered *part* of the story of the Trojan War, a connection which is being shown by the repetition of Achilles' κλέα ἀνδρῶν here. Clearly we should take this as a catch-phrase for all epic poetry, especially in that Demodocus here combines the heroes of both the Homeric epics into a single poem about the strife between them, a subject that does not come up anywhere else in extant Greek poetry, according to the commentaries.[25]

Cretheus' use of *arma virum* recalls all three of these Homeric singers, and so extends the meaning of Virgil's programmatic phrase. In the opening line of the *Aeneid*, *virum* was accusative, but in Cretheus' song the word is genitive plural, 'of men'—thus in the first line of the *Aeneid* the word translates exactly the first word of the *Odyssey*, and in Cretheus' song it translates exactly the genitive plural ἀνδρῶν of κλέα ἀνδρῶν. The *virum* of *arma virum* thus translates the subject of the *Odyssey* or the subject of the *Iliad*, as conceived by Achilles, depending on whether it is taken as accusative or genitive. If genitive, the metonymy between *arma* and the *Iliad* tightens considerably—*arma virum* becomes a paraphrase for κλέα ἀνδρῶν, with *arma* filling in for the κλέος of the war. And since Demodocus conceives of κλέα ἀνδρῶν as a phrase for *all* epic poetry, *arma virum* signals not only Virgil's imitation of the Homeric epics but his conception of the *Aeneid* as part of the same poetic milieu as Homeric poetry.

There are other signs of this positioning as well. Demodocus' third song in *Odyssey* viii is about the Trojan horse (*Odyssey* viii 499–520), and Cretheus' poetry is not limited to *arma virum* but to *equi* as well. In other words, Cretheus does not seem just to know about the current mission of the Trojans in Italy, but about the whole story of Troy, including, we might imagine, the *Iliad* itself. He is a poet who brings the *Iliad* and the *Aeneid* together into one poem. The often observed connection between Cretheus and Virgil is justified, for Virgil is a poet who accomplishes the same feat. In fact the above connections indi-

25 Nagy 1999:42–58 discusses this passage at some length.

cate that the phrase *arma virum* marks passages in which Homeric precedents may be particularly keenly felt.

Now to a slightly more complex example: In Book 11 of the *Aeneid* the Amazon warrior Camilla slays many Trojans in the course of her *aristeia*. Just how badly things are going for the Trojans is made clear when Orchilochus' death under Camilla's spear is described in the language of the *Aeneid's* proem: tum validam perque arma viro perque ossa securim . . . congeminat ("Then she hacked powerfully again and again with her axe, through the man's arms, and then through his bones"; *Aeneid* XI 696–698). But the tide begins to turn against Camilla when the Etruscan general Tarchon, in order to spur on his troops to come to the aid of the Trojans, stages a dazzling coup. He snatches his opponent Venulus off his horse and wrestles with him on his own horse as he leads his men into battle: volat igneus aequore Tarchon arma virumque ferens ("Like a fire Tarchon flies across the plain, carrying arms and the man"; *Aeneid* XI 746–747). Thus Tarchon carries as his battle standard a physical manifestation of the phrase *arma virumque* that embodies the Trojans' destiny and their necessary victory. There is no Homeric precedent for the spectacular feat of wrestling one's opponent off his horse and onto one's own[26] and here we are to imagine that Tarchon knew he would have to do something truly unheard of in order to rally his troops. Tarchon's charge, in particular his creation of the imagery of the proem of the *Aeneid*, inspires the Trojans to redouble their efforts in the battle against Camilla; Arruns immediately starts plotting her downfall, which sets into motion the final stages of the conflict and the poem.

What does have a Homeric precedent in this passage is the simile of the eagle and the snake, which describes Tarchon and Venulus wrestling on the horse:

> utque volans alte raptum cum fulva draconem
> fert aquila implicuitque pedes atque unguibus haesit,
> saucius at serpens sinuosa volumina versat
> arrectisque horret squamis et sibilat ore
> arduus insurgens, illa haud minus urget obunco
> luctantem rostro, simul aethera verberat alis.

> And just as when a tawny eagle, flying on high, carries off a snake he has caught by winding his feet around it and clutching it with his claws, but when the wounded snake bends his winding coils and

26 The closest parallel is the simile in *Iliad* XV that compares Ajax jumping from ship to ship to a man who can jump from horse to horse while they run (*Iliad* XV 679). But Ajax does not actually jump from horse to horse—he is only capable of this metaphorically.

> bristles with raised scales and hisses with its mouth, striking forcefully, no less does he press it as it struggles with his curved beak as he beats the air with his wings.
>
> *Aeneid* XI 751–756

The event described in this simile is found in the *Iliad* in Book 12, when the Trojans, hesitating before pressing on toward the Greek ships, see an eagle carrying a snake. The snake bites the eagle and the eagle drops it and flies away (*I*liad XII 200–207). Polydamas interprets this to mean that the Trojans may reach the ships but will not be able to return home with their booty; Hector dismisses him as superstitious and presses on. Polydamas is correct that the portent is ominous for the Trojans; they do not, in the end, destroy the ships, and although many do escape, probably just as many die. Tarchon creates a similar oracle to encourage the Trojans, the difference being that he does not drop his prey, Venulus, even though he fights back fiercely. The Trojans of the *Iliad* were doomed, and the dropped snake of their oracle reflects that, but the Trojans of the *Aeneid* must triumph; Tarchon knows that as long as he can hold on to his snake, as it were, his homemade oracle will be effective in portending Trojan victory.

In fact, we never find out what happens to Tarchon and Venulus; after the simile the narrative shifts to Arruns and Camilla. This lack of resolution in a passage that refers to an eagle seizing prey recalls another Homeric omen that ends with an unresolved image. At *Iliad* II 308–319 the Greeks, debating their future at Aulis, see a snake eat nine sparrows and their mother, after which Zeus turns the snake to stone as a monument for all time. Calchas interprets this to mean that the Greeks will take Troy in the tenth year; the omen is their assurance that Troy will soon fall. Tarchon and Venulus may not be turned to stone in the narrative of the poem, but the only image of them that the poetry provides is of them wrestling, without end. This limited perspective is a type of petrification—the words on the page describe the state in which Tarchon apparently remains, triumphantly clutching *arma virumque*. It is a portentious image, as the simile of the snake and the eagle, in connection with their Homeric precedent, shows, and it is a frozen image, like that of the snake in Book 2 of the *Iliad*. And just as Odysseus reminds the Greeks in *Iliad* II that after nine years only one remains, the Trojans here may sense that they are nearing the end of their conflict; Turnus' death and the end of the war are only a book away.

This network of passages is perhaps less than spectacular in its depth, for it only involves one or two Homeric precedents for a Virgilian scene. Still, it shows some ways that we can build an interpretation of a particular Virgilian passage such as that of Camilla and Tarchon out of the network of Homeric passages invoked by those scenes. A potentially more fruitful network takes shape in *Aeneid* VI: while traveling through the underworld, Aeneas and the Sibyl reach "the most distant fields, separate [from the rest of the underworld], which the famous war heroes populate" (*Aeneid* VI 477–478). Aeneas stops and talks to the Trojan heroes, who in turn are eager to speak with him. The reaction of the Greeks, however, is quite different.

> at Danaum proceres Agamemnoniaeque phalanges
> ut videre virum, fulgentiaque arma per umbras,
> ingenti trepidare metu; pars vertere terga,
> ceu quondam petiere rates, pars tollere vocem
> exiguam; inceptus clamor frustratur hiantis.
>
> But the Greek noblemen, and Agamemnon's soldiers, as they saw the man and his arms flashing through the shadows, shook with great fear. Some turned and fled, as when they had run for their ships, some lifted a faint shout; but the cries, only begun, stuck in their gaping throats.
>
> *Aeneid* VI 489–493

This variation of *arma virum* has a Homeric quality to it—the epics make clear that one aspect of rhapsodic virtuosity was to reshape formulaic language into different metrical units for different narrative situations. The Greeks feel fear on several occasions in the *Iliad*, but this passage refers specifically to the Greeks' flight to their ships in Book 15 shortly before Patroclus asks Achilles for his armor: "The Achaeans fled because of their weakness, for Apollo sent fear upon them, and gave honor to the Trojans and Hector" (XV 325–327). The implication is that Aeneas appears to the Greeks in the underworld as Hector appeared to them on that day.

But even as they connect Aeneas to the heroism of his ancestors, these passages recall several Homeric scenes that work together to foreshadow Aeneas' future heroism. The phrase *fulgentia arma* is something of a formulaic phrase in the *Aeneid*, appearing ten times in various contexts. By comparison, the Homeric equivalent, τεύχεα παμφανόωντα, appears only twice. One of those appearances comes in Thetis' plan to request arms for Achilles from Hephaestus in *Iliad* XVIII: εἶμι παρ' Ἥφαιστον κλυτοτέχνην, αἴ κ' ἐθέλῃσιν / υἱεῖ ἐμῷ δόμεναι κλυτὰ τεύχεα παμφανόωντα ("I will go to the famous smith Hephaestus, to see if he would be willing to give to my son glorious shining armor"; XVIII 143–144). Here the network of connections takes the kind of turn I am interested in, one that shows how Virgil integrated the Homeric structure into his own; the Virgilian passage, via *fulgentia arma*, recalls a Homeric passage, Thetis' request for Achilles' arms, which then evokes a Virgilian passage, Venus' request to Vulcan for Aeneas' arma: "arma rogo, genetrix nato. te filia Nerei, te potuit lacrimis Tithonia flectere coniunx" ("I ask for arms, a mother for her son. The daughter of Nereus and Tithonus' wife were able to convince you [to do this] with their tears"; *Aeneid* VIII 383–384). I call attention to this passage because Virgil explicitly invokes the *Iliad* and the epic cycle; the wife of Tithonus refers to Aurora, who in the *Aethiopis* requests armor for her son Memnon. If more of the *Aethiopis* had survived than the four lines we have, we could follow this reference into that poem as well. As it is, I can only observe that Virgil had not only Homer but the whole epic cycle as the structure under his work.

The other instance of τεύχεα παμφανόωντα in the *Iliad* comes in Book 5: ἤριπε δ' ἐξ ὀχέων, ἀράβησε δὲ τεύχε' ἐπ' αὐτῷ / αἰόλα παμφανόωντα, παρέτρεσσαν δέ οἱ ἵπποι / ὠκύποδες ("He fell from the chariot, and his arms rattled on him, shimmering and flashing, and the swift-footed horses swerved in fear"; *Iliad* V 294–296). This is the death of Lycaon at the hands of Diomedes, which may at first seem like an interpretive dead end, but the passage connects back to the *Aeneid* in a startling way: it is Aeneas who arrives to defend the body of Lycaon, and for the first but not last time in the *Iliad*, he only narrowly escapes death with divine aid and is thus able to go on to found the Roman race. So while this Homeric passage does not actually invoke any Virgilian passages, it nevertheless is an extremely important passage for the story of Aeneas.

To return to Aeneas' encounter with the Greeks in the underworld, we find a similar network in an Odyssean passage alluded to there, namely the appearance of Heracles in the Nekuia: "Around him there was the screaming of the dead, as of birds fleeing terrified in every direction" (*Odyssey* xi 605). We may conclude that in some sense Aeneas in the underworld is a Heracles figure. But we can go further, because this Homeric passage gestures back, as it were, to a Virgilian passage: we make the connection between the Virgilian Aeneas and the Odyssean Heracles, and can then make a further connection between Aeneas and the Virgilian Hercules of *Aeneid* VIII. Hercules is a legendary hero for Rome before it was Rome, and so will Aeneas be a legendary hero for the next stage of the history of the site of Rome, the stage in which Rome reaches the height of its glory. And without the Homeric connection of Aeneas to Heracles, the resonance of this connection between Aeneas and Hercules in Book 8 could not be felt. And I have only scratched the surface of this network—as I mentioned earlier, the phrase *fulgentia arma* is repeated nine more times in the *Aeneid.* Aeneas' encounter with the Greeks in the underworld refers to all nine, and each of those scenes marks the start of yet another path through the Homeric and Virgilian worlds.

One final example shows how dense the network of meaning can be, how the trail of reference can lead from the *Aeneid* into Homer and then back to the *Aeneid*, connecting Virgilian passages that would have no connection without the Homeric intermediary. Again we start with *arma virum*, as Dido, unable to convince Aeneas to stay in Carthage, resolves to kill herself and gives Anna instructions:

> tu secreta pyram tecto interiore sub auras
> erige, et arma viri thalamo quae fixa reliquit
> impius exuviasque omnis lectumque iugalem,
> quo perii, super imponas.
>
> Build a pyre secretly in the inner parts of the house, in the open air, and place on it the man's arms, which he wickedly left hanging in the wedding chamber, along with all his spoils, and the wedding bed, on which I was destroyed.
>
> *Aeneid* IV 494–497

Dido is trying to convince her sister that burning Aeneas' possessions will quench her love, but in reality she is planning her own death—the whole tragedy of Book 4, the inability of Aeneas to be what Dido wants him to be, is contained in her contemptuous use of the phrase *arma viri*, which is here used with Aeneas as the referent of *vir* for the first time in the narrative. The phrase recurs in reference to another pyre, this time in Book 6. Before Aeneas can enter the underworld, he must bury Misenus, who lies dead on the beach, killed when he challenged Triton to a trumpet-playing match. After his men perform most of the preparations for the pyre, Aeneas adds the finishing touch: At pius Aeneas ingenti mole sepulcrum imponit suaque arma viro remumque tubamque ("But Aeneas dutifully placed the tomb on a huge pile, along with the man's arms, his oar, and his trumpet"; *Aeneid* VI 232–233). This pyre for a deceased companion calls to mind many Homeric scenes; the burial of Elpenor, killed when he fell from the roof of Circe's house in a drunken stupor; the burial of Patroclus, killed and stripped by Hector; the burial of Hector himself; the burial of Greeks and Trojans during the temporary truce of *Iliad* VII; Agamemnon's description of the burial of Achilles in the underworld in *Odyssey* xxiv; and Andromache's burial of her father, Eetion. Of these pyres I want to highlight Elpenor's and Eetion's because, like Misenus' and Dido's pyres, they include arms, Elpenor's because he did not die in battle and Eetion's because Achilles did not take them.

First, Elpenor: αὐτὰρ ἐπεὶ νεκρός τ' ἐκάη καὶ τεύχεα νεκροῦ, / τύμβον χεύαντες καὶ ἐπὶ στήλην ἐρύσαντες / πήξαμεν ἀκροτάτῳ τύμβῳ εὐῆρες ἐρετμόν ("But when the corpse and the dead man's arms were burned, after raising a mound and dragging a gravestone upon it, we planted a well-shaped oar on the top of the mound"; *Odyssey* xii 13–15). This passage is itself a Homeric doublet: Elpenor requests to be buried this way at *Odyssey* xi 74. Heubeck *ad loc.* notes that Elpenor may have had arms, but that he was not a warrior at all, but merely an oarsman. Misenus, trumpeting on the beach while his companions made camp, is a similar sort of man. We could ask then what it means for the programmatic phrase of the *Aeneid* to appear in a description of a pyre that commemorates a man manifestly different from the heroes of the Trojan war, Achilles, Patroclus, and Hector, whose arms could not be included in their funeral, and that rather honors a man who died an unnecessary, natural (and therefore somewhat cowardly) death. Misenus' funeral-with-*arma* also recalls that of Eetion, described by his daughter Andromache in *Iliad* VI as she begs Hector not to return to the fighting.

> κατὰ δ' ἔκτανεν Ἠετίωνα,
> οὐδέ μιν ἐξενάριξε, σεβάσσατο γὰρ τό γε θυμῷ,
> ἀλλ' ἄρα μιν κατέκηε σὺν ἔντεσι δαιδαλέοισιν
> ἠδ' ἐπὶ σῆμ' ἔχεεν·
>
> [Achilles] killed Eetion. And he did not strip his armor, because he honored him in his heart. But he burned him with his cunningly wrought arms and placed over him a tomb.
>
> *Iliad* VI 416–418

Another reference to Eetion comes in *Iliad* XXII, as Andromache, lamenting the death of Hector, calls her father δύσμορος (XXII 481). And in this same speech Andromache describes what will be the pyre for her absent spouse: "But in your house there are clothes, fine and pleasing, made by the hands of women. But I will surely burn all of these things in a blazing fire—they are no use to you, since you will not lie in them" (XXII 510–514). Through this connection we come back to Dido's pyre, which twists the details of the Homeric scene: Aeneas, the spouse, is absent, as Hector was, but Dido, unlike Andromache, burns herself: "We were both born for a single destiny," mourns Andromache at *Iliad* XXII 477—one of suffering. Dido, too, was born for suffering, but the problem is that she and Aeneas were born for *separate* destinies. We might infer that she had wanted Aeneas to be another Hector, and she had wanted to be his Andromache. Now she sees the impossibility of this arrangement, that Aeneas cannot be another Hector. The damage has been done, though, and ironically she can only perish in anguish, like Andromache. Another relevant feature of Andromache's speech is her lament for her son: "For even if he escapes the sorrowful war with the Achaeans, there will always be toil for him, and troubles in the future" (*Iliad* XXII 487–488). She goes on to describe the loneliness Astyanax will face, the alienation, the roaming. This passage reminds me, at least, of another passage from *Aeneid* IV, which would not have been recalled by the *Aeneid*'s pyre scene alone, Dido's raving wish that she and Aeneas had produced a son: "At least if some offspring had been conceived in me from you before you fled, if some little Aeneas were playing in my courtyard, whose face would remind me of you, I would not seem to have been so completely deceived and abandoned" (*Aeneid* IV 328–330). The irony, of course, is that Aeneas *does* have a son, Ascanius, whose promised future is a factor in the decision to leave Carthage; Mercury tells Aeneas, "If the glory of such great things does not move you, think of Ascanius, growing up, and the hope of your heir Iulus" (*Aeneid* IV 272–274). Ascanius' future as the first king of Alba Longa and the forefather of a distinguished race is quite the opposite of what Andromache expects for Astyanax, but like Andromache Dido is left with no future. This is a particularly striking effect because it is generated by a network between passages that starts in *Aeneid* IV, moves by allusion to *Odyssey* xii, to *Iliad* VI, to *Iliad* XXII, and then back to a different passage in *Aeneid* IV, a move not possible if we rigidly take the *Aeneid* to refer only to the *Iliad* as an earlier text, rather than as part of the same network of meaning created by the Homeric poems. And we can even form further links between these passages and those previously discussed. As we learned in *Iliad* IX, Achilles got the lyre with which he sang the κλέα ἀνδρῶν when he sacked the city of Eetion (*Iliad* IX 188), whose pyre (after Achilles killed him) forms one of the crucial links in the network under discussion here.

If we return to our original passage, Dido's lament, we can follow this network in yet another direction. When Dido uses the words *lectum iugalem* ('marriage bed', *Aeneid* IV 496), she calls to mind the marriage bed of Odysseus, which Penelope uses as the final test to determine whether Odysseus is really who he says he is (*Odyssey* xxiii 205–206). But while the marriage bed of Odysseus and Penelope serves as a symbol of their undying love and a verification of their reunion, the *lectum iugalem* of Aeneas and Dido is a symbol of the impossibility of their having such a relationship; indeed, Aeneas would deny that it was *iugalis* at all. Consequently Dido burns it on a pyre reminiscent of the pyre on which Andromache burned Hector's possessions, which she described as οὐδὲν σοί γ' ὄφελος ("No use to you"; *Iliad* XXII 513). But through this connection Aeneas is not completely absent. Odysseus describes how he built the olive-tree bed at *Odyssey* xxiii 200–201: "inlaying it with gold and silver and ivory," among other things. Dido's first view of Aeneas after he emerges from Venus' cloud is described in these same terms: "for his mother had shed upon her son beauty . . . the beauty the hand gives to ivory, or when silver is set in yellow gold" (*Aeneid* I 592–593). Dido's ironic, and pitiful, invocation of the marriage bed of Odysseus thus becomes an invocation of Aeneas himself.

These four sample passages—Cretheus, Camilla, Aeneas in the underworld, and Dido's pyre—generate their own networks of meaning, and yet the four are not unconnected; indeed, they are all part of the network of meaning around *arma virum*, a phrase that appears several more times in the poem. That is, all four of these examples can be seen as part of the same network of meaning, which, I am arguing, is as interpretively robust as any that has been found in Homeric poetry. Along the way I have indicated some ways I think these networks could be interpreted; as for the overarching network around *arma virum*, it would be interesting to see how the meaning of that phrase changes throughout the poem, as Aeneas and the Trojans fulfill their destiny.

And so I return to my original question about whether Virgil understood the nature of Homeric poetry. The connections between repeated language and themes in the *Aeneid* can stand up to the same scrutiny as those in Homer, and Homer's poetry itself is a critical part of these networks. As for Virgil's understanding, I see three possibilities. First, perhaps Virgil understood nothing, and it just looks like he did because the networks I have described are in fact a feature of *all* language. In this case the distinction between oral and written poetry is perhaps not so defined as some might like. The second possibility is that perhaps Virgil *did* understand Homer as a formulaic poet, along with all the resonances that an Archaic Greek audience would have felt. In this case (and I do not think it is too much of a stretch to claim) Virgil was the most attentive, versatile, and hard-wired audience that Homer ever had. A third possibility is that he did not understand anything about formulaic poetry, but that it did not matter: his imitation of Homer was *so* thorough that he unwittingly, as it were, created a piece of literature that functioned, in this respect at least, as a truly formulaic poem would.

Bibliography

Albrecht, E. 1881. "Wiederholte Verse und Verstheile bei Vergil." *Hermes* 16:393–444.

Bloch, Alfred. 1970. "*Arma Virumque* als heroisches Leitmotiv." *Museum Helveticum* 27:206–211.

Clay, Jenny Strauss. 1983. *The Wrath of Athena: Gods and Men in the Odyssey*. Princeton.

Conte, Gian Biagio. 1994. *Latin Literature: A History*. Trans. J. B. Solodow, D. Fowler, and G. W. Most. Baltimore.

Goold, George P. 1977. "The Nature of Homeric Composition." *Illinois Classical Studies* 2:1–34.

Hainsworth, Bryan. 1993. *The Iliad: A Commentary. Volume III: Books 9–12*. Cambridge.

Hardie, Philip, ed. 1994. *Virgil: Aeneid IX*. Cambridge.

Knauer, Georg Nicolaus. 1964. *Die Aeneis und Homer; Studien zur poetischen Technik Vergils, mit Listen der Homerzitate in der Aeneis*. Hypomnemata 7. Gottingen.

Kopff, E. Christian. 1981. "Virgil and the Cyclic Epics." *ANRW* 2.31.2:919–947.

Levitan, William. 1993. "Give Up the Beginning?: Juno's Mindful Wrath (*Aeneid* 1.37)." *Liverpool Classical Monthly* 18.1:14.

Lord, Albert. 2000. *The Singer of Tales*. Harvard Studies in Comparative Literature 24. 2nd ed., with introduction by S. Mitchell and G. Nagy. Cambridge, MA.

Miller, D. Gary. 1982. *Homer and the Ionian Epic Tradition*. Innsbrucker Beiträge zur Sprachwissenschaft 38. Innsbruck.

Moskalew, Walter. 1982. *Formular Language and Poetic Design in the Aeneid*. Mnemosyne Supplement 73. Leiden.

Nagy, Gregory. 1990a. *Pindar's Homer: The Lyric Possession of an Epic Past*. Baltimore.

———. 1990b. *Greek Mythology and Poetics*. Ithaca.

———. 1996a. *Poetry as Performance: Homer and Beyond*. Cambridge.

———. 1996b. *Homeric Questions*. Austin.

———. 1999. *The Best of the Achaeans: Concepts of the Hero in Archaic Greek Poetry*. 2nd ed. with new introduction. Baltimore.

———. 2003. *Homeric Responses*. Austin.

Oliensis, Ellen. 2004. "Sibylline Syllables: The Intratextual *Aeneid*." *Proceedings of the Cambridge Philological Society* 50:29–45.

Schlunk, Robin. 1974. *The Homeric Scholia and the Aeneid*. Ann Arbor.

Scodel, Ruth. 2004. "The Modesty of Homer." *Oral Performance and Its Context* (ed. C. J. Mackie) 1–19. Mnemosyne Supplement 248. Leiden.

West, Martin L. 1985. *The Hesiodic Catalogue of Women*. Oxford.

Wills, Jeffrey. 1996. *Repetition in Latin Poetry: Figures of Allusion.* Oxford.

Zetzel, James E. G. 1984. "Re-Creating the Canon: Augustan Poetry and the Alexandrian Past." *Canons* (ed. R. von Hallberg) 107–130. Chicago.

8

The Homeric Hymn to Apollo

Translated by Rodney Merrill

Translator's Note

My main aims in translating this hymn are similar to those I have set forth at some length in the translator's introduction to my version of the *Odyssey* (Ann Arbor, 2002, 64–85), and more briefly in the introduction to my version of the *Iliad* (Ann Arbor, 2007, 1–22). They have to do with conveying the formal, one should even say musical, aspects of the work, which seem to me to have a direct and profound bearing on its overall significance. These hymns, whether considered as independent works or as proems to a recitation of epic, seem to require such understanding at least as much as the epic itself, for their ritual qualities, explicit or implicit, underlie their narratives and qualify both their drama and their humor. From the translator's point of view it does not greatly matter whether those qualities derive from actual performance as ritual, or whether they constitute a literary convention. By the same token, we do not need to decide conclusively whether these poems began existence as oral poems—"composition in performance"—or as literate derivatives of the great tradition of oral epic. In either case what we have are poems in which, as in Homeric oral epic, repetition plays an important part; repetition, moreover, that is given life and validated by a specific insistent meter, so that the aural music of the poem plays a crucial role both in its meaning and in its reception by the audience.

My use of an English accentual version of the dactylic hexameter meter, therefore, is far from arbitrary or decorative. Whatever the merits of my particular realization may be, it seems essential to make the reader aware of the musical power of the repeated elements on every level, whether of particular words, formulaic phrases, whole lines, or even passages. This has two dimensions: one, internal, relates to the coherence of this particular poem; the other, external, relates this poem to the whole corpus of Homeric poetry, with which it shares a large proportion of the formulaic phrasing as well as more extensive passages. Both qualities are immediately evident to anyone who reads the poem in the original. To begin with the most obvious aspects of the external dimension, the epithets applied to people, places, and things are often the same as those that occur in the epics—e.g. "far-shooting Apollo," "Hera of white arms," "sandy-soiled Pylos," "sea-faring galleys." The catalogs of places in lines 30–44, 216–244, and 409–429 recall those of the *Iliad* and the *Odyssey* not merely in describing journeys around various places but in some of their particular phrasing. Then there are lines and even passages that echo those of an epic. Perhaps the most striking occurs when Apollo, in the form of a youth, questions the merchants from Crete whom he intends to make his priests—he "quotes" four lines (452–455) that occur twice in the *Odyssey*.

> "Strangers, who are you? And whence do you sail on the
> watery pathways?
> Have you affairs in trading, or do you recklessly wander
> over the seas in the manner of pirates who wander at
> random
> putting their lives in danger and visiting evil on strangers?"

In one of the Odyssean passages (iii 71–74), Nestor questions Telémachos and Athena (disguised as Mentor) when they arrive in Pylos; in the other (ix 252–255), Polyphemos interrogates Odysseus and his companions as soon as he catches sight of them in his cave. Nestor's inquiry comes only after his visitors have received a meal, as the culmination of the elaborate ritual of hospitality (*xenía*) so important in the moral universe of Homeric epic. Then when Polyphemos uses the same lines, the extensive repetition reminds us how completely both sides are ignoring that ritual, Odysseus and his men by invading and robbing their host's dwelling, Polyphemos by launching his inquiry before any welcome has been given. In the *Hymn*, Apollo's abrupt questioning, though disingenuous—he knows quite well who they are—resembles Polyphemos' far more than Nestor's. So if this extended quotation can be taken as an allusion, it might well add to our sense of how forcibly the god has abducted these merchants, playing the very pirate he speaks of. The allusive contrast with the courteous hospitality of Nestor might also be underlined by the fact, twice mentioned (398–399, 470; the name "Pylos" occurs twice in 424 as well) that these Cretans were bound for Pylos when Apollo co-opted them into his service.

Whether such echoes in oral epic should be read as allusions may remain a matter for discussion, but their overall importance in integrating this hymn with the large corpus of Homeric poetry can hardly be doubted. For this reason, I have used the formulaic phrasing of my translations of the *Iliad* and the *Odyssey* in all places, brief or extended, where the context allows it. My hope is that readers of the three translations will be able to grasp this relationship almost as immediately and as musically as would the audience of the original works. I readily admit that sheer economy of effort makes this an attractive proceeding, as it surely did for the original poets; but beyond that, one of the important pleasures of this large literary corpus derives from coming across a familiar phrase or passage in a different setting—"repetition" on a grand cultural scale, both synchronic—in many places at the same moment—and diachronic—a literary impulse flourishing across generations, even centuries.

The other, internal, dimension, is equally important but harder to characterize briefly; and only for purposes of analysis can it be separated from our overriding sense of epic diction. To make a beginning, however, both the meter and the repetition founded on that meter give the poem a stylistic coherence and intensity appropriate to the invocation of a god. For example, we hear the phrases "far-shooting Apollo" or "the Far-shooter" many times, some of them in quick succession, as we do "Phoibos Apollo" and "far-working Apollo"—never do we forget the central subject of the hymn. Even when the action is swift, as in line 440, when Apollo leaps from the Cretans' ship, we get the full phrase, "the lord far-working Apollo." Other such formulaic phrases also recur, especially in relation to the other gods and goddesses—Zeus, Leto, Helios. Longer passages as well both unify and ritualize the poem. One of the most notable is lines 22–23, characterizing Apollo's wide-spread predominance in song, repeated exactly only 120 lines later, at 144–145. Another is the question at line 19—"How shall I sing of you who are in all ways worthy of singing?"—repeated in the second part of the poem, at line 207; in both cases the answer leads to the narratives that form the bulk of the hymn. (Without going into the question, I simply note that the hymn as we have it can best be regarded as one poem in two parts of unequal length, the shorter first part celebrating the birth of Apollo on Delos, the second the foundation of his oracle at Delphi.) Evidently the exact repetition of the line is far from casual; in both places the ritual requires the recognition of the god's greatness, a corresponding expression of the singer's humble stance before a plethora of possibilities, and an eventual choice of the most significant among them. For this reason it is important to accentuate musically the quasi-ritual nature of the question and its poetic consequences. Much the same thing holds for other places in the poem. One important example is the extensive repetition in the passages relating Apollo's intentions for his projected temples, first at Telphoúsa, where the spring, wanting to keep the place for her own glory, causes him to abandon the project, and then in Krisa, where he achieves it (247–255; cf. 287–295). How better to dramatize the ritual of this foundation than to show it in the same lines, first frustrated and then carried to fulfillment?

Beyond the repetition itself, the strict yet flexible meter in which it is couched conveys the sort of decorum, the satisfaction in traditional expectations fulfilled, that characterizes all ritual. This is true throughout the hymn, even in non-repetitive passages—the musical rhythm deeply conditions the poem's overall significance as a work of archaic Greek art. I hope that this English version, however much it falls short of the original, will help contemporary readers grasp that significance.

I have relied mainly on the text published in the edition of T. W. Allen, W. R. Halliday, and E. E. Sikes, 2nd. ed. (Oxford, 1963), 20–42, with commentary. The four lines in square brackets (81a, 317a, 539a–b) are based on no textual authority; the Greek lines were suggested, mainly by Allen, to fill lacunae in the manuscripts and are printed in the text of the older Loeb edition, ed. and trans. Hugh G. Evelyn-White (London and Cambridge, MA, 1914). Line 325a is so numbered because it occurs only in one group of manuscripts and was omitted from early editions. I have also consulted the more recent Loeb edition, ed. and trans. Martin L. West (Cambridge, MA, 2003). West characterizes lines 211–213 as "deeply obscure"; corrupt might be a better word—the sense of the original is as unclear as that of my rendering. The diacritical marks over some Greek names are intended, as in my translations of the epics, to help readers pronounce these names with correct accentuation and thereby maintain the dactylic meter. They appear only on names whose pronunciation might not be clear to some readers of English—Apollo, Athena, Artemis, etc., have no marks. The first syllable of two-syllable names always receives the stress. The acute accent (´) indicates stress; a few names have two such accents. The grave accent (`) appears over final -e to indicate that it is pronounced. The diaeresis (¨) over the second of two contiguous vowels indicates that it is to be pronounced separately.

I.

I will remember, nor could I forget, far-shooting Apollo,
whom gods tremble before as in Zeus's abode he is striding—
then as he comes up close to the place they are sitting, they leap up,
all of them, out of their seats, as he stretches his glittering bow back.
Leto alone stays there beside Zeus the great thunderbolt-hurler;
she unloosens the bowstring and closes the lid on his quiver;
taking his arrows and bow in her hands from his powerful shoulders,
she hangs them on the pillar by which his father is sitting,
high on a gold-wrought hook; to a chair she guides him and seats him.
Then, in a goblet of gold, sweet nectar his father presents him,
making his dear son welcome; and straightway the other immortals
sit down there in assembly, and Leto the lady is gladdened,
seeing that she has brought forth so mighty a son and an archer.
Hail and rejoice then, Leto the blessèd, for glorious children
you bore, lordly Apollo and Artemis shooter of arrows,
her in Ortygia, him brought forth in Delos the rocky,
while you reclined on a great tall peak of the Kynthian highland,
close to a date-palm tree by the streams of the River Inópos.
How shall I sing of you who are in all ways worthy of singing?
For to you, Phoibos, melodious songs are intoned the world over,
both on the mainland, nurturing heifers, and over the islands;
all of the crags are delightful to you, and the sharp promontories
jutting from steep high mountains, and rivers that flow to the seabrine,
beaches that slope down into the water, and deep sea harbors.
Shall it be how first Leto delivered you, gladdening mortals,
when by the mountain of Kynthos she lay, on the rock-strewn island

Delos begirt by the sea, with a black wave surging on either
hand to the dry land under the shrill sharp breath of the
stormwinds?
Thence indeed having risen, you rule over all of us mortals,
over the people who dwell in Crete and the district of
Athens,
also the isle of Aigína and galley-renownèd Euboía,
Aigai, Eíresiaí, and Pepárethos, close to the sea-brine,
also Thracian Athos and Pelion's towering summits,
Thracian Samos as well, and the shadowy highlands of Ida,
Skyros as well as Phokaía, the highland of steep Autokánè
also, and firm-set Imbros and inhospitable Lemnos,
sacred Lesbos, the dwelling of Makar, Aíolos' scion,
also Chios, the brightest of islands that lie in the sea-brine,
Mimas, rugged and rocky, and Kórykos' towering summits,
shimmering Klaros as well, and the highland of steep Aisagéa,
also watery Samos and Mýkalè's steep high headland,
then Milétos and Kos, that town of Meropian people,
then too steep high Knidos and wind-blown Kárpathos
island,
Naxos and Paros as well, and the rock-strewn isle of Rhenaía—
even so far did Leto, in birth-pangs with the Far-shooter,
wander to seek a land willing to serve as a home for her dear
son.
They were all dreadfully trembling and fearful, and none of
them dared to
take in Phoibos the lord, not even the richest among them,
not until finally Leto the lady, arriving on Delos,
made inquiry of her, as in these winged words she addressed
her:
"Delos, if you would be willing to be the abode of my dear son
Phoibos Apollo, and here to establish for him a great sumptuous
temple—
since no other will touch you; of that you will not be unmindful,
nor, I believe, will you be at all wealthy in cattle and sheep
flocks,
nor will you bring forth grapes or produce an abundance of
produce—
if you contain, however, the shrine of far-shooting Apollo,

people will all be bringing to you their hecatombs hither,
when they gather together; the measureless savor of fat will
always rise from the fires—your inhabitants you will be feeding
out of those foreigners' hands, for in truth your soil is not fertile."
So did she say; then Delos was gladdened and made her an answer:
"Leto, the greatly illustrious daughter of powerful Koios,
gladly indeed to your offspring, the lord far-shooting, would I grant
welcome, because it is terribly true that of evil repute I
am among men—thus I would become universally honored.
But this saying I tremble at, Leto, and I will not hide it:
for they say that Apollo will be of a haughty and reckless
temper, and greatly will he dominate both among the immortals
and among men who are mortal upon these grain-giving plowlands.
Therefore am I most terribly fearful in mind and in spirit,
lest as he looks for the very first time on Helios' sunlight,
he will dishonor the island because I am rugged and rocky,
overturn me with his feet, thrust me to the depths of the seabrine;
there will the great high billows forever be breaking above me,
over my head; he will go to another land, one that will please him,
there to erect his temple and found his forested woodland.
Sea-polypuses will build upon me their bedrooms, and black seals
also will make me their carefree dwelling, because I lack people.
Yet if you deign now, goddess, to swear me an oath of the strongest—
it will be here that he first will erect a most beautiful temple
which will for all mankind be an oracle—afterward, surely,
81a [let him erect more temples and found more forested woodlands]
widely among all men, for in many a name will he glory."
So she spoke; the great oath of the gods did Leto then swear her:

"Now Earth witness to this, and the wide sky stretching above us,
so too the water of Styx, down-flowing; for this is the greatest
oath and the oath most dreadful among us blessèd immortals:
surely forever will be right here on this island the fragrant
altar and precinct of Phoibos; and you above all will he honor."
But then, when she had sworn and had brought her oath to completion,
Delos was gladdened indeed at the birth of the lord, the Far-shooter;
Leto was yet nine days and as well nine nights by unwonted
birth-pangs pierced to the core; and the goddesses were on the isle with
her, all those who were noblest, as were Diónè and Rhea,
Themis of Ichnai also and thunderous Ámphitrítè,
all of the rest of the goddesses too, save Hera of white arms,
for she sat in the halls of the great cloud-gathering god Zeus;
Eíleithýia the goddess of childbirth alone did not know it,
for she sat in the gold clouds high on the peak of Olympos
by the contrivance of Hera of white arms, who out of envy
kept her away from the place: to a son both faultless and mighty
Leto of beautiful tresses was just then going to give birth.
Then from the firm-set island the goddesses sent away Iris,
Eíleithýia to fetch by promising her a great necklace
fastened together with gold-spun threads, nine cubits extended,
bade her deliver the summons apart from Hera of white arms,
lest with her words that goddess should afterwards turn her from coming.
But then, when to these things swift wind-footed Iris had listened,
she began running, so quickly accomplishing all of the distance.
But then, when she arrived at the seat of the gods, steep Olympos,
straightway Eíleithýia away from the chamber she summoned
out of the door, and in winged words there she spoke and addressed her

all that the goddesses having their homes on Olympos had ordered.
In this way she persuaded the heart in the breast of the goddess;
then they departed on foot, in their steps like timorous pigeons.
Soon as had set foot there on Delos the goddess of childbirth
Eíleithýia, the pangs seized Leto, who yearned to deliver.
Throwing her arms then around a date-palm, she fell to her knees right
there on the soft meadowland, and the earth began smiling beneath her;
he leapt forth to the light; all the goddesses cried out rejoicing.
Thereupon, glorious Phoibos, the goddesses purely and cleanly
bathed you in beautiful water and swathed you in whitest apparel,
delicate, recently woven, and fastened about you a gold band.
Nor was Apollo the god of the gold sword nursed by his mother;
rather, of nectar and lovely ambrosia Themis provided
him a due share with her deathless hands; then Leto was gladdened,
seeing that she had brought forth so mighty a son and an archer.
But then, Phoibos, as soon as you ate the ambrosial victuals,
then no longer the gold cords held you, panting and struggling,
nor did the bonds restrain you, but all their knots were unloosened.
Then to the deathless goddesses spoke forth Phoibos Apollo:
"Ever belovèd to me may the kithara be, and the curved bow;
I will declare to mankind great Zeus's infallible purpose."
So having spoken began to go forth on the earth of the wide ways
Phoibos of hair unshorn who shoots from afar; and at him then
marveled the goddesses all; and with gold all Delos was heavy
laden as she caught sight of the offspring of Zeus and of Leto,
gladdened because it was she that the god had chosen as dwelling,
over the islands and mainland—she loved him the more in her spirit,

blooming, as when with its woodland flowers a mountain-top
blossoms.
You then, silvery-bowed far-shooter, the lordly Apollo,
sometimes strode on your way over Kynthos, rugged and rocky,
sometimes you would go roaming about among islands and
peoples.
Many indeed are your temples and many the forested
woodlands;
all of the crags are belovèd to you, and the sharp promontories
jutting from steep high mountains, and rivers that flow to the
sea-brine;
but in your heart by Delos especially you are delighted,
Phoibos, for there long-robed Ionians gather together,
they themselves and as well their children and virtuous
bedmates.
There in remembrance of you they give you delight with their
boxing
matches and dancing and singing, whenever they set
competitions.
One would suppose them immortal and ageless forever
and ever,
he who had come upon those Ionians meeting together;
he on beholding the grace of them all would delight in his
spirit,
as at the men he gazed, and the women with beautiful girdles,
and at the ships, swift-sailing, as well as their many possessions.
Then there is this great marvel, of fame which never will
perish—
it is the Delian girls, handmaids of the great Far-shooter;
these, whenever at first in a hymn they have lauded Apollo
also Leto the goddess and Artemis shooter of arrows,
calling to memory tales of the men and the women of old times,
straightway a hymn they sing, enchanting the nations of
mankind.
They know how to impersonate all men's voices and all their
musical vocalizations, and each would imagine himself as
sounding the words—so suited to them is their beautiful
singing.
But come, be you propitious, Apollo, and Artemis also;

farewell, all of you maidens; and me then, even hereafter,
call to your memory, when someone among men on the earth, some
much-tried suffering stranger, arrives here making inquiry:
"Maidens, for you which singer is it of men wandering hither
who is the sweetest in song, and by whom you most are delighted?"
Then do you all, each one, make answer and tell him about me:
"It is a blind man dwelling in Chios, rugged and rocky,
whose songs, every one, are the best both now and hereafter."
Yours is a fame, in turn, I will carry around as I wander
over the earth to the well-inhabited cities of mankind;
they will indeed be persuaded, for this is the truth of the matter.
Never will I cease lauding in hymns far-shooting Apollo,
god of the silvery bow, whom Leto of beautiful hair bore.

II.

Oh Lord, you possess Lykia, lovely Maionia also,
then Miletos, delectable city that borders the seabrine,
but over wave-washed Delos yourself you splendidly govern.
Glorious Leto's son, as he plays a refrain on his hollow
lyre, sets forth on his journey to go toward Pytho the rocky,
clad in ambrosial fragrant apparel; and under the golden
plectrum the lyre in his hands sends forth a delectable clangor.
Thence from the earth he departs to Olympos as speedy as thought and
goes to the palace of Zeus and the rest of the gods in assembly;
straightway to the immortals the lyre and the song are enthralling;
all of the Muses together in lovely antiphonal voices
hymn the ambrosial gifts that the gods enjoy, and the sorrows
which men under the hands of the deathless gods ever suffer,
living without understanding and helpless, nor are they ever
able to find any cure for their death or defense against old age.
Meanwhile the Graces with beautiful hair and the jovial Seasons,

Hebè, Harmonia too, and the daughter of Zeus, Aphrodítè,
enter the dance—by the wrists of their hands they hold one another;
singing and dancing with them is a maid not ugly or little,
rather indeed very tall to behold, and of wondrous appearance,
Artemis shooter of arrows, the maid brought up with Apollo;
Ares among them too, and the keen-eyed slayer of Argos,
frolic, the while on his lyre Lord Phoibos Apollo is playing,
high and resplendently stepping, with radiance shining around him,
glittering bright from his feet and his skillfully woven apparel.
Deep in their great hearts then as they look upon him are his mother,
Leto with tresses of gold, and his sire, Zeus counselor, gladdened,
watching their much-loved son as with deathless gods he is sporting.
How shall I sing of you who are in all ways worthy of singing?
Shall I sing about you as a wooer, in loving liaisons,
how you would go forth courting the daughter of Azan along with
godlike Ischys, the well horsed son of Elátios, or with
Phorbas, a scion of Triops' lineage, or with Ereútheus,
or else along with Leukíppos, to Daphne the wife of Leukíppos . . .
you on foot, he in chariot, nor did he come short of Triops.
Or about how at the first all over the earth you were ranging,
seeking an oracle-place for mankind, far-shooting Apollo?
Then to Piéria first you went, straight down from Olympos,
striding along beside sand-strewn Lectos and through Ainiénai
and the Perrhaibians' country; and swiftly you came to Iólkos,
set foot then on Kenaíon in galley-renownèd Euboía,
stood on the Lélantine plain—but it did not please you in spirit
there to erect your temple and found your forested woodland.
Over the Eúripos thence you crossed, far-shooting Apollo,
then climbed up the divine green mountain; and swiftly from there you

journeyed, and reached Mykaléssos and then Teuméssos the grassy.
Next you arrived in Thebè's abode, all covered in forests,
since no one among men yet dwelt in Thebè the holy,
nor at the time were as yet any footpaths nor any roadways
there across Thebè's wheat-bearing plain—it was covered in forest.
Now yet farther from there you went, far-shooting Apollo,
coming to Onchestos, the resplendent grove of Poseidon;
there where a colt, new-broken, recovers his breath from the pain of
drawing a beautiful chariot; though he is skillful, the driver
leaps from the car-box and goes on his journey; and meanwhile the horses
rattle the empty conveyance, bereft of a master to guide them.
Should they shatter the chariot there in the forested woodland,
men take care of the horses, the car they tilt and abandon;
for it was so in the earliest ritual; then do the drivers
pray to the lord; as the share of the god is the chariot guarded.
Now yet farther from there you went, far-shooting Apollo;
then you arrived at the beautiful stream of the River Kephísos,
which pours out of Lilaía its beautiful current of water.
Stepping across, Far-worker, you passed Okaléa of many
towers; proceeding from there you reached Haliártos the grassy.
Toward Telphoúsa you went; it was pleasing to you, a propitious
place to erect your temple and found your forested woodland;
close to her side you stood, and in these words spoke and addressed her:
"Here, Telphoúsa, am I intending a beautiful temple
now to erect, to serve men as an oracle; then they will always
bring here honoring me their hecatombs full and effective—
both those having abodes in the fertile Péloponnésos,
and those dwelling in Europe and over the wave-washed islands—
looking for oracles; then it would be infallible counsel
I would deliver to all of them here in my sumptuous temple."
So spoke Phoibos Apollo, and laid out there the foundations,
broad and exceedingly long throughout; Telphoúsa, observing
this, grew angry in spirit and spoke these words to Apollo:

"Phoibos the lord, Far-worker, advice for your mind will I give you,
since you intend to erect here now a most beautiful temple,
which is to serve all men as an oracle; always will they bring
hither in honor to you their hecatombs full and effective.
But I say to you plainly, and you keep this in your mind now—
always will cause you affliction the clattering of the swift horses
and of the mules which here at my sacred fountain are watered;
then anyone among men will prefer much more to observe those
well-made chariots here, and the swift-hoofed clattering horses,
than to observe the great shrine and the numerous treasures within it.
But if at all you will heed me—as far more mighty and potent,
Lord, you are than I am, yours surely the strength that is greatest—
do you in Krisa erect it, below a ravine of Parnassos.
There will no beautiful chariots ever be dashing, or swift-hoofed
horses be clattering loudly, surrounding your well-built altar;
rather, to you great gifts will the glorious nations of mankind
bring, as Iḗpaíán, Hail Healer; delighting in mind you
then will receive fine victims from all of the neighboring peoples."
Thus she persuaded the mind of the great Far-shooter, that fame might
be Telphoúsa's alone in the country, and not the Far-shooter's.
Now yet farther from there you went, far-shooting Apollo;
next you arrived at the city of arrogant Phlégyan people,
who, not caring at all about Zeus, inhabit the country
there quite near the Kephísian lake in a beautiful valley.
Thence you swiftly advanced, rushing up to the ridge of the mountain;
Krisa at last you reached, underneath snow-covered Parnassos;
it is a slope that is turned toward the west wind; high up above is
hanging a cliff overhead, and beneath it runs a deep valley,
hollow and rugged, and there then resolved Lord Phoibos Apollo
he would erect a delectable temple, and thus he asserted:
"Here is the place I intend to erect a most beautiful temple

now that will serve all men as an oracle; then they will always
bring here, honoring me, their hecatombs full and effective—
both those having abodes in the fertile Péloponnésos,
and those dwelling in Europe and over the wave-washed islands—
looking for oracles; then it will be infallible counsel
I will deliver to all of them here in my sumptuous temple."
So spoke Phoibos Apollo, and laid out there the foundations,
broad and exceedingly long throughout; and upon them a stony
footing was solidly laid by Trophónios and Agamédes,
who were the sons of Ergínos and dear to the gods undying.
Then out of well-wrought stones did the numberless nations of mankind
raise that temple entire, to be always a subject for singing.
Near that spot was a spring, fair-flowing, and there with his mighty
bow by the lord, that scion of Zeus, was slaughtered a dragon,
bloated, enormous, a terrible monster that many an evil
wrought to the people who lived on the earth, to themselves very many,
many to long-shanked sheep, since she was a bloody affliction.
She once, receiving the infant from gold-throned Hera, had brought up
dreadful and cruel Typháön to be an affliction for mankind;
him once Hera had borne, in her anger at Zeus the great father,
when by the scion of Kronos was brought forth honored Athena
out of his head; then straightway Hera the lady was angry,
so that among the assembled immortals she spoke, and addressed them:
"All of the gods and the goddesses all, now listen and heed me,
how dishonored I am by the great cloud-gathering god Zeus
first, even after he made me his bedmate skillful in virtue;
separate now from myself he has brought forth bright-eyed Athena,
who is to be outstanding among all the blessèd immortals;
meanwhile indeed, disabled and weak among all of the gods that
child of my own is, Hephaistos, the cripple-foot creature I brought forth,

[who is a shame and disgrace in heaven to me, so that straightway,]
picking him up in my hands, I hurled him into the broad sea;
but by Thetis of silvery feet, great Nereus' daughter,
he was received; then she with her sisters provided his nurture.
Would that in some other fashion the gods in bliss she had pleasured!
Mischievous, sly in devices! What else will you now be devising?
How by yourself did you dare it, to bring forth bright-eyed Athena?
Would not I have brought forth? Yet nevertheless I am called your
consort among the immortals, the gods who hold the broad heaven.
Take heed now, lest for you I devise some evil hereafter.
Yes, it is true: now I will contrive that a child of my own be
born who will be outstanding among these gods, the immortals;
I will not shame the divine bed-covenant you and I plighted,
neither will I climb into the bed with you, rather will stay far
distant from you and abiding among these gods, the immortals."
So having said, from the gods she departed, enraged in her spirit.
Then straightway began praying the ox-eyed queen, lady Hera,
striking the ground with her hand flatwise and in these words speaking:
"Listen to me now, Earth, and the broad Sky stretching above us,
Titans as well, you gods who beneath earth have habitation
there about huge Tartaros, and from whom both mortals and gods are!
All of you, listen and hear what I say now: grant that a child be
mine without Zeus, nor at all in his might any weaker than he, but
let him be stronger, as much as wide-thundering Zeus is than Kronos."
These words when she had spoken, the ground she lashed with her stout hand;
then was the life-bearing Earth agitated; and when she observed it,

she in her spirit rejoiced, for she thought that it would be accomplished.
Then in fact from that time for a year's full circle of seasons,
never at all she came to the bed of great Zeus of the counsels,
never at all she took the elaborate throne where aforetimes
she had been seated, devising for him grave counsels of prudence;
rather indeed in her temples, in which pray many to her, kept
staying, by offerings gladdened, the ox-eyed queen, lady Hera.
But when finally all of the months and the days were completed,
after the year had revolved and the seasons again were returning,
then did she bring forth one like neither to gods nor to mortals,
fearful and cruel Typháön, to be an affliction to mortals.
Straightway taking the creature the ox-eyed queen, lady Hera,
carried and gave to one evil another: the dragon received him.
Many the evils she wrought on the glorious nations of mankind;
he who encountered the dragon, the day of his doom would remove him
always, until a strong arrow the lord far-working Apollo
shot at the dragon; and there by her horrible agony shattered
she lay wretchedly gasping and rolling about all over.
Then was the noise unspeakable, wondrous, as she in the woodland
hither and thither was writhing incessantly: life she abandoned,
breathing it bloodily forth; thus triumphed Phoibos Apollo:
"Now then, putrefy here on the earth which nourishes people!
Nor will you live any more as an evil affliction to mortals,
those who, eating the fruit of the earth's all-nurturing bounty,
hither will carry to me their hecatombs full and effective;
nor any way against death most cursèd will either Typhóeus
be of avail, or Chimaíra so evil of name, but on this spot
you will be putrefied by the black Earth and the radiant High Lord."
So triumphing he spoke, and her eyes were both covered in darkness.
Her did the sacred power of Helios cause putrefaction,
wherefore Pytho the place is now called, and the lord himself they

call by another cognomen, the Pythian, since it was there that
monster was putrified then by Helios' penetrant power.
Straightway then in his mind it was known by Phoibos Apollo
how that spring with its beautiful stream had entirely beguiled him;
so in his wrath he approached Telphoúsa, and quickly arriving,
stood very close to her there, and in these words spoke and addressed her:
"Not by beguiling my mind, Telphoúsa, were you to reserve so
lovely a place for yourself, your fair-flowing water to pour forth.
This spot also for me will be glorious, not for you only."
Thus, and upon her a crag did the lord, far-working Apollo,
thrust in a rocky deposit, her streams entirely concealing,
there too, an altar he made for himself in the forested woodland
close to the beautiful stream of the spring; there now to the lord do
all men pray, and exalt the Telphoúsian god, as they call him,
since it was there he humbled the streams of the holy Telphoúsa.
Straightway then in his heart began pondering Phoibos Apollo
who were the men he should bring in there to be priests of the temple,
making oblations and doing him service in Pytho the rocky.
As he revolved these things, he perceived a swift ship on the wine-dark
seaway and saw inside of her men both many and noble,
Cretans from Knossos the city of Minos, who for the lord make
sacred oblations, and also as messengers bring the decrees of
Phoibos Apollo the god of the gold sword, which he declares as
oracles out of the laurel below the ravines of Parnassos.
These, pursuing their commerce and profit, were now in a black ship
making a voyage to sandy-soiled Pylos and seeking the people
native to Pylos; but they were encountered by Phoibos Apollo;
down on the sea he suddenly leapt, in his shape like a dolphin,
on the swift galley, and lay there, a monster enormous and fearful;
then whoever of them took thought in his mind to observe it,

every way it shook him about as it rattled the ship-beams.
Silently there on the ship they sat, all quaking in terror,
nor did they loosen the tackle throughout their black hollow galley,
nor in the dark-prowed ship did they slacken and lower the canvas,
but in the way they had rigged it first with the cables of ox-hide,
so they sailed, and behind the swift ship the impetuous south wind
hurried it onward; and first they coasted the Máleian headland,
passed the Lakonian country, and to the sea-garlanded town on
Taínaron's cape and the country of Helios who delights mortals
they came, where there are always deep-fleeced sheep of the lordly
Helios browsing for forage—they have a delectable country.
There they wanted to haul in the galley, and then, disembarking,
ponder upon the great marvel, and also observe with their own eyes
whether the monster would stay on the deck of the hollow galley,
or leap away, back into the waves of the fish-thronged sea-brine.
But to the tiller the well-built galley would not be responsive,
rather she kept to the side of the fertile Péloponnésos
taking her way; and with breezes the lord far-shooting Apollo
easily guided her onward; advancing her journey the galley
came to Arena and to the delectable town Argyphéa,
Thryon, the ford of the Álpheios River, and well-built Aipy,
sandy-soiled Pylos as well, and the men who are native to Pylos.
Next past Krounoi she went, then Chalkis as well, and past Dýmè,
then by illustrious Elis, in which the Epeíans are rulers.
When toward Pherai she headed, exulting in Zeus-sent breezes,
under the clouds the steep mountain of Ithaka showed to the sailors,
then Doulíchion, Samè, and also wooded Zakýnthos.
Finally, when they had passed the whole coast of the Péloponnésos,
then, toward Krisa, the measureless gulf came into their vision,
that which cuts from the mainland the fertile Péloponnésos;

then behind them by the order of Zeus came a strong clear west wind,
rushing along through the air in a blustery gale, so that swiftly
running the ship would accomplish her course on the salt seawater.
Finally they went back once more toward dawn and the sunrise,
voyaging; leading the way was the lord, Zeus' scion Apollo;
then they arrived in Krisa the sun-bright, wealthy in vineyards;
there on the sands in the harbor was grounded the sea-faring galley.
Thereupon leapt from the galley the lord far-shooting Apollo
much like a star in the midst of the daylight: many the flashing
sparks which flew from him then, and the radiance rose to the heavens.
Into his shrine he entered between two valuable tripods.
Thereon a blaze he kindled, revealing his shafts in their splendor;
Krisa entire was replete with the radiance; then ululated
all the Krisaíans' bedmates and daughters with beautiful girdles
under the impulse of Phoibos, for he upon each threw a great fear.
Swift as a thought he thence leapt speeding again to the galley,
seeming in likeness a man of enormous vigor and power
just in his prime—with his hair were his broad young shoulders enveloped;
raising his voice he spoke, and in these winged words he addressed them:
"Strangers, who are you? And whence do you sail on the watery pathways?
Have you affairs in trading, or do you recklessly wander
over the seas in the manner of pirates who wander at random
putting their lives in danger and visiting evil on strangers?
Why do you sit thus feeling so timorous, not on the land yet
disembarking, and not in the black ship stowing the tackle?
This indeed is the custom among all grain-eating mortals,
that whenever they come in a black ship out of the seaway

onto the land, worn out with their labor, at once in their spirits
does a desire for delectable food take hold of their senses."
So did he utter, and into their breasts great courage he planted.
Then in return spoke, giving him answer, the chief of the Cretans:
"Stranger—although in no way you appear like men who are mortals
either in stature or form, but instead like gods, the immortals—
hail to you, greatly be glad, may the gods endow you with blessings.
Truthfully speak to me now about these things, so that I know well
what is this land, what country, and what men here are the natives,
since quite otherwise thinking did we set sail on the great gulf
going to Pylos from Crete, that country we claim as our birthplace;
now instead with the ship we have come here, not at all willing—
wanting to finish our journey—another way, different sea-paths;
but an immortal has guided us here, though we did not wish it."
Speaking to them made answer the lord far-shooting Apollo:
"Strangers who had your dwellings about well-forested Knossos
earlier, but who will now no longer again be returning,
each of you, back to your loveable cities and beautiful houses,
or to your dear bedmates, but instead my sumptuous temple
here you will keep and attend, that among many people is honored.
I am the scion of Zeus, and the name I claim is Apollo;
now I have guided you hither across the great gulf of the deep sea,
not as intending you harm—instead, my sumptuous temple
here you will keep, that among all people so greatly is honored;
then you will know the immortals' purposes; so at their pleasure
all of your days and forever, unceasingly, you will be honored.
But come, just as I say it to you, very swiftly obey me:
first now, lower the sails, untying the cables of ox-hide,

then drag out the swift galley and pull her up on the dry land,
take out all of your goods and the gear of the balanced galley;
there too, an altar erect on the tide-heaped sand of the seashore,
kindle a fire thereon, white barley-meal offer upon it,
pray then, standing beside each other, surrounding the altar;
then inasmuch as I first, on the seaway misty and murky
made my appearance and leapt on the swift ship shaped like a dolphin,
so do you pray to me here as Delphínios; so will the altar
also forever be called Delpheíos and Great Overseer.
Then, while eating a meal on the shore by the swift black galley,
pour out wine to the blessèd immortals who dwell on Olympos.
When you have quite satisfied your appetites, eating the sweet food,
follow me then as you sing "Iḗ Paián, Hail to the Healer,"
till you arrive at the place you will keep my sumptuous temple."
So did he say; they carefully listened to him and obeyed him.
First they lowered the sails, untying the cables of ox-hide,
let down the mast with the fore-stays, positioning it on the mast-crutch,
then themselves disembarked on the tide-heaped sand of the seashore.
Out of the seabrine onto the land they dragged the swift galley
high up onto the sand, and they fixed tall props underneath her;
there too, an altar they made on the tide-heaped sand of the seashore,
kindled a fire thereon, white barley-meal offered upon it,
praying as ordered, beside each other, surrounding the altar.
Thereupon, taking a meal by the side of the swift black galley,
they poured wine to the blessèd immortals who dwell on Olympos.
When they had quite satisfied their appetites, drinking and eating,
they set forth; they were led by the lord, Zeus' scion Apollo,
who in his hands was holding a lyre and delightfully playing,
high and resplendently stepping; and marching in rhythm the Cretans

followed to Pytho and sang "Iḗ Paíán, Hail to the Healer,"
like those Cretans, the singers of paeans, in whom has the Muse put
into their breasts, that goddess, the honey-voiced talent of singing.
They on their feet, unwearied, advanced to the ridge, and Parnassos
rapidly reached, and as well the delectable place in which he was
going to dwell and be honored among such numerous peoples;
leading them there, he showed them his sanctum and sumptuous temple.
Then indeed in the breasts of the men their spirits were stirred up,
so that the chief of the Cretans addressed him, making inquiry:
"Lord, since far from our friends and the land of our fathers you now have
brought us—to you this seemed to be best somehow, in your spirit—
how shall we live here now? We urge you, consider the matter.
This is a land not pleasing for vineyards or good for its pastures,
so that from it we can live well here and do service for mankind."
Smiling at them thus answered the lord, Zeus' scion Apollo:
"Simpletons truly you are, most miserable, who desire such
troublesome cares in your heart, such difficult toils and restrictions!
Easily I will inform you of this, in your minds I will place it:
if in your right hands each of you taking a knife were to slaughter
sheep incessantly here, unstinted the victims would all yet
be, so many the glorious nations of mankind bring me;
you keep guarding the temple, receiving the nations of mankind
who come gathering hither, especially showing my guidance
[clearly to mortals; and take to your hearts just customs.
But if in mindlessness someone not obey but ignore me,]
or if at all some word or some action be idle and useless,
or an outrage, as is common among you men who are mortal,

then over you will there be other men as instructors and masters,
under whose forcible hands you will all of your days be subjected.
All these things have been told to you now: guard them in your spirits."
So to you too farewell, great scion of Zeus and of Leto;
but about you and about some other song I will be thinking.

Contributors

CURTIS DOZIER received his Ph.D. in Classics from the University of California, Berkeley, and is Visiting Assistant Professor of Latin at Vassar College. His research focuses on the social context of Latin poetry: where and in what format Romans encountered it, what intellectual and social role it played in Roman society, and how Roman social practices shaped its interpretation.

DAVID LARSEN is a Postdoctoral Associate of Yale University's Whitney Humanities Center. In 2009 his translation of al-Ḥusayn ibn Aḥmad ibn Kh̲ālawayh's *Names of the Lion* was released by Atticus/Finch Books (Seattle). He is currently at work on a comparative study of Greek- and Arabic-language semiotics.

RODNEY MERRILL, Ph.D., Stanford 1970, is an independent scholar and translator of the *Odyssey* (University of Michigan Press, 2002) and the *Iliad* (University of Michigan Press, 2007). Works in progress include translations of the *Argonautica* of Apollonius Rhodius and plays by the three great Athenian tragedians.

JACK MITCHELL is an Assistant Professor of Classics at Dalhousie University in Halifax, Nova Scotia. His research focuses on poetical and oratorical performance in Mediterranean educational contexts in the Hellenistic and Imperial periods.

TIMOTHY PEPPER is a doctoral candidate in Classics at the University of California, Berkeley. He is currently interested in the overlap of literature, social interaction, and models of behavior in ancient societies. He is completing his dissertation on the construction of ambition among social strata in early Ptolemaic Egypt.

DAN SOFAER is a poet whose work has been published in *Fulcrum: An Annual of Poetry and Aesthetics*. His current research interest is the *Odyssey*.

CHARLES STOCKING is Visiting Lecturer in the Department of Classics, University of California, Los Angeles.

THOMAS R. WALSH is Senior Faculty emeritus at Occidental College, after serving as Associate Professor in the Department of Comparative Literature and in the Department of English and Comparative Literary Studies. He is now a research associate at the University of California at Santa Cruz, where he teaches Greek, Latin, and ancient literature as the need arises. He is currently working primarily on a series of essays in Homeric studies and the comparative literature of ancient societies.

General Index

ʿAbīd b. al-Abraṣ, 14, 33n58

ʿĀʾis̲h̲ā bt. Abī Bakr, 29, 36

Achilles, 126n35, 131–166 passim, 178n15, 199–200, 205–207

Aegisthus, 122, 124

Aegyptids, 112, 116, 118, 119

Aegyptus, 111

Aeneid: as synchronic snapshot of Homer, 197; inconsistency in, 196n16

Aeschylus, 105–127. *See also titles of individual plays*

Aethiopis, 204

Agamemnon (tragedy), 121

Ajax, 201n26

Alcaeus, 89

Alcibiades, 170

allusion, 36, 75, 96, 151n30, 169, 194n5, 197–198, 204, 207, 212–213

Amphiaraus, 50

amphoras, 170–173, 171 figs. 1–2, 173 fig. 4a, 174, 174 fig. 5a–b, 175 fig. 6. *See also* wine

anankē ('necessity'), 125

Andromache, 206–208

anger: concrete vs. abstract forms, 110; divine , 112, 113, 121; of Achilles, 149–152; of Zeus, 105–107, 112, 113, 114, 115, 116, 117–118, 126; philosophy and, 107; poetic lexicon of terms for, 106, 125, 126, 127; politics and, 105, 109, 113n13; power and, 110, 120. See also *kholos*; *kotos*; *menos*; *menis*

aoidos ('professional solo performer'), viii–ix, 52, 71, 72, 86, 87, 88

Apollo, 51n5, 111, 121, 124; inspiring *mantis*, rhapsode, poet, 53–54, 71

Archilochus, 169, 182–188; Fr. 2 West, 182–187

Argives, 105

Aristophanes, 76–77, 81–82, 84–85, 91–92, 93, 98. *See also titles of individual plays*

arma virumque ('arms and the man'): as translation of Homeric language, 198; as Virgilian *klea andrōn*, 199–200; repeated in the *Aeneid*, 198

Ascanius, 207

General Index

Index Locorum

Literary Sources

Aeschylus
Agamemnon 456–457: 119–120; 459, 463–465: 120; 634–635: 121 with n27; 763–771: 120–121; 1211: 121
Eumenides 219–224: 124 with n32; 314: 126n34; 425–426: 125; 499–501: 125–126; 800: 126n35; 942: 125n34
Libation Bearers 23, 31–41: 121–122; 946–952: 122–123; 1024–1027: 124
Suppliants 1: 114; 333–336: 111; 343–344: 112; 347: 105–107, 112; 360: 113; 375–376: 113, 120; 385–386: 106–107, 113–114, 116; 418–437: 114–116; 474–477: 116; 478–479: 106, 117; 615–618: 106, 117; 743–745: 118–119
Fr. 148 Smyth: 123
Ps.-Aeschylus
Prometheus 163, 165–166, 602: 126n35
Alcman
Fr. 1.98 Page: 83n21
Anacreon
PMG 417.6: 91n44
Archilochus
Fr. 2 West: 169 with n2, 182–187; fr. 5 West: 182, 183, 186; fr. 114 West: 184n40, 185
Aristophanes
Birds 39–41: 79; 123: 82n20; 156: 98; 251: 95; 317: 79; 413–433: 80 with n14; 451–459: 85–86; 469: 82n20; 610–618: 96; 677–684: 86–87, 91n45; 685–687: 81; 699: 91n45; 724: 96; 737: 96; 737–752: 87–90; 774: 89; 784: 97; 904–910, 915–919, 924–931: 92–94; 1058–1064: 90–91; 1088–1089: 95; 1300: 94–95; 1313–1322: 94; 1332: 97; 1377–1407: 95; 1437: 80; 1744: 80
Frogs 844, 846: 127n36
Peace 709: 86n32; 796–801: 76n5
Wasps 200: 87n34
Fr. 30 K-A: 82n20; fr. 101 K-A: 79n11; fr. 225.3 K-A: 170n4; fr. 334.2 K-A: 171n4

Epigraphic and Papyrological Sources